T0305132

STRATEGY, STRUCTURE AND STYLE

THE STRATEGIC MANAGEMENT SERIES

Series Editor
HOWARD THOMAS

Further titles in preparation

THE STRATEGIC MANAGEMENT SERIES

STRATEGY, STRUCTURE AND STYLE

Edited by

HOWARD THOMAS, DON O'NEAL AND
MICHEL GHERTMAN

JOHN WILEY & SONS

Chichester · New York · Weinheim · Brisbane · Singapore · Toronto

          National   01243 779777
          International   (+44) 1243 779777
          e-mail (for orders and customer service enquiries): cs-books@wiley.co.uk
          Visit our Home Page on http://www.wiley.co.uk
                              or http://www.wiley.com

The individual copyright to Chapter 14 has been retained by the authors as detailed on the chapter title page.

Other Wiley Editorial Offices

John Wiley & Sons, Inc., 605 Third Avenue,
New York, NY 10158-0012, USA

Jacaranda Wiley Ltd, 33 Park Road, Milton,
Queensland 4064, Australia

John Wiley & Sons (Canada) Ltd, 22 Worcester Road,
Rexdale, Ontario M9W 1L1, Canada

John Wiley & Sons (Asia) Pte Ltd, 2 Clementi Loop #02-01,
Jin Xing Distripark, Singapore 129809

VCH Verlagsgesellschaft mbH, Pappelallee 3,
D-69469 Weinheim, Germany

Library of Congress Cataloging-in-Publication Data

Strategy, structure and style/edited by Howard Thomas, Don O'Neal and
    Michel Ghertman.
        p.   cm.—(The strategic management series)
     "Papers presented at the 14th International Conference of the
    Strategic Management Society, held in Paris, September 20–23, 1994"—
    Pref.
      Includes bibliographical references
      ISBN 0-471-96882-X (alk. paper)
      1. Strategic planning—Congresses.   2. Industrial management—
    Congresses.   I. Thomas, Howard, 1943– .   II. O'Neal, Don.
    III. Ghertman, Michel.   IV. International Strategic Management
    Society Conference (14th : 1994 : Paris, France)   V. Series.
    HD30.28.S7399   1997
    658.4'012—DC20   96-36291
                                                               CIP

British Library Cataloguing in Publication Data

A catalogue record for this book is available from the British Library

ISBN 0-471-96882-X

Typeset in 10/12pt Palatino by Footnote Graphics, Warminster, Wiltshire

Printed and bound by Antony Rowe Ltd, Eastbourne

Contents

Contributors

JAY B. BARNEY
Professor & Bank One Chair of Strategy, Department of Management and HR, Fisher College of Business, The Ohio State University, 356 Hagerty Hall, 1775 College Road, Columbus, OH 43210, USA.

PAMELA BARR
Assistant Professor of Organization and Management, Roberto C. Goizueta School of Business, Emory University, 1602 Mizell Drive, Room 312, Atlanta, GA 30322–2710, USA.

WILLIAM BOGNER
Assistant Professor, Department of Management, Georgia State University, PO Box 4014, Atlanta, GA 30303, USA.

CLIFF BOWMAN
Cranfield School of Management, Cranfield University, Bedford MK43 OAL, UK.

BRIAN K. BOYD
Arizona State University, Tempe, AZ, USA.

JORDI CANALS
IESE, Pearson, 21 Avenida, Barcelona 08034, Spain.

W. OTTO CARROLL
Department of Management, College of Business and Public Administration, Old Dominion University, Norfolk, VA 23529–0223, USA.

SIMON CARTER
Cranfield School of Management, Cranfield University, Bedford MK43 OAL, UK.

BALA CHAKRAVARTHY
Spencer Chair Professor of Technological Leadership, Carlson School of Management, University of Minnesota, 271 19th Avenue South, 871 Management and Economics Building, Minneapolis, MN 55455, USA.

JANE F. CRAIG
Lecturer, General Management, Australian Graduate School of Management, The University of New South Wales, PO Box 1, Kensington, NSW 2033, Sydney, Australia.

RICHARD D'AVENI
The Amos Tuck School of Business, Dartmouth College, 100 Tuck Drive, Hanover, NH 03755, USA.

MAGALI DELMAS
HEC Graduate School of Management, 78351 Jouy-en-Josas, Cedex France.

DAVID FAULKNER
University of Oxford, UK.

STEVEN W. FLOYD
The University of Connecticut CT, USA.

MICHEL GHERTMAN
Professor, Strategic Management and International Business, HEC Graduate School of Management, 78351 Jouy-en-Josas, Cedex France.

XAVIER GILBERT
The Lego Professor, International Institute for Management Development, PO Box 915, 23 Chemin de Bellerive, Lausanne, CH-1001, Switzerland.

KAREN GOLDEN-BIDDLE
Emory University, 1602 Mizell Drive, Atlanta, GA 30322, USA.

KNUT HAANES
Doctoral Fellow, Norwegian School of Management, PO Box 580, 1301 Sandvika, Norway.

TAIEB HAFSI
Ecole des Hautes Etudes Commerciales, Montreal, Canada.

MARK H. HANSEN
Texas A & M University, TX, USA.

BRUCE HEIMAN
University of California, Berkeley, CA, USA.

MARLA HOWARD
Department of Management, College of Business and Public Administration, Old Dominion University, Norfolk, VA 23529–0223, USA.

BALAJI R. KOKA
J. M. Katz Graduate School of Business, 251 Mervis Hall, University of Pittsburgh, Pittsburgh, PA 15260, USA.

PETER LORANGE
The Maucher-Nestlé Professor, International Institute for Management Development, PO Box 915, 23 Chemin de Bellerive, Lausanne, CH-1001, Switzerland.

BENTE R. LOWENDAHL
Associate Professor, Norwegian School of Management, PO Box 580, 1301 Sandvika, Norway.

RAVINDRANATH MADHAVAN
University of Illinois, Department of Business Administration, 317B David Kinley Hall, 1407 W. Gregory Drive, Urbana, IL 61801, USA.

PABLO MARTIN DE HOLAN
Faculty of Management, McGill University, Montreal, Canada.

MICHAEL MAYER
Glasgow Business School, University of Glasgow, Glasgow G12 8QQ, UK.

JOHN MCGEE
Warwick Business School, University of Warwick, Coventry CV4 7AL, UK.

KIRK MONTEVERDE
Research Director, The Access Group, 1411 Foulk Road, Box 7430, Wilmington, DE 19803–0430, USA.

JOHN E. PRESCOTT
J. M. Katz Graduate School of Business, 252 Mervis Hall, University of Pittsburgh, Pittsburgh, PA 15260, USA.

HAYAGREEVA RAO
Associate Professor of Organization and Management, Emory University, 1602 Mizell Drive, Atlanta, GA 30322, USA.

RAYMOND A. THIÉTART
Department of Strategic Management, ESSEC, BP 105, 95021 Cergy Pontoise, Cedex, France.

HOWARD THOMAS
Dean, College of Commerce and Business Administration, 1206 S. 6th Street, 260 CW, Champaign, IL 61820, USA.

RICHARD WHITTINGTON
New College, Oxford OX1 3BN, UK.

BILL WOOLDRIDGE
University of Massachusetts, MA, USA.

LILLIAN CHENG WRIGHT
605 South Willis Avenue, Champaign, IL 61821, USA.

RUSSELL W. WRIGHT
Assistant Professor, Department of Business Administration, University of Illinois, 1206 S. Sixth Street, 165 CW, Champaign, IL 61820, USA.

JEAN-MARC XUEREB
Associate Professor, ESSEC, BP 105, 95021 Cergy Pontoise, Cedex, France.

PHILIP W. YETTON
Commonwealth Bank Professor of Management, Australian Graduate School of Management, The University of New South Wales, PO Box 1, Kensington, NSW 2033, Sydney, Australia.

Series Preface

The Strategic Management Society was created to bring together, on a worldwide basis, academics, business practitioners, and consultants interested in strategic management. The aim of the Society is the development and dissemination of information, achieved through its sponsorship of the annual international conference, special interest workshops, the *Strategic Management Journal*, and other publications.

The Society's annual conference is a truly international meeting, held in recent years in Stockholm, Barcelona, Toronto, London, and Chicago. Each conference deals with a broad, current theme, within which specific sub-themes are addressed through keynote speeches and discussion panels featuring leading experts from around the world.

This volume is the fourth in the series representing Strategic Management Society annual conferences. Papers and panel discussions presented at these conferences address not just the conference themes but, more importantly, discuss "live" issues—those that are currently confronting the Society and its members. In this context presenters feel more freedom to step outside the "boiler-plate" type issues that sometimes discourage dialectic discussion, and utilize these conferences as opportunities to take chances—to address issues that are more "interesting", though perhaps less conventional.

This type of conference format provides the editors with a broader range of ideas, thoughts and themes from which to select papers, and the opportunity to make available an interesting and intriguing selection of conversations to anyone interested in joining the dialog or in just reading about the discussions.

Attending a conference at which a number of presentations are occurring simultaneously requires attendees to make choices and, in the process, inevitably miss some presentations that they may have found interesting and useful. This results in most conference presentations playing to only a few or, at most a few dozen, of those who might be interested. This volume, as do others in the series, offers the opportunity for hundreds of interested individuals to, in effect, attend a number of thought-provoking conference presentations. At the same time it offers much wider exposure to a selection of papers deemed likely to be of interest to a broader audience.

This conference*, entitled "Strategy Styles: Management Systems, Types and Paradigms", was intended to explore management styles, systems, processes, and paradigms, and how the emphasis in global competition shifts from one style to the next as firms in one country see their counterparts in other nations become increasingly effective by using different formulas for competing. The Conference Steering Committee reviewed several hundred papers, ultimately selecting around 150 for presentation at the conference, along with around 20 panel discussions. We believe that the wisdom contained in the rich body of research and experience benefited all the participants, and will be a major contribution to better understanding the significance of the contributions of strategic management.

With so many worthwhile contributions to consider a decision was made, early in the editorial process, not to attempt to select a set of "best" papers from the conference. Judging which presentations are best is highly subjective and, moreover, unlikely to provide the balance of content that will make the volume interesting and useful to a broad range of Society members.

With that in mind, a theme was selected that is consistent not only with the theme of the conference but also with the mission of the Society. Presentations were selected with the additional consideration that they represent some of the more significant issues currently facing business strategists. The result is, we feel, an interesting and effective integration of strategic perspectives that exemplifies many of the most important issues facing strategic management, both now and in the future.

An eclectic ensemble of contributors, including academics, business executives, and consultants, addresses one of the Society's primary concerns—building and maintaining bridges between management theory and business practice.

Editorial commentary provides integration among contributions, resulting in a volume that is more than a collection of currently relevant discussions, to be read once and perhaps forgotten. It is, instead, a collection of thoughts on and approaches to management issues that are timeless in their nature and importance.

---

* The 14th International Conference of the Strategic Management Society, held in Paris, 20–23 September 1994, was attended by several hundred delegates from both the academic and the business worlds.

Introduction

As an early proponent of the need for corporations to have explicit strategies, Tilles suggested that such need ". . . stems from two key attributes of the business organization: first, that success depends on people working together so that their efforts are mutually reinforcing; and second, that this must be accomplished in the context of rapidly changing conditions" (1966, Making Strategy Explicit, in Ansoff, H.I. (ed.), 1969, *Business Strategy*: 181). Tilles described a long-range plan as "At its worst, . . . an extrapolation of past performance . . . into the future, . . . , and expressed in purely numerical terms," and "At its best, . . . a statement of strategy, sequenced over time, expressed in terms of resource requirements and funds flows, and representing a consensus to the top-management team" (Ibid:182). These observations seem as relevant to today's firms and managers as they were 30 years ago, with competitive success still dependent upon strategic issues such as cooperative efforts focused on organizational objectives, effective use of resources, and managing change. Although it is impossible to include in one volume the full breadth of ideas under discussion in the area of strategic management, the editors have selected contributions that offer interesting food for thought in three currently crucial strategic conversations:

1. *Strategy.* Chapters in this section aptly demonstrate the diversity of research topics in strategy. Included are discussions of trust between trade partners, CEO duality, excess capacity, dynamic strategies, distinctive competences, and strategic windows.
2. *Structure.* Perhaps nothing is more important to (helping or hindering) the implementation of corporate strategy than organizational structure. Will it complement or confound the strategy? How should it be changed? How can resistance to change be overcome? Chapters in this section demonstrate cognitive processes, strategic alliances, the M-form organization, and a new theory of the firm.
3. *Style.* Style—management or corporate—is not often discussed directly in strategic management literature, though its presence and effects are pervasive. Chapters in this section discuss style from the perspectives

of the global manager, government policies, executive education, government leadership, reducing uncertainty/complexity, and gaining management consensus.

Section I

Strategy

Managers formulate competitive strategies that they hope will provide their firms with some degree of competitive advantage in their chosen markets. Generalization about corporate strategy beyond that point is difficult, due to the heterogeneity of firms and the different sets of resources they bring to the formulation process. In other words, there is no universal recipe for an effective strategy. Some researchers suggest that strategy may, in fact, be more often a trial-and-error process than precise execution of a carefully crafted plan. Quinn's theory of "logical incrementalism" suggests that, in the absence of overwhelming crises, managers attempt to ". . . sense new strategic needs well in advance, . . ." and ". . . avoid early identification with specific solutions to maintain flexibility, . . ." (*Strategies for Change: Logical Incrementalism*, 1980: 204, 205). The chapters in this section add an interesting variety of perspectives to the continuing conversation in competitive strategy.

Barney and Hansen identify three forms of trust in economic exchanges—weak, semi-strong, and strong—and the conditions under which each can be a source of competitive advantage. This is an extension of transactions cost theory, suggesting that finding nonopportunistic exchange partners can enable firms to gain all the advantages of trade, without the costs associated with governance.

Boyd, Howard, and Carroll empirically examine CEO duality in six European countries (Belgium, France, Italy, Spain, Switzerland, and the UK) and conclude that, contrary to the exhortations of governance-reform advocates, duality has a limited, positive relationship with return on investment.

Canals suggests that the nature of excess capacity differs between industries depending on the nature of competition, globalization and government policies. Clear links between the industry and the capacity adjustment process suggest that long-term solutions lie in rethinking how the firm adds value for customers.

Chakravarthy describes differences in how American and European top management teams leading corporate transformations typically respond to the perceptions of external and internal stakeholders. In American firms the focus of attention is more on shareholders, while European firms appear to take a more balanced approach to the needs of all stakeholders. The author then examines two cases involving European firms, one using the traditional European approach and the other using essentially the American approach, in an attempt to resolve this apparent contradiction and to define what American managers can learn from each case.

D'Aveni suggests that the key to competitive success resides in dynamic strategic interactions in four arenas: cost and quality, timing and know-how, strongholds, and deep pockets. In a dynamic environment a firm's movement and relative position in any of these four arenas is critically important. D'Aveni argues that the only source of truly sustainable advantage is the firm's ability to manage its dynamic strategic interactions with competitors through frequent movements that maintain a relative position of strength in each of the four arenas. In other words, to sustain dominance, firms must seek a series of unsustainable advantages.

Monteverde argues that each organization has a unique set of communication codes that is an idiosyncratic asset upon which the firm can build sustainable competitive advantage. To capitalize on these assets, practitioners are advised to investigate the information flows of the organization and limit the firm to functions that require unstructured interaction.

Wright and Wright introduce a conceptual framework for the analysis of strategic windows, and then discuss the opening and closing of strategic windows as a function of the rate of market growth and competitor imitation. They test the model with an empirical analysis of data on consecutive product generations in the personal computer and semiconductor industries.

Overall, these chapters extend the conversation on corporate strategy and describe current trends in research in the area. The following readings are recommended for those who desire additional background information in this area:

- One of the early studies linking strategic planning and profit performance is described in "Impact of Strategic Planning on Profit Performance" (*Harvard Business Review*, March–April 1974), in which Sidney Schoeffler, Robert Buzzell, and Donald Heany discuss the initial phases of an ongoing study to determine the profit impact of marketing strategies (PIMS).
- In a follow-up article that has become something of a classic, Robert Buzzell, Bradley Gale, and Ralph Sultan, using the PIMS data base, find a positive correlation between market share and ROI ("Market Share—A Key to Profitability", *Harvard Business Review*, January–February 1975).
- A survey of Fortune 1000 firms is the basis of Philippe Haspeslagh's "Portfolio Planning: Uses and Limits" (*Harvard Business Review*, January–February 1982), in which he describes results that suggest that depersonalized, economic approaches can help managers solve the problems of managing diversified industrial companies.
- In "Building Strategy on the Experience Curve" (*Harvard Business Review*, March–April 1985) Pankaj Gemawat suggests that experience curve strategies can improve competitive performance in some clearly defined situations, but cautions that successful use requires understanding: why it works; how it works; and when to apply it.
- To examine the state of research in strategic management, James Fredrickson asked Edward Bowman, David Teece, Richard Daft, Henry Mintzberg, and Donald Hambrick for their perspectives. The result is *Perspectives on Strategic Management* (1990), an interesting discussion of the editor's and authors' perceptions of strategic management research: what they like about it; what they do not like; and what their evaluations mean for the future direction of this line of research.
- Michael Porter's writings on competitive strategy are frequently cited by other researchers, and include *Competitive Strategy: Techniques for*

Analyzing Industries and Competitors (1980), *Competitive Advantage: Creating and Sustaining Superior Performance* (1985), *Competition in Global Industries* (1986), and *The Competitive Advantage of Nations* (1990).

Trustworthiness as a Source of Competitive Advantage

JAY B. BARNEY, MARK H. HANSEN

Significant differences in assumption and method exist between behaviorally-oriented and economically oriented organizational scholars (Donaldson, 1990; Barney, 1990). While these differences manifest themselves in a wide variety of research contexts, nowhere are they more obvious than in research on the role of trust in economic exchanges.

On the one hand, behaviorally-oriented researchers often criticize economic models that assume exchange partners are inherently untrustworthy (Mahoney, Huff, and Huff, 1993) and constantly tempted to behave in opportunistic ways (Donaldson, 1990). These scholars are dissatisfied with economic analyses that suggest trust will only emerge in an exchange when parties to that exchange erect legal and contractual protections (called governance mechanisms) which make it in their self-interest to behave in a trustworthy manner (Williamson, 1975). On the other hand, more economically oriented scholars respond by observing that, at the very least, it is difficult to distinguish between exchange partners that are actually trustworthy and those that only claim to be trustworthy (Arrow, 1974, 1985; Williamson, 1985). Since one cannot reliably distinguish between these types of exchange partners, legal and contractual protections are a rational and effective means of assuring efficient exchange. Trust, many economists would argue, is in fact common in exchange relationships, precisely because of the constant threat of opportunistic behavior, linked with governance (Hill, 1990).

Strategy, Structure and Style. Edited by H. Thomas, D. O'Neal and M. Ghertman
Copyright © 1997 John Wiley & Sons Ltd.

These debates about the role of trust in exchange relationships are interesting, in their own right, but they are not terribly relevant for strategic management research. Much of this research focuses on understanding sources of competitive advantage for firms (Rumelt, Schendel, and Teece, 1991). The effort to understand sources of competitive advantage leads strategy researchers to study differences between firms that enable some firms to conceive of and implement valuable strategies that other firms can either not conceive of and/or cannot implement (Barney, 1991). Debates between behavioral and economically-oriented researchers about how trustworthy individuals or firms are fail to point to these kinds of differences. Moreover, while the behavioral and economic approaches suggest very different processes through which trust emerges in economic exchanges, both these approaches assert that trust in economic exchanges will be very common. Such common attributes of exchange relationships cannot be sources of competitive advantage for individual firms (Barney, 1991). To be a source of competitive advantage, trust must be available to only a few firms in their exchange relationships, not to most firms in most exchange relationships (Peteraf, 1993). The purpose of this chapter is to understand the conditions under which trust and trustworthiness in exchange relationships can, in fact, be a source of competitive advantage for firms.

DEFINING TRUST AND TRUSTWORTHINESS

Numerous definitions of trust and trustworthiness have been presented in the literature (Bradach and Eccles, 1989; Gambetta, 1988; Lewicki and Bunker, 1994). For purposes of this discussion, Sabel's (1993: 1133) definition of trust has been adopted: trust is the mutual confidence that no party to an exchange will exploit another's vulnerabilities.

Parties to an exchange can be vulnerable in several different ways. For example, when parties to an exchange find it very costly to accurately evaluate the quality of the resources or assets others assert they will bring to an exchange, these economic actors are subject to adverse selection vulnerabilities (Akerlof, 1970). When parties to an exchange find it very costly to accurately evaluate the quality of the resources or assets others are actually offering in an exchange, these economic actors are subject to moral hazard vulnerabilities (Holmstrom, 1979). Also, when parties to an exchange make large, asymmetric transaction-specific investments in an exchange, they are subject to hold-up vulnerabilities (Klein, Crawford, and Alchian, 1978). According to Sabel, when parties to an exchange trust each other, they share a mutual confidence that others will not exploit any adverse selection, moral hazard, hold-up, or any other vulnerabilities that might exist in a particular exchange.

A definition of trustworthiness follows directly from Sabel's definition of trust. As the word itself implies, an exchange partner is trustworthy when it is worthy of the trust of others. An exchange partner worthy of trust is one that will not exploit others' exchange vulnerabilities. Notice that while trust is an attribute of a relationship between exchange partners, trustworthiness is an attribute of individual exchange partners.

TYPES OF TRUST

While trust is the mutual confidence that one's vulnerabilities will not be exploited in an exchange, different types of trust can exist in different economic exchanges. These different types of trust depend on different reasons parties to an exchange can have the confidence that their vulnerabilities will not be exploited. At least three types of trust can be identified: weak form trust, semi-strong form trust, and strong form trust.

WEAK FORM TRUST: LIMITED OPPORTUNITIES FOR OPPORTUNISM

One reason that exchange partners can have the mutual confidence that others will not exploit their vulnerabilities is that they have no significant vulnerabilities, at least in a particular exchange. If there are no vulnerabilities, then the trustworthiness of exchange partners will be high, and trust will be the norm in the exchange.

This type of trust can be called weak form trust because its existence does not depend on the erection of contractual or other forms of exchange governance. Nor does its existence depend on commitments by parties to an exchange to trustworthy standards of behavior. Rather, trust emerges in this type of exchange because there are limited opportunities for opportunism. Parties to an exchange, in this weak form context, will gain all the benefits of being able to trust their exchange partners without substantial governance or other costs.

Of course, weak form trust is likely to emerge in only very specific kinds of exchanges, i.e. exchanges where there are limited vulnerabilities. In general, whenever the quality of goods or services that are being exchanged can be evaluated at low cost, and whenever exchange partners do not need to make transaction-specific investments to obtain gains from an exchange, vulnerabilities in that exchange will be limited, and weak form trust will be common. Easy-to-evaluate quality effectively eliminates adverse selection and moral hazard vulnerabilities; no transaction-specific investment effectively eliminates hold-up vulnerabilities. In this sense, weak form trust is clearly endogenous, i.e. it emerges out of a very specific exchange structure.

Given this analysis, an important question becomes: how often will weak form trustworthiness exist? While, ultimately, this is an empirical question, it seems likely that weak form trust will be the norm in highly competitive commodity markets (Williamson, 1975). Examples of such markets include the market for crude oil and the market for soy beans. In all these markets, it is relatively easy for buyers and sellers to evaluate the quality of the goods or services they are receiving. Moreover, in all these markets, there are large numbers of equally qualified buyers and sellers. Thus, firms do not have to make transaction-specific investments to trade with any one firm. Since parties to exchanges in these kinds of markets are not subject to significant exchange vulnerabilities, weak form trustworthiness is usually the norm.

SEMI-STRONG TRUST: TRUST THROUGH GOVERNANCE

When significant exchange vulnerabilities exist (due to adverse selection, moral hazard, hold-up, or other sources), trust can still emerge, if parties to an exchange are protected through various governance devices. Governance devices impose costs of various kinds on parties to an exchange that behave opportunistically. If the appropriate governance devices are in place, the cost of opportunistic behavior will be greater than its benefit, and it will be in the rational self-interest of exchange partners to behave in a trustworthy way (Hill, 1990). In this context, parties to an exchange will have the mutual confidence that their vulnerabilities will not be exploited because it would be irrational to do so. This type of trust can be called semi-strong trust, and is the type of trust emphasized in most economic models of exchange (Hill, 1990).

A wide range of governance devices have been described in the literature. Economists have tended to focus on market-based and contractual governance devices. One market-based governance device is the market for reputations (Klein, Crawford, and Alchian, 1978). Examples of more contractual forms of governance include complete contingent claims contracts, sequential contracting, strategic alliances, and hierarchical governance (Williamson, 1985; Hennart, 1988; Kogut, 1988). Contractual governance devices explicitly define what constitutes opportunistic behavior in a particular exchange and specify the economic costs that will be imposed on offending parties (Williamson, 1979).

Recently, this economic focus on market-based and contractual governance devices has been criticized as being badly undersocialized (Granovetter, 1985). Several authors have suggested that a variety of social costs can also be imposed on exchange partners that behave in opportunistic ways. In this sense, these social costs can be seen as a form of governance.

One implication of including governance devices that impose social costs on opportunistic exchange partners, instead of just economic costs, is the expectation that opportunistic behavior will be unusual, even in settings where few market-based or contractual governance devices are in place, as long as these more social forms of governance exist (Granovetter, 1985). However, while this more social approach to governance broadens the range of governance devices that should be studied, the trust that emerges among parties to an exchange with these social governance mechanisms in place is of the same type as the trust that emerges with only economic governance devices in place. In both cases, trust emerges because rational actors find it in their self-interest, for both economic and social reasons, not to behave opportunistically.

Like weak form trust, semi-strong trust is endogenous, i.e. it emerges out of the structure of a particular exchange. However, unlike weak form trust, the structure of that exchange is modified, in the semi-strong case, through the use of governance devices of various types. If parties to an exchange create and/or exploit the correct governance devices, then opportunistic behavior in that exchange will be unlikely, and trust—albeit of the semi-strong variety—will exist.

Of course, the creation and exploitation of different forms of governance are not costless. The costs of market-based and contractual forms of governance are well documented (Williamson, 1985). While social forms of governance have fewer direct costs associated with them, they are nevertheless costly, in the sense that the use of these forms of governance requires one to only engage in exchanges where potential partners are embedded in specific broader social networks of relations. This limitation on potential exchange partners is an opportunity cost of using social forms of governance.

Traditional transactions cost logic suggests that rational economic actors will insist on just that level of governance necessary to ensure the semi-strong trustworthiness of exchange partners. One implication of this form of analysis is that there may be some potentially valuable exchanges that cannot be pursued. Whenever the cost of governance needed to generate semi-strong trust is greater than the expected gains from trade, an exchange with semi-strong trustworthy partners will not be pursued. This can happen in at least two ways. First, the expected gains from trade may be relatively small, in which case even modest investments in governance mechanisms may not pay off. Second, the expected gains from trade may be very large, but so may be the exchange vulnerabilities in that trade. In this type of exchange, the high cost of governance may still be greater than the expected value of exchange, even if that expected value is large. Indeed, as Grossman and Hart (1986) suggest, there may be some exchanges where no governance devices will create semi-strong trust (i.e. where the cost of governance is infinitely high). If the only types of trust that can exist in economic exchanges are of the weak and semi-strong types, then these valuable, but costly to govern, exchanges may have to remain unexploited.

STRONG FORM TRUST: HARD CORE TRUSTWORTHINESS

Strong form trust emerges in the face of significant exchange vulnerabilities, independent of whether or not elaborate social and economic governance mechanisms exist, because opportunistic behavior would violate values, principles, and standards of behavior that have been internalized by parties to an exchange. Strong form trust could also be called principled trust, since trustworthy behavior emerges in response to sets of principles and standards that guide the behavior of exchange partners. Frank (1988) might call strong form trust "hard core trust." Hard core trustworthy exchange partners are trustworthy, independent of whether or not exchange vulnerabilities exist and independent of whether or not governance mechanisms exist. Rather, hard core trustworthy exchange partners are trustworthy because that is who, or what, they are.[1] In this sense, strong form trustworthiness is clearly exogenous to a particular exchange structure. Strong form trust does not emerge from the structure of an exchange, but rather reflects the values, principles, and standards that partners bring to an exchange.

The Strong Form Trustworthiness of Individuals

While the existence of strong form trustworthiness is ultimately an empirical question, research from a variety of disciplines can be helpful in answering the existence question. If exchange partners are individuals, then research in developmental psychology suggests that strong form trustworthiness can exist in at least some people.

Developmental psychologists have studied the stages of moral development in children and young adults. (Kohlberg, 1969, 1971). A simplified version of these stages is summarized in TABLE 1.1. When children are very young they are unable to make moral choices. In this stage, decision making and behavior are essentially amoral. However, as children mature, they often have to decide whether or not to conform their choices and behaviors to a set of values, principles, and standards. In the conventional morality stage (Kohlberg, 1969), children conform their choices and behaviors to a set of values, principles, and standards in order to avoid the costs imposed on them by others for failing to do so. In this stage, children are moral because the costs of being caught violating principles and standards (i.e. punishment) are too high. In the post-conventional morality stage, choices and behaviors conform to a set of values, principles, and standards because they are internalized by individuals. While external costs could still be imposed on choices and behaviors that do not conform to these principles and standards, avoiding these costs is not the primary motivation for moral behavior. Rather, the primary motivation for such behavior is to avoid internally imposed costs, including a sense of personal failure, guilt, and so forth.

TABLE 1.1 Parallels between stages of moral development and types of trust

Stages in moral development	Types of trust and trustworthiness
Amoral stage: when there are no moral choices to be made	**Weak form trust:** limited opportunities for opportunism
Conventional morality: decisions and behaviors conform to standards in order to avoid the cost of being caught violating standards	**Semi-strong form trust:** trust emerges in response to social and economic governance mechanisms that impose costs on opportunistic behavior
Post-conventional morality: decisions and behaviors conform to standards because they have been internalized as principles and values	**Strong form trust:** an exchange partner behaves in a trustworthy manner because to do otherwise would be to violate values, standards, and principles of behavior

Some obvious parallels, identified in TABLE 1.1, exist between the types of trust and trustworthiness identified here and the stages of moral development identified in developmental psychology. The amoral stage in the moral development literature is analogous to weak form trustworthiness. Just as young children cannot violate moral standards when they are unable to make moral choices, individuals in exchange relationships cannot act opportunistically when there are no opportunities to do so. Conventional morality is analogous to semi-strong trustworthiness. In conventional morality, individuals make choices to conform their behavior to a set of principles and standards in order to avoid the cost of failing to do so; in semi-strong trust, opportunistic behavior is avoided because of the economic and social costs imposed on such behavior by governance mechanisms. Finally, post-conventional morality is analogous to strong form trustworthiness. In both cases, choices and behavior conform to a set of principles and standards because those principles and standards have been internalized. While external costs may be imposed on individuals that violate these principles and standards, avoiding these external costs is not the primary reason choices and behavior conform to them. Rather, the avoidance of internally imposed costs—including a sense of personal failure and guilt—provide the primary motivation for this type of principled behavior.

Psychologists have shown that post-conventional morality is not uncommon (Kohlberg, 1971). In order for post-conventional morality to lead to strong form trustworthiness, all that is additionally required is that some of these values, principles, and standards suggest that exploiting an exchange partner's vulnerabilities is inappropriate.

The Strong Form Trustworthiness of Firms

At the individual level, the existence of strong form trustworthiness in at least some people seems plausible. However, that individuals—as exchange partners—can be strong form trustworthy does not necessarily imply that firms—as exchange partners—can be strong form trustworthy. Firms, as exchange partners, can be strong form trustworthy for at least two reasons. Either a firm may possess a culture and associated control systems that reward strong form trustworthy behavior, or the specific individuals involved in a particular exchange may, themselves, be strong form trustworthy.

Zucker (1987) has shown that firm founders can have a very strong impact on the culture and other institutional attributes of firms. This impact can continue, even if these individuals have been dead for many years. If these and other influential individuals were themselves strong form trustworthy, they may have created an organizational culture characterized by strong form trustworthy values and beliefs. These strong form trustworthy values and beliefs may also be supported and reinforced by internal reward and compensation systems, together with decision-making mechanisms that reflect strong form trustworthy standards. A firm with these cultural and institutional mechanisms in place will often behave in a strong form trustworthy manner in exchange relationships.

Moreover, exchanges between firms are, more often than not, actually exchanges between small groups of individuals in different firms. For example, when an automobile company signs a supply agreement with a supplier, the two groups of individuals most directly involved in this agreement are the purchasing people, in the automobile company, and the sales people, in the supply company. While the firms in these exchanges may not have strong form trustworthy cultures, the specific individuals that are most directly involved in these exchanges may, themselves, be strong form trustworthy. Exchanges between strong form trustworthy individuals in different firms can lead to strong form trust, even though the firms, themselves, may not be strong form trustworthy.

TRUST AND COMPETITIVE ADVANTAGE

Trust can emerge in economic exchanges in any of the three ways discussed. However, these three types of trust are not equally likely to be sources of competitive advantage.

WEAK FORM TRUST AND COMPETITIVE ADVANTAGE

The exchange attributes that make weak form trust possible suggest that weak form trust will usually not be a source of competitive advantage. As suggested earlier, weak form trust is most likely to emerge in highly competitive commodity markets. It is well known that exchange partners in highly competitive commodity markets can expect to gain few, if any, competitive advantages (Porter, 1980). In particular, while those participating in these markets will be able to rely on the existence of weak form trust in their exchange relationships, the advantages of weak form trust will accrue to all exchange partners in these markets equally, thereby giving no one of them a competitive advantage.

SEMI-STRONG FORM TRUST AND COMPETITIVE ADVANTAGE

Semi-strong trust in exchange relationships is economically valuable, in the sense that its creation assures parties to an exchange that their vulnerabilities will not be exploited. However, the ability to create semi-strong trust in economic exchanges depends on several important governance skills and abilities that parties to an exchange must possess. For example, for semi-strong trust to emerge, exchange partners must be able to accurately anticipate sources and levels of opportunistic threat in the exchanges in which they may participate. Also, to create semi-strong trust, exchange partners must be able to rely on existing social governance mechanisms and/or to conceive of, implement, and manage the appropriate market-based and contractual governance mechanisms. Only if exchange partners can accomplish these tasks will the "right" types of governance be chosen to create semi-strong trust and the value of semi-strong trust be realized.

However, for semi-strong trust to be a source of competitive advantage, there must be heterogeneity in the exchange governance skills and abilities of competing firms (Barney, 1991). If most competing firms or individuals have similar governance skills and abilities, they will all be equally able to create the conditions under which semi-strong trust will emerge in their exchange relationships. Moreover, the cost of creating semi-strong trust will also not vary dramatically across these equally skilled competitors. Since these competitors do not vary in their exchange governance skills, no one of them will be able to gain a competitive advantage based on the semi-strong trust that they are able to create with these skills.

Of course, there is no reason to believe, a priori, that competing exchange partners will be equally skilled or able in creating the conditions necessary for semi-strong trust. For example, some exchange partners may have developed a high degree of skill in managing, say, intermediate market forms of governance (e.g. equity joint ventures). These highly skilled actors may be able to create semi-strong trust using these intermediate market forms of governance in economic exchanges where less skilled actors may be forced to use hierarchical forms of governance. If intermediate market forms of governance are, in fact, less costly than hierarchical forms of governance, those that obtain semi-strong trust through intermediate market forms will have a competitive advantage over those that must obtain trust in that exchange through hierarchical forms of governance. Similar reasoning could apply to those that are highly skilled in managing contractual forms of governance (e.g. complete contingent claims contracts) compared to those that are only able to use more costly intermediate market forms of governance or hierarchical forms of governance.

Moreover, not only must these special skills and abilities be heterogeneously distributed across time, they also cannot rapidly diffuse among competitors and still be a source of sustained competitive advantage (Barney, 1991).

In general, whenever exchange partners possess rare and costly to imitate governance skills and abilities, they may be able to use those abilities to gain competitive advantages in creating semi-strong trust. On the other hand, when competing exchange partners possess similar governance skills and abilities, the creation of semi-strong trust will generate only competitive parity.

STRONG FORM TRUST AND COMPETITIVE ADVANTAGE

For strong form trustworthiness to be economically valuable, all those with a significant stake in an exchange must be strong form trustworthy. If one or more parties to an exchange may behave opportunistically in that exchange, then all parties to that exchange will need to invest in a variety of social and economic governance mechanisms to ensure semi-strong trust. Any potential economic advantages of being strong form trustworthy are irrelevant when semi-strong governance protections are erected and exploited, since strong form trustworthy parties are forced to behave as if they were only semi-strong trustworthy.

Economic Opportunities in Strong Form Trust Exchanges

On the other hand, if all those with a significant stake in an exchange are strong form trustworthy, some important and valuable economic opportunities may exist. These opportunities reflect either the governance cost advantages that strong form trust exchanges may enjoy over semi-strong form trust exchanges and/or the ability that strong form trustworthy exchange partners may have to explore exchange options not available to semi-strong form trustworthy exchange partners.

When two or more strong form trustworthy individuals or firms engage in an exchange, they can all be assured that any vulnerabilities that might exist in this exchange will not be exploited by their partners. Moreover, this assurance comes with no additional investment in social or economic forms of governance. As long as the cost of developing and maintaining strong form trustworthiness in an individual or firm, plus the cost of discovering strong form trustworthy partners, is less than the cost of exploiting or creating semi-strong form governance devices, those engaging in a strong form trustworthy context will gain a cost advantage over those exchanging in a semi-strong trustworthy context.

Perhaps even more important than this governance cost advantage, those engaging in strong form trust exchanges may be able to exploit exchange opportunities that are not available to those who are only able to engage in semi-strong trust exchanges. It has already been suggested that valuable semi-strong exchanges will not be pursued when the cost of governance needed to generate semi-strong trust is greater than the expected gains from trade. While semi-strong trust exchanges will not be pursued in these situations, it may be possible to pursue strong form trust exchanges. In this sense, strong form trustworthiness may increase the set of exchange opportunities available to an individual or firm, compared to those who are only semi-strong trustworthy (Zajac and Olsen, 1993; Ring and van de Ven, 1994).

Consider, for example, several competing firms looking to cooperate with one or more of several other firms in the development and exploitation of a new, and sophisticated, technology. Suppose that only a small number of these two sets of firms are strong form trustworthy, that the technology in question has significant economic potential, but that there are enormous exchange vulnerabilities in the technology development process. Semi-strong trustworthy firms, in this setting, will need to invest in substantial amounts of costly governance to try to create semi-strong trust. It may even be the case that no form of governance will create semi-strong trust (Grossman and Hart, 1986). The potential economic return that could be obtained from this exchange will need to be reduced by an amount equal to the present value of the cost of governing this exchange. Moreover, the present value of this exchange will also have to be discounted by any residual threat of opportunism. The reduced value of this exchange could lead semi-strong trustworthy firms to decide not to pursue it, even though substantial economic value may exist.

On the other hand, exchanges of this sort between strong form trustworthy firms are burdened neither by the high cost of governance nor any residual threat of opportunism. Strong form trustworthy firms will be able to pursue these valuable but highly vulnerable exchanges, while semi-strong form trustworthy firms will be unable to pursue them. This may represent a substantial opportunity cost for semi-strong trustworthy exchange partners and a source of competitive advantage for strong form trustworthy exchange partners.

Traditional transactions cost logic suggests that, when faced with these valuable but highly vulnerable exchanges, exchange partners will opt for hierarchical forms of governance and use managerial fiat as a way to manage trustworthiness problems (Williamson, 1985). However, hierarchical governance is not always a solution to these problems. First, there may be important legal and political restrictions on the use of hierarchical governance. For example, one cannot acquire a direct competitor if such actions lead to unacceptably high levels of industry concentration. Also, firms may be required, for political reasons, to maintain market or intermediate market relationships with an exchange partner (e.g. when entering into a new country market).

Second, as Grossman and Hart (1986) suggest, hierarchical governance does not necessarily "solve" opportunism problems. Rather it simply shifts those problems from a market or intermediate market context to inside the boundaries of the firm. Where, in market-based exchanges, firms face the threat of opportunism in exchanges with other firms, bringing these transactions within the boundaries of a firm can simply lead to a division facing the threat of opportunism in exchanges with other divisions. Put differently, hierarchical governance does not automatically create strong form trust exchanges (Ouchi, 1980).

Where hierarchical governance may not always be a solution to the threat of opportunism, exchanges between strong form trustworthy exchange partners—whether those exchanges are within the boundary of a single firm or not—will, in general, create strong form trust. Strong form trustworthy individuals or firms will often be able to gain governance cost advantages over semi-strong trustworthy individuals or firms. Moreover, strong form trustworthy individuals or firms will often be able to engage in economic exchanges that cannot be pursued by semi-strong trustworthy exchange partners. Put differently, the level of vulnerability in some economic exchanges may be greater than the ability of any standard governance devices to protect against the threat of opportunism. The only way to pursue these exchanges is through strong form trustworthiness.

Of course, if most competitors are strong form trustworthy, and engage in exchanges with others that are also strong form trustworthy, then the advantages of strong form trustworthiness would only be a source of competitive parity, and not competitive advantage. However, while the number of strong form trustworthy exchange partners in a particular segment of the economy is ultimately an empirical question, it seems like a reasonable guess that strong form trustworthiness in at least some segments of the economy is probably rare, and thus (assuming exchanges with other strong form trustworthy exchange partners are developed) at least a source of temporary competitive advantage for strong form trustworthy individuals and firms.

Locating Strong Form Trustworthy Exchange Partners

Given the important competitive advantages that may attend exchanges between strong form trustworthy exchange partners, an important question becomes: how can strong form trustworthy exchange partners recognize each other? This process is problematic, since exchange partners that are not strong form trustworthy have a strong incentive to assert that they are.

Of course, a simple solution to this adverse selection problem would be to directly observe whether or not a potential exchange partner is strong form trustworthy, and respond appropriately. Unfortunately, the individual and organizational attributes that create strong form trustworthiness are difficult to directly observe. At an individual level, the values, principles, and standards around which strong form trustworthy individuals organize their lives are clearly not directly observable. At the firm level, an organization's culture, and associated control systems, may be difficult to observe, and their implications for individual behavior ambiguous—at least to those not deeply embedded in this culture and control system. Moreover, if the development of strong form trust depends on the strong form trustworthiness of small groups of people in a larger organization, evaluating the individual values, principles, and standards of these people remains difficult.

Even with these challenges, strong form trustworthy exchange partners can still be found. It will often be the case, for example, that exchange partners will begin a relationship assuming that others are at least semi-strong trustworthy. As this relationship evolves over time, parties to an exchange may be able to gain sufficient information to accurately judge whether or not others are strong form trustworthy. If two or more parties to an exchange discover that they are strong form trustworthy, any subsequent exchanges between these parties can generate strong form trust, and these exchange partners will subsequently obtain all the advantages of strong form trustworthiness.

Notice that this process of discovering strong form trustworthy exchange partners assumes that one's trustworthiness type does not automatically change as a result of experience in a semi-strong trust relationship. If the creation of semi-strong trust exchanges inevitably led exchange partners to become strong form trustworthy, then all exchanges would inevitably be characterized by strong form trust, and strong form trustworthiness would not be a source of competitive advantage to any individual or firm. Rather than changing an exchange partner's trustworthiness type, the creation of a semi-strong trust exchange creates an opportunity for exchange partners to more directly observe another's trustworthiness type.

This search for potential strong form trustworthy exchange partners can be shortened through the use of signals of strong form trustworthiness

(Spence, 1973). Signals of strong form trustworthiness must have two properties: (1) they must be correlated with the underlying (but costly to observe) actual level of strong form trustworthiness in a potential exchange partner, and (2) they must be less costly to exchange partners that are actually strong form trustworthy than they are to exchange partners that only claim they are strong form trustworthy (Spence, 1973).

Several behaviors by exchange partners qualify as signals for strong form trustworthiness. For example, a reputation for being strong form trustworthy is a signal of strong form trustworthiness. Gaining a reputation as a strong form trustworthy exchange partner occurs, over time, as an exchange partner confronts situations where opportunistic behavior is possible, but chooses not to engage in opportunistic activities. There are no opportunity costs associated with a strong form trustworthy individual or firm not behaving opportunistically, since such behavior is not in this kind of exchange partner's opportunity set. On the other hand, nonstrong form trustworthy exchange partners will have to absorb opportunity costs each time they decide not to behave in an opportunistic way. These opportunity costs make it more costly for an exchange partner that is not strong form trustworthy to develop a reputation as strong form trustworthy, compared to an exchange partner that is actually strong form trustworthy.

While a reputation for being strong form trustworthy is a signal of strong form trustworthiness, it is noisy. In particular, this reputation cannot distinguish between those exchange partners that are actually strong form trustworthy and those that are not strong form trustworthy, but have yet to engage in an exchange where returns to opportunistic behavior are large enough to motivate opportunistic behavior. While a reputation for being strong form trustworthy does eliminate those exchange partners who have acted opportunistically, it does not eliminate those exchange partners who might act opportunistically, given the right incentives.

Another signal of strong form trustworthiness is being open to outside auditing of the exchange relationship. This is less costly to strong form trustworthy exchange partners, compared to those that are not strong form trustworthy, since trustworthy exchange partners were not going to behave opportunistically anyway. One would expect to see strong form trustworthy firms and individuals to be very open to outside auditors, perhaps even paying the cost of outside auditors chosen by potential exchange partners.

A third signal of strong form trustworthiness might be to make unilateral transaction-specific investments in an exchange before that exchange is actually in place. Gulati, Khana, and Nohira (1994) have found, for example, that it is not uncommon for firms with a strong track record of successfully engaging in joint ventures to sign long-term third-party supply contracts that are only valuable if a particular joint venture actually goes forward— before that joint venture agreement is complete. Such unilateral transaction-specific investments are less costly to strong form trustworthy firms, since they were not going to behave in an opportunistic manner in developing this joint venture anyway. These investments foreclose opportunistic opportunities for firms that are not strong form trustworthy, and thus represent significant opportunity costs to these firms.

If strong form trustworthiness is relatively rare among a set of competitors, and if two or more strong form trustworthy exchange partners are able to engage in trade, then these strong form trustworthy individuals or firms will gain at least a temporary competitive advantage over individuals or firms that are not strong form trustworthy. For this competitive advantage to remain, however, the individual and organizational attributes that make strong form trustworthiness possible must also be costly to imitate and immune from rapid diffusion. Fortunately, the individual and organizational attributes that make strong form trustworthiness possible (i.e. individual values, principles, and standards; an organization's culture and associated control systems) reflect an exchange partner's unique path through history (path dependence) and are socially complex and thus are immune from competitive imitation (Barney, 1991; Arthur, 1989; Dierickx and Cool, 1989).

DISCUSSION

Trust, in economic exchanges, can be a source of competitive advantage. However, trust in these exchanges is not always a source of competitive advantage. Weak form trust is only a competitive advantage when competitors invest in unnecessary and costly semi-strong governance mechanisms. Semi-strong trust is only a source of competitive advantage when a small number of competitors have special skills and abilities in conceiving of and implementing social and economic governance devices and when those skills and abilities are immune from low cost imitation. Strong form trust is a source of competitive advantage when two or more strong trustworthy individuals or firms engage in an exchange, when strong form trustworthiness is relatively rare among a set of competitors, and when the individual and organizational attributes that lead to strong form trustworthiness are immune from low cost imitation.

This analysis has important implications for research in organization theory and strategic management. For example, these ideas can be seen as an extension of transactions cost theory—an extension that makes this form of analysis strategically more relevant. Where transactions cost economics implicitly assumes that the skills and abilities needed to conceive of and implement governance mechanisms are constant across individuals and firms (Williamson, 1985), this approach suggests that these skills and abilities may vary in some strategically important ways. Also, where transactions cost theory assumes either that all potential exchange partners are equally likely to behave opportunistically or that one cannot distinguish between those that will behave opportunistically and those that will not (Williamson, 1985), this analysis suggests that potential exchange partners' opportunistic tendencies may vary, and that these differences can be discovered.

Thus, consistent with many of the more behaviorally-oriented organizational scholars cited earlier, the approach in this chapter rejects both the assumption that all exchange partners are likely to engage in opportunistic behavior and the assumption that it is not possible to know how opportunistic a particular exchange partner is likely to be. However, these transactions cost assumptions are not replaced by equally extreme, if opposite, assumptions that most exchange partners are trustworthy most of the time. Rather, the approach adopted here is that the trustworthiness of exchange partners can vary and that how trustworthy an exchange partner is can be discovered.

This analysis also points to two important exchange processes that have not received sufficient attention in the organization and strategy literatures. First, the argument suggests that semi-strong trust can be a source of competitive advantage if competing exchange partners vary in their skills and abilities in conceiving of and implementing governance mechanisms. What these specific skills and abilities might be, and why they might develop in some economic actors and not others, are unexplored issues in this chapter. What these skills are, and how they develop and evolve, are important research questions.

Second, the argument suggests that strong form trustworthy exchange partners may be able to discover other strong form trustworthy exchange partners. Once discovered, these kinds of exchange partners can gain important competitive advantages from working with each other. However, much more empirical work needs to focus on the process through which strong form trustworthiness evolves in an economic actor.

By examining the competitive implications of different types of trust in economic exchanges, it becomes clear that extreme assumptions about potential exchange partners—that most are trustworthy and that most are opportunistic—are overly simplistic. Rather, the trustworthiness of exchange partners may vary, and in that variance, the possibility of competitive advantage may exist.

NOTE

1. In principle, some level of compensation will always exist where strong form trustworthy exchange partners will abandon their values, principles, and standards of behavior, and act in opportunistic ways. This level of compensation might be called the "Faustian" price. However, this level of compensation is *much* higher for a strong form trustworthy exchange partner, compared to a semi-strong trustworthy exchange partner.

REFERENCES

Akerlof, G.A. (1970) "The Market for 'Lemons': Quality Uncertainty and the Market Mechanism", *Quarterly Journal of Economics*, **84**, 488–500.

Arrow, K.J. (1974) *The Limits of Organization*. New York: W.W. Norton.

Arrow, K.J. (1985) "The Economics of Agency", in J.W. Pratt and R.J. Zeckhauser (eds), *Principals and Agents: The Structure of Business*. Boston, Mass.: Harvard Press.

Arthur, W.B. (1989) "Competing Technologies, Increasing Returns, and Lock-in by Historical Events", *Economic Journal*, **99**, 116–131.

Barney, J.B. (1990) "The Debate between Traditional Management Theory and Organizational Economics: Substantive Differences or Intergroup Conflict?" *Academy of Management Review*, **15**, 382–393.

Barney, J.B. (1991) "Firm Resources and Sustained Competitive Advantage", *Journal of Management*, **17**, 99–120.

Bradach, J.L. and Eccles, R.G. (1989) "Price, authority, and trust", *Annual Review of Sociology*, **15**, 97–118.

Dierickx, I. and Cool, K. (1989) "Asset Stock Accumulation and Sustainability of Competitive Advantage", *Management Science*, **35**, 1504–1511.

Donaldson, L. (1990) "A Rational Basis for Criticisms of Organizational Economics: A Reply to Barney", *Academy of Management Review*, **15**, 394–401.

Frank, R.H. (1988) *Passions within Reason*. New York: W.W. Norton.

Gambetta, D. (1988) *Trust: Making and Breaking Cooperative Relations*. New York: Basil Blackwell.

Granovetter, M. (1985) "Economic Action and Social Structure: The Problem of Embeddedness", *American Journal of Sociology*, **91**(3), 481–510.

Grossman, S.J. and Hart, O. (1986) "The Costs and Benefits of Ownership: A Theory of Vertical and Lateral Integration", *Journal of Political Economy*, **94**, 691–719.

Gulati, R., Khana, T., and Nohira, N. (1994) "Unilateral Commitments and the Importance of Process in Alliances", *Sloan Management Review*, forthcoming.

Hennart, J-F. (1988) "A Transaction Costs Theory of Equity Joint Ventures", *Strategic Management Journal*, **9**, 361–374.

Hill, C.W.L. (1990) "Cooperation, Opportunism, and the Invisible Hand: Implications for Transaction Cost Theory", *Academy of Management Review*, **15**(3), 500–513.

Holmstrom, B. (1979) "Moral Hazard and Observability", *Bell Journal of Economics*, **10**, 74–91.

Klein, B., Crawford, R.A., and Alchian, A.A. (1978) "Vertical Integration, Appropriable Rents, and the Competitive Contracting Process", *Journal of Law and Economics*, **21**, 297–326.

Kogut, B. (1988) "Joint Ventures: Theoretical and Empirical Perspectives", *Strategic Management Journal*, **9**, 319–332.

Kohlberg, L. (1969) "Stage and Sequence: The Cognitive-developmental Approach to Socialization", in D.A. Goslin (ed.) *Handbook of Socialization*. New York: Rand McNally, pp. 347–489.

Kohlberg, L. (1971) "From Is to Ought", in T. Mischel (ed.) *Cognitive Development and Epistemology*. New York and London: Academic Press, pp. 151–236.

Lewicki, R.J. and Bunker, B.B. (1994) "Trust in Relationships: A Model of Trust Development and Decline", Working paper, Department of Management and Human Resources, The Ohio State University.

Mahoney, J.T., Huff, A.S., and Huff, J.O. (1993) "Toward a New Social Contract

Theory in Organization Science", Working paper 93-0136, Department of Management, University of Illinois at Urbana-Champaign.

Ouchi, W.G. (1980) "Markets, Bureaucracies, and Clans", *Administrative Science Quarterly*, **25**, 121–141.

Peteraf, M.A. (1993) "The Cornerstones of Competitive Advantage: A Resource-based View", *Strategic Management Journal*, **14**, 179–192.

Porter, M. (1980) *Competitive Strategy*. New York: Free Press.

Ring, P. and van de Ven, A. (1994) "Developmental Processes of Cooperative Interorganizational Relationships", *Academy of Management Review*, **19**, 90–118.

Rumelt, R., Schendel, D., and Teece, D. (1991) "Strategic Management and Economics", *Strategic Management Journal*, **12**, 5–29.

Sabel, C.F. (1993) "Studied Trust: Building New Forms of Cooperation in a Volatile Economy", *Human Relations* **46**(9), 1133–1170.

Spence, A.M. (1973) *Market Signalling: Information Transfer in Hiring and Related Processes*. Cambridge, Mass.: Harvard University Press.

Williamson, O.E. (1975) *Markets and Hierarchies: Analysis and Antitrust Implications*. New York: Free Press.

Williamson, O.E. (1979) "Transaction-cost Economics: The Governance of Contractual Relations", *Journal of Law and Economics*, **22**, 233–261.

Williamson, O.E. (1985) *The Economic Institutions of Capitalism*. New York: Free Press.

Zajac, E. and Olsen, C.P. (1993) "From Transaction Cost to Transaction Value Analysis: Implications for the Study of Interorganizational Strategies", *Journal of Management Studies*, **30**, 131–145.

Zucker, L.G. (1987) "Institutional Theories of Organization", *Annual Review of Sociology*, **13**, 443–464.

2

CEO Duality and Firm Performance: An International Comparison

BRIAN K. BOYD, MARLA HOWARD, W. OTTO CARROLL

INTRODUCTION

CEO duality exists when a firm's chief executive also serves as chairman of the board of directors. Governance reform advocates in the USA, UK, and elsewhere argue that duality enables CEOs to abuse their power, and recommend separation of these two positions. However, there is virtually no empirical evidence to support this recommendation. We develop comparative statistics on the occurrence of duality in 2097 firms in six European countries, and report that duality has a limited, positive relationship with return on investment.

The 1990s have been a period of heightened visibility for boards of directors in the USA and abroad. This upswell of interest—by both academics and the popular business press—is due in part to several recent trends. First, institutional investors have sought an increasing involvement in the management of their holdings as their portfolios have become less mobile. Second, shareholder activism has matured from a grass-roots phenomenon to a major factor in shareholder meetings and proxy contests. Mirroring the US experience, shareholder activism is also spreading through Europe. Third, there is a greater interest in both regulatory (e.g. new Securities and Exchange Commission (SEC) proxy requirements) and quasi-regulatory (e.g. the Cadbury recommendations in the UK or the Hilmer study in Australia) oversight of corporate boards. Finally, prominent corporate crises across the globe—including General Motors and Digital Equipment Corporation in the USA, Maxwell in the UK, Metallgesellschaft and Schneider in Germany, Alcatel in France, and Itowan in Japan—have raised concerns about the governance of these firms (*The Economist*, 1994).

It is not surprising, then, that this heightened visibility had led to extensive criticism: boards have been questioned in the press, at shareholder meetings, and in courtrooms regarding their decisions over corporate strategy, executive compensation, or even the composition of the board itself. One of the broadest criticisms is that chief executives dominate boards to their own advantage; this perception is the basis for governance reform efforts in many nations (Dalton, Kesner, and Rechner, 1988). Recently, retirement funds and shareholders' associations have targeted poorly performing firms—and the passive endorsement of CEO decisions—by demanding active, independent monitoring and evaluation of top management.

One area, CEO duality, has come under particular fire from reformers. Duality exists when a firm's chief executive also serves as chairman of the board of directors. It has been argued that duality is a cause of poor performance and the inability of US firms to keep up with the need to change (*Wall Street Journal*, 1992a). Most academic researchers have also supported separation of these positions: Michael Jensen (1993), for example, has argued that duality is simply inconsistent with the notion of good internal control. Similarly, Jay Lorsch (1989: 184–185) recently recommended "One major need is to diminish the CEO's power as leader of the board. . . . Providing a leader separate from the CEO could significantly help directors prevent crises, as well as to act swiftly and effectively when one occurs." In the 1993 proxy season, resolutions to separate chief executive and chairman positions emerged at Chrysler, Advanced Micro Devices, Champion International, Sears & Roebuck, and other major firms. Additionally, concern over duality has surfaced outside the USA as well: in the UK, the Cadbury Report, the Pensions Investment Research Consultants (PIRC) (a research arm of UK pension funds), and the Institutional Stockholders Committee have all proposed separation of chief executive and chairman positions (*Corporate Governance*, 1993; Oxford Analytica, 1992; Stiles and Taylor, 1993). Similar proposals have been made regarding the boards of both Australian (Donaldson and Davis, 1991) and Canadian firms (Conference Board of Canada, 1995). However, despite the seemingly reasonable plea by shareholder activists and governance experts to separate the positions of CEO and chairman, empirical evidence to date lends little or no support that such separation is associated with improved or higher levels of firm performance.

While relatively little is known about the causes and consequences of duality in the USA, even less is known about this topic in other countries. We attempt to rectify this research gap by studying duality in six European countries: Belgium, France, Italy, Spain, Switzerland, and the UK. Our goal is to develop comparative statistics on duality for these countries, examine the effect of duality on performance, and to extend the theoretical foundation for future research.

LITERATURE REVIEW

While the combination of CEO and chairman positions has drawn considerable attention in the popular press and from governance reform advocates, the topic has received relatively little attention by business researchers. Not only is academic study on this topic fairly sparse, but it is also compounded by two substantial limitations—a nearly exclusive focus on US firms, and a lack of theory development. We explore each of these issues in the following paragraphs.

First, while there is an extensive literature on boards of directors, the vast majority of this research is focused on the boards of US firms—including studies of CEO duality. Consequently, many authors (e.g. Demb, 1996; Zahra and Pearce, 1989) have called for more emphasis on boards outside the USA. In general, comparative research on issues across national boundaries is notedly difficult to perform; questions of both data collection and the context of research abound (Boyacigiller and Adler, 1991). With regard to boards of directors, there are three main reasons why researchers often limit their focus to the USA: perceived uniqueness, researcher ethnocentrism, and data availability (Boyd, Carroll, and Howard, 1996). Faced with these limitations, it is not surprising that there is very little work available on duality in other countries. Dalton and Kesner (1987) provided comparative data on the frequency of duality in Japan, the USA, and the UK, while a subsequent paper (Dalton, Kesner, and Rechner, 1988) discussed the context and implications of duality in other countries. Finally, several authors (e.g. Mills, 1981; Spencer, 1983) have provided very different estimates of the frequency of duality in the UK. While review and conceptual papers address the potentially adverse consequences of CEO duality—Sykes (1994: 118), for example, mentions the "unease over this concentration of power"—no prior studies have documented performance disparities or actual governance failures attributed to duality among non-US firms.

Despite the challenges of international board research, the effect of duality on performance abroad is a relevant and timely question. Despite claims of uniqueness, certain consistencies surrounding boards of directors in different nations have been found. One primary role of boards is decision making with limited information. This is readily identifiable regardless of the board structure or composition (Demb and Neubauer, 1992). That this is true for different models of corporate governance may be due in part to the increasing globalization of products and markets (*The Economist*, 1994), as well as the increased globalization of capital structures (Carroll, 1995). With respect to industrialized economies, the context of decisions has been found to be more important than nationality (Everett, Stening, and Longton, 1982; Hoffman and Hegarty, 1989). This is especially applicable to the current sample, as the same corporate philosophical underpinnings are present (Tricker, 1994). In addition, the validity of cross-national board research has been demonstrated by prior research (Demb, 1996; Demb and Neubauer, 1992). Other common functions of corporate boards across nations and even legal systems include evaluation and control of company management (Dalton and Kesner, 1987).

The second limitation of most prior studies of duality is the emphasis on performance outcomes versus development of a theoretical framework of *how* and *why* duality should affect performance. The need for a solid theoretical framework is particularly important as empirical studies of US firms have yielded largely inconsistent results: some studies (Berg and Smith, 1978; Rechner and Dalton, 1991) have reported negative relationships between duality and performance, one study (Donaldson and Davis, 1991) reported a small, positive relationship, and other studies (Cannella and Lubatkin, 1993; Mallette and Fowler, 1992; Rechner and Dalton, 1989) have reported a minimal relationship. A recent meta-analysis integrated these findings and reported an aggregate effect size of -0.02 between duality and performance (Boyd, 1995). In the absence of any clear empirical or theoretical rationale for or against CEO-chairs, it is therefore impossible to develop useful normative guidelines for effective board structure. Boyd (1995) addressed this theory vacuum, and argued that these disparate findings could be resolved via the integration of two different perspectives: agency theory and stewardship.

Agency theory is founded on economics-based research on risk sharing. An agency problem exists when an agent (e.g. a CEO) has established goals which conflict with that of a principal (e.g. shareholders). Agency problems are more likely to occur when an agent has little or no financial stake in the outcome of his decisions (Fama and Jensen, 1983)—a common scenario in many large US corporations (Boyd, 1994; Lewellen, Loderer, and Rosenfeld, 1985). Thus, an agent may be tempted to maximize his power or personal wealth at the expense of the corporation (Fama, 1980; Ichan, 1986).

Corporations attempt to prevent agency problems by delegating *decision management* to the CEO, and *decision control* to the board. Thus, the CEO is responsible for initiation and implementation of strategic decisions, while the board is responsible for ratifying and monitoring decisions by the CEO. The board is viewed as the primary internal control mechanism for aligning the different interests of shareholder and top management (Mizruchi, 1983; Walsh and Seward, 1990).

The consolidation of the two positions provides the CEO with a broader power base (Hambrick and Finkelstein, 1987; Harrison, Torres, and Kukalis, 1988; Patton and Baker, 1987), the appearance of unity of command (Finkelstein and D'Aveni, 1994), and weakens decision control by the board (Boyd, 1994; Morck, Shleifer, and Vishny, 1989). This reduction in board control better enables the CEO pursue his own agenda at the expense of shareholder goals (Mallette and Fowler, 1992). Agency problems and the corporate governance failures have been linked with numerous adverse outcomes, including higher levels of executive compensation (Boyd, 1994), golden parachute provisions (Singh and Harianto, 1989), antitakeover "poison pills" (Mallette and Fowler, 1992), greenmail payments (Kosnik, 1987), and wealth-diluting acquisitions (Lewellen, Loderer, and Rosenfeld, 1985). Thus, agency theory would propose that combination of CEO and chairman positions would weaken board control, and negatively affect firm performance.

In comparison, the stewardship model argues that duality offers many benefits, and is a mechanism which can be used to improve firm performance. One assumption of the agency model is that executives are inherently opportunistic agents who will capitalize on every chance to maximize personal welfare at the expense of shareholders. Donaldson (1990) voiced concern with the inability of agency theory to address and integrate related research in organizational theory and organizational behavior. The desire to maximize income, for example, might be counterbalanced by "a much larger range of human motives, including needs for achievement, responsibility, and recognition, as well as altruism, belief, respect for authority, and the intrinsic motivation of an inherently satisfying task" (Donaldson, 1990: 372). Thus, Donaldson proposes a very different model—that the CEO "far from being an opportunistic shirker, essentially wants to do a good job, to be a good steward of the corporate assets" (Donaldson and Davis, 1991: 51). Stewardship theory asserts that CEO duality would facilitate effective action by the CEO, and consequently lead to higher performance.

Support for the stewardship model is provided by other research on corporate governance. Resource dependence theory (Pfeffer and Salancik, 1978) proposes that corporate boards are a mechanism to manage external dependencies and reduce environmental uncertainty, and that characteristics of an effective board will vary as a function of environmental conditions. Resource dependence has been supported by several studies linking board composition and environmental conditions (e.g. Boyd, 1990; Pfeffer, 1972, 1973; Pfeffer and Salancik, 1978). Given the large and intertwining web of institutional cross-holdings common among European companies, resource dependence theory seems especially applicable to the European context.

Resource dependence would therefore suggest that CEO duality might actually improve organizational performance in certain contexts (Boyd, 1995): leaders with greater discretion would be better able to overcome organizational inertia, and hence more likely to implement their strategic decisions (Pfeffer and Salancik, 1978). Duality also increases chief executive discretion by providing a broader power base and by weakening the relative power of other interest groups (Hambrick and Finkelstein, 1987: 379). A single leader will improve responsiveness to external events, and facilitate accountability of decision making (Pfeffer and Salancik, 1978). Duality also centers authority (Perrow, 1986); for example, duality has been found to facilitate replacement of the CEO when faced with poor corporate performance (Harrison, Torres, and Kukalis, 1988). Boyd (1995) argued that the competing views of agency and stewardship regarding duality could be integrated via a contingency model, as shown in FIGURE 2.1. He noted:

> . . . the agency model of the CEO-Chair as the opportunistic, self-maximizing, shirker is as extreme a model as stewardship's depiction of the CEO-Chair as the altruistic, self-sacrificing steward of corporate assets. In practice, elements of both theories are likely to be present. The critical question, therefore, is under what circumstances does the consolidation of power and decision-making afforded by duality outweigh the potential abuses described by the agency model?

The paper argued that the benefits of duality (i.e. the stewardship rationale) would outweigh the costs (i.e. the agency rationale) in markets which would require a strong CEO and fast strategic decision making. Using Dess and Beard's (1984) model of organizational environments, duality was positively linked with return on investment (ROI) under conditions of resource scarcity (low munificence) and intense competition (high complexity). While the link between duality and ROI in volatile environments (high dynamism) was in the expected direction, this relationship was not statistically significant.

What other factors might moderate the costs and benefits associated with duality? Relevant research suggests that the international dimension may be an important element in the duality–performance relationship. In the USA, we saw that duality and performance were moderated by market characteristics. Under the conditions when the benefits of stewardship

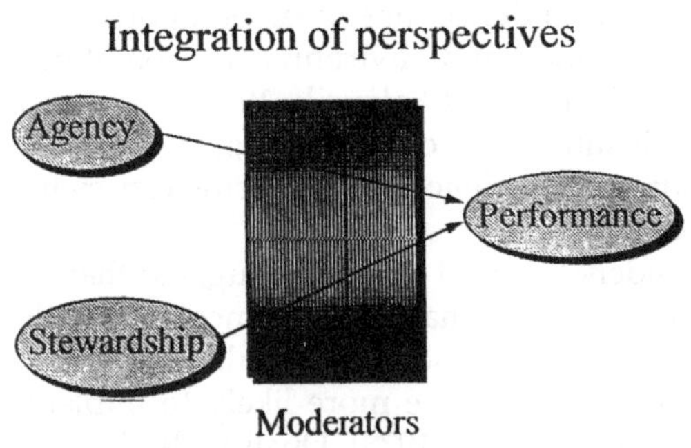

FIGURE 2.1   A contingency model of duality and performance

outweigh the costs of the agency model, there is a long-run positive return to having a combined CEO-chair. Ultimately, both agency and stewardship are models of organizational behavior—dependent on characteristics such as altruism versus opportunism, or individualism versus collectivism. Because these characteristics stem from culture and national management styles, the likelihood of agency abuses may be greater or lower in one country than another, and the benefits of stewardship may also vary from one country to the next.

Self-maximization is a fundamental assumption of the agency model, and such behavior is likely to depend heavily on whether a culture emphasizes individuality or collectivism. Hofstede's (1980) study shows the USA ranking much higher on the "individualism" value index than the European counterparts. Additionally, European executives have been found to have fewer lifetime employers and a longer duration of employment than their American counterparts. These statistics are relevant to agency theory in two ways: first, the stability of employment is likely to foster greater loyalty to the firm; this, in turn, creates a disincentive for agency problems. Second, the longer duration of employment is associated with a longer planning horizon, and less individual accountability regarding short-term performance (Pennings, 1993). Thus, sacrificing the firm's long-term profitability for short-term gains is likely to be less acceptable or desirable in the European context than the US. An additional measure of support for stewardship models is provided by d'Iribarne (1994), who found that the "honor principle" guides much management activity in France. In this setting, workers and managers internalize the roles and expectations necessary for the successful operation of their firm.

Not only is there a lesser likelihood of self-interested behavior among European managers, but equity practices ensure a climate more conducive to effective monitoring and control. While corporate ownership in the UK is more dispersed than in other European countries, it is still much more concentrated than in the USA (Li, 1994; Sykes, 1994). Ownership structure plays an important role in the agency–stewardship debate, as without separation of ownership and management, the presumption of an agency problem is absent. Additional limitations on agency problems in Europe are generated by the ongoing relationships and cross-holdings among companies. After the original Berle and Means (1932) thesis, separation of ownership and control also implies an ease of transfer of ownership which is not met currently in Europe. Restrictions on transferability arise either from the state (*Wall Street Journal*, 1994) or banks and other industrial cross-holdings (Scott, 1987; Sykes, 1994). Another case for the minimization of agency costs is when the CEO is also a major shareholder (Fama and Jensen, 1983). This is often the case in Europe, as family corporations are more prevalent than in the USA (Banai and Levicki, 1988). The need for monitoring of agency costs may be less in the smaller companies common in Europe which allow an atmosphere of trust to exist (Barkema, 1995). A comparison of the following agency outcomes suggests that—in general— the European context is less susceptible to agency problems than the United States.

EXECUTIVE COMPENSATION

Levels of CEO compensation are often viewed as an indicator of agency problems (Fama, 1980; Fama and Jensen, 1983). Drastic differences in the levels of total CEO compensation, i.e. $717 237 in the USA, versus $439 441 in the UK, $463 009 in Italy, or $479 772 in France*, suggest that agency problems may be less prevalent in Europe than the United States (*Wall Street Journal*, 1992b). Similarly, CEOs of US firms have been characterized as trying to manipulate the board in effort to maximize their personal wealth (Boyd, 1994; Walsh and Seward, 1990). Compensation is viewed very differently in Europe, however. For example, French executives have described high levels of compensation as "scandalous" and "demoralizing" (Pennings, 1993: 271), and "[European] Executives, including the CEO, are motivated by a mixture of immaterial income, such as challenge, pride, freedom, resources, and so on" (Pennings, 1993: 272). Pennings concludes that "discussion of agency theory in these countries is ill-fitting or even irrelevant" (1993: 276–277). Additionally, Barkema (1995) questioned the strict applicability of agency theory's economic underpinnings to top managers. In his study of Dutch executives, he found that other incentives— such as social contracts with subordinates—may be more effective than compensation packages.

DIVERSIFICATION

While individual shareholders can diversify their financial risk by investing in several firms, top managers do not have this flexibility. Rather, they derive much of their wealth from the firm they manage. Agency theory proposes that these managers—in the absence of a substantial ownership stake or external monitoring—will attempt to reduce this business-specific risk via diversification. Thus, greater emphasis on unrelated versus related diversification is viewed as a symptom of agency problems (Eisenhardt, 1989; Jensen and Meckling, 1976). The agency model of diversification has been supported in one empirical study of US firms (Amihud and Lev, 1981). In support of our culture-based model, American firms have been found to have fewer single/

---

* These estimates are based on comparably sized firms, and include cash, stock options, benefits, and perks.

dominant product firms, and higher levels of unrelated diversification than their counterparts in the UK (Jammine, 1984; Rumelt, 1982).

Consequently, the likelihood of agency problems would appear to be much less for European firms than the USA. In contrast, the European management styles described previously would appear very much in accordance with the stewardship model. Therefore, we propose the following hypothesis:

H1: CEO duality will be positively associated with firm performance in European firms.

METHOD

One criticism of international board research is the inconsistent degree of coverage for boards in different countries (Boyd, Carroll, and Howard, 1996). In Europe, for example, the vast majority of studies examine either the UK or Germany, with relatively little attention devoted to other members of the European community. Data were collected for companies in six European countries: Belgium, France, Italy, Spain, Switzerland, and the UK; this sample was intended to provide a more detailed and comprehensive view of European governance practices. We excluded countries which require two-tier boards (e.g. Germany) and those which impose restrictions against combined CEO-chairs (e.g. duality is prohibited in most Scandinavian nations, except for smaller firms).

All firms in the sample were publicly held, and data for all variables were collected from the *Disclosure WorldScope* CD-ROM database. All data collected were for 1991, and companies with missing data were either deleted from the sample, or supplemented with additional data from company annual reports or Moody's *International Manual*.

Duality was coded as "1" if the firm's chief executive also served as chair of the board of directors, and "0" otherwise. Performance was operationalized using ROI. Given international differences in profitability norms and accepted accounting practices, we analyzed data from each country separately, and in their own currencies. Then, results from each country were aggregated using the meta-analysis procedure described by Hunter, Schmidt, and Jackson (1982). Additional variables (e.g. firm sales, industry affiliation) were collected for use in descriptive analyses.

RESULTS

Complete data were collected for 2097 firms. The majority of these were UK firms ($N = 1137$), followed by France ($N = 385$) and Italy ($N = 195$). The sample firms represented a broad array of industry types; from primary materials, to manufacturing, service, and finance. Banking and financial services (SICs 60 to 69) were the most common industry type, comprising 25% of our sample. Manufacturing (SICs 30 to 39) was the next most common, comprising 22% of the sample. Distribution of the sample by industry type and country is shown in TABLE 2.1.

TABLE 2.1   Sample by country and industry code

SIC codes	Belgium	France	Italy	Spain	Switzerland	UK	Column total
01–19	11	36	14	12	3	102	178
20–29	18	74	37	19	24	203	375
30–39	29	86	50	21	41	232	459
40–49	12	24	12	18	19	51	136
50–59	10	46	8	2	20	175	261
60–69	51	94	67	25	36	245	518
70–79	1	22	7	1	5	91	127
80–89	0	3	0	1	0	34	38
90–99	1	0	0	0	0	4	5
Row total	133	385	195	99	148	1137	

Next, we analyzed the frequency of duality by country. As shown in FIGURE 2.2, duality was prevalent in France (70% of firms have combined CEO-chairs), yet relatively rare in Italy (18% firms) or Spain (11% of firms). Our sample reported duality in 22% of UK firms, a smaller estimate than the 30% reported by Dalton and Kesner (1987). However, their estimate was based on a 1986 sample of 50 of the largest UK firms.

Hypothesis 1 stated that CEO duality will be positively related with firm performance in European firms. The following element of our analysis was to compare performance levels of firms with CEO-chairs against those with independent boards. These results of these analyses are shown in FIGURE 2.3. While firms with CEO-chairs had higher levels of ROI in four of the six countries (Spain, Belgium, Italy, and the UK), this effect was statistically significant only for the UK sample ($p = 0.01$).

To aggregate these results, we used the meta-analysis procedure described by Hunter, Schmidt, and Jackson (1982): the t-tests for each country were first transformed into the effect size r (analogous to the Pearson correlation). The six estimates of r were then aggregated, weighted by sample size. The overall effect size of the relationship between duality and performance was 0.09. Thus, on average, there was a limited, positive effect of duality on ROI. These findings offer limited support for hypothesis 1.

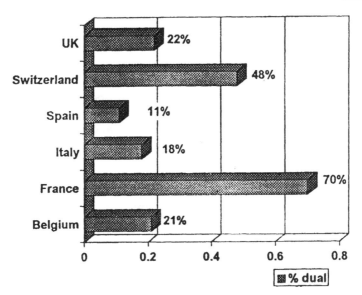

FIGURE 2.2   Occurrence of duality by country

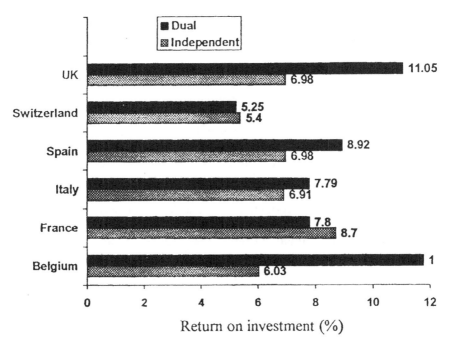

FIGURE 2.3   Duality and performance by country

Discussion

Governance reform advocates worldwide have recommended unilateral separation of the chairman and chief executive positions, despite the absence of any quantifiable link to firm performance. Our results indicate that the dangers of CEO duality among European firms are largely illusory. Consequently, any movement toward the Scandinavian model (i.e. mandatory separation of chief executive and chairman positions) would not improve returns to stockholders, and may even diminish the rate of return.

While these findings may be of modest statistical significance, they do yield important insights into two theoretical perspectives which are applied to top managers. First, our results offer a significant, empirical confirmation of Pennings' (1993) conclusion regarding the limited applicability of agency theory to European executives. While agency theory would predict sizable adverse consequences, the meta-analysis indicates a small, positive effect of duality. Thus, investigating the generalizability of agency theory beyond the US border is an important agenda for future research.

These findings question the generalizability of stewardship theory as well. Given the loyalty, long-term perspective, and collective orientation of the "typical" Euromanagers, they would have the promise of making much better "stewards" than their American counterparts. However, the magnitude of the return to duality is much smaller than expected. One possible explanation lies in other cultural traits identified by Hofstede (1980). For example, scores on Hofstede's "uncertainty avoidance" value index indicate that many Europeans are substantially more risk averse than their American counterparts. Similarly, the "masculinity" scores—which reflect the importance of success and achievement—are much higher for American than European executives. A likely scenario, then, is that the power, discretion, and latitude afforded by duality is of little benefit if the chief executive is unwilling to exert that power. Stated bluntly, a risk averse and non-achievement oriented steward may be little better than no steward at all. Future studies could address this issue using finer-grained approaches based on case studies or interviews with CEO-chairs of European firms.

As mentioned in the introduction, General Motors is frequently used as an example of a corporate governance failure. The unchallenged leadership of Roger Smith who maintained tight control over GM and its board has been cited as an example where one well-intentioned man would let nothing stop him from excessive spending in negative net present value (NPV) projects. Key information for directors was withheld until shortly before board meetings and the meeting times were scheduled rigidly with little time for discussion. He expected ratification from his loyal directors. Jensen (1993) questions what if GM had acquired Toyota and Honda, total equity value of $26.2 billion in 1985, instead of spending the $67.2 billion in research and development and investments in excess of depreciation between 1980 and 1990, inclusive. Would an independent chairman of the board have broken Smith's power barrier? In 1994 GM issued board guidelines after thoughtful consideration of its governance system. The first guideline addresses CEO duality by stating that the board should retain the freedom to make the choice they deem appropriate and also there shall be no requirement that the chairman of the board be a nonemployee. However, many of the remaining 27 guidelines provide alternative control mechanisms including a routine of periodic monitoring of management and assessment of directors and of management. The policies of scheduled regular meetings of outside directors, a lead outside director, and independent key committees provides internal control, and can offset any loss of control associated with the consolidation of CEO and chairman positions (*Directors & Boards*, 1994). Similarly, Boyd (1994) demonstrated that duality is just one element of the firm's internal control system. His study concluded that control is determined by a number of factors, including duality, director equity holdings, board representation by ownership groups, the ratio of insiders, and levels of director compensation. Thus, by guiding the design of these other aspects of board structure, firms can gain the benefits of duality without sacrificing control.

A greater understanding of how companies throughout the world balance the entrenchment avoidance and unity of command dilemma should be sought by examining the duality–performance relationship in the context of independence, activity level, qualifications or reputation, and incentives of other members of the board. The comparative picture of corporate governance is incomplete without a careful historical analysis of corporate and regional cultures including the role of government, debt holders, institutional investors, employees, and other stakeholders in monitoring corporations across the world. Different nations' corporations are characterized by very different capital structures, financial reporting and audit requirements, firm size, capital, labor, and product markets. Family-controlled corporations are more prevalent in Europe than in the United States and corporate cross-holdings are commonplace. These factors, which are very different from US corporate characteristics, may dominate the management control issue, making both the agency and the stewardship theories of CEO performance trivial in some nations.

In spite of differences from country to country, this study and related comparative research can provide useful insight as national barriers of the capital, labor, and product markets fade away and changes in business result. Globalization is here to stay and is the most prevalent reason that systems of corporate governance are converging in the industrialized world. The analysis by Oxford Analytica (1992: 1) summarizes key changes across the G7 to be "greater accountability, broader representation of stakeholder interests, and an enhanced role for the board in strategic direction."

Perhaps the benefits of stewardship and trust will exceed the agency costs regardless of national culture as these changes and convergence occur.

Finally, the experience and results of studies on board roles and structure is of imminent interest in nations which are beginning to privatize and where equity ownership is a novelty. The entire corporate ownership and governance system is being shaped in new market economies. Why should they not learn from the experience of centuries of market economies taking into account their own circumstances as Demb (1996) suggests? In fact, the Russian Privatization Bureau invited a working group from the West to draft a corporate governance system for Russia; evidence of the importance of further research of internal control systems (Monks and Minow, 1995). After all if we agree that there is a common problem set—defined by Demb (1996: 105) that "All boards are groups of individuals engaged in complex judgments about ill-defined issues!"—then we should be able to learn from others and from comparative research.

ACKNOWLEDGEMENT

This project was funded by a grant from Old Dominion University's Bureau of Research, College of Business Administration.

REFERENCES

Amihud Y. and Lev, B. (1981) "Risk Reduction as a Managerial Motive for Conglomerate Mergers", *Bell Journal of Economics*, **12**, 605–617.

Banai, M. and Levicki, C.J. (1988) "Europe", in R. Nath (ed.) *Comparative Management: A Regional View*. Cambridge, Mass.: Ballinger Publishing Company, pp. 97–137.

Barkema, H.G. (1995) "Do Top Managers Work Harder When They Are Monitored?" *Kyklos*, **48**(1), 19–42.

Berg, S.V. and Smith, S.K. (1978) "CEO and Board Chairman: A Quantitative Study of Dual vs. Unitary Board Leadership", *Directors & Boards*, **3**, 34–39.

Boyacigiller, N.A. and Adler, N.J. (1991) "The Parochial Dinosaur: Organizational Science in a Global Context", *Academy of Management Review*, **16**, 262–290.

Boyd, B. (1990) "Corporate Linkages and Organizational Environment: A Test of the Resource Dependence Model", *Strategic Management Journal*, **11**, 419–430.

Boyd, B.K. (1994) "Board Control and CEO Compensation", *Strategic Management Journal*, **15**, 335–344.

Boyd, B.K. (1995) "CEO Duality and Firm Performance: A Contingency Model", *Strategic Management Journal*, **16**, 301–312.

Boyd, B.K., Carroll, W.O., and Howard, M.H. (1996) "International Governance Research: A Review and Agenda for Future Studies", *Advances in International Comparative Management*. Greenwich, CT: JAI Press, pp. 191–215.

Cannella, A.A. and Lubatkin, M. (1993) "Succession as a Sociopolitical Process:

Internal Impediments to Outsider Succession", *Academy of Management Journal*, **36**, 763–793.

Caroll, W.O. (1995) "Corporate Governance Reform across Nations: A Review", Paper presented at the annual meeting of the International Association of Business and Society, Vienna.

Conference Board of Canada (1995) *Corporate Governance: Improving the Effectiveness of Crown Corporation Boards*. Ottawa: Self-published.

Corporate Governance: An International Review (1993) "Corporate Governance update", **1**(1), 48–50.

Dalton, D.R. and Kesner, I.F. (1987) "Composition and CEO Duality in Boards of Directors: An International Perspective", *Journal of International Business Studies*, **18**(3), 33–42.

Dalton, D.R., Kesner, I.F., and Rechner, P.L. (1988) "Corporate Governance and Boards of Directors: An International, Comparative Perspective", *Advances in International Comparative Management*, **3**, 95–105.

Demb, A. (1996) "Phasing and Focusing research: Accelerating along the Learning Curve", *Advances in International Comparative Management*, Greenwich, CT: JAI Press, pp. 101–125.

Demb, A. and Neubauer F.F. (1992) *The Corporate Board: Confronting the Paradoxes*. New York: Oxford Press.

Dess, G.G. and Beard, D. (1984) "Dimensions of Organizational Task Environments", *Administrative Science Quarterly*, **29**, 52–73.

Directors & Boards (1994) "The GM Board Guidelines", **18**(4), 5–9.

D'Iribarne, P. (1994) "The Honour Principle in the 'Bureaucratic Phenomenon' ", *Organization Studies*, **15**, 81–97.

Donaldson, L. (1990) "The Ethereal Hand: Organizational Economics and Management Theory", *Academy of Management Review*, **15**, 369–381.

Donaldson, L. and Davis, J.H. (1991) "Stewardship Theory or Agency Theory: CEO Governance and Shareholder Returns", *Australian Journal of Management*, **16**, 49–64.

Eisenhardt, K. (1989) "Agency Theory: An Assessment and Review", *Academy of Management Review*, **14**, 57–74.

Everett, J.E., Stening, B.W., and Longton, P.A. (1982) "Some Evidence for an International Managerial Culture", *Journal of Management Studies*, **19**, 153–162.

Fama, E.F. (1980) "Agency Problems and the Theory of the Firm", *Journal of Political Economy*, **88**, 288–307.

Fama, E.F. and Jensen, M.N. (1983) "Separation of Ownership and Control", *Journal of Law and Economics*, **26**, 301–325.

Finkelstein, S. and D'Aveni, R. (1994) CEO Duality as a Double-edged Sword: How Boards of Directors Balance Entrenchment Avoidance and Unity of Command", *Academy of Management Journal*, **7**, 1079–1108.

Hambrick, D.C. and Finkelstein, S. (1987) "Managerial Discretion: A Bridge between Polar Views of Organizational Outcomes", *Research in Organizational Behavior*, **9**, 369–406.

Harrison, J.R., Torres, D.L., and Kukalis, S. (1988) "The Changing of the Guard: Turnover and Structural Change in the Top-management Positions", *Administrative Science Quarterly*, **33**, 211–232.

Hoffman, R.C. and Hegarty, W.H. (1989) "Convergence or Divergence of Strategic Decision Processes among 10 Nations", in C.A.B. Osigweh, Yg (ed.) *Organizational Science Abroad*. New York: Plenum Press, pp. 97–115.

Hofstede, G.H. (1980) *Culture's Consequences*. Beverly Hills: Sage.

Hunter, J.E., Schmidt, F.L., and Jackson, G.B. (1982) *Meta-analysis: Cumulating Research Findings across Studies*. Beverly Hills: Sage.

Ichan, C. (1986) "What Ails Corporate America—and What Should Be Done?" *Business Week*, October 27, 98–104.

Jammine, A.P. (1984) "Product Diversification, International Expansion and Performance: A Study of Strategic Risk Management in UK Manufacturing", unpublished doctoral dissertation, London Business School.

Jensen, M.C. (1993) "The Modern Industrial Revolution, Exit, and the Failure of Internal Control Systems", *The Journal of Finance*, 48(3), 831–880.

Jensen, M.C. and Meckling, W.F. (1976) "Theory of the Firm: Managerial Behavior, Agency Costs, and Ownership Structure", *Journal of Financial Economics*, 3, 305–360.

Kosnik, R.D. (1987) "Greenmail: A Study of Board Performance in Corporate Governance", *Administrative Science Quarterly*, 32, 163–185.

Lewellen, W., Loderer, C., and Rosenfeld, A. (1985) "Merger Decisions and Executive Stock Ownership in Acquiring Firms", *Journal of Accounting and Economics*, 7, 209–231.

Li, J. (1994) "Ownership Structure and Board Composition: A Multi-country Test of Agency Theory Predictions", *Managerial and Decision Economics*, 15, 359–368.

Lorsch, J.W. (1989) *Pawns or Potentates: The Reality of America's Corporate Boards*. Cambridge: Harvard Business School Press.

Mallette, P. and Fowler, K.L. (1992) "Effects of Board Composition and Stock Ownership on the Adoption of 'Poison Pills' ", *Academy of Management Journal*, 35, 1010–1035.

Mills, G. (1981) *On the Board*. London: George Allen.

Mizruchi, M.S. (1983) "Who Controls Whom? An Examination of the Relation between Management and Boards of Directors in Large Corporations", *Academy of Management Review*, 8, 426–435.

Monks, R. and Minow, N. (1995) *Corporate Governance*. Cambridge: Blackwell Business Publishers.

Morck, R., Shleifer, A., and Vishny, R.W. (1989) "Alternative Mechanisms for Corporate Control", *American Economic Review*, 79, 842–852.

Oxford Analytica (1992) *Board Directors and Corporate Governance: Trends in the G7 Countries over the Next Ten Years*. Oxford: Self-published.

Patton, A. and Baker, J.C. (1987) "Why Won't Directors Rock the Boat?" *Harvard Business Review*, 65(6), 10–12, 16, 18.

Pennings, J.M. (1993) "Executive Reward Systems: A Cross-national Comparison", *Journal of Management Studies*, 30, 261–280.

Pfeffer, J. (1972) "Size and Composition of Corporate Boards of Directors: The Organization and its Environment", *Administrative Science Quarterly*, 17, 218–228.

Pfeffer, J. (1973) "Size, Composition, and Function of Hospital Boards of Directors: A Study of the Organization–environment Linkage", *Administrative Science Quarterly*, 18, 349–364.

Pfeffer, J. and Salancik, G. (1978) *The External Control of Organizations: A Resource Dependence Perspective*. New York: Harper and Row.

Rechner, P.L. and Dalton, D.R. (1989) "The Impact of CEO as Board Chairperson on Corporate Performance: Evidence vs. Rhetoric", *Academy of Management Executive*, 3, 141–143.

Rechner, P.L. and Dalton, D.R. (1991) "CEO Duality and Organizational Performance: A Longitudinal Study", *Strategic Management Journal*, 12, 155–160.

Rumelt, R. (1982) "Diversification Strategy and Performance", *Strategic Management Journal*, **3**, 359–370.

Scott, J. (1987) "Intercorporate Structures in Western Europe: A Comparative Historical Analysis", in M.S. Mizruchi and M. Schwartz (eds) *Intercorporate Relations*. Cambridge: Cambridge University Press, pp. 208–232.

Singh, H. and Harianto, F. (1989) "Top Management Tenure, Corporate Ownership Structure and the Magnitude of Golden Parachutes", *Strategic Management Journal*, **10**, 143–156.

Spencer, A. (1983) *On the Edge of Organization: The Role of the Outside Director.* New York: Wiley.

Stiles, P. and Taylor, B. (1993) "Benchmarking Corporate Governance: The Impact of Cadbury Code", *Long Range Planning*, **26**, 61–71.

Sykes, A. (1994) "Proposals for a Reformed System of Corporate Governance to Achieve Internationally Competitive Long-term Performance", in N. Dimsdale and M. Prevezer (eds) *Capital Markets and Corporate Governance*. Oxford: Clarendon Press, pp. 111–127.

The Economist (1994) "Watching the Boss: A Survey of Corporate Governance." January 29, 1–18.

Tricker, R.I. (1994) "The Board's Role in Strategy Formulation: Some Cross-cultural Comparisons", *Futures*, May, 403–415.

Wall Street Journal (1992a) "Other Concerns Are Likely to Follow GM in Splitting Posts of Chairman and CEO", November 4, B1, B11.

Wall Street Journal (1992b) "Managers' Incomes Aren't Worlds Apart", October 12, B.1.

Wall Street Journal (1994) "France's Bureaucracy Finds It Hard to Stop Meddling in Industry", June 17, A1, A6.

Walsh, J.P. and Seward, J.K. (1990) "On the Efficiency of Internal and External Corporate Control Mechanisms", *Academy of Management Review*, **15**, 421–458.

Zahara, S.A. and Pearce, J.A. (1989) "Boards of Directors and Corporate Financial Performance: A Review and Integrative Model", *Journal of Management*, **15**, 291–334.

Excess Capacity and Global Competition: A Resource-based Approach

JORDI CANALS

INTRODUCTION

Rivalry in many industries in Europe has increased dramatically in recent years. Reports related to excess capacity in industries such as automobiles, steel, chemicals, consumer electronics, personal computers or commercial banking are common.

Firms that compete in these industries find themselves in a difficult and complex situation. On one hand, they are pursuing a higher market share and contributing to a downward pressure on prices, due to fierce competition. On the other hand, many of those firms lack the operational flexibility they need, their production costs are high and difficult to curb, their margins are declining and many of them are losing money.

The degree of excess capacity in Europe is not easy to measure. Let us have a quick look at the automobile industry. It was estimated to have a total installed capacity of about 13.5 million cars at the end of 1994. That same year little more than 10 million units were sold, so excess capacity was around 3.5 million units.

However, those estimates present limitations. First, some companies have manufacturing facilities that can work in several shifts per week, and this must therefore be taken into account when measuring total installed

Strategy, Structure and Style. Edited by H. Thomas, D. O'Neal and M. Ghertman
Copyright © 1997 John Wiley & Sons Ltd.

capacity. The second limitation refers to the export capacity of other countries to the European market and its measurement. Exports from third countries contribute to increase excess capacity.

In any case, it is obvious that excess capacity in those industries leads to price wars among competitors that hope to maintain their market share. Price wars partially explain the losses experienced by several companies. Consequently, the problem of excess capacity in Europe is a serious one for many companies and, indirectly, for governments as well.

The purpose of this chapter is to examine the roots of excess capacity in Europe in the 1990s, as well as the steps that companies can take to solve this problem. Our principal argument is that efforts to rationalize capacity by restructuring or downsizing firms are important, but not always sustainable. The factors that lead to sustainable competitive advantage are innovation and investment (in new capacity). Excess capacity can be better understood if we approach it and link it up with innovation and investment decisions. To develop this argument, we will use some of the contributions from the resource-based view of the firm.

The outline of this chapter is as follows. The origin and nature of excess capacity are developed in the next section and then the adjustment in capacity at the industry level is discussed. The following section reviews some of the firms' reactions to excess capacity. The analysis is enriched here with the experience of some European companies. The resource-based perspective of excess capacity is offered next, and in the final section we present a managerial approach to excess capacity and investment decisions.

THE ORIGIN AND NATURE OF EXCESS CAPACITY IN EUROPE

Ghemawat and Caves (1986) show that profitability decreases as competition to expand capacity increases. The origin of heightened competition in different industries is, in general, not related to price-cutting strategies but to a massive increase in capacity investment. Some contributions from industrial economics offer a first explanation of the phenomenon's roots.

This growth in capacity may be the result of a deliberate strategy of incumbent companies to deter the entry of new competitors in their industry (Dixit, 1980; Gilbert and Harris, 1984; Spence, 1977). However, this behavior is not the most frequent case. The reasons are numerous. For example, many industries have more than two competing companies, while the majority of models of capacity expansion designed to deter the entrance of potential competitors assume only two companies. Also, efforts to discourage the entry of these competitors are usually very expensive for those companies that undertake them, as has been pointed out by Johnson and Parkman (1983) and Porter and Spence (1982). This is a reason why that behavior is not observed in many industries. Another reason that explains

TABLE 3.1 Some explanations for excess capacity in Europe

External factors	Internal factors
Foreign direct investment	
Deregulation	Biased forecasts
New competitors	Excess investment
Economic cycle	Scale
Changes in demand	Barriers to exit
Changes in technologies	

the high cost of this strategy is that some of those models assume the existence of perfect information, while in many industries the increase in capacity is subject to several uncertainties, among others that of adverse selection (Ghemawat, 1987).

Nevertheless, empirical evidence shows that the development of installed excess capacity in European industries stems from other causes, different from the entry deterrence story. We shall distinguish, in the first place, between causes external to companies that compete in an industry and causes internal to these companies (TABLE 3.1). Let us begin with external causes.

EXTERNAL DRIVERS OF EXCESS CAPACITY

The first factor to be considered is the increase in foreign direct investment (FDI) in European Union (EU) countries, coming both from other EU countries, as well as from third-party countries, such as Japan and the United States.

When the goal of direct investment has been the acquisition of existing companies, production capacity, in general, has not increased. However, when direct investment has created new companies, the capacity in the industry has increased. The case of the automobile industry in Europe is a clear example of the increase in production capacity provoked by direct investment, coming from other European countries, as well as from Japan or the United States.

A second factor to examine is deregulation. Deregulation in many industries (banking, telecommunications, or medical equipment) has spawned new possibilities to compete within countries (for instance, with price competition) and across countries. In general, the optimal level of capacity in a regulated industry is higher than in more competitive industries.

Another reason for the increase in capacity in Europe is the emergence of new, export-led competitors, outside of the EU countries. In fact, the growing liberalization of international trade, the emergence of new exporting powers like South Korea, Taiwan and Singapore, and the opening up of EU countries with respect to Central and Eastern European countries, have generated a considerable increase in installed capacity in certain industries.

More specifically, the increase in capacity is especially apparent in products which compete primarily on costs and in those where technological innovation is low or slow to come about. The new export-led countries enjoy important advantages, due to their low labor and social costs.

Technological change introduced in production processes, generated from the application of the new information technologies and the growing use of robotics, has also brought about an interesting phenomenon: the existence of excess installed capacity that is unuseable due to its high costs, above the industry average cost (Bianchi and Volpato, 1990). In other words: this capacity is obsolete, and companies consider it worthless, due to the fact that improvements in the production processes developed in recent years make older facilities uncompetitive. The reasons for this obsolescence may be economic (the old production processes are not competitive in costs) or marketing-led (the old production processes cannot guarantee a minimum product quality, offered by other companies in the industry).

The appearance of worthless production capacity ("the wrong kind of capacity") has also been spurred by important changes in the demand for certain products. In the automobile industry this change has been particularly intense: the growing demand for better quality and improved car performance has rendered obsolete production facilities that did not meet these objectives at levels similar to those of the competition.

When substitute products appear, or demand changes, previous investments lose part of their value. The launch of new products to substitute for existing ones (for example, medical diagnosis based on computerized scanning or magnetic resonance have replaced traditional radiologic diagnostics and, therefore, the demand for X-ray equipment) or the introduction of more efficient production processes, explain how new competitors or the established companies that lead this change show advantages in costs, in product quality or in both attributes over other companies that are slower to react.

One last external factor, of a cyclical nature, that has contributed to the present excess capacity in Europe is the economic recession of 1992–94 which has provoked a significant decline in consumer demand. Companies dependent upon the evolution of the economic cycle have found themselves with unexpected excess capacity.

INTERNAL DRIVERS OF EXCESS CAPACITY

The second set of reasons for the increase in production capacity in Europe has to do with internal factors within the companies themselves. In the first place, we must point out the expectations created around the Single European Market. When, back in 1986, the EC began to approve the Directives that would lead to the creation of an internal market for the member countries, many companies in different industries saw that circumstance as an opportunity for investment and growth. Some companies opted for acquiring others. On the other hand, other companies tried to grow internally. This internal growth was also stimulated by the strong economic growth in Europe during the second half of the 1980s.

In the end, this factor is related to an exceedingly optimistic sales forecast, that led to the belief that the economic growth in the second half of the 1980s would last for many years. Baden-Fuller (1990a) has argued that these exceedingly optimistic forecasts for growth in demand were also the cause of excess capacity in certain industries after the first oil crisis in the 1970s.

This phenomenon has been analyzed in detail by Ghemawat (1987), who points out that the uncertainty surrounding certain investment decisions creates more chances of bad choices. In this case, companies with more optimistic forecasts are the ones that tend to invest in excess capacity. This explanation coincides, to a great extent, with the phenomenon known as "the winners' curse": in an auction, the winner is usually the one whose forecasts are the most optimistic.

A second phenomenon related to the creation of a single market in Europe was the general belief that economies of scale would be the key success factor in the integrated European economy. This assumption led many companies to expand their capacity, and increase their minimum scale, while thinking that the previous scale was not efficient. This factor, while critical for some companies and industries, was not so for all. In fact, the minimum efficient scale in many European industries was lower than expected and had already been reached by many companies. The general acceptance of the phenomenon of economies of scale was a strong incentive for many companies to increase installed capacity.

Another reason for the perpetuation of this excess capacity in certain sectors is the difficulty companies have in abandoning the industries in which they operate. Barriers to exit are enormous in many cases. Part of these barriers to exit is related to the strength of the unions, the capacity for self-deception by governments that think that certain problems of capacity can be resolved through more subsidies, and the difficulty that companies face in recovering the investments they have made over the years. It is interesting to observe that the entry and exit patterns of companies in certain industries present characteristics specific to the country in which they operate. Thus, Daems (1990) observes that different national labor legislation and the regulation of bankruptcies lead to different exit patterns in the same sector.

Finally, one aspect that explains excess capacity in certain industries is the firm's lack of the right type of production capacity. Its excess capacity

TABLE 3.2   Barriers to change and exit

Internal	External
Management Expectation of competitors Financial resources High sunk costs Past success	Legal system Industrial policy Social attitudes Competitors' reactions

corresponds to obsolete capacity. The barriers that block this transition are numerous and include, in general, factors internal to the company itself, such as an absence of managerial capabilities, the expectation that other companies will fail first, the lack of financial resources for investment, the inability to incorporate new technologies or the dependence on a single product (TABLE 3.2).

External factors include obstacles imposed by the legal system for restructuring companies, the obstruction of unions and governments in effecting the necessary adjustments in production capacity or the existence of public subsidies that perpetuate business crisis. The impossibility of effecting this transition has led many companies to end up displaced from the market in some products or even to disappear altogether.

EXCESS CAPACITY IN ACTION: AUTOMOBILES AND BANKING

After having discussed some explanations for excess capacity, we wish to briefly refer to the nature of this problem in two industries in Europe: the automobile and the banking industries. In TABLE 3.3 we summarize the main explanations.

It is interesting to note some similarities and differences among these industries. The first is that the increase in excess capacity in banking is mainly due to the deregulation experienced in each national market, and not so much to an increase in foreign competition. In fact, foreign penetration in the different national banking markets is still low (Canals, 1993) and, in the best cases—with the exception of Britain—does not even reach 15% of market share in many of the activities of commercial banks.

On the other hand, in the automobile industry, excess capacity has been provoked both by an increase in the capacity of national manufacturers, as well as by strong growth in investments from abroad and exports from third-party countries—mainly Japan.

Second, excess capacity in banking does not stem from an inappropriate response to new trends in demand. In other words, the network of retail banking offices—to a greater or lesser extent—is a competitive network,

TABLE 3.3   The roots of excess capacity in some industries

Banking	Automobiles
Deregulation	FDI
FDI	Obsolete investments
Capital movements liberalization	Manufacturing management
Obsolete capital	Drop in demand
New IT	Shorter product cycle
New rivals	Range of models
Substitution	Global competition
	Imitation

although its productivity should improve. On the other hand, for many European automobile manufacturers, their existing capacity is not, in many cases, technologically updated. In other words, their capacity is not competitive compared to the best automobile producers, either in quality or in costs.

Third, an important phenomenon is taking place in the banking industry: the substitution of certain financial products traditionally offered by banks for other financial products offered by different financial intermediaries—for example, insurance companies—or even by nonfinancial companies—such as credit cards offered by large department stores or automobile manufacturers.

On the other hand, what is occurring in the automobile industry is, essentially, an imitation, a "me-too" effect. Certainly, some producers like the Japanese have introduced breakthrough processes that have led to a spectacular improvement in the quality and the performance of cars, but the automobile continues to carry out, roughly speaking, the same functions and is manufactured by the same companies. In this industry, what takes place is a very rapid process of imitation, so that the best production practices and the best designs spread quickly.

Therefore, this process of imitation leads to excess capacity. To the degree to which a company has the people and the resources necessary to adjust to the changes that others bring about, it will continue to be competitive. The difficulties presently being experienced by some European automobile manufacturers are the result of internal organizational obstacles and limited resources which prevent them from responding to this change with greater celerity.

DIFFERENT PATTERNS FOR ADJUSTING EXCESS CAPACITY AT THE INDUSTRY LEVEL

The experience in adjusting capacity in different industries leads to a distinction between procedures for the whole industry and practices at the company level. Let us note that excess capacity can be a problem shared by many companies in an industry. However, sometimes the problem presents special challenges for companies depending on their resources and capabilities. In this section, we will explore solutions at the industry level. In the next section, we will discuss how to deal with the problem at the firm level. From the point of view of an industry, we can distinguish between three generic methods of adjusting excess capacity.

PRODUCT-MARKET COMPETITION

The first method is through more intense competition in the product market. Rivalry will lead efficient companies to survive and less efficient ones to abandon the industry. This is the solution that the model of perfect competition offers which, in an implicit or explicit way, arises in various industries (from soft drinks to numerical control equipment) not subjected to direct government interference.

This procedure has a positive dimension: it guarantees an efficient resource allocation, at least in the short term. However, its presents two problems. First, from the point of view of efficiency, it is possible that, in a situation of excess capacity, price wars will also lead more efficient companies to cut back production capacity, while those that are less efficient resist doing this. In fact, the more efficient companies may have a greater incentive to reduce capacity (Ghemawat and Nalebuff, 1985). Secondly, this mechanism presents important social problems in Europe, which might end up affecting, in one way or another, the social and work climate that companies face. Here we enter into a question that goes well beyond the goal of this work: the role of trade unions and the public sector in order to facilitate a less painful adjustment transition.

CAPITAL MARKETS DISCIPLINE

The second generic mechanism of adjusting the production capacity of an industry, in the case of publicly traded companies, operates through capital markets. In fact, excess capacity can be one of the reasons for some firms' decreasing profitability. If this factor affects share price, another company could launch either a hostile or a friendly takeover bid, which could signal the beginning of a restructuring process. This restructuring will probably include a reduction in idle capacity.

The discipline provided by capital markets offers a guarantee for an efficient use of financial resources and helps align shareholders and managers' interests and becomes a tool for corporate governance. On the other hand, this mechanism requires large and efficient capital markets, with many listed companies. This factor helps explain partially why capital markets discipline does not operate in Europe to the extent it does in the United States. It is also important to note that takeovers, especially, hostile takeovers, while attempting an increase in efficiency, might destroy trust and the work atmosphere in the firms involved. In several cases, this cost has not been negligible.

GOVERNMENTS' INTERVENTION

The third generic mechanism consists of some type of coordinated action between the public sector and companies within an industry. Some of these actions fall under the generic name of industrial policy: subsidies to failing companies so that they can carry out their reorganization or continue selling below cost, cooperative agreements to reduce capacity of companies in the industry, agreements that include financial firms to lend funds for restructuring (Kester, 1991) or, simply, tariff barriers that protect the national industry from foreign competition.

The efficiency of this solution to the excess capacity problem depends on the nature of the industry. In TABLE 3.4 we distinguish four categories of industries, according to two criteria: the geographical scope of the industry and the government policy towards the industry. When an industry is operating in a global environment and the government intervenes in the restructuring process, the most efficient solution tends to be a concerted action between the government and the companies to cut capacity. If, on the other hand, the industry has a local scope, government assistance tends to consist of subsidies that help perpetuate the problem.

When the government decides not to intervene in the industry, the product market—or capital markets—will unleash their mechanisms to adjust capacity. Once again, it is necessary to distinguish between industries with global competition and industries where competition is more local. In the

TABLE 3.4 The nature of the industry matters: who leads the adjustment process?

Geographical scope of the industry	Government policy	
	Activist industrial policy	No industrial policy
Global	Coalition of government and firms (national interest)	Product market Capital markets Alliances
	Alliances among firms	Corporate governance
Local	Coalition of governments and firms	Corporate governance New investment

TABLE 3.5   The nature of the industry matters

Geographical scope of the industry	Government policy	
	Activist industrial policy	No industrial policy
Global	*Trade policy:*	
	Automobiles	Soft drinks
	Computers	Consumer goods
	Airlines	Investment banking
	Telecommunications	
Local	*Subsidies, regulation:*	
	Telecommunication (national services)	Construction
	Pharmaceuticals	Commercial banking
	Textiles	Publishing

first case, capital market adjustments (mergers or acquisitions) are usually more frequent. In the second case, along with capital markets, competition in the product market pushes the restructuring process, so that less efficient companies will see their market share reduced over time.

In industries with a global scope and an activist government intervention public authorities step in using trade policy, especially nontariff barriers. In the case of a more local industry, government policies tend to consist of subsidies, regulatory measures and voluntary cuts in capacity (TABLE 3.5).

A coordinated intervention between the government and local companies can be an acceptable solution in the short term (Bower, 1990), as long as this action does not lead to the artificial survival of companies—protecting them from free competition—that financial assistance be directed toward extraordinary costs and that the agreement be of a cooperative and voluntary nature. Should one of these conditions be missing, what normally happens is that these measures are nothing more than patches that do not fix the problem at its root.

CORPORATE REACTIONS TO EXCESS CAPACITY

The second category of solutions corresponds to those applied by firms affected by excess capacity. The main course of action oriented toward correcting this excess capacity can be of two types. First, a mere restructuring to adjust current capacity to what the markets can absorb, keeping in mind the new competitive climate. The second step includes innovation. In fact, the basis of any sustainable advantage demands that firms be able to offer products that have real value for their customers, a superior quality or higher performance. Normally, excess capacity assumes the entry of new companies in the industry with the same product already being offered by existing companies, at similar prices. If the demand for this product does not grow or decreases, excess supply is inevitable.

In order to escape this impasse, reducing a company's capacity may be a necessary measure, but one that is not sufficient and only of a temporary nature. The viability of a company in the long run is based on innovation and investment. Only if a company offers something different from other firms, will it be able to escape price wars. The need for differentiation requires the development of resources and investment in them. In this context, a company has to create a balance between its resources and capabilities and evaluate whether it can develop on its own those that it needs to continue in the market.

Independently of the mechanisms deployed by governments to assist firms to adjust capacity, in a first approach we can distinguish between several options that companies beset by excess capacity can choose from to get out of this hole.

DOWNSIZING

Downsizing, restructuring or refocusing are different versions of the first generic reaction to excess capacity. Normally, it is triggered by a sharp decrease in sales, a loss of market share or a significant decrease in profitability. In these circumstances, firms attempt to cut costs—principally, indirect ones—in order to immediately improve their profitability.

Along with this reduction, firms usually reevaluate the set of businesses in which they compete and the profitability of the different products that they offer. These occasions are normally used by companies to restructure their portfolio of products and business. Firms shut down certain businesses, reduce their range of products and concentrate their efforts on those in which they truly are or can be competitive.

The decision to restructure a company as a solution to problems of capacity has been widely studied. The literature on this subject (Bowman and Singh, 1993) usually distinguishes between the restructuring of the company's portfolio of businesses (normally, to reduce its degree of diversification) and mere financial restructuring (oriented toward using debt as a mechanism to impose more discipline on managers).

Also, restructuring can be initiated by causes external to the company, for example a process of deregulation that leads to excess capacity. On the other hand, it can be brought about by the initiative of managers themselves or by that of the board of directors (Gibbs, 1993; Johnson, Hoskisson, and Hitt, 1993). Together with cost cutting, firms normally choose to freeze investments, or selectively increase some critical assets for a later relaunch of the company.

In order to discuss this option in more detail, we will look briefly at the restructuring of Seat, a subsidiary of the Volkswagen Group. Its problems in 1994 were twofold. First, those experienced by the industry as a whole in Europe (falling demand, high costs and increasing rivalry). Second, there was Seat's expensive and inefficient production structure. This problem was concentrated mainly in one of its two assembly plants, in Zona Franca in Barcelona (Spain). This plant, more than 30 years old, was, until 1993, Seat's only plant, with a production capacity of half a million vehicles per year. In January of 1993, a new plant was opened in Martorell (Barcelona). It incorporated all of the advances in automobile production and assembly, with an initial capacity to produce 300 000 cars per year, although, with additional investments, it could reach up to almost half a million. In other words, with this investment Seat was almost doubling its production capacity.

This capacity was not, however, homogeneous. Production at the old plant was more expensive and its internal processes less efficient. On the other hand, components were very expensive, for two reasons. First, they were purchased in Germany through the Volkswagen Group—at higher prices and with German D-marks, more expensive in relation to the peseta. Second, logistically, this arrangement was not at all efficient, due to the considerable physical separation between the supplier and Seat.

The new plant was, therefore, the future of the company. Because of strong growth in sales between 1989 and 1991, Seat managers thought that it would be possible to keep both plants operating at full capacity. However, the fall in demand, the overall excess capacity in the industry and the strong price war in the European market since 1991 made such a goal unviable. Seat lost $1300 million in 1993.

After intense negotiations between the parent company, Seat, the unions and the different governments involved, a restructuring plan was designed by the end of 1993, with the following principal elements: the concentration of the production of the four Seat models in Martorell, with a progressive dismantling of production in Zona Franca; a reduction in staff from more than 23 000 workers to about 14 000; a reduction of indirect costs; a relaunching of the company's brand image, which was seriously damaged by the crisis; finally, the establishment of stricter financial controls on the part of the parent company in order to identify early possible deviations from the results that they were experiencing.

An interesting point worth mentioning is the flexibility that companies with several production plants have compared to companies that have only one plant. If Seat had confronted the crisis of 1993 with a single plant—the obsolete plant at Zona Franca—most likely the only solution would have been the ultimate dismantling of the company. The reason for this is that the Zona Franca plant could not be easily transformed and adapted to modern production and assembly practices. The existence of one or more plants with greater efficiency allows a company to focus production on these new technologies to the detriment of the less efficient ones. This possibility gives a company breathing space because it does not find itself condemned to abandon the industry. This result coincides with similar experiences in other industries (Baden-Fuller, 1990a).

REENGINEERING

The reengineering or reconfiguration of a firm entails a new way of organizing operational processes with the goal of increasing efficiency, obtaining cost reductions and improving customer service. Reconfiguration involves, therefore, an analysis of the company's chain of activities, from the purchasing of raw materials to the after-sales service—if it exists—that it offers to its customers. Each one of the company's activities is analyzed, according to the following criteria.

First, how does an activity's efficiency in Firm A compare with that of the most efficient firm in the industry? Second, can the company improve its efficiency service by itself? Third, should the company enter into an alliance with other companies to develop necessary capabilities and thus improve the efficiency of operations? Fourth, should the company continue to develop this activity, or, on the other hand, is it advisable that the company farms this activity out?

These criteria lead to a reshuffling of, at least, two areas of a company's activities. First, the realm of internal processes, in particular the organizational design and control systems. In fact, the reduction or elimination of hierarchical levels within the company are the result of this approach. The growing use of information technologies allows a company to confront these changes.

The second area of action is the degree of vertical integration that the company needs in each one of its stages or activities, not only in the purchasing or manufacturing of certain raw materials or auxiliary products. In the end, the classic "make or buy" decision (Williamson, 1975) acquires extraordinary force in the reconfiguration of a company provoked by significant excess capacity in an industry.

Reconfiguration decisions bring up, in some cases, the need to enter into alliances with other companies. In this sense, the reconfiguration of a company's activities can be considered as an option for improving its operations with the help of a partner (Kogut, 1991; Hurry, 1993). In order to discuss this option in depth, we shall present the case of Indo, a European company that manufactures lenses (the fourth largest European producer), eyeglasses and beveling machines (the second largest European producer) for optics. This company had practically doubled its sales between 1985 and 1993, reaching an annual turnover of $160 million at the end of that year, with a return on equity of about 20%.

The stagnation of the European market, the economic crisis in the early 1990s and the growing foreign competition—principally in the eyeglasses industry—brought about an overhaul of the industry—some smaller companies had to abandon the industry altogether—and damaged Indo's performance. In view of its deteriorating performance, management at Indo designed a two-phase strategy. The first phase consisted of a restructuring plan similar to that of Seat: concentration of production in the more efficient plants, reduction of staff, containing indirect costs and implementing stiffer financial controls.

However, Indo's managers realized that these actions had a limit: costs could not be reduced indefinitely. Indo began to work seriously on reconfiguring the company, a strategy that encompassed five important areas. First, a turnaround of the eyeglasses production processes, the company's least profitable division, whose production and assembly process could involve 180 different steps before the product was considered finished. With this goal, Indo redesigned its production process by establishing work groups that did assembly from beginning to end, including quality control. Thus it abandoned its traditional assembly production line. It is estimated that its production efficiency improved by 30%.

The second decision consisted of the search for a cheaper geographic location for manufacturing some products whereby the cost of labor was very important. With this goal, at the end of 1993 it began producing lenses in Morocco, where the cost of labor was 10% of what it was in the average EU country.

The third decision consisted of subcontracting manufacturing cheaper lenses to more efficient specialists, in order to later distribute them through its distribution network.

The fourth decision consisted of evaluating possible alliances for Indo's beveling machines division. The importance of R&D for the design of high quality machines required bigger volumes, so that the company could absorb these fixed costs.

Finally, there was a significant management reorganization. In fact, up until 1992 management at Indo never considered its three divisions as units in different businesses. The existence of some synergies among the three led them to share technical and financial resources and management expertise. Growing competition in each one of its businesses and blurring responsibilities forced Indo's management to propose a sharper distinction between those divisions, with a different management team ultimately responsible for each one of them, preserving certain coordinating elements that were considered to be indispensable. These actions reflect, therefore, a complete redesign of the organization of the company's different activities and functions, and question previous decisions concerning the degree of vertical integration.

Finally, let us emphasize two additional points that this case presents. First, a company with several business units must rethink its organizational structure in response to a change in the industry. With a centralized management, Indo was able to compete satisfactorily in the three businesses when competition was not very intense. At times when there is excess capacity and competition is rapidly increasing, the survival of each business depends on being as competitive as the most specialized company in that business. This condition may require a significant reorganization of the company. Second, the reconfiguration or reengineering of a company will, on many occasions, be preceded by its restructuring. These are not, therefore, two mutually exclusive options, but reengineering on many occasions requires and entails restructuring as an initial step.

THE WAY TO THE FUTURE: INNOVATION AND INVESTMENT

Those actions geared toward downsizing or reconfiguring a company help cut costs and improve the efficiency in production or distribution to the level of the most efficient companies, or even surpass them. However, in industries affected by a high level of excess capacity, the threat of price wars, especially on the part of companies that are most reluctant to reduce capacity, may provoke an erosion of those that attempt a restructuring.

On the other hand, from a conceptual point of view, it is useful to recall that superior returns are always the outcome of innovation, either in products or in processes. What has happened with some firms' downsizing or reengineering processes is that their sales have fallen quicker than their cost structures and the effort to increase efficiency has become a major task that staves off or blocks thinking about the future, and stops innovation and investment. Hence, a company competing in an industry affected by excess capacity should ask itself not only what it should do to increase efficiency, but also how to innovate and in what areas to innovate in order to overcome some of the problems that excess capacity generates. As Hamel and Prahalad (1994) point out, innovation is the key when competing for the future.

Normally, innovation requires a process of investment, either in new production plants and equipment, new products, R&D, brand reputation, new business design or capabilities that people must learn in order to deal with new problems. Therefore, reinventing the company always requires investment.

Let us briefly discuss a successful case of innovation in an industry with excess capacity: Banco Popular. It was, in 1988, the second most profitable retail bank in Europe. It focused its activities on retail banking and did not intervene in capital markets and corporate finance, unlike other banks.

In the light of increasing rivalry in the industry many banks opted for the path of growth and the objective of a larger market share in order to confront shrinking profit margins. As a result of this option, all of these banks experienced a significant reduction in profitability between 1989 and 1994.

Banco Popular adopted a completely different strategy. In response to growth, it put first return on equity. To achieve that goal, it did not participate in price wars to grab market share, but instead designed an innovative marketing strategy focused on offering very attractive financial products to groups of customers that shared common features: high-school families, passengers of certain airlines, automobile dealers, repair shops or members of some professional associations. Customer satisfaction was the key criterion for its managers.

In short, together with significant innovation in its products, Banco Popular reinvented the way to compete in a very crowded industry. It also redesigned its business by launching new products, figuring out how these products would reach potential customers through the appropriate segmentation of customers and the search for networks of customers with similar financial needs. Through this strategy, the bank has not only escaped price wars, but has also saved resources in advertising and distribution costs.

Its profitability (return on equity) has grown threefold between 1989 and 1994, reaching 29% before taxes, its market capitalization has not stopped growing and it has twice been named the best managed bank in the world. All of this has occurred at a time when profitability in the banking sector in all of Europe has fallen dramatically, and while large banks like Crédit Lyonnais and Banesto were facing serious crises.

MANAGING CAPACITY

The options just outlined that companies may undertake to adjust capacity can be related to some generic strategies that have been developed in the literature on excess capacity. We refer to those presented by Harrigan (1982, 1990). She suggests that firms' reactions to excess capacity in an industry can be grouped under the following categories: increase investment in production capacity, maintain it, decrease it, exploit existing capacity to the maximum, divest from or abandon the industry.

The principal characteristic of this set of possible decisions with regard to excess capacity is that the determining variable is excess capacity itself. Thus the insistence on investment or divestment in excess capacity is a natural outcome. However these categories do not distinguish whether or not the excess capacity is obsolete capacity, a fundamental distinction to be made. Neither do the models developed in game theory, principally those that explain attempts to deter the entrance of other rivals.

A clear example of this is the model developed by Fudenberg and Tirole (1984), consisting of two companies that compete over two time periods, by choosing capacity. However, in the real world this variable is not homogeneous, not the same for all companies being considered and its use will depend on the firms' capabilities.

Neither does this classification delve into a fundamental aspect of any adjustment process: the necessary reconfiguration of certain processes to regain competitiveness. Finally, it seems that the company's only competitive weapon is spare capacity and, indirectly, the lower prices that this capacity permits. The critical question of innovation is not addressed, although it is necessary for generating new competitive advantages that lead to sustainable performance.

However, by making a slight modification in the model proposed by Harrigan, we can relate the conceptual model that we presented earlier to her categories. This attempt is reflected in TABLE 3.6. The key variable that links both models is investment. In fact, innovation in products or processes assumes investment. Therein lies an important difference between both models: in the one we discuss here, investment is oriented toward innovation in products or in production processes; in other words, its driving force is entrepreneurship and differentiation. On the other hand, in the Harrigan model, investment is considered essentially a competitive weapon for increasing production capacity, in the hope of reduction in costs and/or the deterrence of current or potential competitors in order to increase capacity.

To conclude this section, we consider some relationships that we may observe between the external forces that provoke the change due to excess capacity, and the possible corporate reactions to these changes, according to the type of external forces that stir up the reaction. We single out some firms that can be grouped—with prudence—under some of those categories.

In TABLE 3.7 we present the principal driving forces that facilitate change:

TABLE 3.6 Relationships between strategic reactions and Harrigan's options

Harrigan's options	Strategic reactions			
	Innovation	Restructuring	Downsizing	Exit
Increase investment	X			
Hold investment			X	
Decrease investment		X	X	
Harvest investment		X	X	
Divest			X	X

TABLE 3.7   Relationships between the forces of capacity adjustment and corporate reactions

Forces of change	Corporate reaction			
	Downsizing	Restructuring	Innovation	Exit
Product markets	Volkswagen	Barclays	Nokia	National firms
Capital markets	Daimler-Benz	Philips	–	–
Industrial policy	Crédit Lyonnais	Fiat	–	State-owned companies
Corporate governance	Lufthansa	Siemens	Glaxo	NatWest

competition in the market for products, actions in capital markets, industrial policy and a board of directors that promotes change. From the information gathered in TABLE 3.7, we can draw some tentative hypotheses about the drivers of change. First, pressure coming from capital markets or government intervention is more decisive in forcing a firm's downsizing, reengineering or exit, but there are not many successful experiences of a firm's reinvention coming from those forces. Second, reinvention seems to emerge naturally from product market competition, or corporate governance, rather than capital market constraints. Third, capital market competition seems more effective in pushing for a firm's reengingeering or downsizing, but does not have the same efficiency in forcing exit.

EXCESS CAPACITY FROM THE RESOURCE-BASED PERSPECTIVE

One of the major effects of excess capacity on firms is the fall in their profitability. In other words, firms saddled with excess capacity no longer generate a satisfactory profitability. The potential roots of firms' profits are: (1) monopolistic profits that stem from a monopoly position that firms enjoy; (2) profits stemming from the innovation, insight and ability of entrepreneurs or the ownership of valuable resources (Ricardian rents).

Excess capacity tends to erode both types of profit. Deregulation allows for entry in an industry and puts an end to monopoly privileges in markets such as telecommunications, postal services or airlines. Excess capacity also makes it more difficult for entrepreneurs to generate new rents from some business activities, especially when there is an abnormal concentration of competitors vying for the same customers in the same markets with the same products.

In general, economic performance is dependent upon the level of rivalry in product markets (Porter, 1980) and in factor markets (Dierickx and Cool,

1989). As has been discussed in the past few years in the strategy field, economic rents and the sustained competitive advantages that performance reflects (Barney, 1991) depend upon the stock of resources and capabilities a firm has accumulated.

Firms not only differ in terms of economic performance. They differ in performance because they show important differences in the stock of resources and capabilities they have accumulated (Nelson, 1991). As Penrose (1959) explained, the heterogeneity of the services available (or potentially available) from its resources gives each firm its unique character.

The resource-based approach to strategy explains superior economic performance, not in terms of industry attractiveness or the ability that a firm has to fix consistently higher prices, but in terms of the resources and capabilities that make it possible for a company to offer lower prices, higher quality or both.

Resources are valuable as far as they are scarce, untradeable, show externalities and complementarities with other products and are difficult to imitate and substitute (Barney, 1991; Mahoney and Pandian, 1992; Amit and Schoemaker, 1993, Peteraf, 1993). In general, sunk costs tend to be a source of value for many resources because they define the type of rivalry in many industries (Sutton, 1991). Sunk costs and their importance in competition bring forth the need to consider the commitment of factors (Ghemawat, 1991). These factors tend to be sticky. The reason is that investment or divestment in those factors is not flexible nor frictionless.

Nevertheless, a stock of resources is not enough to generate superior economic performance. History shows that firms with formidable resources—capital or technology—have been unable to successfully compete with other companies endowned with an apparently lower stock of resources. Recent stories of competition in different industries, like personal computers, copiers or information services, reveal that truth.

The missing step is capabilities. Capabilities express the ability that a firm has to use and deploy its resources in product markets. Capabilities allow a firm to use its stock of resources efficiently, and, in this way, it might achieve a better performance than direct competitors.

Amit and Schoemaker (1993) distinguish between resources, capabilities and strategic assets. Resources are converted into products or services for the product market. Capabilities refer to the firm's ability to deploy those resources. They involve tangible and intangible processes developed by people working in the firm. In general, those processes entail generating and exchanging information about products, production processes, procedures, views of the competition and the industry or ways of serving new or old customers' needs. Finally, strategic assets are a set of scarce resources and capabilities that are difficult to trade, imitate and substitute for. Those strategic assets are the source of a firm's sustainable competitive advantage.

In this context, it seems plausible to state that capacity is an important strategic asset in many companies. Nevertheless, its economic value—as the economic value of any other resource or capability—hinges upon its scarcity, the difficulty imitating it and substituting for it. In some industries it is possible to argue that the very same concept of excess capacity seems to state that capacity is not a strategic asset, because it is no longer scarce at the industry level. In an industry with excess capacity, scarcity is the absent factor.

Nevertheless, a general situation of excess capacity in a certain industry does not preclude the idea that some companies may enjoy valuable, scarce, and difficult to imitate, difficult to substitute, capacity. Examples are numerous. In the personal computer industry, saddled with excess capacity, strong rivalry and brutal price wars, Compaq has emerged as one of the leading world producer. Among the factors explaining such a success, we can immediately single out a careful assessment of capacity investment, with a combination of simple operational policies and flexibility that allows the firm to develop, manufacture and distribute competitive products at a quick speed and, simultaneously, enjoy one of the lightest cost structures in the industry.

The automobile industry also presents the same striking evidence. In Europe, it is possible to observe companies like Volkswagen or Ford with idle capacity and high costs. One might suggest that it is because both firms are very strong and entrenched in the German market, with high production costs and slow growth. The question is that in that very same market the observer can identify a successful company: Opel-GM Europe. This company undertook a careful and well-planned series of investment decisions in new automobile models and new plants in the late 1970s and in the 1980s. It entered the turbulent and recession-prone 1990s with the most efficient, most economical and most flexible manufacturing and assembly plants in the European car industry.

The resource-based view helps us to understand the excess capacity problem better by pointing out, not only that excess capacity shows, by itself, a lack of scarcity and the problem of imitation. The other dimension it highlights is the coincident existence in the same industry, in the same geographical context and at the same time, of companies with the right and the wrong, outdated, types of capacity. The former have the modern kind of capacity, based upon resources and capabilities that are rare, difficult to acquire, imitate and substitute. In the same industry there might also coexist firms with the wrong, obsolete kind of capacity, because they are based upon resources and capabilities that are abundant, easy to acquire or imitate, or already obsolete.

This striking comparison, that can be observed in several industries—as we have previously shown in the automobile and banking industries—stresses the key role of capacity in creating and sustaining a competitive advantage. Capacity can be recognized as an important strategic asset, once it is considered from the resource-based perspective. This approach also sheds light on and confirms the critical role assigned in game theory to capacity competition. On the other hand, this approach also delves into the roots and true problems of excess capacity: the lack of scarcity and the easiness in trading resources and capabilities that sustain certain types of capacity in underperforming companies.

It is now clearer, from this perspective, that classic solutions to the problem of excess capacity, like agreements in cutting down capacity, quotas, fixing prices or restructuring, are short-term, evasive solutions. The reason is that the roots of the problem are not just more intense competition or a capacity expansion by previously existing companies. The real roots lie in the eroding value of the resources and capabilities embedded in companies with the capacity problem.

If this analysis is correct, we can also immediately conclude that solutions like restructuring, downsizing or subcontracting might help the company get out of a hole for a short time. But they are not, and could not be, by definition, sources of competitive advantage. Every other company can do the same thing, imitating the first mover. The only real, long-term solution is to generate and accumulate new resources and capabilities—or revitalize the old ones in a new, useful, economically valuable, ways—that will pave the way for new capacity that is modern, difficult to imitate and difficult to trade. In some sense, this is another perspective to the problem of competing for the future discussed by Hamel and Prahalad (1994).

Capacity is also a combination of sticky resources embedded in a firm. It is also firm-specific in so far as it operates in combination with other resources. New capacity means investment in resources and capability development. Investment—in general, the resource allocation process within a company—turns out to be a key strategic decision that will determine in many ways the evolution of the company in the future (Bower, 1970; Baldwin and Clark, 1992).

The ability to evaluate new investment decisions is critical for a company's performance, especially investment in new capabilities. Its relevance also highlights the need to establish investment practices within companies that are favorable to create and support key resources and generate new capabilities. Investment decisions are critical strategic decisions a firm should think carefully about. On the other hand, these are decisions that will lock the company into a certain pattern of behavior for a rather longer period of time, the longer the more specific and scarcer the capacity (Ghemawat, 1991).

We can conclude that investment may have an effect on excess capacity, but its true relevance for a company goes beyond that. Investment becomes the process by which many competitive advantages a firm may enjoy come to life.

A MANAGERIAL APPROACH TO EXCESS CAPACITY AND INVESTMENT DECISIONS IN CAPACITY

In the previous sections, we have presented the problem of excess capacity and potential solutions elaborated from different perspectives: traditional management prescriptions (like downsizing or restructuring), industrial policy recommendations (like coalitions between governments and companies to shut down capacity) and game theory and its discussion of capacity and excess capacity as strategic weapons companies should consider.

The perspective offered by the resource-based view of the firm presented in the previous section (and its relations with the problem of excess capacity) signals the importance of capacity investment in resources and capabilities. Those resources could become strategic assets and sources of sustainable competitive advantage.

If we agree on recognizing the importance of investment in capacity, the next natural step is to try to understand and figure out the effects of those decisions in a wider managerial framework. It is also relevant to try to envisage the potential effects of those decisions. The following step should be how to evaluate those strategic decisions. It seems quite natural that if investment decisions are strategic, they cannot be left to the firm's financial or planning department, and consider the decision only from the financial perspective. Neither can it be left to the marketing department, in the case the investment decision involves, not only new production processes, but also new products.

If those decisions are bound to be critical, they need an integrative approach that considers the wholeness of the firm, both internally—in relation to the people and resources of all types the company has—and externally—in relation to customers, rival companies and suppliers. Some methodological approaches to those problems have been offered. Ghemawat (1991) proposes an innovative framework and distinguishes different perspectives in the decision process: positioning in the product market, sustainability of its performance and flexibility.

Canals (1995) presents a decision process which is made up of the following steps: industry analysis, financial analysis, resource analysis, value-based judgements and contingency analysis. Those viewpoints about complex decisions seem to be useful in practice and help not to overlook key factors. Nevertheless, managers need to have a framework that relates excess capacity and capacity decisions to economic performance from a decision perspective, not just from a logical viewpoint. This perspective is offered in FIGURE 3.1. This framework tries to incorporate the contributions from the industrial economics approach to strategy. It can be seen in the upper part of the figure: industry attractiveness and relative positioning (Porter, 1980). But this framework also wants to capture the key role played by resources and capabilities in both shaping industry

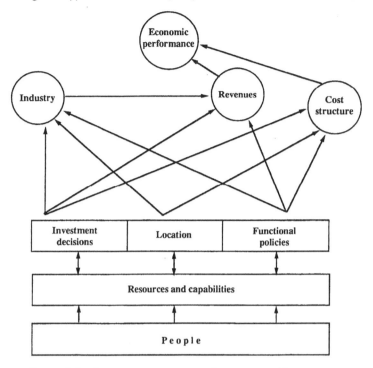

FIGURE 3.1 Strategy, corporate performance and investment

attractiveness and achieving a relative, comfortable positioning within the industry.

Resources and capabilities are deployed in three different types of decision: investment decisions, location decisions and functional decisions. In the first category, we distinguish between investment decisions in assets like capacity, new product development or R&D. Investment decisions pave the way for the future of a firm in one way or another. They involve significant resources and are not easy to reverse. In general, investment decisions are more difficult to change than pricing or purchasing decisions.

Location choices are the second type of decision. Location has to do not only with the cost of factors that a certain location has in relation with alternative "loci", but also market opportunities offered by the sheer fact of being close to a certain territory. Location decisions have a tremendous effect on corporate performance. Once a company has decided to enter into a new market (especially if the entry decision involves investment in production facilities) the decision to pull back is difficult to implement. Total irreversibility does not exist, but it is true that some entry decisions are difficult to reverse.

The opposite is also true. Some successful location decisions—either for cost reasons or for market reasons—contribute to explain the superior economic performance of some companies. Wal-Mart's decision to invest in the early 1970s in cities with a total population lower than 100 000 people and, later on, in smaller towns, preempted new entry in markets, because they could accommodate only one discounter, but not two.

Among the third category of decisions, we highlight many of those decisions that we call functional or operational policies. Within the context of operational decisions we include all the day-to-day decisions made in the different departments: production, purchasing, logistics, pricing, advertising, etc. We argue that functional decisions have a clear impact on a company's performance. But for our purpose, their main feature is that functional policies are easier to imitate and reverse. It is true that some companies have a special knack in marketing or technology, and decisions related to those areas are more difficult to imitate successfully. Usually, in that case, the truth about those companies is that they are the market leaders in several dimensions and rivals can imitate their pricing policies, but not the organizational capabilities needed to make that policy the most appropriate. In that case, what is scarce is people's competences and the set of organizational capabilities that support and complement those policies, not the policies themselves.

On the other hand, in relation to investment decisions (Amit and Schoemaker, 1993 speak about strategic assets and investment in strategic assets: the meaning is the same), the opposite is true. Investment decisions in new products or production processes are more difficult to imitate. Even if a rival firm has the financial muscle to do it, it may not have the organizational capabilities to run it as efficiently as the other firm. Or, what happens sometimes is that companies do not have the managerial capabilities to screen and efficiently evaluate investment decisions.

Those investment decisions have, at least, three effects. First, they shape the cost structure of a company or, at least, of certain products offered by a company. Second, if the decisions involve products or services, they configure and define the revenue structure of the firm, which will depend on how that product competes and compares with other companies' similar products. Third, investment decisions, either in products or new production processes, contribute to mould the structure of the industry, making it more or less attractive to the firm itself and to other competitors. Investment decisions imply sunk costs that shape the nature of rivalry within the industry.

When the investment decision has to do with investment in production capacity, the effects are amplified for several reasons. First, the company is stuck with a production process that incorporates a certain level of technology. Corporate learning depends upon it. If the choice of process or technology is not satisfactory, the owner is not only stuck with those inefficient assets, but also corporate learning might fade away, impoverishing the ability of the company to improve its technological foundations.

Second, investment decisions in production capacity create additional inertia within the firm. If a manufacturing plant becomes obsolete and its technology is substituted by a new and better one, the company's ability to change depends not only on its financial resources, but also on the managers' and employees mindset. This is a key reason why companies find change so hard, especially when that change involves a breakup with policies and practices that were successful in the past. Again, problems that large companies face with change have less to do with financial resources than with corporate routines and internal culture.

Third, investment in capacity has a big impact on the structure of the industry, in several ways: expanding capacity, setting new cost benchmarks for other companies or making other firms' plants obsolete. In some cases, the changes that investment decisions bring about in existing industries might generate a problem of excess capacity in the whole industry. In that case, we should distinguish among companies that lead the change in the industry, companies that are followers, and companies that do not react and leave change aside. We may observe the three types of company in the same industry, affected by the excess capacity problem. Companies in the third group face the most serious and obvious hurdle.

From this discussion, we would like to draw some conclusions. First, not all types of investment lead to the problem of excess capacity as it is usually understood. Many times, a revolutionary investment means a shift in paradigm in the industry, and not just a problem of excess capacity. In that case, it is possible to support the idea that excess capacity is not generated from investment; rather it is generated by the lack of innovative investment.

Second, the only way to get out of the excess capacity problem is to invest in new assets, resources and capabilities that may lift the company up and separate it from the "me-too" spiral of imitation and price wars.

Third, from the model presented in FIGURE 3.1 and the subsequent discussion, it is clear that we can assert that the effects of investment decisions go beyond theorical considerations or superior resources or capabilities, but go to the heart of the major factors that determine corporate performance.

SOME FINAL CONCLUSIONS

In this chapter we have discussed the roots of one of the most important problems currently affecting many industries in Europe: excess capacity, and the specific way some companies are confronting this problem. Excess capacity has been generated by firms' internal factors, such as the inability to meet customers' needs or excess investment, and by external factors, such as the deregulation and the heightened competition that globalization has brought about. In short, the critical question in many industries is that there is an excessive number of companies competing with the same products for the same customers.

In some industries a substitution effect is also taking place, whereby old products or production processes are being replaced by new ones. This phenomenon indicates that many companies not only have a problem of excess capacity, but also that this capacity is not qualitatively adequate to meet the new demands of customers.

In this chapter we have also discussed approaches at the industry and the firm levels to tackle the problem. The discussion has led us to focus on the role of resources, capabilities and investment to better understand the problem of excess capacity and its potential solutions.

When resource analysis is introduced in discussing the excess capacity problem, it is possible to observe an additional perspective. Capacity can be considered as an important strategic asset. The resource-based approach sheds light upon one of the main dangers of excess capacity: its abundance (or lack of scarcity) and flexibility.

From this perspective, classic solutions to the problem of excess capacity like quotas or restructuring appear to be very weak. If the problem is the eroding value of the resources owned by companies, the focus of the problem should shift toward innovation and investment in new resources, and leave aside questions such as how to cut down installed capacity.

REFERENCES

Amit, R. and Schoemaker, P.J. (1993) "Strategic assets and organizational rent", *Strategic Management Journal*, **14**, 33–46.

Baden-Fuller, C.W.F. (ed.) (1990a) *Managing Excess Capacity*. Oxford: Basil Blackwell.

Baden-Fuller, C.W.F. (1990b) "Competition and Cooperation: Restructuring the UK Steel Castings Industry", in Baden-Fuller, C.W.F. (ed.) *Managing Excess Capacity*. Oxford: Basil Blackwell.

Baldwin, C. and Clark, K. (1992) "Modularity and Real Options: An Exploratory Analysis", mimeo, Harvard Business School.

Barney, J. (1991) "Firms Resources and Sustained Competitive Advantage", *Journal of Management*, **17**, 99–120.

Bianchi, P. and Volpato, G. (1990) "Flexibility as the Response to Excess Capacity: The Case of the Automobile Industry", in Baden-Fuller, C.W.F. (ed.) *Managing Excess Capacity*. Oxford: Basil Blackwell.

Bower, J.L. (1970) *Managing the Resource Allocation Process*. Boston: Harvard Business School Press.

Bower, J.L. (1990) "Management Revolution: The Response to Global Glut", in Baden-Fuller, C.W.F. (ed.), *Managing Excess Capacity*. Oxford: Basil Blackwell, pp. 19–39.

Bowman, E.H. and Singh, H. (1993) "Corporate Restructuring: Reconfiguring the Firm", *Strategic Management Journal*, **14**, Special issue, 5–14.

Canals, J. (1993) *Competitive Strategies in European Banking*. Oxford: Oxford University Press.

Canals, J. (1995) "Strategy and Investment Decisions", mimeo, Barcelona: IESE.

Daems, H. (1990) "Industry and Country Exist: Reflections on International Differences in Exit Behaviour", in Baden-Fuller, C.W.F. (ed.), *Managing Excess Capacity*. Oxford: Basil Blackwell, pp. 59–74.

Dierickx, I. and Cool, K. (1989) "Asset Stock Accumulation and Sustainability of Competitive Advantage", *Management Science*, 35, 1.504–1.511.

Dixit, A. (1980) "The Role of Investment in Entry Deterrence", *Economic Journal*, 90, 95–106.

Fudenberg, D. and Tirole, J. (1984) "The Cat Effect, the Puppy Dog Play and the Lean and Hungry Look", *American Economic Review*, 74, May, 361–368.

Ghemawat, P. (1987) "Investment in Lumpy Capacity", *Journal of Economic Behaviour and Organisation*, 8, 265–277.

Ghemawat, P. (1991) *Commitment*. New York: Free Press.

Ghemawat, P. and Nalebuff, B. (1985) "Exit", *Rand Journal of Economics*, 16(2), 184–194.

Ghemawat, P. and Caves, R. (1986) "Capital Commitment and Profitability: An Empirical Investigation", in Morris, D.J. et al. (eds), *Strategic Behaviour and Industrial Competition*, Oxford; Clarendon Press, pp. 94–110.

Gibbs, P.A. (1993) "Determinants of Corporate Restructuring: The Relative Importance of Corporate Governance, Takeover Threat and Free Cash Flow", *Strategic Management Journal*, 14, Special issue, 51–68.

Gilbert, R.J. and Harris, R.G. (1984) "Competition with Lumpy Investment", *Rand Journal of Economics*, 15, Summer, 197–212.

Hamel, G. and Prahalad, C.K. (1994) *Competing for the Future*. Boston: Harvard Business School Press.

Harrigan, K.R. (1982) "Exit Decisions in Mature Industries", *Academy of Management Journal*, 25(4), 707–732.

Harrigan, K.R. (1990) "Implementing Endgame Strategies for Declining Industries", in Baden-Fuller, C.W.F. (ed.), *Managing Excess Capacity*. Oxford: Basil Blackwell, pp. 193–211.

Hurry, D. (1993) "Restructuring in the Global Economy: The Consequences of Strategic Linkages between Japanese and US Firms", *Strategic Management Journal*, 14, Special issue, 69–82.

Johnson, R.A., Hoskisson, R.E., and Hitt, M.A. (1993) "Board of Directors Involvement in Restructuring: The Effects of Board versus Managerial Controls and Characteristics", *Strategic Management Journal*, 14, Special issue, 33–50.

Johnson, R.A. and Parkman, A. (1983) "Spatial Monopoly, Non-zero Profits and Entry Deterrence: The Case of Cement", *Review of Economics and Statistics*, 65.

Kester, C. (1991) *Japanese Takeovers*. Boston: Harvard Business School Press.

Kogut, B. (1991) "Joint Ventures and the Option to Expand and Acquire", *Management Science*, 37(1), 19–33.

Mahoney, J.T. and Pandian, J.R. (1992) "The Resource-based View within the Conversation of Strategic Management", *Strategic Management Journal*, 13, 363–380.

Nelson, R. (1991) "Why Do Firms Differ?', *Strategic Management Journal*, Special Issue.

Penrose, E.T. (1959) *The Theory of the Growth of the Firm*. New York: John Wiley & Sons.

Peteraf, M.A. (1993) "The Cornerstones of Competitive Advantage: A Resource-based View", *Strategic Management Journal*, **14**(3), 179–192.

Porter, M.E. (1980) *Competitive Strategy*. New York: Free Press.

Porter, M.E. and Spence, A.M. (1982) "The Capacity Expansion Process in a Growing Oligopology: The Case of Cornwet Milling", in McCall, J.J. (ed.), *The Economics of Information and Uncertainty*, Chicago: University of Chicago Press, pp. 259–294.

Spence, M. (1977) "Entry, Capacity Investment and Oligopolistic Pricing", *Bell Journal of Economics*, **8**, 534–544.

Sutton, J. (1991) *Sunks Costs and Market Structure*. Cambridge, Mass.: MIT Press.

Williamson, O. (1975) *Markets and Hierarchies*. New York: Free Press.

Managing Corporate Transformation: Two Contrasting Leadership Styles

BALA CHAKRAVARTHY

INTRODUCTION

Corporate transformation is a major preoccupation of many of our most admired corporations. Once excellent companies have seen their growth slow down and profits decline dramatically in the past decade. The experiences of firms like IBM, Philips, Honda, and others from all three industrial triads, form the bases for numerous models of corporate transformation that are offered by consultants and academics alike.

Transformation is typically viewed in these models as a multistage process (see FIGURE 4.1), following a sequence of restructuring, revitalization, and renewal (Kelly and Gouillart, 1995). The first stage of *restructuring*, also called "awakening" (Tichy and Sherman, 1993) or "simplification" (Baden-Fuller and Stopford, 1994), is especially relevant to underperforming firms. This stage involves a major downsizing of the firm, pruning of its business portfolio and an overhaul of its structure and management processes. A successful restructuring will restore the firm's profitability at least to the minimum threshold that is appropriate for its industry context, albeit at the cost of growth (see FIGURE 4.1). However, this in itself is not enough to restore the firm's competitiveness. In addition, the transformation process must also help the firm rejuvenate its strategies and renew its

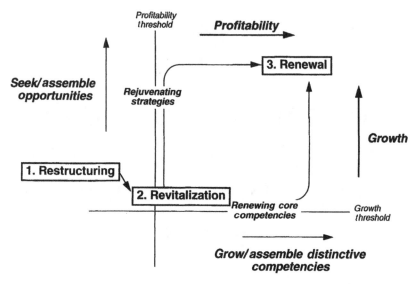

FIGURE 4.1   A multistage process of corporate transformation

core competencies (Hamel and Prahalad, 1994). This is called the *revitalization* stage. The effort here may include both in-house attempts at identifying new business opportunities and developing new competencies, as well as acquisitions and strategic alliances that enable the firm to access these opportunities and competencies with the help of others. The third and final stage of the transformation process is *renewal*, a stage in which the firm seeks to be continuously engaged in identifying and eliminating waste, building and sharing new capabilities, and rejuvenating its strategies—thus embodying aspects of both restructuring and revitalization at the same time.

The model proposed above assumes a seamless progression from one stage of transformation to the next, triggered by the firm's improving performance. Unfortunately, this smooth transition is a rarity. The primary difficulty appears to be in the inability of top management to maintain its legitimacy with the firm's employees through the restructuring stage. The legitimacy of corporate leadership can be measured both in commercial and social terms. Commercial legitimacy refers to the support that a top management team can garner from its shareholders, bondholders, customers, and suppliers. It is a measure of how well the top management team manages the economic activities of a firm. Social legitimacy, on the other hand, refers to the degree of commitment that top management is able to generate among the firm's employees and host communities for the firm's mission and strategies. Unlike the commercial stakeholders, who have more of a transactional association with the firm, the social stakeholders of a firm have an emotional relationship with it.

Commercial and social legitimacy are unfortunately at odds with each other, especially during the restructuring stage of the transformation process. In trying to improve its commercial legitimacy, top management may cause irrevocable damage to its social legitimacy. Social legitimacy once lost is difficult to rebuild. Rejuvenating a firm's strategy and renewing its competence platform depend critically on committed employees. Without such a commitment, corporate transformation can stall after a successful restructuring.

Scholars of European management (Calori and de Woot, 1994) have observed that social legitimacy thresholds are a lot higher for European CEOs than they are for their American counterparts. There is more concern in Europe for the fulfillment of employees and the well-being of host communities than in the USA. In contrast, creating value for the firm's commercial stakeholders is the dominant concern of top management in the USA. Commercial legitimacy thresholds are a lot higher in the USA. FIGURE 4.2 contrasts the two stereotypical contexts.

The differing importance of commercial and social legitimacy in Europe and the USA is also reflected in the corporate governance structures used in the two continents. In a stereotypical European firm, the governance structure focuses on social legitimacy. As Calori, Valla, and de Woot (1994, p. 36) note (see overleaf):

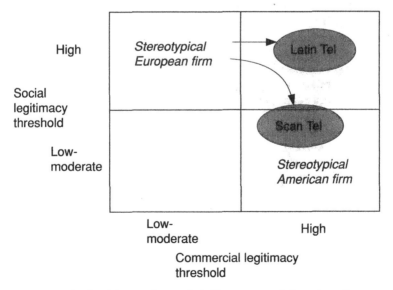

FIGURE 4.2   Legitimacy demands in European and American firms

In Europe, the top management has power, but it has to consult, to negotiate, to convince: There is a need for independence (on the part of stakeholders), authority is questioned. The decisions coming from the top are criticized. People start to involve themselves only after a lot of discussions, dialogues and information.

In Germany and in Scandinavia the governance structure provides a direct voice for the firm's employees. In Spain and Italy, the government regulates employee dismissals. Even where the governance structure or social regulation do not so require, the emphasis on social responsibility is very clear in Europe (Calori and de Woot, 1994). In contrast, in an American firm the governance structure is primarily designed to serve the interests of the firm's shareholders and not its other stakeholders.

This chapter describes the restructuring of two European firms from the telecommunications industry: Latin Tel and Scan Tel, both disguised names. Each is a major player in its home market, with a context that calls for a predominant emphasis on social legitimacy. Both Latin Tel and Scan Tel have powerful employee unions and substantial government interest in their affairs, both because of the strategic importance of their industries and the importance of these firms to the national economy. However, both firms also faced serious performance challenges that threatened their commercial legitimacy. New CEOs were brought in from the outside to deal with this challenge. Hans Anderson, the new CEO of Scan Tel, pursued more of an American approach to corporate transformation (see FIGURE 4.2), focusing primarily on the firm's commercial stakeholders. In three short years, he improved the financial performance of Scan Tel dramatically and leveraged that result with a highly successful stock offering. In contrast, Marc Pujol, the new CEO of Latin Tel, followed a more balanced approach that tried to address the needs of the firm's commercial stakeholders without alienating its social stakeholders. This tightrope-walk clearly delayed the restructuring of Latin Tel, but when completed the firm was better prepared for re-vitalization than Scan Tel. The contrasting leadership styles in the two companies offer some important lessons for managing corporate transformation.

THE SCAN TEL TRANSFORMATION: BUILDING COMMERCIAL LEGITIMACY

A BRIEF BACKGROUND ON SCAN TEL

Scan Tel, a leading Scandinavian telecommunications service provider, was created in 1990 as a majority government-owned monopoly, integrating the erstwhile government-controlled independent regional operating companies. The primary motivation for Scan Tel's creation was to create a national company of critical mass to withstand global competition and to eventually privatize it. In 1991 the Scan Tel group employed 17 900 people and made paltry pretax profits of $200 million on revenues of $2.5 billion. An internal study comparing Scan Tel and 15 other telecommunications companies showed that the firm was in the lowest quartile on all key performance ratios. For example, its return on assets after depreciation was 6.8% and return on equity was 19% while the best companies showed 16.6 and 36.2% respectively. The company was also highly geared. Its solvency ratio (the proportion of the firm's share capital and retained earnings to its total fixed assets) was 23.9%. Industry experts believed that Scan Tel's solvency ratio should have been more in the region of 40%.

Anderson and his team knew there were several difficult challenges ahead. The company would face significant changes in its regulatory environment over the next few years. A number of its businesses would be opened to competition. By 1992 Scan Tel expected to have to compete for nearly 40% of its revenues. One issue for top management was whether the company's investment in technology was sufficient to meet this competitive threat. Scan Tel's network had a mixture of old and new technologies. This meant that Scan Tel would only begin to introduce intelligent network services such as itemized billing and 800 toll free numbers in 1993, while these had been common in other European countries for some years. A study by an outside management consulting company analyzed two liberalization scenarios. Under the more pessimistic scenario competition would capture almost 30% of Scan Tel's revenues by the year 2000.

UNCOMPROMISING DISCIPLINE

A useful first step in any transformation process is to instill discipline in the organization (Ghoshal and Bartlett, 1994). Discipline induces a firm's employees to meet all expectations generated both by their explicit and implicit commitments. Discipline is enhanced if there are clear standards of performance, there is objective and timely feedback against these, and the rewards and sanctions in an organization are tied closely to over- and underachievements against standards. One of the first tasks that Anderson and his team initiated at Scan Tel was to introduce budgetary discipline. Top management knew that it would have to trim costs. Many functions were redundant across the operating companies, these would have to be rationalized.

Given the resistance in the operating companies to centralization and the political influence that they had, this was a particularly difficult task. Budgets became an early test of top management's right to manage. When the regional operating companies first submitted their budgets, they were all routinely rejected. Top management demanded a 5% reduction in all expenses across the board. As Anderson observed later:

> We in top management did not have a choice. Either we had to pick our fight early and hold our ground or we would have been quickly reduced to rubber stamps. Even though we did not know where the savings would come from we were quite confident that they were possible. Our bench marking study told us so.

The operating companies not only complied and made the requested revisions to their budgets but they actually achieved the promised savings as well.

SIMPLIFYING THE STRUCTURE

Baden-Fuller and Stopford (1994) observe how important it is in the restructuring stage to simplify the organization structure, consolidate core businesses, and trim the rest. At Scan Tel, Anderson sought to create separate customer business units, particularly in deregulated markets. He saw this as a means of consolidating businesses that were already subject to competition and giving them a critical mass. While it was difficult for him to divest any businesses from Scan Tel's portfolio, he certainly wanted to isolate the poor performers for eventual downsizing or divestiture.

The mobile operations of the regional companies, which were already subject to competition, were first brought into a single new company, Scan Tel Mobil. The next major reorganization happened in 1992 with the consolidation of the sale of all telecommunications equipment. In 1993, Scan Tel Datacom was established as an independent business unit (IBU). It was responsible for the building, operation, and marketing of the group's data network services. Besides consolidating Scan Tel businesses that were subject to or likely to face competition, Anderson also sought to group activities for better efficiency. Scan Tel EDB was created as a single IBU to provide data processing services to all Scan Tel companies. Similarly, all customer equipment financing was brought into another new company, Scan Tel Finance. As would be expected, the establishment of these IBUs was resisted by the operating divisions. Their managing directors accused Anderson and his team of "hollowing out" the operating companies. It also led to conflicts with the unions, who were concerned about the implications of the move for employee rights, salaries, working hours, pension and other benefits. It must be noted in this context that under the terms of the political agreement that created Scan Tel, despite the stated objective of preparing the company for global competition, its top management was issued the following directive:

When managing the affairs of the Scan Tel group, top management must do so with due regard to the already existing very positive features of the individual telecoms companies. These include company culture, environment, etc. and not least their close relationship with the regions they were serving. So, Scan Tel should not uncritically interfere with the internal affairs of the individual telecoms companies.

Hans Anderson's actions tested this directive to the limit. This left a lot of unhappy social stakeholders. Besides the managing directors of the operating divisions and employee unions, there were several in the government who thought that Anderson's actions were a bit too drastic and insensitive.

Downsizing

Early in 1993, top management asked a consulting firm to conduct a study on Scan Tel's productivity. On the basis of internal benchmarking and the identification of "best practice" within different departments of the company, the consultant concluded that the work force could be reduced by about 4800. This slimming was sought to be achieved through better working methods, improved task definition, and creation of a system of performance objectives. When the unions rejected the report, top management tried to reinforce their case by hiring another consulting firm to validate the figures and methods. The second consultant agreed with 77% of the employee reductions suggested by the first. However, the employee unions remained unmoved.

The unions demanded that Scan Tel find solutions other than dismissal, such as developing new businesses. Suggestions included insourcing work such as the maintenance of Scan Tel's fleet of cars, telephone booths, and other parts of the telecommunications network. They proposed that the new businesses could be financed by the cost savings obtained by not laying off employees, which at that time was three years of salary plus pension. Many of Scan Tel's employees, being ex-government workers, were entitled to a government pension. The liability for this pension was passed on to Scan Tel at its formation.

In June 1993, the five unions representing Scan Tel employees set up their own work-group to analyze and validate the external consultants' reports. The group, called the FEO-group (the Future Efficient telephone Organization), claimed to have found several serious discrepancies in these reports. The FEO findings stated:

> ... we cannot avoid noticing how different departments within Scan Tel have manipulated their numbers in order to make their department look better than others. The consultants have let these mistakes pass by and simply

added more mistakes. The number of mistakes in the sample tests we conducted is incredibly high. How many mistakes there are in the areas we have
not had the chance to examine, we can only guess.

It was not just the unions that opposed the proposed downsizing. The federal government, for obvious political reasons, also balked at the proposal.
Top management reluctantly agreed in October 1993 to put involuntary
attrition on hold until 1997.

PROOF OF THE PUDDING IS IN ITS EATING

Despite the many challenges and delays to top management's plans for
restructuring, there was much that the executive team could feel proud of.
In two short years, headcount was trimmed through natural attrition and
voluntary departures from 17 900 to 16 750. This together with other cost
control initiatives had boosted operating margin from 12.7 to 18.4%. Profit
before tax rose from approximately $200 million to $400 million in 1993.
Long-term debt was cut from $2 billion to $1.5 billion and the solvency ratio
rose to 33.5%. Anderson felt that the timing was right to make a public
offering. When Scan Tel was formed, the government had committed to
bring its equity position down to 51%. However, Anderson had delayed the
public offering not only because Scan Tel's performance was poor in its first
two years, but also to give him time to persuade the government to remove
dividend caps on the shares to be held publicly and give up its right to
repurchase these shares at a future date. Both of these hurdles had been
cleared. Timing was now of the essence, since a number of other European
telecommunications companies were slated for privatization following the
lead of British Telecom. Anderson wanted Scan Tel to be among the early
followers.

In April 1994, Scan Tel offered 49% of the company to the public. The
offering was a huge success. It was oversubscribed 4.3 times. The sale of the
new shares left Scan Tel with over $1 billion for investment in new projects,
after fully funding all of its pension liabilities and trimming long-term loans
to a healthy level. Clearly, the company's commercial stakeholders
approved of Anderson's methods. Scan Tel was financially in excellent
shape and Anderson had established at lest a skeletal framework for its
future strategy and structure. The investor community found this to be a
promising first step in the company's attempts to take on global competition. The Scan Tel story is not new in the American context. If anything,
Anderson may have been slowed down by the firm's governance structure
from achieving even more in the first two years. Is Scan Tel then a role
model for others in Europe? Before one answers that question it may be
informative to look at another European restructuring. The story of Latin
Tel follows next.

The Latin Tel Transformation: Balancing Commercial and Social Legitimacy

A Brief Background on Latin Tel

Latin Tel is the European subsidiary of a large international telecommunications equipment manufacturer. Its turnover in 1994 was over $US1 billion. When Marc Pujol joined Latin Tel as its new CEO in 1984, the company was in trouble. After decades of profitable operation, Latin Tel posted its first loss in 1980. Losses persisted year after year through 1984. Moreover, 73% of Latin Tel's revenues came from one single customer, the national telephone company. The telecommunications market in the country was expected to become progressively open to other European and eventually to global competitors. Latin Tel was at risk by being so heavily reliant on one customer.

In addition to this growing competitive threat, technology was another major change force that affected Latin Tel. The advent of digital technology had revolutionized the telecommunications equipment manufacturing sector. Digital switching rendered nearly 5000 employees (35% of its work force) redundant at Latin Tel. Whereas six employees per 1000 access lines were needed to produce the old electromechanical switches at Latin Tel, the manufacture of the new digital switches was estimated to be eight times more productive.

Pujol's approach to managing transformation was distinct from Anderson's in three respects: (1) his moderation of strict discipline with fairness, (2) his invitation to the firm's key stakeholders for their active participation all through the transformation process, and (3) his emphasis on selective revitalization even during the restructuring stage.

Moderating Discipline with Fairness

One of Pujol's early initiatives was to reorganize the company into four autonomous operating groups and to create a total of 12 businesses within them. Each business was assigned a clear responsibility for performance. Performance against budgets was monitored monthly and managers were encouraged to highlight problems early. A new management-by-objectives system was introduced to assign personal responsibility to individual managers for aspects of business performance. All compensation, either as pay incentives or promotion, was made competitive and tied to results against these objectives. An important consequence of this was that managers at all levels within the company began identifying and surrendering slack resources. Pujol noted:

When you have a huge excess of employees, as we did, the control system breaks down. No matter what the manager does, the business cannot be profitable. We invited our business managers to submit a stretch budget that would show a profit. They very quickly identified large numbers of redundant employees in their businesses. For purposes of internal profit measurement, we did not charge these employees to the business budget. This created a new profit consciousness in the company. The redundancies that were identified also helped convince the unions that we had been inefficient.

The redundant employees were physically relocated to an unused company canteen. The canteen became a powerful visual symbol of the problems facing the company. With the company's approval, some of the redundant workers chose to stay at home. Others found creative ways to while away their time. The unions could not complain since the employees were on full wages. However, they did point out that the arrangement was unfair to those employees stuck in the canteen who had further career aspirations. Top management agreed to have a planned rotation of employees between the redundant pool in the canteen and the factories, even though this was opposed by the shop supervisors on the ground that it was disruptive to their work plans. Each time a worker rejoined the work pool, he/she had to be given training and it took several weeks before the worker could settle into the work rhythm of the team. The rotation plan ensured that no employee would be in the redundant pool for more than 18 months.

This sense of fair play was not an isolated incident. Latin Tel had signed in 1987 a three-year wage contract with the unions. The rising prosperity of the national economy in the following two years, bumped up wages at a considerably higher rate than what the Latin Tel unions had contractually agreed to. Even though the union leaders had used the best available information at the time of negotiating the contract, they were in a difficult position when subsequent events suggested that they may have been poor bargainers. On a matter of principle, Latin Tel management refused to renegotiate the wage contract. But instead they invited the unions to support an employee bonus scheme tied to the company's sales exceeding $1 billion. When the company cleared that mark its employees did receive the special bonus. Not only did this gesture enhance the union's trust in management, it also was a first lesson to employees on how company performance would increasingly influence their compensation in the future.

It is important to note here that top management was not being particularly generous or kind in its gesture. It merely chose not to take full, short-run advantage of an opportunity to gain at the expense of the firm's employees. It was not violating their trust.

GIVING STAKEHOLDERS A "VOICE" IN THE PROCESS

Hirshman (1970) has observed that if the demands of a firm's stakeholders are not satisfied, top management is likely to meet with passive opposition, which under certain circumstances may also become an active challenge to its authority or lead to defections from the organization. He labeled these active responses "voice" and "exit" respectively. While a stakeholder's ability to exert pressure may be negligible, either because of inability to put forward active opposition or because of limited exit options, the discontent is merely bottled up—ready to spill at the first available opportunity. By providing the compensating inducement of voice when plans and budgets are formulated, top management can ensure the continued cooperation of the firm's stakeholders.

Pujol made sure that the key stakeholders were closely involved with each detail of the restructuring plan. Besides giving them a real voice in the decision process, Pujol ensured that there was strict follow-up against all commitments. It is this combination of voice and discipline that the company attributes to the successful cooperation that it has subsequently enjoyed with all of its stakeholders. In describing his style of leadership, Pujol noted:

> I try to keep in close touch with the representatives of all stakeholders. Some are for change. I value their ideas. Others are against it. I value their caution. The fine art of managing any change process is not so much in knowing where to go, but rather what is the prudent speed to get there. I believe in participation. That does slow things down a bit. But whoever said revolutions are the way to go? I believe in evolutionary change.

Pujol's strong belief in participative management began to find broad acceptance within Latin Tel. For example, Latin Tel's vice president in charge of employee relations had daily breakfast meetings with representatives from the unions to deal quickly with any misunderstanding, and to seek their help in resolving difficult problems.

SELECTIVE REVITALIZATION EVEN DURING RESTRUCTURING

Hamel and Prahalad (1994) describe the power of vision, or strategic intent as they call it, to convey: (1) a sense of direction, (2) a sense of discovery, and (3) a sense of destiny. Soon after taking charge of Latin Tel, Pujol attempted to provide such a vision for Latin Tel. It was simple and in many ways obvious. The key elements of the vision were to dominate the local market, expand international revenues, and reduce the dependence on the national telephone company through diversification into other businesses, all to be accomplished within five years. In order to fulfill this vision, Latin Tel would have to improve its productivity to the levels of its global competitors, install a commercial orientation in its businesses and build capabilities in new product development. Each of these goals represented a major "stretch" target for Latin Tel managers.

The emphasis at Latin Tel on a corporate vision early in the transformation process is noteworthy. Latin Tel's poor financial performance and flat sales qualified it for a major restructuring. The more typical emphasis at this stage is on financial performance. Cost cutting and portfolio trimming are the dominant emphases of top management. In contrast, Pujol also chose to focus on growth and productivity improvement—performance targets that are typically pursued in the revitalization stage. He reasoned that a single-minded focus on the denominator, i.e. employee strength, to the exclusion of the numerator, i.e. the revenues that could be additionally generated on any given employee strength, was a perverse way of addressing the productivity problem. Moreover, he felt that it was very important to the morale of the work force that it saw signs of revitalization concurrent with the restructuring of the company. Restructuring would then be seen not as an end in itself, but rather as the flip side of revitalization. With this in mind, Pujol created the IPS Operating Group in 1984. As he noted:

We created Industrial Products and Services (IPS) because of the need to diversify and because it is essential for Latin Tel to grow outside telecommunications and electromechanics. Perhaps at a different time and place, this new group would have made no strategic sense at all. But in the mid 1980s it was very important for Latin Tel to impress the government and the unions that we were not merely downsizing the company but were also very serious about creating new jobs.

By 1989, IPS was providing employment to 638 employees, many of whom had been made redundant by Latin Tel's restructuring plan. Pujol's sponsorship of IPS was at variance from the "sour-first-sweet-later" philosophy advocated by the stage models of transformation. Proponents of this philosophy point out that it is important to focus the energies of the organization on cost savings initially. The results are immediate. However, this approach fails to deal with the resulting redundancies in the work force. IPS's ability to absorb Latin Tel's redundant employees was rather modest, numbering just over 600 at best. But the psychological impact that it created was quite significant. It represented a good faith effort by top management to create new jobs in the company to replace those lost to technological change and growing competition. Restructuring is helped when there are signs of revitalization.

SEAMLESS TRANSITION TO REVITALIZATION

Under Pujol's leadership, Latin Tel's work force was drastically reduced from a complement of 15 633 employees in 1984 to 7178 in 1992. More importantly, the work force was better skilled (31% had high school diplomas in 1992 compared to 11% in 1984). Concurrent with this "right sizing," the company's sales actually expanded from $400 million in 1984 to $1.1 billion in 1992. Net income before transformation costs had grown in the same period from a loss of $5 million to a profit of over $100 million. Employee productivity, as measured by sales per active employee, rose from $25 600 in 1984 to $153 000 in 1992, finally matching that of other international competitors. The company had also diversified its revenue base. The national telephone company's share of Latin Tel's revenues dropped to less than half by 1994, from a high of 73% in 1984. International revenues represented nearly 40% of the total in 1994, growing from 16% in 1984.

What made Pujol particularly proud of Latin Tel's restructuring was that it had been achieved without losing the trust or cooperation of any of the firm's key stakeholders. Also, the process had not merely focused on cost reductions, but had actively supported learning and innovation. The company had launched several new businesses during its restructuring. One such, industrial electronics, had developed rapidly to become a competence center for its parent worldwide. By nurturing trust, cooperation, learning, and innovation through the difficult restructuring stage of the transformation process, Pujol had increased the odds of a successful revitalization and perhaps even renewal at Latin Tel.

The positive impact of this trust-building exercise was evidenced in a number of ways. The labor negotiations with the unions had grown to be amicable. The 1992–93 wage negotiations lasted a mere five minutes. In 1993, Pujol launched a new program called Cenit for revitalizing the company. It sought to empower employees at all levels. In order to facilitate this, he sought from the unions the right to offer differential wages to employees based on their contributions to the Cenit program. The unions agreed, an achievement that would have been unthinkable in the 1980s. Employee satisfaction had also improved despite the downsizing. In a yearly survey conducted by an external consultant, the average index of employee satisfaction had climbed steadily from 5.06 in 1989 to 5.4 in 1994 on a 7-point scale. The increase, though small in absolute terms, was statistically significant. It is also useful to remember that the increase was achieved during a period when the employee strength had dropped from 10 216 to under 7000.

IMPLICATIONS FOR PRACTICE

THE PREDOMINANCE OF COMMERCIAL LEGITIMACY

The transformation of Scan Tel was characterized earlier as an American-style restructuring, because of its predominant emphasis on the commercial stakeholders of the firm (seemingly at the expense of its social stakeholders). It is important to remember here that the Scan Tel board of directors included all of its key social stakeholders. Thus an argument can be made that as long as there are formal checks and balances on leadership actions by these social stakeholders, it is the responsibility of top management to push hard toward the interests of the firm's commercial shareholders. This is exactly what Scan Tel's leadership team did.

A further justification for their actions is the very short lead time that Scan Tel had to improve its financial performance before going to the stock market. Anderson was afraid that the firm's commercial legitimacy had dropped so low that it was time to swing the legitimacy pendulum in favor of commercial legitimacy, albeit at some loss to his social legitimacy. European firms that are faced with restructuring would do well to emulate Scan Tel, especially where their governance structures provide strong voices for their stakeholders. While social legitimacy may be hurt in the process, the very survival of the firm may be at stake without such an action.

THE IMPORTANCE OF BUILDING TRUST DURING RESTRUCTURING

Despite their valiant attempts to journey through the three stages of corporate transformation sketched in Figure 4.1, American managers have typically been stalled after the restructuring stage. Trust, that is so vital to the revitalization and renewal stages, once lost during the restructuring stage is difficult to rebuild. Trust in an organization is defined as a common belief among its stakeholders that each will behave in accordance with its implicit and explicit commitments, and will not take excessive advantage of the other even when the opportunity presents itself. To build trust, an organization needs discipline. This ensures that the commitments of each stakeholder will be monitored closely. However, it is just as important for trust building if selective modifications are allowed to these commitments. Pujol's willingness to introduce job rotation for workers in the surplus pool or his openness to provide a performance bonus for his workers, even though he was not required to do either in a strict contractual sense, are examples of this trust-building process at Latin Tel.

Another vital element for building trust is providing a voice for stakeholders in the transformation journey. The special efforts that Latin Tel's top management took to encourage full participation by the company's stakeholders, helped nurture a cooperative relationship with each of them. Each stakeholder had the right, under the restructuring plan, to file grievances against Latin Tel management with a specially appointed government Commission. The Commission did not receive any complaints about Latin Tel, despite the company's failure to meet some of the conditions under the plan. True cooperation had made contractual obligations superfluous. A third contributor to the trust-building process was the insistence of Pujol and his team that restructuring and revitalization be pursued simultaneously. The creation and subsequent exploits of Latin Tel's IPS division illustrate this emphasis.

If quick performance turnaround is not an imperative, American managers should emulate the Latin Tel approach if they wish to journey through successfully to the renewal stage of the transformation process. The delay in producing short-term performance gains should be traded off against building an organizational trust platform that is essential to revitalization and renewal. Without trust empowerment is an empty slogan, and without empowerment there can be no bottom-up innovation.

REFERENCES

Baden-Fuller, C. and Stopford, J. (1994) *Rejuvenating the Mature Business*. Boston: Harvard Business School Press.

Calori, R., Valla, J.P., and de Woot, P. (1994) "Common Characteristics: The Ingredients of European Management", in R. Calori and P. de Woot (eds), *A European Management Model*. Englewood Cliffs: Prentice-Hall, pp. 31–54.

Calori, R. and de Woot, P. (1994) *A European Management Model*. Englewood Cliffs: Prentice-Hall.

Ghoshal, S. and Bartlett, C.A. (1994) "Linking Organizational Context and Managerial Action: The Dimensions of Quality of Management," *Strategic Management Journal*, **15**, 91–112.

Hamel, G. and Prahalad, C.K. (1994) *Competing for the Future*. Boston: Harvard Business School Press.

Hirshman, A.O. (1970) *Exit, Voice and Loyalty. Responses to Decline in Firms, Organizations and States*, Cambridge, Mass.: Harvard University Press.

Kelly, J. and Gouillart, F. (1995) *Transforming the Organization*. New York: McGraw-Hill.

Tichy, N. and Sherman, S. (1993) *Control Your Destiny or Someone Else Will*. New York: Free Press.

5

Hypercompetition

RICHARD A. D'AVENI

This chapter describes a fundamental shift in strategy in hypercompetition. The goal of strategy has shifted from *sustaining* advantages to *disrupting* advantages. Competition advances through a series of dynamic strategic interactions in four arenas: cost and quality, timing and know-how, strongholds, and deep pockets. In this dynamic environment a company's *movement* and its *relative* position in any of the four arenas are critically important. The only source of truly sustainable advantage is the company's ability to manage its dynamic strategic interactions with competitors through frequent movements that maintain a relative position of strength in each of the four arenas. Ironically, to sustain dominance, companies must seek a series of unsustainable advantages.

Some companies have tried to resist the intensity of competition by clinging tenaciously to their current advantages. These companies have watched their advantages eroded and their positions undermined despite their best efforts. Other companies have tried to slow competition through cooperative strategies, but ultimately these strategies have led to more intense competition as groups of competitors join with one another or new players pick off companies lulled into complacency by cooperative arrangements. In an environment in which every advantage erodes, both clinging to past advantages and trying to slow change are ultimately ineffective. The most effective companies in hypercompetition actively work to disrupt the status quo and undermine current advantages, moving from temporary advantage to temporary advantage.

Companies enhance their ability to disrupt the status quo and seize the initiative through the New 7Ss. These are:

- superior stakeholder satisfaction
- strategic soothsaying

Strategy, Structure and Style. Edited by H. Thomas, D. O'Neal and M. Ghertman

- positioning for speed
- positioning for surprise
- shifting the rules of competition
- signaling strategic intent
- simultaneous and sequential strategic thrusts

Just as companies shaped themselves to sustain advantages by using McKinsey's old 7S framework, they prepare for hypercompetition through using the New 7Ss. The New 7Ss define a vision for market disruption by creating a series of actions that generate superior stakeholder satisfaction, and they carry that vision into the future through strategic soothsaying. The New 7Ss build flexible capabilities of speed and surprise to facilitate the creation of disruption. Finally, the New 7Ss suggest using tactics that shift the rules of competition, signal strategic intent to dominate, and confuse or overwhelm competitors through simultaneous and sequential strategic thrusts that disrupt competitors and seize the initiative away from them.

A New Ideology of Competition

Markets were never really static; they just moved to higher levels of competition so slowly that they appeared to be static. But today markets are driven by the forces of global information processing and technological competitions that have transformed relatively low-intensity static environments to high-intensity dynamic hypercompetition overnight. These forces create opportunities to unseat the established leaders. This has reshaped the competitive options of all companies.

Secure Fortresses

In the old view of markets, companies focused on building monopolies in a specific market or market segment, limiting competition in those segments, and making excess profits by using their monopoly power to raise price, as illustrated by Figure 5.1. If new entrants occasionally shouldered their way into the market, competitors formed oligopolies that essentially limited competition by tacitly colluding to be less competitive. Either way, companies sought to build secure and sustainable fortresses they could defend against competitors without actively fighting. Antitrust laws tried to counter this approach by herding companies toward perfect competition, where excess profits and competitive advantages are nonexistent. A "fair", or "level", playing field was forced upon the players, and the market was frozen in a state where no one dominated. At least, that was the theoretical plan.

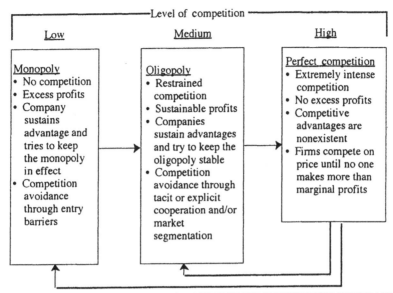

FIRMS SEEK TO MOVE AWAY FROM PERFECT COMPETITION TO GENERATE
PROFITS. PROGRESSION TOWARD PERFECT COMPETITION IS SO SLOW
THAT EACH STAGE APPEARS TO BE A STABLE, STEADY STATE

FIGURE 5.1   Traditional types of competition in a stable world

THE DISRUPTIVE AND THE DEAD

Today the fortresses of the past have crumbled, and the knights who once
defended them are left exposed on the open fields of combat. Monopolies
are virtually nonexistent. Even where they were once protected by government regulations, they have been dismantled through policies of deregulation and privatization in response to competitive pressures. Oligopolies are
also very hard to sustain. They last only as long as all competitors play by
the same rules. If one player steps out of the bargain or a new one enters the
market, all bets are off. In today's markets perfect competition often develops
because firms hold on to their old advantages until their competitors have
imitated them, resulting in bankruptcy or long-term poor performance.

In the current environment companies no longer have the option of
sustaining monopolies or oligopolies. They now have two choices: to
disrupt or to be dead. As shown in FIGURE 5.2, they can choose between
perfect competition or hypercompetition. Hypercompetition does not offer
the excessive profits of monopolies, nor does it offer the sustained profits of
oligopolies. But it does provide intermittent profits through temporary
advantages. Stringing together these advantages is the best strategy for

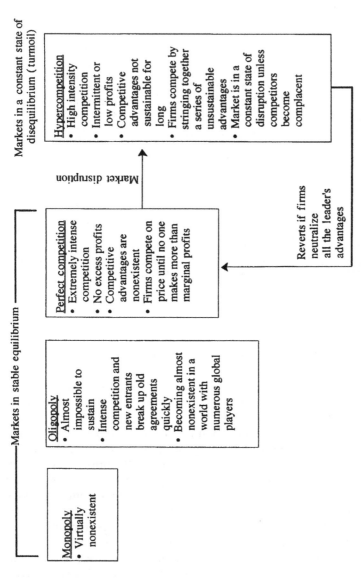

COMPANIES WOULD PREFER TO MOVE OUT OF PERFECT COMPETITION TO STABLE MONOPOLIES AND OLIGOPOLIES, BUT THESE PATHS ARE BLOCKED. THEY ARE FORCED TO MOVE INTO HYPERCOMPETITION BY CONSTANTLY DISRUPTING THE BALANCE AND STABILITY OF PERFECTLY COMPETITIVE MARKETS

FIGURE 5.2   New realities of competition driven by changes in the technological, global and information processing environments

long-term success in an environment that would otherwise offer few opportunities for using old strategies designed to create and defend monopolies or oligopolies. In other words, companies have little choice but to enter hypercompetition because it is superior to the state of perfect competition that would result if firms were left to imitate each other and reach a state of stable equilibrium. Disrupting that equilibrium by using the New 7Ss is essential to break out of it.

THE DANGER OF SHORT-TERM PROFIT ORIENTATIONS

Traditionally, oligopolistic and monopolistic strategies are preferred to hypercompetition by American business. These corporations seek the greater short-run profits provided by seeking oligopoly and monopoly. However, over the long run, profits and market position require a longer-term view of what happens when firms are trying to compete by avoiding competition. The aggressive firms eat their lunch, leaving devastation and starvation where once short-run profits prevailed.

The United States has been criticized for its short-run profit orientation, and researchers have blamed the problem on the stock market and government policy. The real problem is the American ideology of maximizing profits by *avoiding competition*. Instead firms should be maximizing their hypercompetitiveness to protect their relative strategic positions in their markets by racing up the escalation ladders faster than competitors do and by heating up the competition to even higher levels.

THE END OF A CHIVALROUS AGE

The rise of hypercompetition and the subsequent erosion of the fortresses of monopolies and oligopolies have brought an abrupt end to the age of chivalry. The gentility of tacit collusion and avoiding head-on competition is gone. The days in which it was uncouth to destroy a competitor are gone. Similarly, the usefulness of antitrust laws designed to protect "fair play" by pitting equally weighted players against each other is gone. The world of strategy has moved away from an ideology where "fair" competition was supposed to be like fixing wrestling matches between wrestlers of equal weight. It has moved to a new view where winners take all and combatants of unequal weight use any tactic available to them.

This shift in the definition of competition has been relatively rapid and was largely unexpected. It is no wonder that both managers and regulators have been slow to acknowledge this new vision of what competition is and should be. Companies can no longer compete according to the old ideology of fair play and chivalry. They are increasingly realizing the need for a new

The traditional American ideology	Hypercompetition in a global market
• Fair play and chivalry (e.g. do not use predatory and exclusionary practices)	• Winner takes all and "all is fair in love and hypercompetition "
• Domestic tranquillity	• Global business war
• Strong antitrust	• Relax antitrust to build national champions
• Not Darwinism, so protect the small company	• Darwinistic survival of the fittest
• Cannot use aggressive metaphors	• Use of new metaphors to motivate seizing the initiative and aggressive action
• The goal of antitrust is static efficiency and fair play	• The goal of antitrust is dynamic efficiency and meritocracy
• The concept of strategy as it is practiced today by many firms (e.g. long-range plans, sustainable advantage, use of generic strategies and barriers to entry)	• New concept of strategy (based on the New 7Ss and escalation ladders)
• Profits are bad and should be punished because they result from monopolistic practices	• Profits are rewards for behaviors that create jobs in the United States and satisfy customers better than anyone else in the world
• America is assumed to be eternally prosperous with plentiful high-paying jobs in the USA	• America is losing jobs to low labor cost locations overseas so corporate America must protect US jobs even at the expense of profits

FIGURE 5.3   Contrasting ideologies of the past and future

ideology of hypercompetition. The most aggressive firms have already given up the traditional ideology that guided strategy and policy in a chivalrous age. They realize that they are not fighting on the contained fields of combat of relatively tranquil and insulated domestic markets. They are in the midst of the head-to-head, fight-to-the death, global business war. They are now adopting a new ideology more appropriate to the hypercompetitive environment of all-out war, as summarized in FIGURE 5.3. As Ernesto Martens, CEO of Vitro (one of North America's largest firms) said, "You could actually feel it sweep through the company, this realization that the world was becoming a different place" (Nichols, 1993).

HYPERCOMPETITIVE EXHORTATIONS TO BATTLE

Cooperation and chivalry are not the model for the future of competition, even though cooperation and fair play have been the American tradition. The new model is Honda's battle cry of *Yamaha o tsubusu!* ("Annihilate, destroy, and crush Yamaha!") during the H–Y War or Komatsu's motto *Maru C* ("Encircle Caterpillar").

The signs of a more aggressive approach to competition can already be seen and heard across the United States. Employees in an AT&T factory are exhorted to "declare business war" against Northern Telecom (Schwartz, 1992). United Parcel Service, in its intense competition with

Federal Express and others, asserts in its television advertising, "The arms race may be over, but the package race is just heating up." Edward E. Crutchfield, chairman and CEO of First Union Corporation, comments on the shifting financial service industry: "We bankers are throwing snowballs [at each other] and there's someone out there with an Uzi" (Brannigan and de Lisser, 1993). Robert Lutz, president of Chrysler, declares, "The war isn't over but we've definitely landed on the beaches" (Greenwald, 1993).

There is a new intensity of competition. There is a new recognition of the demands of hypercompetition. There is a growing realization that chivalry is dead.

KILL OR BE KILLED

This new aggressiveness of competition is perceived by some as a ruthless drive to dominate. An industry analyst described the strategy of Intel as "a scorch, burn and plunder strategy with one aim: Kill off competitors. If you think Grove is determined to control the future of computing hardware, you're absolutely right" (Wrubel, 1993).

But Intel CEO Andrew Grove does not see himself as a ruthless and powerful Visigoth preparing to sweep through the countryside. He is fighting for survival. As he commented in a 1993 article, "The history of hightech industries is filled with the cadavers of companies that lived for a while and are no longer around. I drive up and down this peninsula and see the buildings of companies that are now on their third owner. The previous owners are gone. I have daily reminders of the mortality rate when you live in the fast lane" (Wrubel, 1993).

In this environment it is kill or be killed. The aggressiveness of hypercompetition demands a new ideology. The business environment today is as untamed as the Wild West. Entry barriers and deep pockets are leveled. The rich and poor are equally in danger as they ride through the sagebrush. It takes a new breed of rugged and fearless competitor to survive. And it takes a new ideology of competition.

This recognition of the need for a new ideology is by no means universal. But as those fighting by the old rules of chivalry take a beating in world markets, it is becoming harder to avoid acknowledging the reality of hypercompetition. Still, it is not clear that US managers and policymakers understand the full depth of the changes in the current competitive environment. Such a recognition is vital to the future competitiveness of the nation.

HYPERCOMPETITIVE NATIONS

In hypercompetition the advantages of nations are just as unsustainable as the advantages of companies. The past success of US companies in world markets is no guarantee of their future success, as the rise of strong competitors from Europe and Asia has demonstrated. Nor is Japan's success any indication of its future prospects; it is still unclear what Korea and China have in store for Japan and America. In the past decade America watched helplessly as control over key industries shifted to foreign competitors. Giants such as IBM and GM stumbled. This era was the Vietnam of US business history—demoralizing and confusing.

The only meaningful prospect for future success results from corporate strategies and government policies that encourage companies to adopt this new ideology of no-holds-barred hypercompetition. As Michael Porter comments on the results of his exhaustive four-year study of 10 nations in *The Competitive Advantage of Nations*, "Companies and economies flourish because of pressures, challenges, and new opportunities, not a docile environment or outside 'help' that eliminates the need to improve. Progress comes from change, not from a preoccupation with stability that obstructs it" (Porter, 1990). US managers and policymakers must promote a dynamic environment that is the best hope for the US economy and its companies.

MEETING THE CHALLENGE

The United States cannot afford to move back to aggressive attacks on its large, successful corporations by antitrust regulators. Antitrust laws often served to protect the underdog competitor from what was labeled a "predatory" firm. Yet it is this hypercompetitive predatory firm that survives in today's world. The government must untie the hands of our best hope for winning against global forces such as NEC, ABB, and others. Managers also cannot be content to focus on sustaining their current advantages. They must actively develop a series of advantages by using the New 7Ss.

Managers must abandon old strategic tools and theories that no longer apply in hypercompetitive environments. They must, for example, reconsider the use of the following strategic frameworks and maxims.

Commitment

Traditionally, increasing commitment by investing in fixed equipment or plants is thought to signal intent and increase focus. But in hypercompetition a rigid commitment tends to make the firm inflexible and predictable. The more a firm is locked into a specific course of action, the more competitors can maneuver around the firm in creating new advantages. Also, long-term commitments tend to lock the company into a specific advantage rather than allow it to move flexibly from advantage to advantage. In hypercompetition the flexible, unpredictable player has the advantage over the inflexible, committed opponent.

Long-term Planning

Traditionally, managers are exhorted to develop long-term plans that set the company on a steady course for the future. All parts of the plan consist of and build upon each other over time. Instead managers need to plan to be opportunistic and flexible in hypercompetition; they need to plan for change rather than consistency. Good competitors will destroy your plans. (There is an old military saying: A good plan lasts only until contact with the enemy.) Because long-term success depends on a series of short-term advantages, the exact nature of which cannot always be seen at the outset, the company needs to create a process of developing a series of advantages. This is in contrast to planning for specific goals and results under traditional approaches to long-range planning. In hypercompetition managers need to ask themselves what skills or assets are necessary to ensure that the company will have the necessary flexibility to meet the demands of building a series of advantages. In particular, they need to focus on how they can best develop the New 7Ss to prepare for the long-term process of hypercompetition.

Generic Strategies

Traditionally, selection of generic strategies, such as being a differentiator or low-cost producer, was recommended, but in hypercompetition these positions are only a short-term strategy at best. Firms actually move between such positions in the course of the evolution of the industry. Sometimes companies occupy two positions at once. The actions of competitors can move a company from one position to another without any action on the part of the company. Consistent strategies of being a follower or first mover are too static in hypercompetition. Companies shift from being first movers to followers and then back to first movers. In hypercompetition the advantage goes to the firm that keeps moving up the escalation ladder—not to the firm that locks into a fixed position like one of the generic strategies.

Building Entry Barriers

In hypercompetition managers seeking to build entry barriers or relying on entry barriers for protection against competitors will be frequently disappointed. Even the most persistent entry barriers and strongholds are beginning to fall. In hypercompetition the best barrier to entry by new companies or expansion by existing players is for the company to move aggressively from advantage to advantage. Notice that this is not really a defensive barrier, since companies keep on attacking, rather than defending, their current turf. This forward momentum and aggressive competition give a clear sign to would-be competitors that entry will be a challenge. It also offers fewer windows of opportunity for competitors.

In hypercompetition the advantage goes to the party with the initiative, not the player playing defense, using entry barriers to exclude players.

SWOT (Strengths, Weaknesses, Opportunities and Threats) Analysis

Analyzing a competitor's current strengths and weakness and playing strengths against weaknesses may work in the short term but is not an effective long-term strategy in a dynamic environment. Consistently playing against the weaknesses of a competitor is both predictable and a strategy that ultimately builds its weaknesses into strengths. A tennis player who serves to his opponent's weak backhand will eventually force the opponent to develop a stronger backhand. Then the first player faces a rival with a strong forehand and a strong backhand.

NPV Analysis

This method of analyzing projects to see if they generate a positive net present value (NPV) is predictable and fails to recognize the dynamic role that competitors play in shaping cash flows. Companies that use this model for capital budgeting will adopt a project only if the proposed project generates a positive NPV. In markets where opponents are willing to fight vigorously against a proposed investment, they can depress the expected cash flows for the company basing its decisions on NPV analysis and make the project look less attractive. On the other hand, if opponents do not fight, they allow their rival to have cash flows and to undertake this investment. Thus, in a dynamic environment the hypercompetitive opponent can actually decide where the company using NPV analysis competes. Further, using NPV analysis on one project at a time (as is done in most firms) does not allow the company to see the big picture needed to develop an effective competitive strategy wherein some projects are undertaken despite their negative NPV for the larger strategic purpose of disciplining the expectations of an opponent, letting it know its NPV for certain projects will be negative because of the competitive reaction to those projects.

Power over Buyers and Suppliers

Traditionally firms are taught to gain power over buyers and suppliers, but this ignores the reactions of the buyers and suppliers. General Motors had power over its dealers. It squeezed their margins and off-loaded inventory onto them without much concern for their risks of bankruptcy. The response was that dealers picked up Toyotas and Nissans to give themselves power over GM and to play each off against the other. This dynamic reaction to a temporary GM advantage destroyed the advantage.

In hypercompetition the advantage does not go to firms that squeeze dealers and suppliers but to firms that enlist them in the effort to create new advantages through using the New 7Ss.

To revert to old strategic doctrines, no matter how successful they were in the past, can be futile. Even to stand still in this environment is to move backward. As Ernesto Martens, the CEO of Vitro, said: "Our challenge is to change who we are without losing sight of what we are all about. . . . My challenge is to convince the people here that we can no longer be complacent in the face of world competition" (Nichols, 1993).

Our corporate and political leaders need to have the courage to address this new competitive environment by adopting a new view of competition that welcomes it and encourages it even if the business-is-war metaphor scares them or has an unpleasant sound to them.

Many companies and policymakers realized that change was needed. Forward-thinking companies have restructured themselves to become leaner. Courts and enforcers backed away from aggressive antitrust actions in the light of the decline of once-powerful corporations in hypercompetition.

The danger now is that we may misinterpret the lessons of the 1980s. We may be tempted to see these changes as a single anomaly in the environment. For managers it is tempting to think that a single restructuring or intense reengineering process can cut out the fat and set our corporations on an upward course again. It is tempting to limit the erosion of our current advantages through cooperation without hypercompetitive intent.

In politics there is a temptation to see the swing away from aggressive antitrust enforcement as a product of a Republican administration rather than the result of new realities of competition. Instead the shift to less aggressive enforcement of antitrust laws by the judicial and regulatory systems is a recognition of the new realities of hypercompetition. The dragons of monopoly power no longer roam the earth. But the threat of foreign competitors to US jobs is very real. US companies are no longer fighting to build monopolistic empires; they are fighting for survival. If US policy fails to support its corporations in this struggle, we may wake up too late to find that the corporate giants of the world have died or moved overseas. The outcome of this struggle affects US jobs, competitiveness, and the economy. The antitrust implications of hypercompetition must be addressed by regulators more explicitly.

The challenge facing the United States today is whether it can recognize the reality of hypercompetition and rise to meet the demands of this new environment. The United States must have the courage to overcome the tired ideologies and policies that made it successful in the past but are now keeping it in that past. America's old advantages are running out. The United States now must move on to its next advantage: the creative ability of its people to disrupt markets with sudden and overwhelming force through using the New 7Ss.

LEAN AND MEAN: HYPERCOMPETITIVE INTENT

The New 7Ss are the smelling salts that can wake up the sleeping giants of industry after a long period of sleep. Those large and small companies that wake up and fight will be the ones to succeed in the intense competition ahead. Instead of defending the status quo with entry barriers, the New 7Ss encourage the next generation of advantages, not sustain those of the past.

During the 1980s US corporations became leaner. Now they must become meaner, adopting a hypercompetitive intent to dominate. This does not mean engaging in endless price wars, however. Jumping to new or recently dormant arenas of competition is a good option. So too is restarting the cycles within each arena. The key is to dominate in each arena by having the superior position relative to the competition. If it moves, the firm must move, and preferably in a way that seizes the initiative (as the New 7Ss suggest). Reactive moves and playing catch-up are not enough.

The process of becoming leaner has stripped away the structures and strategies designed to support and sustain old advantages. Like mollusks that have shed their old shells, companies now have a critical decision. They can seek to create new shells, new, rigid structures and strategies to support and "sustain" a new advantage. These structures and strategies will soon become as stifling as their pursuit of their old advantage had been. Or these companies can use their newly found leanness to become aggressive hypercompetitors, flexibly and unpredictably moving from advantage to advantage.

Becoming hypercompetitive may appear to be a risky route for corporations. Certainly stable, consistent, long-term plans sound more rational, less risky, and less costly than jumping from advantage to advantage. A natural sense of conservatism may cause some companies to opt for the seemingly safer option of shoring up and sustaining an old advantage. But becoming mean by using the New 7Ss and pursuing a series of temporary advantages, as dangerous as this may be, is far less dangerous than being trapped in a rigid company trying to sustain an advantage long after it has begun to slip away. Companies that choose this latter route could find themselves the next IBM, valiantly defending the mainframe business throughout the 1980s even as it evaporates beneath them.

A SLEEPING GIANT AWAKENS

There is new evidence that US companies, despite the regulations that often hold them back, can seize the initiative and win in global competition. US companies are becoming more hypercompetitive without moving across the line into antitrust violations. In the first five months of 1992, *Business Week* reports, US car makers seized 72.4% of the domestic auto and light truck market, up 1.6 points from a year earlier. At the same time, Japanese automakers lost 1.4 points (Kerwin and Treece, 1992). In 1992 the Ford Taurus moved ahead of the Honda Accord as the best-selling US passenger car for the year. The Saturn is a roaring success. Lou Gerstner has a new vision for IBM that no longer defends mainframes, but moves on to what IBM is now calling "power architecture". Clearly the American dinosaur is not dead but is evolving to meet the new demands of its environment.

In 1993 US companies began to see growing profits and investments (Mandel, 1993). The United States was making gains across a wide range of industries, including autos, steel, food, computers, chemicals, semiconductors, telecommunications, and banking. Analysts predicted that the largest US industrial corporations were "poised for a comeback". General Motors actually led the *Fortune 500* in sales in 1992, and old-line companies such as Gillette, Whirlpool, and Union Carbide made great gains through stronger attention to customers, technological advances, and other moves (Faltermayer, 1993).

US companies increasingly are using the New 7Ss to boost stakeholder satisfaction, engage in strategic soothsaying, increase speed and surprise, shift the rules, signal, and use simultaneous and sequential strategic thrusts. They are moving ahead in the four arenas of competition by competing more aggressively on price and quality, timing and know-how, attacking strongholds, and building and using deep pockets.

Meanwhile, Japan has stumbled, and its bubble economy has been deflated. Most of what has been lost is the sense of invincibility gained during its rise after World War II—what has been called the Godzilla myth (Church, 1993). Toshiba, Honda, and other large corporations are changing their approaches to business (Gross, 1992). They are discovering, as US firms did during the 1980s, that all advantages are temporary. What worked in the past must be rethought to seize the advantage in the future. As always in hypercompetition, the vanquished have the chance to rise like a phoenix from defeat while the victors have the potential to lose their dominance because their hubris causes them to sustain their old ways of doing things.

ONLY THE DYNAMIC SURVIVE

Political and regulatory shifts will most likely occur too slowly to meet the immediate challenges of hypercompetition. Companies cannot wait. Of course, no one should intentionally break the law, but the dangers of standing still in hypercompetitive environments outweigh the dangers and costs of provoking an antitrust investigation by the government or a lawsuit from a competitor. The most aggressive companies realize this. Throughout its history General Electric, for example, has been no stranger to antitrust controversies.

American Airlines and Microsoft must continue to move as quickly up the escalation ladders as possible, to act decisively and aggressively, despite carrying the weight of government investigations or private lawsuits. (American had this point driven home when it began relying almost solely on price competition to win and its smaller competitors, which had been nipping at its heels, suddenly took a bite out of its rear, contributing to American's substantial losses in early 1993 (Solomon, 1993).) The antitrust actions may have had a dampening effect, but they seem not to have affected the most aggressive companies' fundamental approach to competition. Remember, the courts are beginning to come down on the side of antitrust defendants in many situations that were previously thought to be illegal (so consult legal counsel on current law). Most of all, remember that you are helping America when you are hypercompetitive because winning in the marketplace will defend US jobs and pursue dynamic efficiencies.

The world has moved forward and continues to move forward into hypercompetition. For US managers and policymakers the choice is clear. We can stand still and allow this wave of constant change to wash over us. We can try to resist the dynamics of the environment by clinging to concepts of sustainable advantages, by believing in the power of entry barriers. Or we can actively embrace the environment and take advantage of its opportunities. We can actively seek to disrupt current advantages, build new ones, and move competition up the escalation ladders. There is only one course that leads to long-term survival and success in hypercompetition. In a dynamic world only the dynamic survive.

REFERENCES

Schwartz, J. (1992) "IBM, Please Call AT&T", *Newsweek*, 28 Dec., 44.
Brannigan, M. and de Lisser, E. (1993) "Two Big Rival Banks in Southeast Take on New-Age Competitors", *Wall Street Journal*, 8 July, A1.
Greenwald, J. (1993) "Motown Turns a Corner", *Time*, 26 July, 52.
Wrubel, R. (1993) "Scorch, Burn and Plunder", *Financial World*, 16 Feb., 29.
Porter, M.E. (1990) *The Competitive Advantage of Nations*, 735, New York: Free Press.
Nichols, N.A. (1993) "From Complacency to Competitiveness", *Harvard Business Review*, Sept.–Oct., 163–165.
Kerwin, K. and Treece, J.B. (1992) "Detroit's Big Chance", *Business Week*, 29 June, 82.
Mandel, M.J. (1993) "This Rebound Just May Be for Real", *Business Week*, 11 Jan., 56.
Faltermayer, E. (1993) "Poised for a Comeback", *Fortune*, 19 Apr., 174–175.
Church, G.J. (1993) "Goodbye to the Godzilla Myth", *Time*, 19 Apr., 43.
Gross, N. (1992) "Toshiba: Rethinking the Way It Does Business", *Business Week*, 27 Apr., 55.
Solomon, S.D. (1993) "The Bully of the Skies Cries Uncle", *The New York Times Magazine*, 5 Sept., 14.

6

Mapping the Competence Boundaries of the Firm: Applying Resource-based Strategic Analysis

KIRK MONTEVERDE

INTRODUCTION

This chapter suggests one way in which the resource-based approach to strategy may be put into practice. A method is suggested which, although practitioner-oriented, is also grounded in empirically tested theory. This theoretical base is constructed by first examining the relationship between the resource-based strategy literature and the economic literature on transaction costs. The economic construct "asset specificity" (particularly of the human capital type) is viewed through a resource-based lens and certain of the empirical findings of the transaction costs literature are reinterpreted. This reinterpretation supports a hypothesis that it is an organization's unique set of communication codes which represent the idiosyncratic asset upon which a firm may build sustainable competitive advantage. Thus, the practitioner is advised to investigate the information flows of the organization and to limit the firm to functions which require unstructured interaction. These are the only exchanges which may be expected to benefit from the unique strategic asset of firm-specific communication codes. Evidence drawn from the American semiconductor industry is used to demonstrate application of the approach.

Even when explained particularly well and aimed at a general manage-

Strategy, Structure and Style. Edited by H. Thomas, D. O'Neal and M. Ghertman
Copyright © 1997 John Wiley & Sons Ltd.

ment audience (Wernerfelt, 1989), the resource-based strategic framework remains relatively inaccessible to most business practitioners. Better known in business circles is its perhaps less academically examined cousin, "core competence" (Prahalad and Hamel, 1990, 1994). It is the goal of this chapter to offer a means, both theoretically based but practitioner-oriented, of employing a resource-based framework to address a specific management issue—mapping the *boundaries* of firm competence. Key to this approach is a focus on only one of the many insights that may be derived from the resource-based strategic model. This focus is developed by a review of selected empirical studies in what is argued to be a closely related economics literature, that employing the transaction costs paradigm. Review of this economic literature is prerequisite to an application of the resource-based model.

The first step in application of the resource-based approach to strategy is discovery of those exceptional attributes (resources) of one's firm that hold the potential upon which to build a sustained competitive advantage. A summary of the basic guidelines to searching for these unusual resources is given by Barney (1991: 105–106):

> To have this potential (of sustained competitive advantage), a firm resource must have four attributes: a) it must be valuable, in the sense that it exploit opportunities and/or neutralizes threats in the firm's environment, b) it must be rare among a firm's current and potential competition, c) it must be imperfectly imitable, and d) there cannot be strategically equivalent substitutes for this resource that are valuable but neither rare or imperfectly imitable.

The concept of a firm's set of "exceptional strategic resources" as defined by the four considerations above has a parallel in the transaction costs literature as the economic construct, "asset specificity". The transaction costs literature hinges much of its explanation for the very existence of firms on the notion that certain transactions, for minimum-cost execution, require an investment in unique assets whose value is fully realizable only in a specific context, time, and place. Because markets will typically fail to exist for such assets, alternative institutional means of managing transactions (including, notably, that which we recognize as the common business firm) are said to develop around those investments necessary to realize least cost. Investment in these "specific assets" are surely valuable (they are, by construction, required for minimum-cost execution), and their uniqueness guarantees rarity and imperfect imitability. "Strategic substitutes", alternatives to any *given* idiosyncratic investment, may exist. However, any such alternative (that is, any other resource investment which enables least cost production) will also be rare and imperfectly imitable; otherwise, no idiosyncratic investment would have been contemplated in the first place. If a firm can avoid making an idiosyncratic investment while still obtaining least cost production, it will choose to do so. Nonrare, perfectly imitable resources are those transacted particularly well across markets. In short, those resources the strategist is told constitute his firm's source of potential sustained competitive advantage are the same as those the transaction costs economist would say are housed within the firm in the first place because they support transactions which could not be executed efficiently in the marketplace.

Fortunately, there is a growing body of empirical work in the transaction costs literature which can be interpreted in a way that (1) is consistent with the newer resource-based paradigm and (2) may serve as a set of case narratives to promote understanding of resource-based strategy among a practitioner audience. Specifically, several studies have presented evidence suggesting that investment in specific *human* capital may be key to understanding the dimensions of the firm. These include two studies drawing data from the auto industry (Monteverde and Teece, 1982a; Masten, Meehan, and Snyder, 1989), one each from the aerospace (Masten, 1984) and naval shipbuilding (Masten, Meehan, and Snyder, 1991) industries, and a study of the decision among electronic components distributors to integrate their marketing function, i.e. hire a sales force (Anderson and Schmittlein, 1984). Although originally inspired by the transaction costs model, each of these studies may be reinterpreted through a resource-based lens. The specific human capital investment hypothesized in these studies to have required a hierarchical governance structure (e.g. integration of effected transactions within the firm), may *also* be interpreted as that valuable, rare, only imperfectly imitable, nonsubstitutable asset upon which an organization's sustainable competitive advantage may be built.

But what is the exact nature of this pivotal human capital investment? Recently, specific human capital investment in the form of *firm-specific shared communication codes* (Monteverde, 1995) has been featured in an empirical investigation of the changing structure of the semiconductor industry. In this study, the statistically supported hypothesis is that the higher the level of required "unstructured technical dialog" accompanying an exchange, the higher the likelihood of integration of that exchange under an organizational hierarchy. The reasoning lying behind this hypothesis is that an "organization" will be uniquely efficient in accommodating unstructured dialog because of an investment in unique codes for communication, "short-cuts" to understanding one another, understood fully only by organization members. Given a resource-based interpretation, these shared communication codes (qualifying under the four criteria listed earlier) are the firm's source of potential sustainable competitive advantage. Furthermore, where a firm's boundaries incorporate exchanges which *do not* draw upon these unique communication codes in any important way, the firm may be said to be operating beyond its "core" competency. Thus, the implied prescription for practitioners is to limit operations of a single organization to those production stages which require unstructured communication between human agents in adjacent production steps. All other transactions, that is, those *not* requiring dialog, do not benefit by being carried out within a hierarchy and might best be exchanged using the market mechanism ("outsourced").

REINTERPRETING EARLIER EMPIRICAL TRANSACTION COSTS RESULTS

Before proceeding with a more detailed look at the application of resource-based analysis, a review of some of the earlier empirical work in the transaction costs tradition would seem appropriate. How can these results be reinterpreted within the resource-based approach? And, although these studies may not have addressed it, can *firm-specific communication code* be used to explain their findings?

First, it is important to realize that the resource-based framework assumes *less* about the nature of human behavior than does the brand of transaction costs economics employed in the early studies. Specifically, much transaction costs research has relied upon the construct of "appropriable quasi-rents" (Klein, Crawford, and Alchian, 1978) which *opportunistic* human agents are assumed willing to grab if they can do so without penalty. Investment in assets specific to a particular transaction ("asset specificity") creates quasi-rents. Quasi-rents are defined as the dollar amount of the specialized asset in its first-best use versus its value in its second-best use. Transactions which create high appropriable quasi-rents are those which the theory suggests will be housed within organizations in order to avoid appropriation. In contrast, a resource-based approach does not rely upon a necessary assumption of opportunism and the resultant fear of quasi-rent appropriation.

Interestingly, most transaction costs studies have not attempted to *directly* measure the dollar magnitude of appropriable quasi-rents created by investment in specific assets (one exception is Monteverde and Teece, 1982b). Proxies for quasi-rents have been especially necessary when the studied investment is in idiosyncratic *human* capital. For example, in the first empirical study of the transaction costs literature, Monteverde and Teece (1982a: 207) hypothesized (and found statistical support for) the following proposition:

> The greater is the applications engineering effort associated with the development of any given automobile component, the higher are the expected appropriable quasi rents and, therefore, the greater is the likelihood of vertical integration of production of that component.

The level of applications engineering, the directly measured independent variable, is taken as a surrogate measure for the magnitude of appropriable quasi-rents; it is the latter which transaction costs theory predicts should be related to the likelihood of vertical integration. However, it is possible that the directly measured construct, the magnitude of applications engineering, is related to a different intervening variable than that which the paper originally asserted. For example, it may proxy for the magnitude of necessary unstructured technical dialog between engineers in adjacent workflow steps. This interpretation, one inspired by the resource-based framework, is consistent with the statistical results reported in the paper, but does *not* require an assumption of opportunism and a consequent fear of quasi-rent appropriation. Instead, it may be the case that components produced internally by the auto companies are those whose efficient design and production requires dialog between engineers who, if they work within the same organization, have come to use the same firm-specific communication codes.

Anderson and Schmittlein (1984) found a relationship between the likelihood of employing an integrated sales force (their dependent variable) and a measure of human capital-based asset specificity constructed using an average of respondents' answers to six questions. Among the six questions was at least one which explicitly attempted to measure the level of required learning on the part of a new salesperson of the firm-specific routines of the company he or she was to represent either as an employee (the integrated choice) or as an independent manufacturers' rep (the market exchange alternative). Specifically, respondents were asked on a semantic differential scale whether they disagreed or agreed (1 to 7) with the statement, "It's difficult to learn all the ins and outs of our company that a salesperson needs to be effective." Neither the quasi-rents construct nor an assumption of opportunism is needed to explain the positive relationship of at least this first element of the constructed asset specificity measure and sales force integration (although the authors assume opportunism, they themselves do not talk about their measures as proxying for the dollar magnitude of appropriable quasi-rents). Viewed from a resource-based perspective, the relationship may be interpreted, for example, to support a hypothesis that integration is more likely the more specialized are the routines (or ways of communicating and interacting) within a company. The more specialized the routines or communication protocols, the higher the cost of not belonging to the organization in which these routines may be most efficiently learned (as a joint product of simply doing one's job). This sales force integration choice, predicated upon the most efficient way of gaining organization-specific know-how, does not require any assumption as to whether or not individuals act opportunistically.

For a final example consider the much more recent research of Masten, Meehan, and Snyder (1991). Although not abandoning quasi-rents and the fear of their appropriation as a possible explanation for integration of production, the authors argue that this cost of using the marketplace must be considered in conjunction with the cost of organizing exchange within a hierarchy (e.g. a firm). Indeed, using a two-stage econometric technique borrowed from labor economics and data from the naval shipbuilding industry, the authors' striking results indicate "that the correlation between human capital specificity and the likelihood of integration . . . is a consequence of a *decrease* in internal organization costs rather than the increase in the costs of market exchange . . ." (p. 19, emphasis added). Ironically, although the authors title their article "Costs of Organization", their findings might perhaps be more appropriately labelled the *"Benefits* of Organization." Their principal finding suggests that transactions involving a high degree of human capital specificity are vertically integrated not necessarily because of fears of using the marketplace, but because it is somehow beneficial having such transactions executed within organizations. The authors offer one explanation of this result, speculating that perhaps "workers with more specific skills are less costly to manage" (p. 18). Human capital-sourced asset specificity was measured in the study by asking respondents to rate each sample task or component on a 10-point scale as to "the degree to which the skills, knowledge, or experience of workers are specific to this application" (p. 14). Given the manner in which the asset specificity construct was thus operationally measured, it is also possible to give a communication code, resource-based interpretation to the results of this study. Perhaps workers performing tasks judged to be "specific" work efficiently together not just because they are easier to manage but because they also understand one another particularly well. That is, it may be the case that the tasks judged to be firm-specific are also those which demand the most intense unstructured dialog between workers and are therefore integrated under a hierarchy because workers in a single organization can most efficiently acquire the common communication codes needed to accommodate such unstructured dialog.

COMMUNICATION CODE AS A SOURCE OF A SUSTAINABLE COMPETITIVE ADVANTAGE

If, as suggested above, dialog between people in adjacent production steps is an important motivation for housing these steps within the same organization, it must be because that dialog is somehow more efficient between individuals working within a single organization. That which makes this dialog uniquely efficient in an organization has been labeled the organization's specific communication codes. An important feature of these codes is that they are an asset not associated with any particular individual nor any identifiable subset of individuals in the organization. They are a "corporate" asset. Following Becker (1962), Arrow notes that a significant amount of human capital accumulation consists of training specific to a single firm and suggests that "learning the information channels within a firm and the codes for transmitting information through them is indeed a skill of value only internally" (Arrow, 1974: 56). It may even be argued that this form of idiosyncratic human capital investment is the defining essence of what we recognize as organizations:

> . . . The learning of a code by an individual is an act of irreversible investment for him. It is therefore also an irreversible capital accumulation for the organization. It follows that organizations, once created, have distinct identities (Arrow, 1974: 55).

Under this characterization, then, organizations are distinguished by the codes, the specific business dialect, their members use. Drawing upon the equivalence argued earlier between firm-defining specific assets and a firm's core strategic resources, this shared business dialect becomes our focus in mapping the boundaries of core competence. If the firm's shared communication codes are its key strategic resource, then a map of the intensity of the exercise of these codes—a map of the intensity of dialog within the firm—can help define the boundaries of firm competence.

Consider the opposite extreme of a hypothetical firm in which individuals communicate with one another without "dialect", that is, communicating without assuming the other party is aware of any of the firm's organization-specific routines, personnel, past history, or protocols. To push the example a bit further, assume that employees lack a common social setting (as if they are all "telecommuters" or never venture from their offices) and never learn anything much about the personalities of their fellow employees that might facilitate communication. Communication between "employees" under these circumstances may be supposed to resemble the more formal communication employed between individuals in different firms executing market transactions. By construction, this set of employees (this "firm") cannot be expected to be able to accomplish anything that could not be accomplished by independent entrepreneurs transacting in the marketplace; indeed, the extreme example constrains these "employees" to communicate as if they were *not* part of a larger organization. In order for this collection of individuals to be capable of producing more than the sum of what they could produce individually, there must be some advantage to their working together in teams over time. The most straightforward source of such synergy is the learned ability of the team to communicate in "dialect" among one another, taking for granted a shared understanding of firm-specific routines, etc. (Nelson and Winter, 1982).

"DIALOG" AND STRUCTURAL CHANGE: AN EXAMPLE FROM THE AMERICAN SEMICONDUCTOR INDUSTRY

Because of rapid technological change, the semiconductor industry is one in which competitive competencies have, over time, been narrowing. The result has been the appearance of a "dis-integrating" industry wherein individual stages of production previously integrated together within all firms have today evolved into separate industries. A more detailed examination of one instance of this narrowing, one particularly illustrative of the role of diminished dialog, may be helpful in demonstrating how analysis of dialog patterns can guide practitioners in determining their firm's competency limits.

Integrated circuit (IC) production, broadly defined, traditionally is broken into four fundamental, sequential stages: design, fabrication, package assembly, and test, all of which are *technologically* separable (Kimura, 1988, especially p. 49). It is the *organizational* separation of the first two of these production stages into distinct industries for at least certain classes of ICs (see Monteverde, 1995) that is of interest here. It is hypothesized that the recently observed "fabless" phenomenon (i.e. viable semiconductor firms which do not fabricate; for example, see Ferguson, 1990; Florida and Kenney, 1990; Rappaport and Halevi, 1991) may be explained by technological changes that have enabled exchange between the adjacent stages of design and fabrication now to occur with a minimum of engineering dialog where previously considerable unstructured technical discussion was the norm.

To better picture its *information* flows, the traditional four-part semiconductor production workflow may be recast. Both the design and fabrication stages may be broken each into two substages, design into logic and layout, and fabrication into process development and production fabrication. Important to this analysis is a recognition that process development is upstream from *both* layout and production fabrication. The traditional product flow would emphasize only the latter. FIGURE 6.1 illustrates this revised workflow for contemporary semiconductor firms producing digital logic chips using the most popular type of fabrication process ("CMOS"). This workflow diagram is the same whether the design and fabrication stages of production are integrated within a single firm (perhaps because of historical inertia) or not.

Notable in FIGURE 6.1 are the "interfaces" between the four design and fabrication substages. As is indicated by the double-headed arrows, considerable interactive dialog still exists today between the substages within the ovals, that is, between process development and production fabrication and between logic design and layout. In contrast, the handoffs *across* the oval boundaries are today commonly unidirectional. Indeed, for the two interfaces between the ovals, documentation has largely replaced conversation (at least for CMOS digital logic designs) even among firms whose boundaries

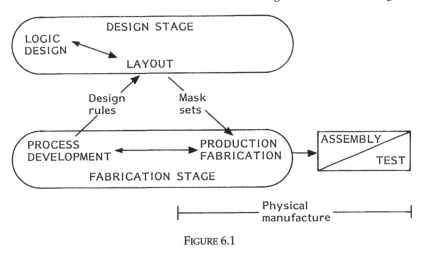

FIGURE 6.1

still encompass both the design and fabrication stages. One handoff, mask creation, has been a well-defined interface devoid of engineering dialog for decades (Hnatek, 1973). The second, design rule capture and analysis, has been an area benefitting significantly from the information technology advances of the last 15 years. It is the lessening of engineering dialog accompanying this second handoff and the substitution of technology for conversation, that has enabled the semiconductor industry to dis-integrate into organizations specializing in the separate competencies of *either* fabrication or design. In effect, an older double-headed arrow relationship between layout and process development, one formerly characterized by significant engineering feedback, has been replaced by an explicit unidirectional information flow, unaccompanied by unstructured technical dialog.

New semiconductor process techniques are continuously being refined by fabrication engineers. Design rules, for any given process, dictate the minimum transistor sizes, spacings between transistors, and overlaps required to ensure connections. Failure to meet the rules *anywhere* on the chip may make the device inoperable (see Trimberger, 1987: 9, 184). Design rules are intended to document all a layout designer need know to successfully execute a design into silicon; they insulate the layout engineer from the chemical and lithographic complexity of fabrication. Codification of these rules into software as automated "design checkers" is a key technological achievement of the past decade and a half. This codification and the sophisticated automated analysis now possible have largely replaced the unstructured interaction between fabrication and design engineers that was common in the industry during the period when both stages were integrated together in all semiconductor firms.

A FURTHER EXAMPLE OF COMPETENCY MAPPING FROM THE SEMICONDUCTOR INDUSTRY

One implication of the above analysis for the practitioner is that the mapping of competence boundaries might best begin with a determination of how information flows within the organization. The first objective is to identify clusters of operations in which individuals continuously communicate (these may or may not correspond to departments on the corporate organization chart). Next, one determines the type and intensity of communication *between* the clusters. Importantly, this cluster analysis may highlight interaction between certain workflow steps that does *not* appear to draw upon firm-specific dialect in any significant way and might just as well, therefore, be "market" interaction. This was the case illustrated above for the interface between IC design and fabrication. The question then becomes whether the firm is attempting to operate, perhaps inadvertently, beyond its "core" cluster of value-adding activities.

Of course, workflow analysis will not always reveal interfaces that have been made as completely unidirectional and devoid of dialog as this chapter has suggested has been the case for IC logic chip design and CMOS fabrication. Nevertheless, an examination of the direction of *change* over time in the type and intensity of information flows may provide important strategic insight. As an example, consider the process of semiconductor design *alone*, illustrated in FIGURE 6.2. In the figure the process has been subdivided into clusters. These clusters represent functions which are either performed by the same person or, if executed by different people, require continuous interaction between those individuals. Notably, loop-backs in the flowchart (which will be familiar to practitioners who have done TQM flowcharting) may be taken as indicative of workflow steps that require feedback. Consequently, process steps between such loop-backs will typically be clustered together on a map of information flows. Using this guidance, the traditional IC logic chip design process is divided here into the clusters: logic partitioning, new cell design, and chip layout/assembly and analysis. FIGURE 6.2 adds to the traditional IC design flow a fourth activity cluster, system design, which immediately precedes chip partitioning.

Next, consider changes in the type and intensity of engineering interaction that have occurred over time in the three interfaces between the four sequential clusters drawn on FIGURE 6.2. Although my evidence is purely anecdotal, supported only by interviews with IC design engineers, it appears that the intensity of engineering dialog has changed markedly for at least some of these handoffs during the decade of the 1990s. The optimal level of unstructured engineering interaction for one handoff has remained fairly stable, that between new cell design and chip layout/assembly and analysis (the handoff denoted in FIGURE 6.1 by a double-headed arrow

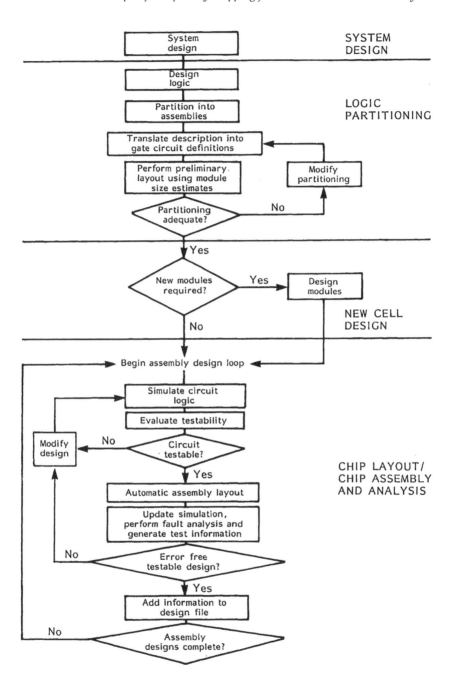

FIGURE 6.2

within the design stage). However, technological advances have allowed for *less* dialog between the operations of logic partitioning and new cell design (operations which were both subsumed under the label of logic design in FIGURE 6.1) while the optimal level of unstructured technical dialog between system design and logic partitioning has risen dramatically. Interestingly, these latter two stages have generally *not* been organizationally integrated; logic partitioning has been traditionally the province of semiconductor firms (either of the fabless or integrated variety) while system design (of, for example, computer or communication equipment) has been the core competency of their customers. But as "systems on a chip" are becoming increasingly commonplace, the necessary dialog between systems designers and chip partitioners has increased. Today, they can sometimes be the same person.

The upshot of this (admittedly preliminary) analysis of information flows in semiconductor design is that competency concentrations may again be shifting. On the one hand competency in what this chapter had labeled "logic design" in FIGURE 6.1 may be narrowing to exclude logic partitioning. On the other hand, because dialog between what had been the distinct disciplines of systems design and chip logic partitioning has been dramatically increasing, these two functions may, in the not too distant future, be most commonly found integrated under common organizational hierarchies where they are not today. The strategic question for a semiconductor company (say of the fabless variety) is where to focus if it is to follow the guidance derived from resource-based analysis that one is best concentrating on clusters of processes that share a common source of sustainable competitive advantage. A fabless semiconductor firm would be advised either to gain systems design expertise to complement its logic partitioning competence (and perhaps give up on the rest of what traditionally has been considered "IC design") or, instead, retreat to the still fairly tightly related operations incorporated within the new cell design and chip layout/ assembly and analysis stages. If a firm were to choose the latter strategy it might be most appropriately called an IC cell archive or, employing the term the industry itself uses, cell "library" firm. This firm would concentrate on predesigning common subsets of complete chip logic (called cells) which various customers would combine together in various ways dictated by their own partitioning preferences and/or system-level requirements.

DISCUSSION

Resource-based analysis has gained tremendous momentum as a new academic strategic paradigm. It has gained attention, in part, because it is largely consonant with a growing body of economic research, prominently the transaction costs literature. Indeed, the advantage this strategic approach enjoys in being able to draw upon a reservoir of economic work raises the possibility of its eventually altering the business policy field as dramatically as did an earlier import from industrial organization economics, the industry analysis framework associated with the writings of Michael Porter (e.g. 1980).

Although empirical research in the transaction costs literature has been active for more than a decade, this literature is virtually untapped as a *direct* tool for the practice of business strategy. This is partially because the transaction costs literature is peppered with such esoteric constructs as "appropriable quasi-rents" and "asset specificity", terms almost guaranteed to turn away the practitioner. Resource-based analysis, because it has been developed within the field of strategic management, uses terminology (such as "sustainable competitive advantage") that is at least familiar-sounding to those in the business community. Nevertheless, resource-based analysis today still remains a strategic framework much more talked about in academic circles than among practicing business strategists. The goal here has been to try and increase the resource-based framework's visibility among practitioners while also clarifying the relationship of some of its terms with those used in transaction costs economics.

As the chapter has attempted to document, it is often possible to give a resource-based interpretation to the empirical work reported in the transaction costs literature, specifically that subset of the literature that employs the construct of human capital-based "asset specificity". This is useful because it opens up an entire set of industry studies to illustrate to practitioners the application of resource-based analysis. Furthermore, one particular form of organization-specific asset is examined which, in the parlance of resource-based analysis, is identified as an organization's key source of potential sustainable competitive advantage. That organization-specific asset is each organization's unique set of communication codes used by members to efficiently interact with one another. Drawing heavily upon the experience of the American semiconductor industry, the chapter argues that the boundaries of a firm's competency may be defined by mapping its information flows and noting where exchange between workflow steps do not, in any important way, draw upon firm-specific communication dialect. In short, it is argued that the boundaries of firm competency are defined where explicit, generally understood "documentation" can replace idiosyncratic "dialog".

REFERENCES

Anderson, E. and Schmittlein, D. (1984) "Integration of the Sales Force: An Empirical Examination", *Rand Journal of Economics*, **15**, 385–395.
Arrow, K. (1974) *The Limits of Organization*. New York: W. W. Norton & Co.

Barney, J. (1991) "Firm Resources and Sustained Competitive Advantage", *Journal of Management* **17**, 99–120.

Becker, G. (1962) "Investment in Human Capital: A Theoretical Analysis", *Journal of Political Economy*, **70**, Supplement, October, 9–49.

Ferguson, C. (1990) "Computers and the Coming of the U.S. Keiretsu", *Harvard Business Review*, July/August, 55–70.

Florida, R. and Kenney, M. (1990) "Silicon Valley and Route 128 Won't Save Us", *California Management Review*, **33**, 68–88.

Hnatek, E. (1973) *A User's Handbook of Integrated Circuits*. New York: John Wiley & Sons.

Kimura, Y. (1988) *The Japanese Semiconductor Industry: Structure, Competitive Strategies and Performances*. Greenwich, Conn.: Jai Press.

Klein, B., Crawford, R., and Alchian, A. (1978) "Vertical Integration, Appropriable Rents, and the Competitive Contracting Process", *Journal of Law and Economics*, **21**, October, 297–326.

Masten, S. (1984) "The Organization of Production: Evidence from the Aerospace Industry", *Journal of Law and Economics*, **27**, October, 403–417.

Masten, S., Meehan, J. Jr, and Snyder, E. (1989) "Vertical Integration in the U.S. Auto Industry", *Journal of Economic Behavior and Organization*, **12**, 265–273.

Masten, S., Meehan, J. Jr, and Snyder, E. (1991) "The Costs of Organization", *Journal of Law, Economics and Organization*, **7**, 1–25.

Monteverde, K. (1995) "Technical Dialog as an Incentive for Vertical Integration in the Semiconductor Industry", *Management Science*, **41**, 1624–1638.

Monteverde, K. and Teece, D. (1982a) "Supplier Switching Costs and Vertical Integration", *Bell Journal of Economics*, **13**, 206–213.

Monteverde, K. and Teece, D. (1982b) "Appropriable Rents and Quasi-Vertical Integration", *Journal of Law and Economics*, **25**, October, 321–328.

Nelson, R. and Winter, S. (1982) *An Evolutionary Theory of Economic Change*. Cambridge, Mass.: The Belknap Press.

Porter, M. (1980) *Competitive Strategy*. New York: Free Press.

Prahalad, C.K. and Hamel, G. (1990) "The Core Competence of the Corporation", *Harvard Business Review*, May/June, 79–91.

Prahalad, C.K. and Hamel, G. (1994) *Computing for the Future*. Boston: Harvard Business School Press.

Rappaport A. and Halevi, S. (1991) "The Computerless Computer Company", *Harvard Business Review*, July/August, 69–80.

Trimberger, S. (1987) *An Introduction to CAD for VLSI*. Boston: Kluwer Academic Publishers.

Wernerfelt, B. (1989) "From Critical Resources to Corporate Strategy", *Journal of General Management*, **14**, Spring, 4–12.

7

Developing and Deploying Corporate Resources in the Technological Race to Market

LILLIAN CHENG WRIGHT, RUSSELL W. WRIGHT

INTRODUCTION

A principal managerial concern in the technological race to market entry is the timing of the entry and the development of sustainable competitive advantage. This issue has taken on paramount importance in the increasingly shortened product life cycles in the global competition of high-tech industries.

Past research in the area of market entry timing provides little definitive insight. Empirical research results call into question the attainability of competitive advantage through market entry timing. Even where a firm develops competitive advantage by entering the market at the "appropriate" time, this advantage eventually erodes. To the extent that all resources, and therefore competences, are ultimately imitable, there is a specific amount of time when firms can benefit from their competitive advantage in the market. It is this period of time which industry practitioners and academic researchers have referred to as a "strategic window" of opportunity.

Strategy, Structure and Style. Edited by H. Thomas, D. O'Neal, and M. Ghertman
Copyright © 1997 John Wiley & Sons Ltd.

Strategic innovations often open windows of opportunity whereby a firm can gain competitive advantage. The duration of that advantage is a function of the rate of competitive imitation as well as the incumbent's ability to erect entry barriers and satisfy market demand. The window eventually closes, the strategic action is diffused and becomes an industry requirement.

Our interest in the concept of strategic windows is the result of three years of field research on product development and introduction practices in the semiconductor and computer industries in the United States, Japan, and Europe. Throughout our interviews and discussions with industry participants, it was evident that their entry and entry timing decisions were based not only on the race to take the technological lead, but also on the concept of strategic windows. There is, however, little theory to guide these managers in identifying the opening and closing of strategic windows, much less factors that can shorten or lengthen the window time frame.

A strategic window is open in a product market when an entry can be made without having to take sales away from an incumbent. After the window closes, an entrant would need to dislodge a competitor at a time when the basis of competition (Birnbaum-More *et al.*, 1994) has widened and there is no clear source of competitive advantage.

In this chapter, we briefly discuss the issues of market entry timing and sources of competitive advantage. We then examine the concept of strategic windows and propose a conceptual framework for strategic window analysis. We discuss the opening and closing of strategic windows as a function of the rate of market growth and competitor imitation. We then show empirical validation of the model using data of consecutive product generations in the personal computer and semiconductor industries.

We examine the principal drivers of strategic windows and demonstrate the phenomenon of strategic windows in terms of the appropriability, transferability, and imitability of resources using the knowledge-based theory of the firm. We conclude the chapter with comments on how a firm can attain competitive advantage by developing and exploiting resources necessary in an industry evolution of continually emerging strategic windows.

MARKET ENTRY TIMING

There continues to be an academic debate on the advantages of market entry timing. Conditions for first mover advantages as well as disadvantages have been specified (Lieberman and Montgomery, 1988). Empirical research has found support for first mover as well as follower advantages.

Robinson and Fornell (1985) contended that pioneers have long-term market share advantages due to "long-lived" marketing mix advantages, cost savings that allow for a stronger marketing mix and relative consumer information advantages. Urban et al. (1986) found supporting evidence in their study of consumer products that the second entrant can only attain 75% of the market pioneer's share of the market and later entrants capture progressively less.

Other empirical studies, however, showed that later entrants have market share advantages, e.g. Birnbaum-More (1990). Lilien and Yoon (1990) reported that success was higher for third and fourth entrants than for first, second, or fifth and later entrants in French industrial markets. Still other researches had mixed findings. Mitchell (1991) introduced the concept of dual clocks where new entrants to a technological subfield enjoy early mover market share advantages whereas incumbents only enjoy market share advantages as early movers relative to other incumbents.

More recent research suggested some of the past research may have been confounded. Golder and Tellis (1993) concluded that pioneers do not enjoy market share advantages since there is a high failure rate among market pioneers. Birnbaum-More (1990) argued that it is the response time to the first entrant, not the order of entry, that determines the market success of entrants. Brown and Lattin (1994) argued that time in the market as well as order of entry determine pioneer advantages which eventually erode with time. Robinson, Fornell, and Sullivan (1992) found support for the notion of changing fit between firm resources and market requirements and concluded that the order of market entry decision is also influenced by luck and situation-specific factors.

These past empirical research results call into question the attainability of competitive advantage through market entry timing. We discuss next the sources of competitive advantage before we return to the question of market entry timing. We will argue that it is not a question of entering first or responding fast, but one of being able to enter while the strategic window is still open.

SOURCES OF COMPETITIVE ADVANTAGE

Porter (1985) argued that the fundamental basis of long-term successful performance for a firm is sustainable competitive advantage. There are two basic types of competitive advantage for a firm: low cost or differentiation with either a broad or a niche focus. The significance of any strength or weakness of a firm, therefore, is ultimately a function of its impact on relative cost or differentiation. A firm's decision to be a low cost or a differentiated producer results from its ability to cope with the major forces in the industry better than its rivals. A potential entrant to an industry, therefore, must possess obvious sustainable advantage over the incumbents, by way of either low-cost or differentiation. Sustainability of the competitive advantage is important for the entrant to have sufficient time to close the market share gap before the incumbent can imitate.

This view of competitive advantage necessarily limits the applicability of the concept to rather static industry environments. The classic economic assumptions under this analysis are that the industry structure has been determined and that changes and evolution are slow. For companies operating in high velocity environments that need to make fast strategic decisions (Eisenhardt, 1989), as are the cases of companies in high-tech industries, this rather static view offers little guidance. The spectrum of possible strategic options is also much wider.

SPEED TO MARKET

With the increasingly shortened product life cycles, companies in high-tech industries engage in ever more fierce competition in their race to market. Much effort has been made to reduce product development time. The assumption is that a firm can obtain a sustainable competitive advantage from being the first to market a technological product.

Lieberman and Montgomery (1988) argue that pioneers only succeed because of specific conditions. The conditions that confer first mover advantages include defensible property rights, the ability to increase buyer switching costs, and the ability to preempt critical assets. Where these conditions are not present, they argue that firms are unable to obtain first mover advantages. In fact, reasons for first mover disadvantages include offering later entrants free rider benefits, having to assume the risks of resolving technological or market uncertainty, potential shifts in technology or consumer needs, and incumbent inertia as a result of heavy, upfront investment.

Sustainable competitive advantage may be a result of changing fit between firm resources and evolving market requirements (Abell, 1978). Some firms possess the resources to benefit as the first entrant in certain industries while others have the ability to compete more effectively as a later entrant. The order of market entry decision is also influenced by luck and situation-specific factors including the entrant's degree of product innovation, available distribution channels, and expected competitive reactions (Robinson, Fornell, and Sullivan, 1992).

FIRM DISTINCTIVE RESOURCES AND CORE COMPETENCE

The literature points to two features of organizational capabilities in their role in conferring competitive advantage: their distinctiveness and the extent to which they are core (Prahalad and Hamel, 1990). The distinctiveness of a capability is its relative performance to that of other firms. The extent to which a capability is core relates to its strategic significance to the firm.

Collis (1991) further specifies the four requirements of a distinctive competence:

- competitively superior and valuable in a product market
- inimitable
- nontradeable
- nonsubstitutable

Since advantages a firm enjoys can be eroded by imitation, resources which give the firm inimitable competence will give the firm sustainable competitive advantages. Once a strategic action is imitated, it becomes part of the basis of competition and the incumbent needs to find other ways of survival.

STRATEGIC WINDOWS

As indicated in the introduction, academics and industry practitioners refer to the period of time when firms can benefit from their competitive advantage in the market as a strategic window of opportunity.

A closer review of the literature on strategic windows shows that the concept has not been clearly defined. Abell (1978) uses the term "strategic window" to indicate the "limited periods during which the 'fit' between the key requirements of a market and the particular competencies of a firm competing in that market is at an optimum". He advises that investment in a product line or a market area should be made when there is such an open strategic window and disinvestment should be considered when the fit no longer exists. Abell delineates four categories of changes that would cause the opening of a strategic window: new market growth opportunities, new competing technologies, market redefinition, and channel changes. These changes are results of market evolution which changes the success requirements for a firm.

Abell's concept of strategic windows is therefore spatial as it relates primarily to new market opportunities in existing industries. Hunger and Wheelen (1993) specifically cited this concept of strategic windows as "market opportunities" through which the first entrant can occupy a propitious niche and discourage competition to the extent that the firm has the required internal strengths.

Hariharan and Prahalad (1992), however, define a strategic window as "the period of time between the arrival of a 'winning' product concept and the time after which the firm will be unable to change the structure of the industry since specific investments tied to a particular standard have been made". A strategic window is therefore the window of opportunity where the industry structure is determined with the market adoption of an industry standard. This concept of strategic window is time-related and is restricted to the early stage of industry development.

Although Abell (1978) and Hariharan and Prahalad (1992) define strategic window differently, both stress the importance of recognizing market evolution and employing dynamic versus static industry analyses.

DIMENSIONS OF STRATEGIC WINDOWS

Three dimensions define strategic windows: technology, market, and time. A strategic window opens and closes as a function of the interaction of technological and market factors. These two factors affect when the window opens and for how long.

We use the term "technology" here broadly to refer to all kinds of know-how. It is when there is a breakthrough in a technological progress that there is a potential for an opening of a strategic window. Technology alone, however, cannot drive the opening of a strategic window. The market must be ready to accept what the technological progress offers before there would be a market opportunity. Grid Computer, for example, launched one of the world's earliest versions of a DOS-based notebook computer at approximately £8 in 1985. The product was expensive due to the high costs of components at the time. The market was not ready for it because few people were dependent enough on a personal computer to want a light, portable machine, much less an expensive one. The result was a failed market entry.

Factors determining market acceptance of a technological product have been examined by researchers of diffusion of innovation and are beyond the scope of this chapter. We will simply argue that both technological and market forces drive market acceptance of a product.

OPENING AND CLOSING OF "WINDOWS"

Strategic windows open when the growth of market opportunities for a technological innovation accelerates. How long this window remains open is a function of the rate of competitive imitation as well as the incumbent firm's ability to erect entry barriers and satisfy market demand. CNN is a first mover in providing 24-hour news broadcasts. The company built its network of resources to enable 24-hour reporting around the world. The barriers it has built for potential entrants are high. Federal Express is another example of an operation which has high specific assets whose operation in certain markets would be difficult to imitate.

Since strategic windows open at the time when entrants have the opportunity to develop sustainable competitive advantage, the window closes when such opportunity ceases to exist. In the case of CNN and Federal Express, the windows that were opened by them are no longer open. Although there have not been major rivals to CNN or Federal Express, they have sufficiently filled the market demand and successfully barred potential entrants from entry before the strategic window closed. Potential entrants in either industry need to find a way to force an opening of a different window, one in which they have the capability to compete.

One can strategically force the opening or the closing of strategic windows by way of stimulating market demand or by erecting effective barriers to entry. Entering after the closing of a window has distinct disadvantages one of which is a higher cost structure. The longer one waits to enter, the more likely that the initial entrants have recouped their investment costs and can sell at lower prices to deter entry. They no longer need the margin to survive as the new entrant does.

A strategic window is open in a product market when an entry can be made without having to take sales away from an incumbent. After the window closes, an entrant would need to dislodge a competitor at a time when the basis of competition has widened and there is no clear source of competitive advantage. One can anticipate a closing of a strategic window when the growth in sales in the product market is predicted to be slower. Slowed growth in a product market can result from large proportion of ready adopters having already adopted the innovation in the market, or the announcement of a next generation of innovation that has caused many potential adopters to want to leapfrog to buy the next generation products. An incumbent can therefore force an early closing of a strategic window by speeding up the innovation–adoption process in the market, assuming finite demand for a generation of products. A strategic window will also close if the component prices are dropping slower than system prices and thus, a later entrant has much less room to recoup fixed investments and incumbents can preempt entry by rapidly dropping prices.

If the argument of fit with market requirement holds, then some firms should aim to be first movers and others should be later entrants. The issue is not one of the order of entry but one of recognizing the strategic window and entering before the window closes. Since the fit between firm resources and market requirements should be considered for market entry within a strategic window, it is too simplistic to view the strategic window as opened or closed. It is perhaps more useful to view it as wide open, open a little, or closed.

The question remains whether there is value in entering after the strategic window closes. Is a failed entry a necessary result? In the following section, we discuss the major drivers of strategic windows and explore this question.

DRIVERS OF STRATEGIC WINDOWS

We identify four major drivers of strategic windows: discontinuous technological progress, incremental technological progress, market redefinition, and channel evolution. Case examples are used to illustrate the phenomenon created by different drivers.

The first two drivers are technology-based. Technology progresses in cycles punctuated by discontinuous innovations (Anderson and Tushman, 1990). A period of ferment where all compete to set the industry standard occurs after a discontinuous innovation. Upon the setting of an industry standard, the industry goes through a period of incremental technological change before another discontinuous innovation disrupts the cycle and begins a new one. Discontinuous and incremental innovations can both drive the opening of strategic windows, though at different scales.

DISCONTINUOUS TECHNOLOGICAL PROGRESS

Although the technology to use magnetic tape as a medium of video recording was available as early as 1957, the critical innovation that created market demand and therefore opened a strategic window did not take place until 1975 when Sony introduced the "time-shift" functionality in its Betamax format video recorder. The "time-shift" functionality allowed the user to record a program broadcast on TV and watch it later (Hariharan and Prahalad, 1992). This "time-shift" innovation, however, was easily imitated by JVC who introduced the VHS format recorder a year later. The VHS format provided the viewers two hours of recording instead of the one by Betamax. JVC also succeeded in getting the backing of a large number of major brand manufacturers in major markets of the world. VHS then won the battle to be the standard of the industry even though Betamax has superior recording quality. The strategic window in which the standard of this industry was set and adopted was open for a mere three years (Hariharan and Prahalad, 1992). The VHS format recording machines continued to grow in market dominance.

INCREMENTAL TECHNOLOGICAL DEVELOPMENT

It is important to define an industry structure by way of being a standard setter benefiting from industry-size strategic windows. There are other strategic windows at other times. Incremental technological innovations which effect different generations of innovations, as in dynamic random access memory semiconductors (DRAMs) and personal computers (PCs), for example, have specific strategic windows. We will explore the role of strategic windows in the DRAM and PC markets more extensively in the next section of this chapter.

The other two drivers of strategic windows are more market-based, in terms of how a product market is defined and how a product is sold.

PRODUCT MARKET REDEFINITION

In existing product markets, firms continue to compete on price, new features, and services, constantly broadening the basis of competition. Some of these can be considered strategic tactics while others truly redefine a product market, erode previous competitive advantage, and allow a new set of entrants thereby creating a new strategic window.

Docutel was a successful vendor of automated teller machines (ATMs), supplying most of the market up to 1974. In early 1975, large computer companies such as Honeywell, IBM, and Burroughs began to provide solutions to banks' total electronic funds transfer system needs. ATMs were one component of a complete system of equipment. These computer firms in essence redefined the product market in terms of total banking solutions for banks (Abell, 1978). Docutel was disqualified as a potential supplier. The ability to provide a complete system of computing equipment became a qualification for entrance in the market. The strategic window was opened in 1975 and closed only a couple of years later.

CHANNEL EVOLUTION

Increasingly, companies compete by their channel strategies. The PC industry offers a good example since a lot of change has happened in a relatively short period of time. Dell Computers entered the PC market in the mid-1980s selling mail-order PCs. This opened a strategic window for mail-order and telemarketing PCs and started a wave of mail-order entrants into the PC market including Club AT, Gateway 2000, Mitsuba, Northgate, and Zeos. These companies have fared well compared with PC vendors who sold through the more traditional dealer channels in the late 1980s. As competition in the PC market became more intense, the leaders of the field, such as Compaq and IBM, began to sell their products through the mail-order and telemarketing channels, thereby forcing a closing of the window and eroding the competitive advantage shared by these firms. Offering PC products through the mail-order or telemarketing channel, providing more direct customer service, has become part of the basis of competition in the PC industry. As a result, the early entrants to the mail-order and telemarketing channels no longer enjoy a competitive advantage.

STRATEGIC WINDOW ANALYSIS

We present in this section our preliminary framework for strategic window analysis. A strategic window is a temporal phenomenon driven by technological and market forces. As described earlier in this chapter, we define technology here broadly to include all kinds of know-how. A technological innovation (within or outside of the industry) sets in motion the race to market entry. The entry or entries that ignites market growth opens a strategic market window. Some may enter the market before the opening of the window and lack the resources to stimulate market demand. Some may enter before the market is prepared to adopt the innovation. These firms will fail at market entry.

The firm or firms which succeed in opening the window do so with a relatively high cost function having to absorb to some extent the costs of market education. The firms also reap relative strategic advantage for early market entry. The strategic market window opens and continues to widen with the momentum of competitive imitation or competitor entries. With the strategic window open, the growth of the market is accelerated at the rate of competitor entry. Each of these entrants will gain strategic advantage relative to their competition outside the window. As more and more industry members enter and obtain relative strategic advantage, the advantage erodes (at the rate of imitation). Given finite market demand in any product market, the growth rate of the market will eventually slow, leading to a closing of the strategic window. After the window closes, the relative strategic advantage continues to erode to the point where the innovation becomes a basis of competition and an industry requirement.

A strategic window opens at the first inflection point when the change in the rate of market growth increases. The window closes when the change in the rate of market growth becomes negative. For ease of demonstration, we will explore the role of strategic market windows in two high-tech industries. Incremental technological innovations dictate the evolution of these two industries. As such, we are able to study the recurrence of strategic windows in a particular market and the effect of market entry timing on the long-term performance of the industry members.

PRODUCT LIFE CYCLES: THE CASES OF DRAMs AND PCs

To demonstrate the phenomenon of strategic market windows, we will examine the DRAM, dynamic random access memory, segment of the semiconductor industry, and the microcomputer or PC segment of the computer industry. We choose to illustrate the strategic window concept with these two industry segments because of their clearly delineated incremental technological generations. In the case of DRAMs, each successive generation is a technological advancement over the previous in the increased density achieved in the integrated circuit (IC). Each generation of PC products is defined by the speed of the central processing unit, the microprocessor.

In both DRAMs and PCs, technological generations of products overlap and each generation of products exhibits a product life cycle (see FIGURES 7.1 and 7.2). Firms in both industries are on a continuous race to speed the latest generation of products to market. Market entry timing has, therefore, been a critical success factor in both industries.

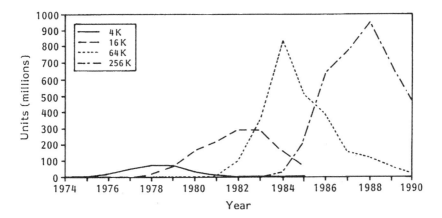

FIGURE 7.1   Worldwide DRAM shipments by density (Source: Dataquest, Inc., reproduced with permission)

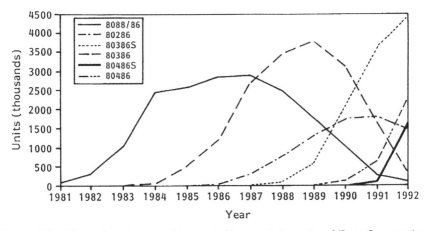

FIGURE 7.2   PC market segment shipments (Source: International Data Corporation, reproduced with permission)

DRAMs

An industry segment originally dominated by US semiconductor firms, the DRAM market was largely lost to Japanese firms in the late 1970s. An account of historical market entry patterns by US and Japanese firms provides some insight to the development of the memory IC market to date (Lamond, 1989). In the 1K DRAM generation introduction in 1970 and the 4K DRAM generation in 1973, US firms held a substantial lead over their Japanese rivals. By 1977, the US market leaders Mostek, Intel, and TI held 80% combined market share. The later entrants, NEC, Fujitsu, and Hitachi, were producing only very small quantities of 4K DRAMs.

A closer look at the early 16K DRAM market reveals the closing of the strategic window in 1977 when the growth rate of the market slowed. Three US firms, Mostek, Texas Instruments, and Intel, introduced 16K DRAM products in 1976 but none was able to deliver in volume due to production problems. Their entrance in the market was effective, however, in opening the strategic market window. NEC, Fujitsu, Hitachi, National, and Motorola had all successfully entered the market by 1977, toward the end of which we saw a change in the growth rate of the market and the strategic window closed. Firms that entered the market after 1977 did not fare well. Of more than 20 semiconductor firms in this market segment, these entrants collectively held some 77% of the 16K DRAM market in 1982 (FIGURE 7.3).

Despite the intense race to lead in entering the subsequent 64K generation, only two US firms, Texas Instruments and Motorola, succeeded in entering the market before the window closed in 1981. Six Japanese firms, Hitachi, NEC, Fujitsu, Mitsubishi, OKI Electric, and Toshiba, had reached volume shipment of 64K DRAM by 1981. As a result, the 64K DRAM

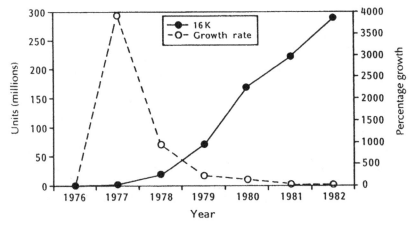

FIGURE 7.3 Worldwide 16K DRAM market (Source: Dataquest, Inc., 1979–82, reproduced with permission)

market was dominated by the Japanese suppliers. With the exception of Texas Instruments, US semiconductor firms did not succeed in entering the 256K DRAM market before the window closed in early 1983. By the beginning of 1985, Japanese firms had taken 98% of the 256K DRAM market.

In all of the entries into these DRAM generations described above, those firms entering within the respective strategic windows continued to hold a market share advantage. The order of entry, however, was much less significant. While Mostek, Intel, and TI were the first entrants to the 16K DRAM market, the market share leaders in 1983 were NEC, TI, Fujitsu, Hitachi, and Motorola. Similarly, in the 64K DRAM market, TI and Fujitsu were the first entrants but the lead in market share was later held by Hitachi and NEC. Hitachi led its competition in being the first to enter the 256K DRAM market but the lead in market share was held by NEC.

SUCCESSIVE GENERATIONS IN THE PC INDUSTRY

The race to enter the market with successive generations of products of higher microprocessor speed has dominated much of the competition in the PC industry in the 1980s. As the time between two successive generations of products shortened (see FIGURE 7.2 on US PC shipment by microprocessor segment), the PC manufacturers' speed in bringing a new generation of products to market became increasingly critical. In the early stages of the industry, practitioners competed to be the first to enter a market. By the second half of the 1980s, engineers in the industry believed there was a window of opportunity whereby one could enter the market and attain market leader status. Indeed, an analysis of firm entries and market share in each generation of product reveals that the failure rate of early entrants is as high as late entrants. Firms bringing their products to market within the strategic window have a greater chance of survival within the processor segment. Successful firms tend to enter the market within the respective strategic windows of the successive product generations.

FIGURE 7.4 (US 80386DX PC shipments) illustrates the growth of the market segment in the first seven years of the product's life cycle. The growth in the market took off in the third quarter of 1986, opening the strategic market window, with Compaq's entry of its first 80386DX PC, the Deskpro 386. The annual growth rate of the market peaked in late 1987 at which point we argue that the strategic window for market entry into this product generation closes.

A handful of firms, Eltech, Data Bank Computer, Inc., and Advanced Logic Research, entered the 386 market before the Compaq entry. Eltech, in fact, entered the market almost a year before Compaq. These three entries, however, did not bring forth significant sales. Compaq was the first

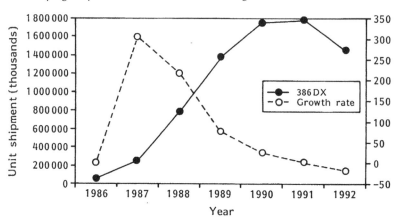

FIGURE 7.4   US 80386DX PC shipments (Source: International Data Corporation, 1986–92, reproduced with permission)

company which succeeded in forcing open the strategic window before industry leader IBM launched its first 386 product. Among the many early entrants of 386DX products, the order of entry for the more established PC manufacturers were Compaq, Bull/Zenith, Acer, Wang, and Wyse. The order of leading 386DX PC market share holders as of 1989 were IBM, Compaq, Tandy, Everex, and Bull/Zenith. At the end of 1990, the top ten 386SX PC manufacturers were IBM, Compaq, Gateway 2000, Tandy, NCR, NEC, Bull/Zenith, Wang, CompuAdd, and Everex. Of these, only Gateway 2000 had missed the strategic window in a substantial way. CompuAdd had entered the market just when the window was closing in November 1987. Gateway 2000 had entered the largest subsegment of the 386DX market, the 386DX/33, within the strategic window, as had all the other top ten 386DX market share holders.

TABLE 7.1 shows the 20 most viable desktop PC manufacturers in the late 1980s. The top nine are ranked in the order of their recent performance in the PC market in late 1995. The rest of the manufacturers had been faced with various levels of financial and operational troubles in the early 1990s. With the notable exception of Packard Bell, the top performers had entered each of the processor segment markets within the respective strategic windows. Hewlett-Packard, AST, and Gateway 2000 had missed the window with their entries into the 386DX market but entered within the windows in the subsequent 386SX and 486DX markets. Packard Bell markets its products through mass merchandisers and typically enters the market late with very low-priced models. One can also argue that Packard Bell operates along a different set of strategic windows, namely those that emerge for the more price-elastic segments of the market. Companies

Table 7.1 Entry dates of leading PC manufacturers in three successive microprocessor segments

Product segments Strategic windows	386DX* Q3 86 to Q3 87	386SX* Q2 88 to Q3 89	486DX* Q1 90 to Q3 90
Compaq	Sep-86	Jun-88	Feb-90
IBM	Jun-87	May-89	Dec-89
Gateway 2000	Sep-88**	Aug-89	Jan-90
Dell	May-87	Apr-89	Jul-90
Packard Bell	Jul-88	Nov-89	Oct-91
Acer	Mar-87	Oct-89	Oct-90
Hewlett-Packard	Feb-88	May-89	Feb-90
NEC	Jul-87	Sep-88	May-90
AST	Jan-88	Sep-89	Jan-90
Bull/Zenith	Mar-87	Oct-89	Nov-90
Zeos	Mar-88	Nov-88	Nov-90
Tandy/Grid	Oct-87	May-89	Feb-90
Unisys	Oct-87	Jan-91	Jul-90
CompuAdd	Nov-87	Sep-89	May-90
ALR	Aug-86	Jul-89	Apr-90
Wyse	May-87	Dec-89	Mar-91
Wang	May-87	Feb-90	Jul-90
Everex	Jul-87	Oct-88	Jun-90
NCR	Sep-87	Jan-89	Apr-90
Tandon	Dec-87	Mar-89	Apr-90

*The opening and closing of the respective strategic windows are estimated using quarterly market data.
**Italicized dates indicate centres after the respective strategic window has closed.
Source: International Data Corporation, 1986–91, reproduced with permission.

that compete in these market segments need to have achieved lower cost functions than their counterparts in the larger PC market.

KNOWLEDGE-BASED VIEW OF THE FIRM

Firms that learn to constantly hit the strategic windows in their industry, open new strategic market windows with their own innovations, have the ability to ride the cycle and compete in an environment where knowledge diffusion is rampant, will achieve sustainable competitive advantage. But what are the capabilities that enable firms to do all these? We argue that it is the firm's organizational level routines and processes that allow it to innovate, and make products better at cheaper prices, that provide the firm with the flexibility it needs to compete in high velocity environments. In other words, it is the firm's ability to build, integrate, and exploit knowledge that gives it the ability to compete.

DEVELOPING AND EXPLOITING RESOURCES

Collis (1991) explains that there are two ways in which extending the scope of the corporation creates value or develops/enhances valuable resources:

> The first is when a corporation leverages its resources by diversifying into markets where those resources contribute to a competitive advantage. This strategy capitalizes on an outward flow of value. The second way to create value occurs when a corporation diversifies in order to build its resources. This involves an inward flow of value. The distinction is between deploying an existing resource into a new market, and entering a new market in order to develop a unique resource. The distinction is important because in the former case, the corporation must directly add value to the business unit it acquires (or establishes), while in the latter case the corporation can actually reduce value in the acquired business unit because it is gaining value elsewhere in the company.

It is the opportunity to develop and exploit resources that we argue is valuable for companies to enter a product market after the strategic window has closed. After the closing of a strategic window, technology has usually diffused and become to a certain extent nontacit, tangible, and transferable. While there is little chance that firms entering after the window has closed could perform well in that product market, entering offers the firm a chance to learn and "exercise its muscles" so it can develop the resources and integrate the "knowledge" to enter the next generation of innovation within the opening of the strategic window. As we have presented above, the Japanese semiconductor companies' late entrance into the 4K DRAM market provided them with the opportunity to develop and enhance necessary resources for future competition.

A DYNAMIC VIEW OF FIRM COMMITMENT

The strategic window concept necessitates a dynamic view in a firm's commitment of resources. In the increasingly competitive global environment today, firms need to recognize that the market is in a state of constant evolution, as is technology. How a firm can continue to invest in developing and exploiting resources to compete in the future will determine its long-term viability in the marketplace.

MANAGERIAL IMPLICATIONS

Managers must evaluate their market positions in their considerations for market entrance. Whether a firm should race to be the first entrant depends on the firm's resources. Compaq, for example, had the resources to force open the strategic window for the 386DX market in late 1986 while most of the other IBM-compatible PC manufacturers would not have been in a position to do so. As other IBM-compatible PC manufacturers developed more resources such as distribution know-how to compete, they became increasingly capable to launch a product to open the window of a new PC market. Gateway 2000 and AST are both examples of successful entrants into the 486DX market segment before either IBM or Compaq had introduced their first 486DX model.

As we have demonstrated in this chapter, some firms have the set of resources to benefit as first entrants. Others would fare better as early followers. The strength of a firm's resource base relative to its competition changes with the intensity of competition. The issue is more one of entering within the strategic market window than the absolute order of entry. It is also important for managers to recognize that any strategic market window has the momentum to open further after it opens, is wide open in the middle of the window time frame, and is on the way to close before it closes. Managers need to decide on whether their firm is entering the market when the window is open, open slightly, or closing. The efforts of market entry may differ at different points of entry as reflected in such entry variables as intensity of promotion, distribution, and pricing.

In FIGURE 7.5 showing the 486DX market segment, we compare the actual 486SX shipment in the first four years and its growth rate with the forecast made by the International Data Corporation as early as 1987. Although the IDC forecast was optimistic, it was accurate in predicting the point when the rate of the market growth would slow. In other words, its forecast, though much higher than the actual market, was useful for estimating the opening and closing of the strategic window. In industries such as the PC industry where the major technological advances are made in upstream industries such as the semiconductor, hard drive industries, the trajectory of technological breakthroughs is mapped to great accuracy. The time difference whereby a PC manufacturer can force open a market window ahead of forecast is not substantial.

Firms entering after the closing of the strategic market window need to recognize the disadvantages of late entry and consider the resources necessary for closed-window market entry. Packard Bell provides a case in point. The company's ability to price its products substantially lower than competition together with its dominance in the mass merchandisers' market enables the firm to compete in the market with late entry. Firms may also use a late entry as an investment to obtain production and market knowledge to enhance their ability to seek early entrances in future generations. This is essentially the choice NEC, Fujitsu, and Hitachi made with their late entry into the 4K DRAM market.

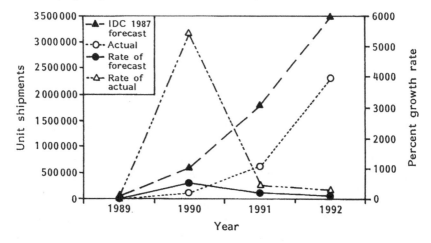

FIGURE 7.5   486DX market segment (Source: International Data Corporation, 1989–92, reproduced with permission)

CONCLUSION

In this chapter, we have examined the phenomenon of strategic market windows. We have identified the dimensions of such strategic market windows and explained the drivers for this phenomenon. We have presented examples to demonstrate the occurrence of strategic market windows under different circumstances. With the preliminary framework of strategic window analysis, we have also discussed the opening and closing of strategic market windows in successive product generations of the DRAM and PC markets.

Only resources that are competitively superior and valuable in a product market, inimitable, nontradeable, and nonsubstitutable can provide a firm with sustainable competitive advantage. Entry into a market within the opening of its strategic window gives the entrant relative strategic advantage *vis-à-vis* its competition outside the window. With competitive imitation as evidenced by market entry, all relative strategic advantage eventually erodes, becomes a basis of competition and an industry standard. Firms need to evaluate the evolution of the market and of technology, continue to develop and exploit resources that could confer this relative advantage in industries that are punctuated by the opening and closing of continually emerging strategic windows.

A firm can effect an opening of a strategic window if it can leverage its resources by diversifying into a different product market, and they can force the closing of a window by erecting specific barriers for entry as well as speeding up the innovation adoption process. A strategic window closes at the point when the growth in sales has slowed. Entry after a strategic window has closed leaves the entrant little chance for market success but it may provide opportunities for developing resources for future competition.

REFERENCES

Abell, Derek F. (1978) "Strategic Windows", *Journal of Marketing*, **42**.

Anderson, Philip and Tushman, Michael L. (1990) "Technological Discontinuities and Dominant Designs: A Cyclical Model of Technological Change", *Administrative Science Quarterly*, **35**, 604–633.

Birnbaum-More, Phil (1990) "Competing with Technology in 8-bit Microprocessors", *High Technology Management Research*, **1**, 1–14.

Birnbaum-More, Phil, Weiss, Andrew, and Wright, Russell W. (1994) "How Do Rivals Compete: Strategy, Technology and Tactics", *Research Policy*, **23**, 249–266.

Brown, Christina L. and Lattin, James M. (1993), "Investigating the Relationship between Time in Market and Pioneering Advantage", *Management Science*, **40**, 1361–1370.

Collis, David (1991) "Corporate Advantage: Identifying and Exploiting Resources", Conceptual Note. Boston, Mass. Harvard Business School.

Eisenhardt, Kathleen M. (1989) "Making Fast Strategic Decisions in High Velocity Environments," *Academy of Management Journal*, **32**, 543–576.

Golder, Peter N. and Tellis, Gerard J. (1993) "Pioneer Advantage: Marketing Logic or Marketing Legend?" *Journal of Marketing Research*, **30**, May, 158–170.

Hariharan, Sam and Prahalad, C.K. (1992) "Strategic Windows in the Structuring of Industries: Compatibility Standards and Industry Evolution", Working Paper. Los Angeles, Calif. University of Southern California.

Hunger, J. David and Wheelen, Thomas L. (1993) *Strategic Management* Reading, Mass.: Addison-Wesley Publishing Company.

Lamond, Annette (1989) "The Loss of US Dominance in DRAMS: A Case History (1976–1984)", HBS Case Note, Boston, Mass.: Harvard Business School.

Lieberman, Marvin B. and Montgomery, David B. (1988) "First-Mover Advantages", *Strategic Management Journal*, **9**, 41–58.

Lilien, Gary L. and Yoon, Eunsang (1990) "The Timing of Competitive Market Entry, An Exploratory Study of New Industrial Products", *Management Science*, **36**, 568–585.

Mitchell, Will (1991) "Dual Clocks: Entry Order Influences on Industry Incumbent and Newcomer Market Share and Survival when Specialized Assets Retain Their Value", *Strategic Management Journal*, **12**, 85–100.

Porter, Michael E. (1985) *Competitive Advantage: Creating and Sustaining Superior Performance*, New York: The Free Press.

Prahalad, C.K. and Hamel, Gary (1990) "The Core Competence of the Corporation", *Harvard Business Review*, May–June, 79–91.

Robinson, William T. and Fornell, Claes (1985) "Sources of Market Pioneer Advantages in Consumer Goods Industries", *Journal of Marketing Research* **22**, 305–317.

Robinson, William T., Fornell, Claes, and Sullivan, Mary (1992) "Are Market Pioneers Intrinsically Stronger than Later Entrants?" *Strategic Management Journal*, **13**(8), 609–624.

Urban, Glen L., Carter, Theresa, Gaskin, Steven, and Mucha, Zofia (1986) "Market Share Rewards to Pioneering Brands: An Empirical Analysis and Strategic Implications", *Management Science*, **32**, 645–659.

Section II

Structure

Among the early, and best-known, discussants of organizational structure was Adam Smith, whose description of the economies of scale that can be made available through division of labor helped lay the groundwork for mass production (1776, *The Wealth of Nations*). Max Weber's bureaucracy, or ideal organization, incorporated Smith's division of labor into a highly standardized organization, featuring a hierarchical organizational structure, rewards and promotions based on objective criteria, and protection of the rights of individuals (1947, *The Theory of Social and Economic Organizations*). The argument of whether Weber's bureaucracy has outgrown its usefulness has continued for years and, although the bureaucratic form remains the dominant form of organizational structure, other types of organizational forms have their enthusiastic proponents, and organization structure remains a primary issue in implementing corporate strategies.

Barr, Bogner, Golden-Biddle, Rau, and Thomas look at the roles that managers' cognitive processes play in their economic assessment of strategic alliances. The authors integrate and synthesize three papers that were presented as part of a panel discussion, and conclude that cognitive insights can help expand our understanding of how alliances are formed and sustained.

Bowman and Carter attempt to provide new insights to the strategy/ structure relationship, by expanding on Danny Miller's earlier attempts to correlate Michael Porter's generic competitive strategies with Henry Mintzberg's definitions of organizational structures. The authors suggest that changes in some of the contingencies on which Mintzberg based his structures may explain the emergence of a new type of structure, the machine adhocracy.

Faulkner and McGee examine 10 international strategic alliances and the relationship between long-term success and economic benefits, alliance form, management process, and learning capacity. They find the most important factor to be the partners' commitment, mutual trust, and flexibility.

Haanaes and Lowandahl discuss limitations of previous theories of the firm, and introduce an alternative unit of analysis—the unit of activity. Linking the unit of activity to the resource-based perspective, the authors argue that it is more suitable for understanding organizational processes (e.g. value-creating activities), whether they are situated inside or outside the boundaries of the firm.

Madhavan, Koka, and Prescott look at the pattern of worldwide strategic alliances among steel industry firms, suggesting that firms that are well positioned in their industry network have superior access to industry resources and capabilities. The authors study how the structure of the strategic alliance network shapes—and is shaped by—industry competition.

Whittington and Mayer suggest that, whereas the M-form organization was once accepted as the universally superior form of organization, today its superiority is in question. They study its progress in France and Germany, during the 1980s and early 1990s, to determine whether its predicted spread has materialized. The authors conclude that, by keeping the strategy formulation process too centralized, and by excessive bureaucratic procedures, the M-form organization may have lost much of its competitive advantage. In fact, at least in Europe, the holding company may offer greater flexibility to market conditions.

One of the traditional conversations in strategic management, the strategy–structure relationship, has inspired extensive research and writing. Following are some examples:

- As an organizational form is bureaucracy still effective, or has its time passed? In "The Coming Death of Bureaucracy" (*Think*, November– December 1966) Warren Bennis offers one of the better-known arguments on the obsolescence of the machine bureaucracy—that it is too mechanical for the modern corporation.
- Countering Bennis' argument, Robert Miewald suggested that Max Weber's objective was to create a logical and efficient organization form and that whatever organizational configuration meets those criteria is a bureaucracy ("The Greatly Exaggerated Death of Bureaucracy", *California Management Review*, Winter 1970).
- Guided by Herbert Simon's "bounded rationality" theory (*Administrative Behavior*, 1945), Jay Galbraith explains why task uncertainty is related to organizational form, and develops a framework for integrating organizational interventions (e.g. information systems, group problem-solving) that have been treated separately before ("Organization Design: An Information Processing View", *Interfaces*, 4(5), May 1974).
- Larry Greiner's model of organization development describes five phases of development that growing organizations experience, each ending in a management crisis. In "Evolution and Revolution as Organizations Grow" (*Harvard Business Review*, July–August 1972) he suggests that a sense of organizational history can help management anticipate the next crisis.
- In "Note on Organization Design" (*Harvard Business School 476–094*) Jay Lorsch argues that an organization is designed to direct its members in achieving organizational goals, and to determine the criteria for selection of people.
- In contrast with the trend toward organizational downsizing, Dwight Gertz and Joao Baptista suggest that no company ever shrank to greatness, and that their study of more than 1000 large companies demonstrates that companies must grow to be great (*Grow to be Great: Breaking the Downsizing Cycle*, 1995).

Cognitive Processes in Alliance: Birth, Maturity and (Possible) Death

PAMELA BARR, WILLIAM BOGNER, KAREN GOLDEN-
BIDDLE, HAYAGREEVA RAO, HOWARD THOMAS

INTRODUCTION

This chapter presents a series of studies all of which look at the role which cognitive processes play in the life of a strategic alliance. These studies were presented in panel form at the 1994 SMS conference. All of these studies look at managerial processes which are at work as managers make sense of and sustain relationships. These processes are seen as functioning in addition to, or ever perhaps in spite of, the inferences which managers would draw from a purely economic assessment of the strategic alliance. The chapter attempts to simultaneously preserve the focus of each presentation, while pointing to the insights that each provides.

This chapter summarizes a panel discussion that took place at the 14th Annual International Conference of the Strategic Management Society. That panel brought together three studies that have implications for the role of cognitive processes in strategic alliances. The purpose of this chapter is to highlight the contribution each makes toward understanding the cognitive process in alliance activities.

There is a need for cognitive considerations within the alliances literature. Current theories of alliances between firms suggest that they are utilized as responses to opportunities and threats that result from the relationship between environmental conditions and firm traits. For example, the trans-

Strategy, Structure and Style. Edited by H. Thomas, D. O'Neal and M. Ghertman
Copyright © 1997 John Wiley & Sons Ltd.

actions costs approach would suggest that alliance choices should be based on gaining efficiencies in marketplace transactions. And the international business literature advises the use of alliances to scale national barriers to entry or to take advantage of global economies (Contractor and Lor˜ge, 1988). What each of these approaches has in common is their focus on characteristics of the firms and industries in which alliances take place as well as on the alliance outcomes themselves. What is not included are the less readily observable interpretive processes that must necessarily be part of that process.

Recent literature on decision making and strategy formulation in organizations has focused on the impact of managerial interpretation in these critical processes (Hall, 1984; Meyer, 1982). That such processes may be important in alliance formation choices can be illustrated by an example based on common themes in the strategy literature. A contingent theory of alliance formation may offer two stylized choice types for incorporating alliances into a firm's competitive strategies: offensive-opportunist (OO) and defensive-controlling (DC). In both cases the goal of top management is to use alliances to exploit strengths and defend against threats in order to improve the performance of firm assets, but the breadth and content of actual alliances vary depending on the posture chosen. The OO approach would suggest using alliances to exploit existing competencies and competitive advantages, while the DC approach would suggest using alliances to shore up competitive weaknesses in existing skills and product lines.

The above prescriptions, however, ignore the cognitive processes of the managers. Though it is sound to suggest that firms in a "strong" competitive position use OO type alliances while those in a "weak" competitive position take a DC approach, actual alliance choices will depend on managerial interpretations. Depending on how managers *interpret* their industry, their competitive position, and the role that alliances in general play in their strategy, very different actions could result under the same circumstances. Such a scenario suggests that understanding how managers interpret concepts such as alliances can make a significant contribution to understanding the alliance choices observed.

The unifying theme of this panel was that to better understand alliance outcomes, cognitive processes must be added to the simple model proposed by current literature and represented in FIGURE 8.1.

The remainder of this chapter summarizes the presentations made during the panel discussion. The first part, "Understanding Alliance Formation Choices", provides a framework for understanding the role of cognitive processes in alliance outcomes by presenting arguments that suggest alliance formation is a function of both economic and cognitive variables. The second section, "Monitoring as Ritual", provides empirical evidence for the importance of loose linkages between core conceptualizations of

FIRM / INDUSTRY   ALLIANCE
TRAITS   ----------------->   OUTCOMES

As indicated by: Types of partners,
transaction costs,   survival, etc.
industrial organization,
international business

FIGURE 8.1   Basic models of Alliance fit

an alliance and its day-to-day activities to the maintenance of alliances. "Sustaining International Linkages", the third section, uses archival data to shed light on the impact learning has on the long-term survival of alliances. Finally, we present a brief discussion highlighting the contributions cognitive processes can make to understanding alliance outcomes.

UNDERSTANDING ALLIANCE FORMATION CHOICES*

In this section we argue for including interpretation processes in a model of alliance formation. We begin with a brief overview of the major findings from the interpretation literature, then outline the three major interpretive points that we argue enter into the alliance formation process.

INTERPRETATION IN ORGANIZATIONS

Interpretation is a cognitive process undertaken to reduce the uncertainty inherent in an ambiguous environment and allow decisions to be made (Cowan, 1986). However, interpretation is a uniquely individual process and, as such, can result in a variety of conclusions across individuals based on what information is sought or noticed, and the meaning imposed on it (Daft and Weick, 1984). This sensemaking process is affected by numerous individual (Kiesler and Sproull, 1986) and organizational characteristics (Starbuck and Milliken, 1988) which affect each stage of the process: noticing, interpretation, and action.

Individuals make sense of their environments under the constraints of limited cognitive capacity (March and Simon, 1958; Schwenk, 1984). Thus, they cannot attend to all informational cues presented by a vast and ambiguous environment. Both organizational and individual mechanisms

---

* This portion of the panel presentation is a summary of a work-in-progress prepared by Pamela Barr and William Bogner.

act to filter and reduce the amount of information attended to by managers to only that which is considered salient. Cues that have relevance for currently held belief systems are more likely to be noticed and remembered. Attention, therefore, is likely to be directed toward information that is related to the firm's current industry, competition, strategies, and objectives.

Once a cue has been selected for attention, it must be analyzed and given meaning. On an individual level, cognitive processes tend to base meaning on previously acquired knowledge and experiences. In other words, it is more common to imbue new information with a meaning that is consistent with currently held beliefs, than it is to change existing belief structures to accommodate new information. Actions undertaken by individuals in organizations follow from the results of the noticing and sensemaking processes. These actions, in turn, trigger new informational cues in the environment that are picked up, interpreted, and acted on by others. It is this cycle of interpretation, action, interpretation that develops and maintains belief systems (Porac, Thomas, and Baden-Fuller, 1989).

INTERPRETATION PROCESSES IN ALLIANCE FORMATION

As illustrated in FIGURE 8.2, we propose that three main points of interpretation moderate the relationship between industry/firm traits and alliance formation outcomes: (1) interpretation of economic and competitive position, (2) interpretation of alliances in general, and (3) interpretation of alliances for the individual firm.

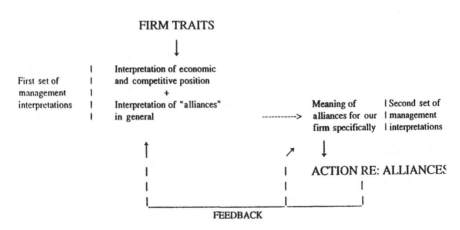

FIGURE 8.2   A cognitive process model

Interpretation of Economic and Competitive Position

Several studies have recently been undertaken to identify the cognitive representations managers have of their competitive fields. In general, this research suggests that industry behavior is dominated by a set of beliefs about industry traits and competitive position that develop over time and are shared by managers across firms (Reger and Huff, 1993; Spender, 1989). Examinations of beliefs managers have regarding their rivals, customers, and suppliers reveal that they are a partial and imperfect representation of what the traditional literature would define as industry and competitive position (Porac, Thomas, and Baden-Fuller, 1989; Porac et al., 1995).

The important implication of this literature is the observation that these shared beliefs are but a subset of what traditional economic theory would identify as the industry and the firm. Managers do not necessarily assess competition on common customers, cross elasticity of demand, or similar types of analyses. Their concepts of rivalry, and the associated direction of attention, are based on different constructs and lead to different definitions. These "belief based" definitions are more compact and are based on only a few highly salient dimensions (Porac et al., 1995; Reger and Huff, 1993). Thus, we would expect that alliance formation choices would be based on management interpretations of industry and firm traits that are more compact than that proposed by economic theory.

Proposition 1 *Managers base alliance formation choices on interpretations of industry traits and competitive position that are more compact and include fewer dimensions than suggested by objective measures of industry structure and competitive position.*

Interpretations of Alliances in General

The interpretation outcome summarized in Proposition 1 is only one that must be developed before managers can construct an alliance formation choice. Incorporating alliances into strategy requires management to develop cognitive conceptualizations about the general role alliances play in firm strategy. Thus, we would expect managers to seek out and analyze information to build an understanding of the concept of "alliances", who uses them, and what they are used for. However, this is not likely to be a straightforward task.

Alliances are a complex and rather ambiguous concept. They cover a wide range of relationships, vary in functional and geographic scope from narrow to broad, and transfer existing products and technology across firm borders. There is also the implication that these agreements are more than a traditional contract between firms; they are "strategic". Successful outcomes are associated with how well managers have used alliances to manage environmental threats, exploit competitive advantage, and/or protect core competencies for their firm as a whole. The wide variation and complexity associated with alliances will quickly result in cognitive overload for managers. Thus, we would expect managers to be selective in their information gathering; to use a limited number of sources of information and to notice a limited number of environmental cues in developing an understanding of alliances. But to which cues will managers attend?

As noted earlier, information search is bounded by current beliefs or activities. Thus the argument can be made that managers will use the same sources of information they use to gather other information about the environment, and will notice those cues that have greatest relevance to the current strategies, goals, and position of the firm. Managers have a limited number of information sources from which they gather the information they need to effectively compete (Porac, *et al.*, 1989). These channels of information gathering are familiar, convenient, and have been successful in providing useful information in the past and, thus, are likely to be used to gather information on alliances. The result of using these sources to build understanding about alliances is that the information gathered is likely to be industry specific, biased by first-mover choices, and feedback is likely to be limited. Thus, the range and scope of alliance use and types identified by managers will be smaller than the total range and use identified in the current literature.

Proposition 2: *Managers' interpretations about the meaning and use of strategic alliances in general will be based on, and biased toward, the information provided by industry sources.*

Interpretation of Alliances for the Individual Firm

The final interpretation we propose is related to alliance formation. Once managers develop beliefs related to industry and competitive position and about alliances in general, they must decide whether alliances are right for their firm. They need to address such question as: (1) are we among the types of firms that use alliances? (2) if so, what type of alliance do we enter, (3) who should we partner with, and (4) what determines success in the alliance?

We propose that the results of this process will strongly reflect the understandings and beliefs developed as a result of the first two interpretive processes. In this way, our model complements the simple FIGURE 8.1 model proposed by the traditional literature: alliance formation outcomes are a function of matching firm and industry traits to alliance options. The difference proposed by the model in FIGURE 8.2 is that the firm and industry traits and alliance options considered by the manager are the result of an interpretive process and are more limited than the vast range proposed by the current literature.

Proposition 3: *Managers' beliefs about whether and how alliances should be used in their firm will be a function of their beliefs about the traits of their firm and industry and their beliefs about the use of alliances in general. Actual alliance formation choice will be more a reflection of this interpretation than it will the prescriptions made by the current literature.*

FROM SENSEMAKING TO SUSTAINING UNDERSTANDING

The model and propositions presented thus far are consistent with the existing interpretation literature. However, alliances have a trait beyond the initial sensemaking that makes them particularly important for strategic success. Alliances are ongoing and, thus, must adapt to the changing competitive environment and to their performance outcomes. It follows that the interpretations presented in FIGURE 8.2 must also evolve as the actions of the alliance change the inputs to those interpretations. Indeed, successful alliances are arguably those that are the most flexible and adaptive, so to sustain an alliance some parts of the system must be adjusted and evolve over time.

In the remainder of this chapter, we focus on this evolutionary process by presenting research from two works-in-progress. The first work highlights the importance of decoupling the actual work from the myth of the alliance so as to maintain the belief that the alliance is fulfilling its intended purpose despite changes in its day-to-day operations. This work suggests that a loose link between actions and subsequent interpretations is better for the alliance. The second work presents evidence linking maintenance of alliance to constant investment in firm competencies. The analysis suggests that alliances are reevaluated as they change over time and that the new understandings of each partner's contributions are necessary if their alliance is to continue. This link ties the understandings presented in FIGURE 8.2 with the more traditional analysis of alliance bases and suggests how the former complements, rather than replaces, the latter.

MONITORING AS RITUAL*

This section presents some preliminary ideas about board governance in large nonprofit organizations. It suggests that the institutional myth of being "volunteer-driven" governs board–staff interactions, and creates a situation in which both staff and board members must maintain a loose

---

* This portion of the panel presentation is a summary of a work-in-progress prepared by Karen Golden-Biddle and Hayagreeva Rao.

coupling between actions and cognitions as they evolve over time if the actual work of the organization is to be accomplished. Although the context of these preliminary ideas is the corporate governance structure, they also have implications for the relationship between alliance partners, and in particular for the managers who are charged with monitoring and evaluating the alliance. The ongoing maintenance of this institutional myth informs the role of managers in an alliance.

Corporate governance in large for-profit and nonprofit organizations is characterized by a chain of agency relationships (White, 1992). As principals, stockholders in for-profits and patrons in nonprofits entrust the responsibility of managing the enterprise to agents called managers and also delegate the responsibility of overseeing managerial performance to another class of agents called directors. Considerable debate centers around the nature of the relationship between boards of directors and top managers: whereas some researchers portray outside directors as *independent and impartial agents* who curtail entrenchment by managers (Fama and Jensen, 1983), others suggest that outside directors are dependent agents prone to serve the interests of long-serving chief executives (Herman and Heimovics, 1990). It is the claim of this presentation that the conceptualizations of organization purpose create strong motivations for the monitors and those being monitored to act in concert with one another to uphold this "institutional myth", and thereby reduce the vigilance of monitoring.

NONPROFIT ORGANIZATIONS AS SELFLESS, VOLUNTEER-DRIVEN ORGANIZATIONS

A striking feature of life in many nonprofit organizations is both staff and volunteer members' depictions of their respective organizations as *selfless, volunteer-driven organizations*. The model of mutual nonprofits as organizations based on altruism and volunteerism can be traced to the nineteenth century (Hall, 1992). During this period, social activists and philanthropists saw themselves as selfless, altruistic stewards of the enterprise and recruited "staff" (managers) to deliver services to needy populations such as "patients", "orphans", and the "deserving poor" (Smith, 1992). Cultural models such as this one, as Meyer and Rowan (1977) observe, become institutionalized myths because of the rationalizing activities of the modern state or the professions. The model of the selfless, volunteer-driven organization, for example, has become codified in the legal and constitutional status of mutual nonprofits as tax-exempt organizations (Hansmann, 1986; Smith, 1992). This "ruling myth" of the organization as selfless, volunteer driven, and mission-based is an important, shared interpretation of the *purpose* of the organization.

CHALLENGING A MYTH

Meyer and Rowan (1977) suggest that when organizations incorporate institutionalized myths into their formal structure it may generate inconsistencies between the formal structure and technical requirements of work. Organizations address conflicts that highlight these inconsistencies by decoupling formal structure from concrete work activities to avoid disruptions in work and to maintain the appearance that the myths work. Organizations decouple formal structures from actual work by creating goals that deflect attention from the measurement of output, avoiding discussions of program implementation, increasing the discretion of professional managers, and relying on human relations (Meyer and Rowan, 1977). Thus, conflicts between perceptions and actions are reduced.

One specific means available to nonprofit organizations of decoupling the formal structure and technical work is by using the institutional myth to shape the formal board role and staff advisory role, but then in everyday, more informal situations to have the staff run the organization. In reality, most volunteers cannot possibly run an organization without seriously disrupting work; they lack the expertise and the time to master the intricacies of program management to really "drive" the organization in any meaningful way. Over time, managers develop greater discretion and both managers and volunteers create informal relationships to make decisions. Consequently, monitoring by the board becomes a ritual that maintains the institutional myth, even in governance issues. However, what would happen if the institutional myth were punctured?

Such an occasion was observed in the midst of a field study being conducted as part of a larger examination of nonprofit institutions. This year-long ethnographic study took place within the confines of a single large nonprofit institution. During the study, the primary investigator observed organization participants in their day-to-day activities, engaged in casual interviews with managers and staff, and studied archival data such as meeting minutes, reports, and internal memos. Careful analysis of fieldnotes and archival data provides insight into how this organization worked to restore faith in the institutional myth by actively managing interpretations and by further decoupling the formal monitoring structure from the day-to-day work of the organization.

As the study was being conducted, the organization suffered a period of resource decline resulting from an increase in competition for contributions from donors. It was during this period that a small percentage of the large volunteer board began to question increases in travel expenditures and administrative expenses that were budgeted by senior board members and the organization's professional managers. It was the concern of these board members that the guiding purpose or "ruling myth" of the organization as selfless and volunteer driven was contradicted by these increases in travel and administrative costs, especially in a period of resource constraints. The senior board members and managers, on the other hand, viewed these increases as normal increases in costs associated with running the organization.

The conflict increased in intensity throughout a six-month period and threatened to become more public, further undermining the cognitive conceptualization of the organization as selfless and volunteer driven. Resolution of the issue occurred when a special committee of personally credible and formally legitimate volunteers was formed to review the proposed budget, and recommended some limited decreases in travel and administrative expenses. Further, a standing "budget review committee" was formed and charged with overseeing the annual budgeting process. This committee, in effect, served as a mechanism to informally resolve disagreements between organizational members regarding how resources were allocated, and thus reduce the opportunity for public questioning of the budget. In sum, the managers of the organization were able to further decouple their day-to-day activities (and spending) from the more general institutional myth by using trusted individuals to provide interpretations of the activities, and their legitimacy, and by providing a mechanism that reduced the perceived need to scrutinize resource allocations.

DISCUSSION

One implication of our preliminary ideas about board–top management relationships in nonprofit organizations is that because institutionalized myths shape agency relationships, monitoring in agency relationships may well be a ritual that is essential to the legitimacy of organizations. Alliances face similar, though not identical, agency relationships. Managers of the alliance itself are frequently monitored by representatives of alliance partners. As alliances interact with their environments they, like any other organization, face continual changes in those environments. Survival thus implies adaptation in the day-to-day activities of the alliance. These changes in the content of the alliance may move it away from the core conceptualizations, or "ruling myths", upon which it was formed. Yet, to satisfy the monitors of the alliance parents, the organization must continue to appear to be fulfilling the myth. The ideas presented here suggest two strategies for maintaining this appearance.

First, a tolerable amount of decoupling between the core conceptualization of the alliance and alliance actions should be anticipated, and even encouraged. Undertaking actions that appear inconsistent with core conceptualizations are often made in response to changes in the environment. Disbanding such an alliance may be unnecessarily destroying a valuable relationship when it was only performing the function for which it was intended. For example, most travel expenses incurred by nonprofit leadership, while on the surface appearing to have been inconsistent with the core conceptualization as a selfless organization, for the most part reflected the necessary costs incurred in promoting the eradication of certain diseases through worldwide education and research. Thus, disbanding an alliance following a tolerable amount of incongruity, rather than working to deliver a new common understanding based on current circumstances, may be akin to throwing the baby out with the bathwater.

The second implication this presentation has for the maintenance of alliances is that alliance managers must actively manage the interpretations that partner representatives have of the activities of the alliance. This is not to say that intentional deception or fraud be engaged in. But, rather, managers must recognize that events are open to different interpretations and that advancing a perspective consistent with the ruling myth is an important management role. It is also true that managers can manage impressions of emerging events in a manner that creates the mutual desire to end the alliance. Most importantly alliance managers should recognize that impressions of ongoing relationships can be managed by all of the parties involved. Ideally partners would be exposed to many different interpretations of the same outcome prior to making decisions about the sustainability of an alliance. Of course, managers are limited in these subsequent evaluations by the same constraints that bound their initial decision making. But knowledge of the dynamic of ongoing common interpretations gives managers the ability to anticipate and seek out new understandings before a decision point is reached.

SUSTAINING INTERNATIONAL LINKAGES: A DYNAMIC COMPETENCE VIEW*

Over time, different levels of power and an unequal transfer of skills may upset both the fairness and the stability of an alliance (Hamel, 1991). In this portion of the panel we present some research suggesting that there are two processes that must be sustained over the course of an alliance relationship. The first was suggested in the prior presentation: an ongoing cognitive interpretation of the relationship. The second, suggested here, is an ongoing development of competencies within the partner organizations. At the end, it is suggested that their combination is mandatory for alliance success. These suggest *why* these relationships become truly "strategic": they involve the development and continual nurturing of each partner's competencies such that, through the alliance, there is continuing sustainable

---

* This portion of the panel presentation is a summary of a work-in-progress paper by William Bogner and Howard Thomas.

competitive advantage in a market for the partners to share. In this presentation we focus on ongoing strategic relationships (OSRs).

PROPOSITIONS AND RESEARCH QUESTIONS

Here we set out the theoretical basis for why partners will want to modify and expand these relationships over time. By inference, we will also be identifying those circumstances when alliances will, in fact, not be renewed or expanded. In developing the propositions about OSRs, we will build on the emerging strategic management view of alliances. Specifically, in developing these propositions we draw on three major concepts in the strategy literature: (1) the role of firm-specific competencies in sustainable competitive advantage; (2) the role of an unknowable and ever changing competitive environment; and (3) the role of ongoing learning among firms about that competitive environment.

Core competencies represent the activities that a firm does particularly well relative to its rivals (Bogner and Thomas, 1994; Prahalad and Hamel, 1990). Competitive advantage results when those competencies are effectively bundled with other product traits in a market of multiple sellers (Bogner and Thomas, 1996). Alliances create the potential for firms with complementary competencies to combine them within a single good or service such that the resulting combination gains greater advantage and commands higher prices. Further, partners who wish to sustain an OSR over time must also sustain the internal unique resources and skills that they contribute to the relationship:

> Proposition 1   *Alliances will be sustained when members continue to bring new and unique skills to the alliance that result in sustained competitive advantage.*

The context in which competitive advantage is sought is constantly changing along several dimensions. Thus, OSRs will always require adjustments and revisions due to the nature of the environments in which they are executed. The competencies that partners contribute to an alliance must evolve in tandem with their environment.

> Proposition 2   *Firms that sustain or improve their alliance relationships in a dynamic environment do so because of their ability to consistently bring new competencies to the OSR.*

Consistent with Propositions 1 and 2, this competence-driven view of OSRs suggests that firms that have either their initial unique contributions copied, or fail to keep their contributions up to date, will have no basis on which to bargain for continuation of the relationship.

Proposition 3   *If firms are unable to constantly bring new competencies to the partnership, then their OSR will end.*

The internal dynamics of continually refining competencies requires experimental learning (Huber, 1991). Importantly, a large, rich portion of this learning takes place through market interactions (Lant, Milliken, and Batra, 1992). Thus, a circular flow results: membership in an alliance gives a firm an enriched market exposure, which enables it to experiment and learn the new unique knowledge needed to sustain improvement in its competencies and, hence, to sustain its future value to (and membership in) the OSR.

Proposition 4   *Firms continually bring new competencies to the OSR through the use of internal learning processes.*

Proposition 5   *The learning that sustains an OSR is driven, in part, by the alliance itself.*

CASES FOR ANALYSIS

The following analysis relates the propositions just presented to eight OSRs. The analysis specifically focuses on relationships that include two firms from different countries and that span a significant period of time. The global pharmaceutical industry was selected because international linkages between leading firms have been regularly occurring since the 1950s and the likelihood of finding several OSRs for comparison was high. The same limitations in collecting data on linkages exist here as with other studies (e.g. Nohria and Garcia-Pont, 1991).

We will first describe the individual cases (these have been significantly edited here due to space limitations). Each of the cases set out here represents an OSR that meets the criteria for study; each involves more than one bargained for agreement, and with one exception the relationships range from about 10 years in length to over 35 years. Four firms are looked at twice. The OSRs have had a wide range of eventual outcomes, including acquisition, dissolution, and ongoing success. Each of the relationships is different. Some are straightforward, others are more convoluted. Some change with the changing competitive fortunes of the parties, others with the changing nature of the competitive environment. This mix of quite different OSRs is particularly gratifying given the research intent of understanding the applicability of the research propositions across all types of OSRs. A summary of each OSR is presented in TABLE 8.1.

TABLE 8.1   Multiple agreements

Firms	Agreements	Surrounding circumstances
Upjohn (US) and Boots Pure Drug Ltd (UK)	1959: Joint venture between Boots and Upjohn of England for marketing of Upjohn chemicals in the UK	Upjohn of England begins construction of facilities in Crawley UK for research and production in 1961
	1974: Upjohn begins selling Boots' discovery, ibuprofen (Motrin), in the US	Motrin is 26% of Upjohn's sales in 1981 when exclusivity ends and Boots enters market with Rufin
	1986: Upjohn and Boots revise marketing agreement for flurbiprofen (Ansaid), son of ibuprofen, giving Upjohn exclusive US rights	Upjohn and Boots both launch OTC version of ibuprofen through licensing agreements with other firms
Upjohn (US) and Hoechst-Roussel (FRG)	1950: Upjohn licenses tolbutamide (Orinase) after conducting clinical trials in the US for Hoechst	Orinase accounts for about 15% of sales in the late 1960s, sales drop in wake of controversy over oral antidiabetic treatments
	1970s: Upjohn licences glyburide (Micronase), son of tolbutamide for the US	Controversy delays regulatory approval until 1983
	1990: Joint marketing agreement for Altace	
	1991: Upjohn licenses glimepiride, third generation antidiabetic for the US	
Abbott Labs (US) and Dainippon (JAP)	1961: Form Nippon Abbott to manufacture radio-chemicals	
	1979: Abbott takes 60% control over the joint venture	Legal changes in 1975 allow foreign ownership of over 50%
	1980s: Product licensing between the parents, formation of another joint venture in Taiwan (70% Abbott)	
	1983: Reorganization of all Japanese operations into Dainabot	

Partners	Events	Comments
Abbott Labs (US) and Takeda (JAP)	1977: Joint venture formed to created TAP 1980: TAP agreement amended to include Latin America	Drugs from Takeda research are put into TAP
American Home Products (US) and Sanofi (FRA)	1981: AHP and Sanofi enter into joint venture 1980s: Marketing agreements entered into between parents 1987: AHP and Sanofi enter into equity agreement, all other agreements are terminated	AHP and Sanofi compete for bankrupt A.H. Robbins in 1989—AHP wins
Merck (US) and Banyu (JAP)	1954: Formation of Nippon Merck-Banyu joint venture 1983: Merck acquires 50.5% interest in Banyu	Japan develops into world's largest antibiotic market Largest acquisition, to date, under new law allowing > 50% foreign ownership
Pfizer (US) and Biogal (HUN)	1980: Pfizer and Biogal agree to joint marketing deal 1991: Pfizer and Biogal form joint venture to market Pfizer products in Hungary, 51% owned by Pfizer	Opening of market to Western investment without loss of control of Hungarian parent firm
Ciba-Geigy (SWI) and Biogal (HUN)	1970s: Ciba-Geigy subsidiary, Zyma, and Biogal enter into numerous production and licensing agreements 1980: New joint venture to build plant and to distribute its output 1991: Ciba-Geigy and Biogal form another joint venture for manufacturing and research. Ciba-Geigy controls 51% of the venture	Joint venture laws liberalized. Hungarian government retains key 1%

Upjohn and Boots Pure Drug

In 1958 a joint venture, Lenbrook Chemicals Ltd, was formed between Boots and Upjohn's English subsidiary in Crawley for the marketing of Upjohn chemicals and bulk pharmaceuticals in the UK. In 1969 Boots launched its anti-inflammatory drug, ibuprofen, in the UK as Brufen. Boots entered into a licensing agreement with Upjohn, who gained regulatory approval in the US for the drug and began selling it under the Upjohn label in 1974 as Motrin. The license to Upjohn was nonexclusive and in 1979 Boots acquired a small pharmaceutical house in the US, renaming it Boots Pharmaceuticals with the intention of launching its own version of ibuprofen. By the early 1980s Boots estimated that Upjohn earned $38.2 million annually on those sales while the royalties and other fees paid to Boots were only $13.2 million Yet by 1983 Boots had achieved US ibuprofen sales of only $35 million dollars, reflecting the firm's inability to build an effective US presence which accounted for 40% of Upjohn's profits that year (Williams, 1984). In spite of their difficulties, in 1986 Boots and Upjohn agreed to revise the licensing agreement as it covered the second generation product, flurbiprofen (Ansaid in the US, Froben in the UK). The revised agreement gave Upjohn the exclusive license for US sales for the new product.

Upjohn and Hoechst-Roussel

This OSR dates back to the 1950s and covers three generations of drugs for the oral treatment of diabetes as well as other product licensing agreements. The original agreement surrounded the drug tolbutamide, which Hoechst developed after the war. (See Sneader, 1985: 217–219 for a brief history of the discovery process.) Upjohn helped conduct the initial tests on tolbutamide for Hoechst and launched it in the US in 1957 as Orinase. In the late 1960s that product and an analog, tolazamide, accounted for about 16% of Upjohn's total sales. Safety questions held up marketing of the second generation diabetes drug, glyburide. It would be 1984 before the product could be introduced as Micronase. Contemporarily in the 1980s, Hoechst had launched a "major expansion drive" in the US (*Business Week*, 1981), building a sales force in the US that would reach about 650 (Teitelman, 1989). Still, in 1990, the two firms agreed to develop and market the third generation antidiabetes product, glimepiride, and to jointly market Hoechst's new hypertension drug, Altace.

Abbott Labs and Dainippon Pharmaceutical

In 1962 Abbott and Dainippon established a joint venture, Nippon Abbott, to manufacture radio-pharmaceuticals. Following legal changes in 1975 that allowed larger ownership of Japanese business, the agreement was renegotiated and by 1979 Abbott had increased its ownership of Nippon Abbott to 60%. In 1983 Abbott's Japanese relationships were realigned. Several units, including Nippon Abbott, were merged into an integrated health care company, Dainabot. Abbott retained "majority interest and management responsibility" in the new firm (1983 Annual Report) and the Dainabot joint venture has undertaken a broader range of drug marketing responsibility for Abbott in Japan. The Abbott– Dainippon relationship has also been the platform for agreements outside of Japan, such as the Taiwan Dainippon Pharmaceutical Co., which is owned 70% by Abbott and 30% by Dainippon.

Abbott Labs and Takeda

Takeda Chemical Industries, the largest pharmaceutical firm in Japan, formed a joint venture with Abbott in 1977. The initial purpose was to provide registration and marketing for Takeda drugs in the US and Canada. The relationship quickly began developing beyond its original scope and by 1980 a second agreement had been announced. This agreement expanded the territory for TAP products to include Latin America and Europe. By 1982 TAP had four drugs in development that had originated from Takeda. When the first product to emerge from TAP research came out in 1986 it was marketed by each parent independently, not by TAP. By 1988 TAP had its own manufacturing plant and a 70-person sales force in Japan.

American Home Products and Sanofi: Sterling (The Takeda–Abbott Joint Venture)

American Home Products (AHP) is a diversified firm with a large stake in pharmaceuticals. Sanofi is a pharmaceutical subsidiary of the French petroleum company. Elf Aquitaine. In 1981 a joint venture was established between the two firms. Sanofi was looking for product links and increased US market access, and AHP was interested in gaining access to the Pasteur Institute and its research in genetic engineering. In addition, the two firms had entered into single product marketing agreements for individual products. In 1987 a new equity agreement was entered into that replaced the previous joint venture and all marketing agreements. Then, late in the year, both AHP and Sanofi made competing bids for the bankrupt A.H. Robbins company, with AHP winning. No further dealings between AHP and Sanofi have been announced and the relationship is effectively terminated.

Merck and Banyu

Merck and Banyu began working together in 1954 when they formed a joint venture called Nippon Merck-Banyu for the manufacture and sale of Merck products in Japan. Banyu's product line was primarily focused on anti-biotics and it had arrangements with other firms as well. In 1983 Merck bought 50.5% of the equity in Banyu in what was at the time the largest acquisition in Japan to that date by a foreign firm. Banyu now exclusively promotes Merck and Banyu products.

Pfizer and Biogal: Ciba-Geigy and Biogal

Hungary has historically had one of the most developed pharmaceutical industries in Eastern Europe and has been able to export about 70% of its production. Biogal has been engaging in OSRs since liberalization of joint-venture laws around 1980. Pfizer's first deal with Biogal was a joint marketing deal in the 1980s. Then in 1991 the two firms formed a joint venture to expand on their prior relationship. Pfizer owns 51% of the new joint venture, which markets Pfizer-originated products in Hungary. A similar pattern of agreements between Biogal and Ciba-Geigy also took place. In the second half of the 1970s a Ciba subsidiary, Zyma, entered into numerous pharmaceutical production and marketing licenses with Biogal. In 1980 the two firms formed a joint venture to build a new plant in Hungary. Under this agreement Zyma owned 49%, Biogal 50% and the Hungarian government 1%. The two principals each agreed to buy and distribute 50% of the output. Then in 1991 Ciba-Geigy and Biogal formed a second joint-venture, Ciba-Geigy-Biogal Pharma Kft, a 51–49 joint venture.

AN AGGREGATE ANALYSIS OF SUSTAINED ALLIANCES

The eight OSRs just summarized all support a role for sustainable competence in multi-agreement relationships. In each relationship the presence of competencies sustained relationships as they were modified or expanded, and their absence led to the end of the relationship in spite of past successes. The first proposition suggested that as long as a partner's contributions are needed to sustain competitive advantage, the parties will seek to continue the relationship. Two relationships involving Upjohn support this view. In these cases, there remained unique traits leading to competitive advantage based on Upjohn's established physician relationships and selling experiences at the time of the latter-generation products. Competitive advantages were sustained in both cases because Upjohn was able to push out the level of its underlying marketplace competencies, as suggested by Proposition 2.

The link between sustained competencies within firms and sustained OSRs between firms was also seen in Abbott's relationships with its Japanese partners, in which the competencies in their partners' research laboratories continually provided new products to the OSR. In these cases, and in the relationships involving Biogal of Hungary, firms expanded their agreements due to the partners' ability to respond positively to changes in technology or the political environment. In each case the firms were able to enter new markets not addressed in the original agreement.

The role of firm-level learning suggested by propositions 4 and 5 was also supported. As previously noted. Upjohn was able to push out its skill advantage in serving physicians. Had it not been for the initial alliances, Upjohn would not have developed the skills that enabled it to present distinctive relationships to its partners as incentive for sustaining the alliance through the subsequent generations of drugs. In a different way the Abbott OSRs also show how learning builds and strengthens the alliance relationship. In the Abbott–Dainippon relationship the alliance itself became the vehicle for new experiences—the founding of new joint ventures in third countries and developing a pool of knowledge and skill *inside* the OSR's joint venture. Importantly, the learning that sustains the value of the relationship was also an outcome of the relationship. By contrast, in the Sanofi–AHP OSR both firms did continue to learn during the period of their relationship, but the learning did not emerge from nor sustain the relationship, consistent with proposition 3.

COMPETENCE EVOLUTION AND COGNITIVE EVOLUTION

The dynamic alliances just discussed depend on cognitive processes of reinterpretation. Clearly as the alliance members developed their competencies, several cognitive changes had to occur. Partners must constantly assess changes in their own competitive positions, the contribution of their assets to the alliance, the competitive position of their alliance partner, and the expected fruits of continuing the alliance. Had these perceptions not developed, it is unlikely that either firm would have continued its relationship. Similarly, the failure of firms to develop competencies will not produce performance, regardless of managers' beliefs about the alliance's potential.

In the second portion of this panel, research was presented that suggested the successful maintenance of alliances occurs through loose coupling between beliefs and actions. Given the relationship between alliance success and competencies demonstrated by this study, and the non-linear way in which competencies evolve, it is likely that loose coupling is the *only type* of relationship that will sustain an alliance. It is important, however, for managers to note when the misalignment between competence evolution and cognitive evolution becomes threatening. Then, as in the situation presented in the second paper, managers must be proactive in realigning the two.

PANEL CONCLUSIONS

The three papers of this panel provide insights that, together, provide a richer understanding of what is occurring in the dynamics of strategic alliance. While the last two studies do not directly address the elements of FIGURE 8.2 from the first paper, they both provide clear insights into the processes that FIGURE 8.2 captures. By bringing together these three papers we sought to use well-grounded research in different areas to provide insights for managers and academics into a new area of inquiry.

The ideas presented here do not replace the insights gained from other models of alliance choice. Rather they complement them. For managers there are insights into why alliances succeed and, more importantly, why they fail when they should succeed. Hopefully these can be used to develop and sustain alliances more effectively in the future. For researchers, the insights here suggest by including cognitive processes, theories of strategic alliances can better explain observed variations in alliance formation, maintenance, and (possible) death.

REFERENCES

Bogner, W. and Thomas, H. (1994) "Core Competence and Competitive Advantage: A Model and Illustrative Evidence from the Pharmaceutical Industry", in G. Hamel and A. Heene (eds) *Competence Based Competition*, London: John Wiley & Sons, pp. 111–144.

Bogner, W. and Thomas, H. (1996) "From Skills to Competencies: The "Play-out" of Resource Bundles Across Firms", in R. Sanchez, A. Heene, and H. Thomas (eds) *Theory and Practice in Competence-Based Competition*, Oxford: Elsevier, pp. 101–118.

Business Week (1981) "A Chemical Giant Leans more Heavily on Drugs", 6 July, 39–40.

Contractor, F. and Lorange, P. (1988) *Cooperative Strategies in International Business*. Lexington, Mass,: Lexington Books.

Cowan, D. (1986) "Developing a Process Model of Problem Recognition", *Academy of Management Review*, 11, 763–776.

Daft, R. and Weick, K. (1984) "Toward a Model of Organizations as Interpretive Systems", *Academy of Management Review*, 9, 284–295.

Fama, E.F. and Jensen, M.C. (1983) "Separation of Ownership and Control", *Journal of Law and Economics*, 26 June, 327–349.

Hall, P.D. (1992) Inventing the Non-profit Sector and Other Essays on Philanthropy, Voluntarism and Non-profit Organizations, Baltimore: Johns Hopkins University Press.

Hall, R. (1984) "The Natural Logic of Policy Making: Its Implications for the Survival of an Organization", *Management Science*, 30, 905–927.

Hamel, G. (1991) "Competition for Competence and Inter-Partner Learning within International Strategic Alliances", *Strategic Management Journal*, Summer, 83–103.

Hansmann, H.B. (1986) "The Role of Nonprofit Enterprise", in S. Rose-Ackerman (ed.) *The Economics of Nonprofit Institutions*, Oxford: Oxford University Press, pp. 57–84.

Herman, R.D. and Heimovics, R.D. (1990) "The Effective Nonprofit Executive: Leader of the Board", *Nonprofit Management and Leadership*, 1(2), 167–180.

Huber, G. (1991) "Organizational Learning: The Contributing Processes and the Literatures", *Organization Science*, 2(1), 88–115.

Kiesler, S. and Sproull, L. (1986) "Managerial Response to Changing Environments: Perspectives on Problem Sensing from Social Cognition", *Administrative Science Quarterly*, 27, 515–538.

Lant, T., Milliken, F., and Batra, B. (1992) "The Role of Managerial Learning and Interpretation in Strategic Persistence and Reorientation: An Empirical Exploration", *Strategic Management Journal*, 13, 585–608.

March, J. and Simon, H. (1958) *Organizations*, New York: John Wiley.

Meyer, A. (1982) "Adapting to Environmental Jolts", *Administrative Science Quarterly*, 27, 515–538.

Meyer, J.W. and Rowan, B. (1977) "Institutionalized Organizations: Formal Structure as Myth and Ceremony", *American Journal of Sociology*, 83(2), 340–363.

Nohria, N. and Garcia-Pont, C. (1991) "Global Strategic Linkages and Industry Structure", *Strategic Management Journal*, 12, Summer, 105–124.

Porac, J., Thomas, H., and Baden-Fuller, C. (1989) "Competitive Groups as Cognitive Communities: The Case of Scottish Knitwear Manufacturers", *Journal of Management Studies*, 26, 397–416.

Porac, J., Thomas, H., Wilson, F., Paton, D., and Kanfer, A. (1995) "Rivalry and the Industry Model of Scottish Knitwear Producers", *Administrative Science Quarterly*, 40, 203–227.

Prahalad, C. and Hamel, G. (1990) "The Core Competency of the Corporation", *Harvard Business Review*, May–June, 79–91.

Reger, R. and Huff, A. (1993) "Strategic Groups: A Cognitive Perspective", *Strategic Management Journal*, 14, 103–124.

Schwenk, C. (1984) "Cognitive Simplification Processes in Strategic Decision Making", *Strategic Management Journal*, 5, 111–128.

Smith, D.H. (1992) "Moral Responsibilities of Trustees: Some First Thoughts", *Nonprofit Management and Leadership*, 2(4), 351–362.

Sneader, W. (1985) *Drug Discovery: The Evolution of Modern Medicines*. Chichester: Wiley Medical.

Spender, J. (1989) *Industry Recipes: An Inquiry into the Nature and Sources of Managerial Judgement*, Cambridge, Mass.: Basil Blackwell.

Starbuck, W. and Milliken F. (1988) "Executives' Perceptual Filters: What They Notice and How They Make Sense," in D. Hambrick (ed.), *The Executive Effect: Concepts and Methods for Studying Top Managers*, Greenwich, Conn.: JAI Press, pp. 35–65.

Teitelman, R. (1989) "Pharmaceuticals", *Financial World*, 30 May, 54–80.

White, H. (1992) *Identity and Control: A Structural Theory of Social Action*. Princeton: Princeton University Press.

Williams, M. (1984) "Early Reports from the War on Painkillers", *Fortune*, 20 August, 101.

9

Organizing for Competitive Advantage: The Machine Adhocracy

CLIFF BOWMAN, SIMON CARTER

INTRODUCTION

In 1979 Henry Mintzberg published an important contribution to our understanding of organization structures. Mintzberg argued the case for a contingency theory of structure: there is no "one best way" to structure an organization, it all depends on the particular contingent circumstances facing the organization. These contingency variables included: the age and size of the organization; the dynamism of the environment; the complexity of the tasks being performed; the technical systems used in the core of the business; and the power relationships (particularly external) affecting the organization (Mintzberg, 1979). Different and coherent combinations of these variables would mean that certain organization forms would be more effective than others.

Mintzberg originally suggested five commonly occurring "configurations" appropriate for different combinations of contingent conditions. These were: the simple (later named "entrepreneurial") form appropriate for tackling simple tasks in dynamic environments; the machine bureaucracy ("machine" organization), a mass-production organization, which is well adapted to a stable environment; the divisionalized organization (often referred to as the M-form, adopted by most diversified corporations); the professional bureaucracy, suitable for tackling complex tasks in stable environments, e.g. a hospital; and the adhocracy (either operating, or

Strategy, Structure and Style. Edited by H. Thomas, D. O'Neal and M. Ghertman
Copyright © 1997 John Wiley & Sons Ltd.

administrative) adapted to cope with complex tasks in dynamic environments. He later added a sixth configuration: the missionary organization (Mintzberg, 1989). Each of these configurations relies on a predominant "coordinating mechanism" which is used to integrate the work, coordinating fragmented tasks and specialized staff. For example, the machine organization relies heavily on the standardization of work processes to effect coordination (e.g. through the use of method study which prescribes precisely how a task should be performed), whereas in the adhocracy coordination is achieved through face-to-face meetings between specialists working in teams (this mechanism is referred to as "mutual adjustment" by Mintzberg).

A year after Mintzberg's book appeared, Michael Porter published *Competitive Strategy* (Porter, 1980), introducing the generic strategy concepts, which have proved to be hugely influential in the strategic management field. Porter argued that, in order to achieve sustainable competitive advantage, the firm must adopt one of three alternative generic strategies: cost leadership; differentiation; or focus (which involves applying one of the other strategies to a narrow market segment). He suggested that failure to do so, or attempting to achieve both cost leadership and differentiation simultaneously, may lead to the firm becoming "stuck in the middle".

It was not part of Mintzberg's intention to relate his work on structures to the problems of delivering competitive strategies. Porter, similarly, devotes very little space in his books (Porter, 1980, 1985) to questions of structure. However, a notable attempt to bring these two contributions together was made by Miller (1986). He suggested that cost leadership is best achieved through the machine bureaucratic structure; and that innovative differentiation requires an operating adhocracy. In other words, the strategy/structure question could be resolved by selecting one of Porter's generic strategies. Once this choice has been made, there are extant and well-understood congruent structural forms that "fit" this choice of strategy.

However, there have been significant developments in both the theory and practice of competitive strategy, and within the field of organization design since Miller's contribution, which suggest that the links between competitive strategy and structure should be reconsidered. This chapter does so and sets out to address the central question: *how should a firm be structured to deliver sustainable competitive advantage?*

The chapter begins with a discussion of recent trends and developments in competitive strategy and in the competitive environment. These changes can be viewed as changes in the contingent conditions facing firms. If these conditions have changed, then arguably either individual firms would have to move to a different configuration to survive (e.g. from a machine organization to a divisionalized structure), or firms that are unable to adapt will go out of business (Hannan and Freeman, 1977). More significantly, it may be that new configurations are required to match new combinations of contingent conditions.

This line of argument is pursued through a consideration of a case of substantial strategy/structure realignment from the manufacturing sector. The case example is then used to develop a generic structure which can help to deliver sustainable advantage. We have labelled this structure the "machine adhocracy". Some complications of these arguments for the management of firms are suggested and finally some suggestions for future research are put forward.

DEVELOPMENTS IN COMPETITIVE STRATEGY AND THE COMPETITIVE ENVIRONMENT

Since the publication of Porter's *Competitive Strategy* (1980) the argument that firms must choose between generic strategies has been challenged (Hill, 1988). Definitional problems with the generic strategy concepts have surfaced and there is evidence that both academics and managers have varying interpretations of these ideas (Cronshaw, Davis, and Kay, 1994; Karnani, 1984; Govindarajan, 1988; Murray, 1988; Mathur, 1988; Miller and Friesen, 1986a,b; Skivington and Daft, 1991; Faulkner and Bowman, 1992). For example, there is debate about whether the "cost leader" strategy involves being low price as well as low cost, and whether the pursuit of cost leadership and differentiation simultaneously inevitably results in the firm being "stuck in the middle".

"Resource-based" theory has emerged which offers a different perspective, arguing that sustainable advantage derives from unique, inimitable competences possessed by firms (Rumelt, 1984; Wernerfelt, 1984; Barney, 1991; Amit and Schoemaker, 1993). Furthermore, the success of many Japanese companies seems to indicate that sustainable advantage is achieved by *combining* cost leadership with differentiation, a view that has some theoretical support (Hill, 1988).

The competitive environment has become more hostile. Increasing competition from rapidly developing nations, globalization of markets and, more recently, the effects of recession have combined to make life more difficult for most firms. Instability in many markets due to political, economic and social upheaval (e.g. Eastern Europe), coupled with the pace of change and shortening product life cycles, has increased uncertainty and dynamism in the environment. Niches that were once safely protected by brand or other entry barriers are being increasingly penetrated. Now no firm seems to be immune from price competition (see the experiences of Mercedes and BMW in the luxury car market under threat from Japanese competition), and being "customer focused" and delivering excellent value (as defined and perceived by the customer) are becoming order-qualifying, rather than order-winning, capabilities.

These developments can be expressed as changes in two of the contingency variables facing firms. Specifically:

- *The environment*: it has become more hostile, more unpredictable and more dynamic.
- *Tasks*: the need for fast-paced innovation, coupled with the need to offer high value at low cost (not necessarily low prices), has increased the task complexity of the firm.

RECENT DEVELOPMENTS IN ORGANIZATION STRUCTURE

Mintzberg identified five basic parts of the organization: the strategic apex (who control the organization); the operating core (the operational heart of the organization); the middle line (the line managers connecting the operating core to the strategic apex); the technostructure (staff analysts who help to achieve the standardization of outputs, work processes, and skills); and support staff (who carry out supporting activities, e.g. staff restaurant, public relations, building maintenance). We can use these categories to explore recent changes in the way firms are organized.

Traditional, hierarchical, functional organization structures have been subject to challenge and change. Delayering and downsizing (or "rightsizing") are banners under which firms have reduced staff numbers (Drucker, 1992; Zeffane, 1992; Neilson, 1990; Quinn, Doorley, and Paquette, 1990; Heenan, 1989). This is usually in response to deteriorating performance, either through the firm's inability to deliver value to customers, e.g. service, new products, or because of pressures to reduce costs. Delayering involves stripping out levels of management (i.e. the middle line has been truncated), whereas downsizing attempts to take out activities previously done within the organization. Downsizing initially impacted upon support staff, particularly those staff whose activities were loosely coupled to the main tasks of the organization.

In the early 1980s many firms subcontracted activities like office cleaning, restaurants and payroll in line with strategies concerned with focusing on the core of the business. More recently, some firms have taken this philosophy into the technostructure and into the operating core, effecting radical reductions in staff numbers. Indeed, some have had to help create new supplying firms because none existed that could deliver the required activities (e.g. BP Exploration).

Due in part to delayering, and encouraged by ideas popularized by management writers like Tom Peters (1988), "empowerment" of junior levels of staff has gathered momentum (Conger and Kanungo, 1988; Bowen and Lawler, 1992). Self-organizing, autonomous teams supported by excellent information systems have challenged the traditional roles of the middle line managers, particularly their role as coordinators through direct supervision. There are also pressures on staff in the operating core to become more flexible, both in terms of their capabilities and their employment contracts (Boynton and Victor, 1991).

Business process redesign (or re-engineering—BPR) requires firms to challenge existing organizational arrangements, particularly functional organization. Because business processes tend to span across existing organizational subdivisions, adopting BPR has usually resulted in a substantial reorganization around more logical groupings of activities (Davenport and Short, 1990; Knorr, 1991; Heygate, 1993). Flexible manufacturing (Parthasarthy and Sethi, 1993; Wheelwright and Hayes, 1985) and the introduction of just-in-time (JIT) systems have led to major restructuring in the operating cores of businesses (Sohal, Keller, and Fouad, 1988). The limitations of functional structures, particularly with regard to new product development, have been exposed (Ruekert and Walker, 1987; Moenaert and Souder, 1990) and cross-functional teams are increasingly required to improve cooperation and coordination in the process of new product development.

These changes can be expressed in terms of Mintzberg's contingency variables as follows:

- *Size*: firms are becoming leaner and smaller.
- *Technical system*: past ways of organizing the operating core are being challenged (by downsizing, and the introduction of BPR, JIT and cross-functional team working).
- *Power*: decentralization of decision making to staff in the operating core, but a shift away from traditional employment contracts.

Clearly, all firms would not experience all these changes in the contingent conditions facing them, but it is worth exploring their implications. As explained earlier, there appears to be a congruence of "fit" between Porter's generic strategies and Mintzberg's configurations (Miller, 1986, 1990). The cost leader adopts the machine form of organization; and the innovative differentiator becomes an operating adhocracy. But if, in order to achieve advantage, the firm needs to combine these two strategies, in an increasingly hostile environment what configuration is appropriate?

In order to explore this question we present a very recent case of a firm that has undergone significant changes to its competitive strategy, and its organization structure. We then use this case to make some tentative suggestions of a new, emerging configuration that can help firms deliver sustainable advantage.

BAXI HEATING

Baxi Heating is an old-established business manufacturing domestic central heating boilers and gas fires. It had developed and grown as a conventional, functionally structured business, employing around 1100 people on four manufacturing sites in north-west England. The company had experienced substantial growth during the period from the mid-1970s to the late 1980s, as growth in the domestic heating market outpaced the economy in general. This was due largely to the UK's conversion to natural gas as the principal domestic fuel source, combined with a rapid expansion in home ownership, house building and house moving during the "boom years" of the mid-1980s. However, by the late 1980s, growth fell away dramatically as the economic downturn began to bite (annual sales at that time were running at around £65m).

During the period 1988–93, the total market demand had fallen by some 25%. The competitive nature of the market-place also changed with some competitors being bought up by new owners. The aggressive entry of new players from mainland Europe led to falling prices and oversupply chasing a reduced demand in a mature market. Distribution channels also changed through the rationalizing and restructuring of the major builders' merchant groups, giving them increased purchasing power, and leading to further pressure on margins. The harmonization of European standards for boilers and the need to develop "green" energy-efficient systems created increased demands on the R&D functions. Baxi was also struggling to contain its cost base, partly because of difficult industrial relations, and also due to the residual momentum of a more relaxed approach to cost control during the boom years. Baxi's cost base was running ahead of the market.

Baxi had attempted to address its manufacturing cost base through a reconfiguration of its manufacturing processes, based around the principles of JIT and a company-wide total quality management (TQM) programme. However, the early gains in local manufacturing areas were being lost as the organization structure and culture "disabled" progress on a company-wide basis. The principal difficulties were:

- the stranglehold of functional hierarchies over empowered operations (see FIGURE 9.1)
- the failure of operational activities to be genuinely customer focused
- inadequate information sharing, in particular the information relationship between customer need/production scheduling and finished goods distribution
- the hierarchical and "controls-driven" functional empires gave no sense of business realism or customer orientation, effectively suffocating the TQM programme at the shop-floor

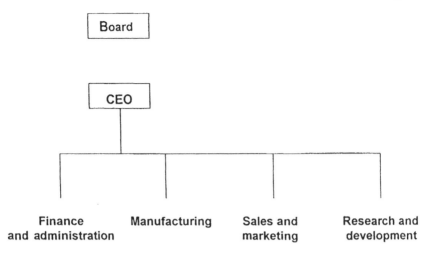

FIGURE 9.1   Baxi: old structure

Having recognized that a new response to the business environment was necessary, there remained a reluctance to face up to the reality that a crisis was building. Indeed, the fact that Baxi had some valuable strengths in its technological competence, excellent product development and deep penetration into its selected market segments all added to the inertia and lack of urgency. The management team continued the pursuit of excellence in areas peripheral to the real strategic need. Baxi had a cultural, structural and organizational blockage to its strategic development.

The solution was a fundamental transformation of the organization structure and systems. This radical change programme was designed to shake out complacency and refocus the business towards customers, to speed up the product innovation programme, improve product and process quality, and increase productivity.

The new structure is based on strategic business units (SBUs), comprising natural product groups, internal supplier groups and support services (see FIGURE 9.2). Each SBU would be self-governing. The product groups had their own dedicated product marketing, new product development, quality control, manufacturing assembly, production engineering, maintenance and management accounting expertise. In effect, the SBUs have become "minibusinesses" within the framework of the company structure, with each unit being fully financially accountable for its own performance.

The new structure has retained some activities as central services, although these were operated as company-wide support groups. These service units include corporate accounting (separated from management accounting, which is an SBU activity), sales (most products from all SBUs

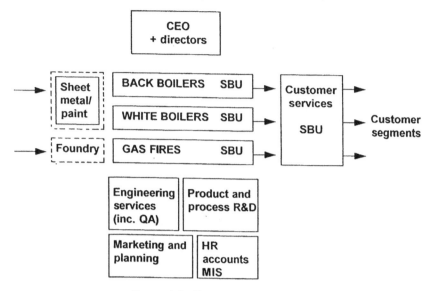

FIGURE 9.2   Baxi: new structure

are sold down the same distribution channels and so separate sales organizations would make no sense at all), procurement (which centrally drove vendor improvement programmes and in-bound quality control), central engineering (retained centrally to handle plant maintenance, civil and project engineering work), and human resources (again, retained centrally to oversee employee relations, training and development, on a company-wide basis). The role of these groups has been to ensure that the customer interface was properly represented and that all operations were subject to market pull, thus escaping the constraints of the old functional empires.

A new group of "irreducible expertise" was also created and brought together as a "university" of know-how. It is here that the organization's core knowledge is pulled together as a centre of excellence. It comprises "blue sky" R&D developing the next generation products and technologies, as distinct from day-to-day R&D which is held within the product groups; manufacturing technology, examining global benchmarking in manufacturing systems and technology; quality systems control, developing systems and auditing conformance to all product, service, plant and environmental standards; management information systems, operating the corporate mainframe and developing user-led information networks; and marketing and economic planning, which holds the market data bases, market trend analysis, and produces the market and economic forecasts. The "university" is a future-oriented unit and provides the base planning data for both the executive group and the operating units.

The role of the board members has changed from being pure functional heads into business-oriented generalists, with each director having specific responsibilities for a portfolio of business unit activities. The board is responsible for overall strategy formulation, providing funding for all operations, cultural development, and the monitoring and control of the business entity as a whole. Each of the SBUs and service centres (each of which also ran as a self-governing business centre with internal rather than external customers) has one general manager at its head for overall accountability. The general managers were supported by specialist or multi-functional teams, each with a team leader. This reduced the management hierarchy from five levels to three.

This combination of flattened hierarchy with multi-skilled teams organized into discrete business units enabled the rapid development of the once faltering TQM programme and achieved the goals of faster product development, improved quality, improved service and sustainable cost reduction. This in turn increased productivity and, more importantly, profitability. Each unit now has a much clearer sense of identity and purpose, strengthening the corporate culture towards customers and the building of a strong team-working culture within the organization.

In the Baxi model, refocusing SBUs towards real customer need and integrating the information links from supplier through to customer (removing all non-value-adding activities) have created the required conditions for a more rapid response to the market environment. Baxi is still far from being the lowest cost producer in the industry, and because of its high cost base, it trades on a premium price basis for higher technology products in its distinctly focused market sectors. However, with the market suffering from oversupply and a continued downward pressure on all market prices from new and existing players aggressively chasing or protecting market share, the financial benefits of Baxi's restructuring enabled it to compete successfully, growing both in profitability and market share as overall market demand fell away.

IMPACT ON MANAGERS

The implications for management roles and behaviour were significant, with the board of directors and the business unit managers in particular taking on broader, generalist roles. Each of these managers had previously operated in a fairly narrow functional speciality and a significant amount of training and support was given to assist in their adjustment to their new roles and responsibilities.

The directors took positions in the new organization which played to their professional strengths and disciplines, and yet avoided the opportunity to revert to safe and familiar old roles. Three directors made a successful transition into their new roles, but two directors, after a period of trying to make it work, eventually left the organization.

The business unit managers received training in three key skills; business strategy and marketing (each unit produced a three-year business plan), finance and accounting, and interpersonal behaviour/team-working skills. The "big bang" approach to the change obviously created some initial anxieties, but the fact that the change was permanent and irreversible allowed managers time to adjust through the period of discomfort and relearning.

Similarly, for the team leaders, the change brought a fresh approach and momentum to the TQM and continuous improvement programmes. The new teams put a great deal of effort into workflow redesign, multi-skilling, and quality systems. This was aided by the fact that in the two years following the organizational restructuring, Baxi spent £1.5m. physically relocating staff and plant so that business teams, management and workforce were both organizationally and physically located in the same areas. More efficient team working permitted a reduction in the number of factory sites from four to three, and later from three to two. The newly empowered and delayered structure had reduced the total number of management roles from 120 to 61 within three years. Managers who were formerly part of the hierarchy now adopted expertise-driven roles within teams.

Perhaps the simplest way of examining the results of the change is to focus upon the impact in three key areas: *process improvement, people* and *profits*.

PROCESS IMPROVEMENTS

Within the first two years, the value and volume of finished goods stock had been halved. The flexible manufacturing system, driven for the first time by "live" customer order data, enabled a rapid response to customer demand. Using two simple measures of performance, CLIP (confirmed line item performance—the product mix variable) and CVP (confirmed volume performance—the daily volume variable), manufacturing teams could manufacture to order any derivative of each product type, in any sequence, within the product SBUs. Using "kanban" pull triggers from the internal supplier groups ensured on-time parts delivery. The throughput time for the manufacture of one boiler fell from 6 hours to 50 minutes; work in progress fell from around 4 weeks to around 2 hours. The manufacturing cycle time was reduced and suppliers were integrated into the continuous improvement process, some of them being trained by Baxi employees, and continuously audited by the purchasing teams. New product introduction process was cut by 18 months and the financial control systems of the business were converted to an activity-based management system.

During the period 1989–93, Baxi increased its share of the UK gas central heating market from 19 to 24%, even though the UK market demand had fallen by around 30% during the same period through the depths of the recession.

PEOPLE

The reorganization into teams had a dramatic effect upon the manufacturing culture. There were between 8 and 10 people in each manufacturing team and approximately 10 elements of work within each team. All team members were trained in all operations and each had to achieve absolute competence in at least five elements. The teams agreed the output levels for the day, the number of productive hours, overtime (and whether or not to be paid for it), holidays, absence, manning rosters, authorize repairs and maintenance, and plan their own training schedule. In addition, teams had responsibility for such matters as first aid, health and safety, product and production modifications, environmental management, layout improvements, and so on.

At its height there were in excess of 130 continuous improvement teams operating across the business. There is flexibility and an absence of demarcation. Improvement ideas flowed, some small and some requiring capital investment. There was a new focus upon employment security rather than job or role security. A huge investment in training and development followed, including the employees establishing for themselves an open learning centre. In order to promote a learning culture within the business, the company, in arrangement with a local college, provided each employee with a voucher to undertake up to 30 weeks' "night school" education in any subject of their choice.

Absence and sickness statistics fell dramatically and safety records improved. The rather Victorian process of "clocking-on" was abolished as employees were trusted to arrive at work and leave when they should. Appraisal and counselling were introduced into the shop-floor areas. The employees established a "return to work" unit to help employees who may have been absent for some time to readjust back into the work environment. At the end of 1993, Baxi Heating was awarded the UK standard "Investor in People".

PROFIT

The organization change occurred on 1 January 1990. For the year ending 31 March 1991 profits increased by 80% from £7.1m. to £13m. largely as a result of the release of latent profitability from process improvement. The sales volumes for the year were slightly down on the previous year. In the following financial year, this high level of profitability was maintained as profits reached £13.9m. on sales turnover level at around £68m. This surge in increased profitability was sustained for a third year as a result of process improvement although declared profits were depressed through volume decline, an acquisition paid for in cash, and a substantial contribution to pension funds resulting from pensions harmonization.

The success of a major change programme, whether it be some form of business process redesign or other transformation, is only sustainable when it properly tunes into the value and belief systems of the employees, and aligns these with the culture and structure of the organization. The organization structural changes within Baxi demonstrate that an appropriate organizational framework is a means to an end rather than an end in itself.

IS THE BAXI CASE EVIDENCE OF A NEW CONFIGURATION OF STRATEGY AND STRUCTURE?

We can use Mintzberg's categorization of the different parts of the organization to explore the new structure that has emerged in Baxi.

The strategic apex has changed quantitatively and qualitatively. The number of executives has been reduced and their roles have changed from functional responsibilities to more integrated product, process or customer-oriented roles. There has also been a more explicit recognition of the longer-term responsibilities of the strategic apex, and a corresponding shift away from intimate involvement in day-to-day concerns.

The operating core has undergone substantial change, involving a regrouping and a reorientation around products. Multi-disciplinary teams have been developed to improve service performance and flexibility. The middle line has been severely truncated. The number of levels in the hierarchy has been dramatically reduced to the point where the middle line almost ceases to be a significant part of the structure. The scope of operations undertaken "in-house" has been reduced within Baxi leading to a substantial reduction in support staff roles.

Baxi, prior to the change, would be classified as a "machine organization" which has an extensive technostructure concerned with work process standardization, budgeting, quality control, etc. These activities are still required but they have, in some cases, been decentralized into the SBUs, and they have taken on a more "business oriented" focus. The relationship between the centralized technostructure activities (quality assurance, personnel, management information systems) has shifted away from a "controlling" approach towards a more supporting and enabling relationship.

So far we have been able to categorize, and then interpret, the new Baxi structure within Mintzberg's categories. However, there appear to be some staff activities in Baxi that do not neatly correspond to either Mintzberg's "technostructure" or the "support staff" category. These are the "university" staff who are concerned with the continual development of processes, products and people in the operating core. They also provide a repository for valuable strategic information (on customers, competitors and the market environment). We believe that this is a different type of staff grouping, and, coupled with the changes in the scope and orientation of the other five staff and line groupings, we suggest that there may be a new "configuration" emerging, which could be labelled the *machine adhocracy*. We believe this new form is a response to the demands of continual product and service innovation at lowest cost, in an increasingly hostile and dynamic competitive environment. In the next section we elaborate this configuration using Mintzberg's approach.

THE MACHINE ADHOCRACY

Mintzberg (1979) argued that the machine organization (or machine bureaucracy) is adapted to tackling simple tasks in stable environments, and the adhocracy form is appropriate for firms dealing with complex tasks in dynamic environments. The machine adhocracy enables a firm to gain the advantages of efficient product/service delivery (at low cost and with high levels of conformance quality) which is a feature of the machine organization, without the stultifying and disabling inflexibility which seems to accompany the machine form. The machine adhocracy has the ability to adapt more readily to a changing task environment, as does the pure adhocracy form. But the pure adhocracy can be an expensive structural solution if it has the potential to tackle much higher levels of change and task complexity than are required by the extant circumstances facing the firm.

The machine adhocracy delivers continuous incremental improvements in the efficiency and effectiveness of the operating core. But, from a day-by-day, short-term perspective there is *stability* in the operating core. This is necessary to achieve the required levels of efficiency. However, either through a continuous series of small adjustments, or through periodic larger-scale changes, the operating core is evolving and not stagnating. The university is the key to this evolutionary process, through its research role and its ability to facilitate learning within the core.

We have used Mintzberg's diagrammatic conventions to depict this new form (see Mintzberg, 1979). The machine adhocracy comprises four

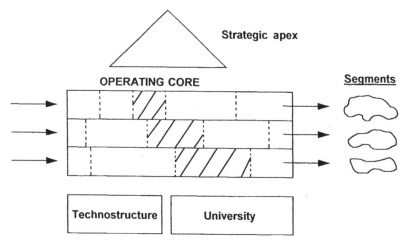

FIGURE 9.3   The machine adhocracy

basic parts (see FIGURE 9.3):

- the strategic apex
- the operating core

- the technostructure
- the university

The first three groupings correspond to Mintzberg's categories, but their roles and responsibilities have been developed and refined. The fourth category, the "university", is a new type of staff grouping. We now explain the roles and characteristics of each grouping.

THE STRATEGIC APEX

The strategic apex has a dual responsibility: first it is required to ensure the efficient management of the current mission of the firm; second, it is responsible for the strategic development of the business. Too often management at the top of the firm focus too much on the day-to-day running of the business at the expense of its strategic development. Specifically, the apex is required to:

- decide what is legitimate activity for the firm (deciding scope, domain, make or buy, diversification)
- fund the operations (financing)
- set the culture and climate
- coordinate and control linkages within the firm and between the firm and suppliers, alliance partners, customers, distribution channels

THE OPERATING CORE

The operating core is the heart of the business. All other staff groups serve the core. People in the operating core are responsible for the efficient delivery of valued products and services to customers. They are concerned with producing high quality products or services (in terms of conformance quality), at lowest costs. In order to deliver valued products, members of the operating core need to understand what it is the customer values, and they need to organize in ways that can most efficiently deliver that value. The operating core consists of a series of linked activities, and it should only undertake those activities in which it can demonstrate competence relative to competitors, or potential suppliers. Thus the operating core of a machine adhocracy focuses on a severely limited range of activities. If there is no strategic advantage in the firm carrying out the activity itself, then it should be subcontracted.

In order to cope with an unpredictable and changing task environment, operatives in the core will need to demonstrate flexibility, either through individuals mastering a wider set of skills (feasible where the tasks are relatively straightforward), or through groups of specialists forming and reforming into teams to tackle varying task requirements. Teams will largely be self-managing, and they are grouped into sets of activities that clearly link together to deliver value to an identifiable customer group (adopting an "SBU" structure within the operating core). Therefore, the machine adhocracy also resembles the divisionalized form of organization. But here the distinctions between SBU groupings tend to be more "fine-grained" than in a typical corporation (which may have within it SBUs with substantially different product/market scopes). And there is more permeability in the boundaries between SBUs with a considerable degree of cooperation between them. Where activities are common across SBU value chains informal coordination processes operate to assist the spreading of expertise and information.

THE TECHNOSTRUCTURE

The technostructure consists of staff whose job is to standardize activities taking place in the operating core. These staff may be standardizing the way the work is performed (e.g. production engineering, operations planning and scheduling), standardizing output (e.g. quality assurance, budgeting and costing), or standardizing skills (e.g. job training, selection). Alongside the operating core, staff in the technostructure are responsible for the efficient delivery of high conformance quality.

THE UNIVERSITY

In contrast to the rather tenuous position of support staff in the machine organization, the staff in the "university" are absolutely key to the future strategic development of the business. The label "university" came from the Baxi case. We have adopted it here because it neatly captures the role these staff play in the firm.

Universities carry out three basic functions for society at large:

- They engage in research (both fundamental research and applied research)
- They teach people new knowledge and skills
- they provide a store of knowledge

The "university" within the firm carries out all these three functions: research into new products, or new processes; helping staff to develop new skills and knowledge, providing valuable information on customers, competitors, markets, etc. University staff cannot impose their solutions on the operating core; they act as facilitators, supporting the direct value creators in the core. The university is vital because its primary focus is on the future. Whereas the operating core and the technostructure concern themselves primarily with the efficient delivery of the current set of products/services, the university is focused on change and development. Its role is to stimulate the continual transformation of activities in the operating core.

The University and Competence Development

We can usefully explore the role the university can play in developing the firm's competences. Competences can be viewed as comprising combinations of:

- *resources* (people, machines, buildings, brands, cash)
- *systems* (e.g. quality, JIT, MRP II—materials requirements planning)
- *Know-how* (special, unique expertise)

Systems are used to deploy resources. Know-how is special knowledge (often implicit or tacit) which enables a firm to operate its systems more effectively than competitors. For example, most auto manufacturers operate some form of JIT system. A few firms seem to be able to reap greater benefits from it than others (e.g. Toyota, Nissan). This special know-how is difficult for competitors to access, hence it can form the basis of a sustained advantage. But, over time this know-how itself may become systematized:

it is made explicit, codified, proceduralized, and is amenable to being taught to others. Once this process develops, the special know-how degrades into an imitable system, which can no longer provide any competitive advantage, because it becomes the norm or the standard practice in the industry.

This suggests that, in order to sustain advantage firms must continually develop unique, not easily imitable know-how. *The university is the engine of know-how development.* Hence, the university continually seeks to "top up" the firm's reservoir of know-how (see FIGURE 9.4). Know-how migrates (or degrades) into "systems" as it becomes teachable, proceduralized and hence more imitable. Unless know-how is either protected or, more

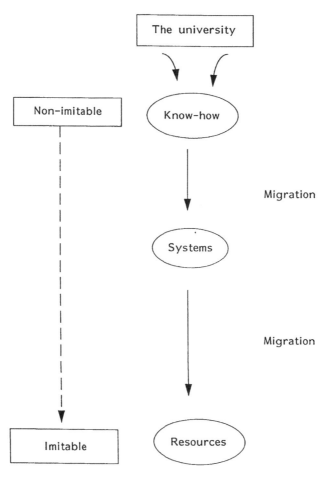

FIGURE 9.4   The university's role as the engine of know-how development

realistically, continually enhanced, the firm will be forced into becoming a "me-too" player. Know-how, as a source of sustainable advantage, must be explicitly and deliberately managed. The university plays a key part in this process. This does not mean, however, that the university is the sole source of expertise in the organization. A major role of university staff is to facilitate the development and dissemination of expertise within the operating core, as well as to learn from others outside the organization.

The university has different roles and relationships with the other parts of the machine adhocracy. It supports the operating core, it cannot dictate to or impose "solutions" in the core. It helps core staff to continually update and improve products and processes, and it also facilitates the sharing of experience and knowledge within the core.

The university's relationship with the strategic apex is essentially to provide timely strategic information, and to conduct strategic analyses to support strategy debate within the apex. Its relationship with the technostructure is similarly supportive, but it also helps the technostructure support the operating core (through assistance with training or with managing the introduction of new systems). It can help all parts of the organization to avoid being overly constrained by beliefs and assumptions (about, for instance, what we think we are good at, or what we believe customers value) and routine ways of thinking, by introducing new information and ideas from outside the organization which may challenge these taken-for-granted beliefs.

The roles undertaken by the university may be filled by staff from other parts of the organization, either as part of their normal workload, or on secondment for a period of time. The movement of staff from the operating core and technostructure in and out of university roles would also facilitate the fostering of a learning orientation throughout the structure.

A "HYBRID" OR A NEW CONFIGURATION?

Whether the machine adhocracy can be regarded as a "hybrid" form, or a new and stable configuration largely depends on the degree to which this structure differs from other configurations. In each of Mintzberg's configurations there is a predominant coordination mechanism (e.g. mutual adjustment in the adhocracy), and there is a staff grouping which is seen to be critical (e.g. the technostructure in the machine organization). What is the primary coordinating mechanism in the machine adhocracy? And what is the critical staff grouping?

In FIGURE 9.5 for each combination of task (simple/complex) and environment (stable/dynamic) the appropriate coordinating mechanism and the corresponding configuration are displayed. We have argued that the machine adhocracy faces a more dynamic environment than the traditional

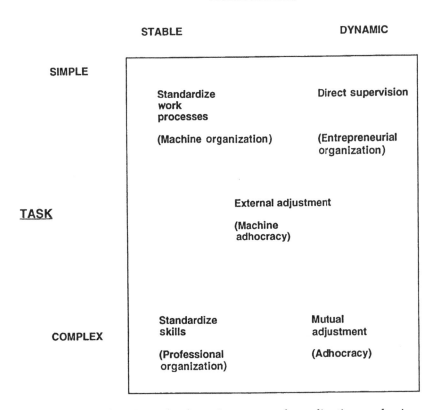

FIGURE 9.5   Combinations of task, environment and coordinating mechanisms

machine structure, and that the complexity of the task facing the organization has increased. The machine adhocracy therefore occupies the centre of
FIGURE 9.5. The main issue facing this organization is the need to continually adapt to a changing competitive environment, while still maintaining
efficient operations (they must be low cost). This is achieved through processes of continual adjustment and learning, throughout the organization.
The challenge is not only to coordinate work efficiently inside the organization, it is to do this and coordinate the whole organization with its marketplace. This external coordination requires excellent information, which is
then used to continually adapt the way the firm works. This coordination
process could be labelled "external adjustment", and the grouping that has
primary responsibility for effecting external adjustment is the university.

Mintzberg also identifies a number of "pulls" (Mintzberg, 1979), e.g. a
pull from the technostructure to standardize activities. We can see in the

machine adhocracy evidence of four "pulls" operating simultaneously in response to the contingent circumstances facing the organization:

- the pull from the operating core to "professionalize" their work through processes of empowerment, decentralization and the reduction of the middle line
- the pull to "balkanize" or divisionalize the organization into quasi-autonomous SBUs; these are a response to the increasing need to focus on different segments of the market and to tailor what the firm does to meet the demands of specific segments
- the pull to "collaborate", to share ideas and expertise across specialisms in order to cope with the demands of the dynamic and increasingly complex task environment
- the pull to "standardize" as the technostructure staff and operating core seek to improve operating efficiency

In other configurations one of these pulls tends to dominate, "pulling" the organization to adopt the corresponding configuration (e.g. the pull to "balkanize" leading to the divisionalized form). But it seems that in the case of the machine adhocracy these pulls are all strong features of the structure, which suggests that this is a different type of configuration.

Hence we would argue that there is sufficient evidence here for us to regard the machine adhocracy as new configuration: it faces a different combination of task and environment from Mintzberg's other configurations (as depicted in FIGURE 9.5); it has a new, key staff grouping (the university); and it displays a new coordinating mechanism (external adjustment).

We further believe that the machine adhocracy will only flourish if there is a strong commitment from the strategic apex to nurture this form of organization. The activities of the university are vulnerable to short-term pressures to cut costs, and, if these university activities are reduced significantly, the organization could easily revert (or convert) into a machine bureaucracy. So although the university is the key part of the structure it has little formal power. The operating core, who "own" the processes, can reject advice and help from the university, as can the apex and the technostructure. The university must *earn* the right to influence these groups by demonstrating how it can add value to the work of these groups.

IMPLICATIONS FOR MANAGERS

There are features of the machine adhocracy that are not new, they merely incorporate trends in organizations already evident. These would include:

- a release of energy, potential knowledge and insight formerly bottled up (and largely disregarded) in the operating core
- non-adversarial relationships with suppliers/distributors: partnerships and alliances
- customer-focused structures; SBU-level accountability

Other aspects of the machine adhocracy are less common, and have interesting implications for the management of organizations:

1. The machine adhocracy is not the "right answer"; thus managers should be encouraged to explore novel forms of structure, as we believe structural innovation can deliver competitive advantage.
2. The critical message of the machine adhocracy is the need to balance today's concerns for efficiency, with explicit attention being paid to building for the future. Individuals need to be tasked, encouraged and rewarded for future-oriented activities.
3. To sustain "university" activities in the face of continual short-term pressures to hit budgets requires a clear vision set at the apex, and supported by overt top team behaviours in line with this intent.
4. To bolster the forward-looking agenda, managers can increase their confidence in sustaining such future-oriented investments by better understanding the firm's current sources of advantage. Managers should get to grips with difficult concepts like know-how, culturally specific ways of doing things, and tacit knowledge, and try to understand what these mean in their particular firm's context.

The machine adhocracy has very few management layers—it is a flat structure. This raises important but difficult questions about more hierarchical structures:

5. What is the "value added" by these layers of management?
6. If the layers go, traditional concepts of a career path go with them, so
7. How to motivate staff in the absence of the prospect (often distant!) of advancement?

This last issue requires some radical thinking about "management" as a career. We believe that many individuals feel uncomfortable in their current managerial roles. They have assumed them because it was expected of them, and there were no other ways of gaining more rewards (including recognition and status).

Coupled with this problem is the increasingly insecure nature of most jobs. "Jobs-for-life" have gone. Baxi talks about *employment* security rather than *job* security. Shorter tenure, and fewer management layers, the need for adaptability coupled with the future-oriented nature of the machine adhocracy would suggest that a more imaginative approach to an employment contract should be explored. The firm can offer good salaries, interesting assignments and can guarantee that the skills and knowledge of employees will be continually developed while they stay with the organization. Status, reorganization and salary increases can be earned by excelling at the tasks in the operating core, university and technostructure, rather than through abandoning task expertise and retreating into management. This is achieved in other arenas like professional sport, and it appears in sales activities (where the best sales person can outearn the CEO), so it can be done.

But, as we have suggested, perhaps the biggest challenge for managers is the willingness and toughness required to sustain future-oriented activities when they are being pressured for short-term bottom line performance. The "softest" most vulnerable budgets tend to be those that are loosely connected (in an explicit causal manner), to the bottom line: training, R&D, market research, etc. But these are the very activities that build the future of the firm. Managers at the apex need well-thought-through strategies, built upon real insights into the nature and sources of advantage to sustain these activities in the short term.

Conclusions

There is evidence to suggest that business organizations have been undergoing significant changes to their structures. In this chapter we have added to the body of empirical evidence through the Baxi case. Clearly, one case example and some generalized evidence of structural change do not amount to conclusive evidence of new configurations of competitive strategy and organization structure. However, we believe that something interesting is occurring and that our machine adhocracy ideal type is a useful "strawman' to encourage debate and further research. There may also be other configurations at business unit and corporate levels that are viable responses to increasingly hostile competitive conditions. In this way the machine adhocracy may be vying with, for example, virtual organizations, alliance networks and forms of "learning organization". Darwinian processes may shake out less viable solutions, and they may encourage the further refinement and adaptation of those new configurations. More case evidence is required to enable us to better identify the contingent circumstances where in the machine adhocracy form might be an effective configuration.

References

Amit, R. and Schoemaker, P.J.H. (1993) "Strategic Assets and Organisational Rent", *Strategic Management Journal*, **14**, 33–46.

Barney, J. (1991) "Firm Resources and Sustained Competitive Advantage", *Journal of Management*, **17**(1), 99–120.

Bowen, D.E. and Lawler, E.E. (1992) "The Empowerment of Service Workers: What, Why, How, and When", *Sloan Management Review*, Spring, 31–39.

Boynton, A.C. and Victor, B. (1991) "Beyond Flexibility: Building and Managing the Dynamically Stable Organization", *California Management Review*, Fall, 53–66.

Conger, J.A. and Kanungo, R.N. (1988) "The Empowerment Process: Integrating Theory and Practice", *Academy of Management Review*, **13**(3), 471–482.

Cronshaw, M., Davis, E. and Kay, J. (1994) "One Being Stuck in the Middle or Good Food Costs Less at Sainsburys", *British Journal of Management*, **5**, 19–32.

Davenport, T.H. and Short, J.E. (1990) "The New Industrial Engineering: Information Technology and Business Process Redesign", *Sloan Management Review*, Summer, 11–27.

Drucker, P.F. (1992) "The New Society of Organisations", *Harvard Business Review*, Sept–Oct, 95–104.

Faulkner, D. and Bowman, C. (1992) "Generic Strategies and Congruent Organisational Structures: Some Suggestions", *European Management Journal*, **10**(4), 494–499.

Govindarajan, V. (1988) "A Contingency Approach to Strategy Implementation at the Business Unit level: Integrating Administrative Mechanisms with Strategy", *Academy of Management Journal*, **31**(4), 828–853.

Hannan, M.T. and Freeman, J.H. (1977) "The Population Ecology of Organisations", *American Journal of Sociology*, **83**, 929–964.

Heenan, D.A. (1989) "The Downside of Downsizing", *The Journal of Business Strategy*, Nov–Dec, 18–23.

Heygate, R. (1993) "Immoderate Redesign", *McKinsey Quarterly*, **1** 73–87.

Hill, C.W.L. (1988) "Differentiation versus Low Cost or Differentiation and Low Cost: a Contingency Framework", *Academy of Management Review*, **13**(3), 401–412.

Karnani, A. (1984) "Generic Competitive Strategies—an Analytical Approach", *Strategic Management Journal*, **5**, 367–380.

Knorr, R.O. (1991) "Business Process Redesign: Key to Competitiveness", *Journal of Business Strategy*, **12**(6), 48–51.

Mathur, S.S. (1988) "How Firms Compete: A New Classification of Generic Strategies", *Journal of General Management*, **14**(1), 30–60.

Miller, D. (1986) "Configurations of Strategy and Structure: Towards a Synthesis", *Strategic Management Journal*, **7**, 233–249.

Miller, D. (1990) *The Icarus Paradox: How Exceptional Companies Bring About Their Own Downfall*, New York: Harper Collins.

Miller, D. and Friesen, P.H. (1986a) "Porter's (1980) Generic Strategies and Performance: an Empirical Examination with American Data Part 1: Testing Porter", *Organisation Studies*, **7**(1), 37–55.

Miller, D. and Friesen, P.H. (1986b) "Porter's (1980) Generic Strategies and Performance: and Empirical Examination with American Data Part 2: Performance Implications", *Organisation Studies*, **7**(3), 255–261.

Mintzberg, H. (1979) *The Structuring of Organisations*, Englewood Cliffs: Prentice-Hall.

Mintzberg, H. (1989) *On Management*, New York: The Free Press.

Moenaert, R.K. and Souder, W.E. (1990) "An Information Transfer Model for Integrating Marketing and R&D Personnel in New Product Development Projects", *Journal of Product Innovation Management*, **7**, 91–107.

Murray, A.I. (1988) "A Contingency View of Porter's 'Generic Strategies'", *Academy of Management Review*, **13**(3), 390–400.

Neilson, G.L. (1990) "Restructure for Excellence", *Management Review*, February, 44–47.

Parthasarthy, R. and Sethi, S.P. (1993) "Relating Strategy and Structure to Flexible Automation: a Test of Fit and Performance Implications", *Strategic Management Journal*, **14**, 529–549.

Peters, T. (1988) *Thriving on Chaos*, London: Macmillan.

Porter, M. (1980) *Competitive Strategy*, New York: Free Press.

Porter, M. (1985) *Competitive Advantage*, New York: Free Press.

Quinn, J.B., Doorley, T.L. and Paquette, P.C. (1990) "Technology in Services: Rethinking Strategic Focus", *Sloan Management Review*, Winter, 67–78.

Ruekert, R.W. and Walker, O.C. (1987) "Marketing's Interaction with Other Functional Units: A Conceptual Framework and Empirical Evidence", *Journal of Marketing*, **51**, 1–19.

Rumelt, R. (1984) "Towards a Strategic Theory of the Firm", in R. Lamb (ed.), *Competitive Strategic Management*, Englewood Cliffs: Prentice-Hall pp. 556–570.

Skivington, J.E. and Daft, R.L. (1991) "A Study of Organisational 'Framework' and 'Process' Modalities for the Implementation of Business-level Strategic Decisions", *Journal of Management Studies*, **28**(1), 45–68.

Sohal, A.S., Keller, A.Z. and Fouad, R.H. (1988) "A Review of the Literature Relating to JIT", *International Journal of Production and Operations Management*, **9**(3), 15–25.

Wernerfelt, B. (1984) "A Resource-based View of the Firm", *Strategic Management Journal*, **5**, 171–180.

Wheelwright, S.C. and Hayes, R.H. (1985) "Competing through Manufacturing", *Harvard Business Review*, **63**(1), 99–109.

Zeffane, E.M. (1992) "Organisational Structures: Design in the Nineties", *Leadership and Organisation Development Journal*, **13**(6), 18–23.

10

Success and Failure of International Strategic Alliances: Evidence from In-depth Case Studies

DAVID FAULKNER, JOHN MCGEE

INTRODUCTION

Until the mid-1980s the strategic alliance as an organizational form was almost universally regarded as a second best, generally transitional, device. It was to be resorted to by companies only if they felt themselves too weak to handle a challenge or an opportunity entirely from their own resources (Harrigan, 1984, 1987; Stopford and Wells, 1972; Collins and Doorley, 1991; Brooke and Remmers, 1970). There was also relatively little attention devoted by researchers to identifying the way in which the apparent high failure rate of alliances could be reduced, or to conducting research to determine the key success factors for the form.

Since that time, however, the reputation of alliances has experienced a notable and positive reversal. The alliance has suddenly become the fashionable international form of the future for would-be global companies (Handy, 1992; Jarillo, 1988; Miles and Snow, 1986; Kanter, 1989), and has become an increasingly favourite topic for academic researchers and practitioner writers (Morris and Hergert at INSEAD, 1987; Glaister and Buckley, 1994).

It has also become common more generally to sing the praises of co-operative strategy to stand alongside competitive strategy as a viable, and

Strategy, Structure and Style. Edited by H. Thomas, D. O'Neal and M. Ghertman
Copyright © 1997 John Wiley & Sons Ltd.

frequently lower-risk path to the Holy Grail of sustainable competitive advantage (Bresser and Harl, 1986; Handy, 1992). It is suggested that use of market competition in all areas is both risky and wasteful of resources, for all but the dominantly strong in all areas of activity, and few companies can confidently meet that claim. By contrast co-operative strategy is more economical because it adds the strengths of one company to those of another in furthering a joint objective (Porter and Fuller, 1986). Prisoner's dilemma considerations (Axelrod, 1984) confirm that two mutually trusting co-operating agents can achieve a higher outcome for their mutual benefit, than distrusting dissimulating ones. Dynamic considerations of mutually reinforcing favourable reputations reinforce this proposition and lead to often dramatic economies in administrative as well as operational areas as trust builds and mutual monitoring becomes unnecessary. Yet the failure rate of alliances is still said to be high, though not as high as that of acquisitions in unrelated industries and fields (Porter, 1987).

It is now commonly recognized that there are a number of external forces that have made the development of alliances more likely than in the past: notably markets (Levitt, 1960 and subsequently, Chandler, 1990; Ohmae, 1989; Hrebiniak, 1992) and technologies (Stopford and Turner, 1985) have become global in nature; (Auster, 1987; Osborn and Baughn, 1987; Pucik, 1988). Life-cycles of products have become shorter, and opportunities for scale and scope economies have become increasingly important in the pursuit of lower unit costs (Porter and Fuller, 1986; Hennart, 1988). Consequently far greater investment needs have faced companies, which have often outstripped their resources. Furthermore the whole economic scene has become more turbulent and uncertain (Astley, 1984) leading to the need for more flexible organizational forms (Contractor and Lorange, 1988; Bartlett and Ghoshal, 1989) than the traditional, hierarchical multinational as described by Chandler (1986).

In response to these external forces firms have faced the imperatives of the "resource dependency perspective" (Pfeffer and Salancik, 1978), which is to say that they have become conscious that they are lacking in all the necessary resources and competencies (Prahalad and Hamel, 1990) to achieve and maintain sustainable competitive advantage. The resource or competence deficiencies may exist in a variety of areas for example, technology, marketing, access to markets, production unit costs, raw materials, special labour skills, information technology (see Paterson, 1992 for 12 distinct reasons cited by 36 separate researchers). Firms are therefore stimulated to find a partner who can supply them, and for whom they have comparably attractive qualities, such that their joint value chains are stronger than either value chain alone (Porter and Fuller, 1986). Complementarities of assets and skills, and the existence of potential synergies are therefore what they look for in a potential partner. However, the partner must have not just complementary assets and needs, but also compatible objectives, and a sensitivity to cultural differences and willingness to learn from them, if the alliance is to achieve its desired objectives and to progress beyond them.

It is one thing to negotiate an alliance, and quite another to make it work successfully. This, it is suggested in the literature, depends upon choosing the appropriate alliance form (Gupta and Singh, 1991), selecting the right partner, setting up the right management systems and then placing a high emphasis on the "softer" more intangible elements of the relationship. These include adopting an attitude of trust (Hill, 1990) and of high commitment from top management down, developing bonding mechanisms to keep the partners together, and adopting a philosophy of continuous learning (Kogut, 1988; Senge, 1992). If such attitudes are genuinely adopted by the partners the key touchstone of success of an alliance is likely to be realized, namely it will *evolve* from its initial limits into something wider, deeper and more important to the partners, probably than that which was initially envisaged (Teramoto, Kanda and Iwasaki, 1991; Bertodo, 1990; Johanson and Mattsson, 1991).

This chapter addresses the problems of achieving long-term success of strategic alliances. Specifically we argue that (a) alliances can be stable and non-transitory, and (b) long-term success is a function of the prospective economic benefits, the form of the alliance, the management processes and systems of the alliance, and the degree to which the partners adopt a positive learning philosophy.

This chapter reports research on 10 international strategic alliances and the nature and strength of the relationship between long-term success and the four categories of key variables; economic benefits, alliance form, management process and capacity to learn.

THE PROPOSITIONS

The propositions considered in this research cover a wide range of issues in the formation and management of alliances. However, they all stem from a central proposition, namely that strategic alliances, if appropriately set up and managed, can be more than mere transitory forms. Moreover, their stability can be as high, or indeed as low, as other more traditional organizational forms. The key to this general proposition lies in four groups of subsidiary propositions concerning the formation of alliances: the economic benefits, the chosen form of the alliance, the management processes of the alliance, and the approach to learning adopted by the alliance. The issue of *formation* concerns the external conditions within which the economic benefits to the alliance are conceived, the internal motivations of the partners, and the partner selection process. The issue of *form* highlights the importance of choosing an appropriate structure within which legal, financial and managerial actions can be taken appropriate to the context of the alliance. The *organization and management* issue relates to the nature of the internal organization structure, the clarity of the management systems and procedures, and the nature of the managerial interaction between the partners. The approach to *learning and evolution* refers to the way in which continuous learning and development take place within the alliance.

The general proposition is that long-term stability and evolution of an alliance are related to certain enabling conditions in alliance formation, the choice of alliance form, the nature of alliance management, and the importance of a positive attitude and approach to learning and alliance evolution. In particular it will be argued that the critical management characteristics include commitment, mutual trust and understanding, and cultural sensitivity, coupled with a positive and productive learning environment.

ALLIANCE FORMATION AND THE ECONOMIC BENEFITS

It is conventionally held that an appropriate strategic fit needs to be struck between the external conditions provoking the need for action, the internal circumstances in the partner companies leading the partners to decide that an alliance between them is the best solution for them to a pressing need, and the structural and organizational form chosen for the co-operative enterprise (Faulkner, 1994). Further to this, we maintain that the nature of external market forces requires that a longer-term view be taken of the development of critical resources and core competences. These competences are not readily found or constructed and therefore companies are impelled to search for partners with whom they can work, from whom they can learn, and critically with whom they can build new, joint competences to create new competitive advantages (Porter and Fuller, 1986; Lorange and Roos, 1992; Lynch, 1990; Bleakley and Devlin, 1988).

Partner selection is a critical element in the success of the enterprise. If the long-term remedying of resource deficiency is the driving force in the search for an ally, the identification in that potential ally of complementary assets and potential synergies is the critical factor in partner selection (Porter and Fuller, 1986; Lorange and Roos, 1992; Lynch, 1990; Bleakley and Devlin, 1988). Other relevant considerations are not to select a partner of very different strength, either stronger or weaker (Bleeke and Ernst, 1991), or the alliance is likely to fall into one-sided dependency (Bertodo, 1990). Similar cultures are not felt to be vital in partner selection but cultural compatibility (or at least sensitivity to cultural differences) must be achieved, otherwise the alliance may be unlikely to succeed (Kanter, 1989;

Lorange and Roos, 1992). The proposition in relation to partner selection is that the key criteria for partner selection are (a) complementary assets (Porter and Fuller, 1986), (b) the existence of synergies between the companies (Lorange and Roos, 1992), (c) approximate balance in size and strength (Bleeke and Ernst, 1991) and (d) "compatible cultures" (Kanter, 1989).

ALLIANCE FORM

The legal form of an alliance provides the framework within which the scope of the alliance and its management processes can be addressed by the partners. In the context of the desired long-term objectives an appropriate form can provide flexibility and decision autonomy whereas an inappropriate form can constrain partners and unduly limit autonomy. There are many ways of classifying alliances. For the purpose of this chapter a very simple and basic classification is made as follows:

1. *Joint ventures*—where two companies set up a separate joint venture company, e.g. EVC is a joint venture formed by ICI and Enichem of Italy.
2. *A collaboration*—where two companies co-operate over a range of activities without forming a separate company, e.g. the Rover/Honda alliance.
3. *A consortium*—where a number of companies set up a new consortium company to carry out a major project or activity, e.g. International Digital Corporation, the Japanese telecommunications consortium set up by Cable and Wireless and a number of Japanese partners including C Itoh and Toyota Corporation.

MANAGING THE ALLIANCE

The management of an alliance concerns the nature of the organizational (as opposed to legal) arrangements both between the partners and internally within the partner companies. Certain principles should underpin the organizational arrangements if friction and other problems are to be avoided; their explicit adoption is important to a smoothly functioning alliance:

- establishment of dispute resolution mechanisms (Spekman and Sawhney, 1991; Collins and Doorley, 1991)
- clear authority vested in the chief executive (Lorange and Probst, 1987)
- an appropriate legal form (Faulkner, 1994)
- a divorce mechanism agreed at the outset (Taucher, 1988)

- processes for wide dissemination of information within the alliance (Kanter, 1989)
- non-conflicting long-term objectives (Spekman and Sawhney, 1991)

An alliance without commitment and trust from the top down may soon wither away in its performance and in its importance to the partner companies (Lorange and Roos, 1992; Kanter, 1989). Furthermore for the alliance to be effective the partners must have positive attitudes towards the alliance, notably:

- a sensitive attitude to national and corporate cultural differences (Kanter, 1989)
- strong commitment by top management in the partner companies (Anderson and Narus, 1990)
- mutual trust (Lynch, 1990)

ALLIANCE EVOLUTION AND THE CAPACITY TO LEARN

An alliance may run effectively for a time but never reach its full potential and ultimately wither away. Such a fate may well be largely dependent upon whether constant attempts have been made to ensure the perpetual evolution of the relationship between the partners (Lorange and Roos, 1992; Achrol, Scheer and Stern, 1990). This may be done by regularly looking for new things that partners can do together, and adopting an exceptionally flexible attitude to change in relation to alliance arrangements (Lorange and Probst, 1987). As Bleeke and Ernst (1991) put it: "The hallmark of successful alliances that endure is their ability to evolve beyond initial expectations and objectives."

For the alliance to succeed long term, it needs to evolve through the partners constantly

- seeking new things to do together (Lorange and Roos, 1992)
- accepting new responsibilities (Achrol, Scheer, and Stern, 1990)
- adjusting flexibly to change (Lorange and Probst, 1987)

In essence, an alliance is a learning arrangement between companies with different things to teach and learn (Hamel, 1991). If the partners enter the alliance understanding this, the continual evolution of the arrangement for mutual benefit is highly probable. A capacity to learn might be indicated by setting up explicit systems to disseminate learning, and explicit reviews of current learning and planned/expected learning (Kogut, 1988; Nelson and Winter, 1982). Therefore, for the greatest prognosis of successful evolution, a philosophy of constant learning (Collins and Doorley, 1991; Teramoto *et al.*, 1991) should be adopted by the partners.

METHODOLOGY

Between 5 and 7 executives from each of the 10 alliances were interviewed in depth to develop a self-assessment and peer review analysis within which the propositions could be addressed. Alliances were then categorized in terms of their degree of long-term success and an attempt was made to explain why differences in long-term performance had arisen. The 10 alliances were set up over a lengthy period in the last 20 years or so. The majority were founded in the last 10 years, however, and all are international, in that there is at least one non-UK partner, or they are operating in the international market. The alliances are listed in TABLE 10.1.

TABLE 10.1   The Alliance Case Studies

Alliance	Parents	Initial focus	Form	Life
ICI Pharma	ICI Sumitomo (Japan)	Pharmaceuticals in Japan	JV	1972–
EVC	ICI Enichem (Italy)	PVC in Europe	JV	1986–
Imperial–Wintermans	Imperial Group Henri Wintermans (Holland)	Cigars in UK	Collaboration	1989–
Dowty–SEMA	Dowty Group SEMA Group (France)	Command and control systems in UK	JV	1982–93
Courtaulds–Nippon	Courtaulds Nippon Paint (Japan)	Marine paint in Japan	Collaboration	1976–
Eurobrek	European food co. American food co.	Breakfast cereals in Europe	JV	1989–
International Digital Corporation	Cable & Wireless Toyota and C. Itoh + 20 others (Japan)	Tele-communications in Japan	Consortium	1986–
Rover–Honda	Rover Honda (Japan)	Automobiles in Europe	Collaboration	1986–94
Royal Bank of Scotland–Banco Santander	Royal Bank of Scotland Banco Santander (Spain)	Banking in Europe	Collaboration with cross-shareholding	1988–
ICL–Fujitsu	ICL Fujitsu (Japan)	Computing in UK	Collaboration with shareholding	1982–

Effectiveness or success was also self-assessed by the respondents who responded to questions covering the following:

1. agreed objectives achieved to a degree acceptable to the partners;
2. spin-off benefits realized;
3. internal morale among alliance personnel is high;
4. the alliance has a good reputation in the partner companies;
5. the reputation of the alliance in the industry is high.

Of these five criteria (Faulkner, 1994), the first two relate to achievements more or less objectively definable. Criteria three, four and five refer to reputational aspects of the alliance perceived in the alliance itself, in the partner companies, and in the industry generally.

An analysis of these responses suggested three categories of alliance according to the level of success achieved. The *limited* alliances were those that met the minimum initial objectives but are felt to have no potential for further development. The *latent* alliances were also successful up to a point, but were held back from enhanced success by one or more factors in relation to how they were set up or run. The *dynamic* alliances were those that had been successful beyond initial aspirations and were continuing to evolve in a positive fashion.

The limited alliances were judged to be ICI Pharma (IP), EVC and Imperial–Wintermans (IW). The latent alliances were Dowty–SEMA (DS), Courtaulds–Nippon Paint (CN), Eurobrek (EB) and Cable and Wireless (CWC), and the dynamic alliances were Rover–Honda (RH). The Royal Bank of Scotland–Banco Santander (RBSS) alliance, and ICL–Fujitsu (IF). A synopsis of each of the 10 case studies is available from the authors but a short description of each alliance is contained in Appendix 1.

TABLE 10.2 illustrates the authors' judgments of the partners' success in what are perceived to be the areas critical to alliance success. As can be seen, the dynamic alliances have a dominance of A judgements, and the latent ones of B judgements. C judgements are strongly in evidence in the limited alliances.

IMPLICATIONS FOR SUCCESS AND FAILURE

LEGAL FORM

Legal form by itself does not appear to have a direct and strong effect on long-term performance. Its effect is more likely to be indirect and to reflect the underlying long-term wishes of the partners. Four of the 10 alliances were joint ventures, one was a consortium, and 5 can be described as collaborations.

TABLE 10.2   The ten alliances: ratings of effectiveness

Alliances	1	2	3	4	5	6	7	8	9	10
Economic benefits	A	B	A	B	A	B+	A	A	A−	A
Top management commitment	C	C	C	C	B+	B−	B	A	A	A
Sensitivity to differences	C	C	B	C	B+	B	A	B+	A−	A
Goal congruence	B	C	C	B	C	A	B	A	A	A
Organizational clarity	C	A	A	C	B+	B	A	B+	A	A
Attitude to learning	C	C	B	C	C	C	B+	A	A−	A
Effectiveness	Ltd	Ltd	Ltd	Lat	Lat	Lat	Lat	Dyn	Dyn	Dyn

Notes: 1 = ICI Pharma; 2 = EVC; 3 = Imperial–Wintermans; 4 = Dowty–SEMA; 5 = Courtaulds–Nippon; 6 = Eurobrek; 7 = International Digital Corporation; 8 = Rover–Honda; 9 = Royal Bank of Scotland–Banco Santander; 10 = ICL–Fujitsu.
Ltd = Limited; Lat = Latent; Dyn = Dynamic.
Source: Authors' assessment except "effectiveness" which is self-assessed in interview/questionnaire.

However, the joint venture (JV) form contains precise commitments and certain constraints which can inhibit the discretion of management and might restrain the development of flexibility required for longer-term evolution (for example, by restricting product or geographic scope). Thus IP, EVC, DS and EB are so confined by their JV agreements so that the climate for developing closer ties and stronger management links between partners is constrained. Perhaps it is not surprising that none of these alliances is perceived to be "dynamic'. In contrast the looser relationships developed by IW, CN, RH and IF seem to permit a more flexible operation both in theory and in practice. The CWC is a clear example of the need to establish a particular legal form to comprehend the variety and diversity of interests of a large number of partners (23 in this case).

ALLIANCE FORMATION AND ECONOMIC BENEFITS

This sample of alliances was selected for the longevity of the relationships and it is no surprise to observe that all have met at least some of their initial objectives. Probably the least successful measured in economic terms are EVC, DS and EB. The nature of the EVC JV forces it to buy raw materials from its shareholders at above market prices and to produce in its partners' factories. This may serve the purposes of the shareholders but limits the independence and the success of the JV itself. DS also lacked its own independent assets and as a JV did not progress beyond a "shop-window"—effective though that role might have been. EB is also perceived as lacking true autonomy and self-sufficiency. Here we see a clear theme— the formation of these alliances contain restrictions on autonomy and independent potential for future growth.

In contrast, the other seven alliances have enjoyed more autonomy and more obvious success. They all exhibit complementary assets, usually technology and production capabilities are matched with market access. In the case of RBSS the initial specification of objectives was less clear and the nature of the asset complementarity was, *ab initio*, not so obvious. Here the immediate economic benefits seem to weigh less heavily than the morale, reputation and other non-economic benefits. At the other extreme, there are two examples where the economic benefits might be calibrated in terms of survival, RH and IF.

These 10 cases demonstrate, not unexpectedly, the importance of strategic considerations being taken into account in the formative stages of an alliance. The nature of and access to markets, the resource characteristics of partners and their risk profiles, and their internal cost structures, and the process of selecting partners all figure very clearly in these cases. However, we see more diversity between the 10 alliances when we look at the ways in which the alliances were managed and their demonstrated capacity to learn and to evolve beyond their initial states.

ORGANIZATION AND MANAGEMENT

The four variables used under this heading are organizational clarity, goal congruence, sensitivity to company differences and top management commitment. The 10 cases break into 2 groups. Five alliances score low on these variables. They are IP, DS, EVC, IW and CN (see TABLE 10.3). A factor common to four of them is the perceived lack of top management commitment. IP's lack seems to stem from their perception of a serious imbalance in the

Table 10.3   Alliance success and failure

Low performers	High performers
ICI Pharma	Eurobrek
EVC	International Digital Corporation
Dowty–SEMA	Rover–Honda
Imperial–Wntermans	RBS–Banco Santander
Courtaulds–Nippon	ICL–Fujitsu

Source: Authors' assessment.

sharing out of the gains. EVC and DS with their lack of independence show a corresponding low level of commitment. The IW alliance is confounded by the conflict of interest on the part of BAT as Wintermans' owners.

Three of the five demonstrate lack of sensitivity to partner issues and concerns. ICI are fundamentally disaffected in their relationship with Sumitomo in IP. ICI and Enichem (in EVC) are each very self-interested, as also were Dowty and SEMA. Goal congruence also scores very low in three of the five. ICI and Enichem (in EVC) have a very limited sphere of agreement focused on the problems of overcapacity in basic chemicals. Beyond this there are few evident areas of common agreement. Similarly Imperial and Wintermans achieved only the initial objectives and found it difficult to see how to develop further common goals given the attitude of Wintermans' parent, BAT. Courtaulds and Nippon found their interests and ambitions to be diverging as Nippon became increasingly globally ambitious whereas Courtaulds wished to operate behind territorial non-competition clauses in the alliance agreement. In contrast ICI and Sumitomo, and Dowty and SEMA had very clear ideas about their competitive strategy agendas in their core businesses.

Organizational clarity showed a greater range of responses for the five low performers. EVC and IW are both very clear about their working arrangements. CN also work well together. However, IP and DS have organizational problems. Of these five, CN stand out as being rather better: their real failure is lack of well-articulated common goals. The others show a wide range of serious organizational deficiencies.

The top five provide a sharp contrast. EB, CWC, RH, RBSS and IF all demonstrate good to excellent ratings on the four principal dimensions. Goal congruence is of particular interest. The partners in these alliances do not just share some common operational goals. They also have long-term goals which are not inconsistent with each other but which can only be secured through mutual sharing of resources. This appears to be the essence of a "good" alliance—helping each other to achieve separate and common goals through sharing of resources and assets. However, there are signs of tensions in this group. Both EB and CWC have some problems with top-level commitment. EB also is only average on sensitivity to partners and on organizational clarity—and is, therefore, the laggard in this group.

Three alliances achieve very high sensitivity scores. CWC and RBSS from the beginning set out to manage the differences between their partners. RH had a very stormy experience in its early days from which a remarkable sensitivity has developed. The loose collaborative structure of RH has meant that its working arrangements (organizational clarity) have not always been clear. But the evidence points to remarkable progress on this as well by virtue of the informal elements in their organization.

RBSS and IF rate very high on all four measures and clearly feel extremely comfortable as partners in their working relationship. This is again remarkable in the case of the two banks because the benefits are much more in the long term with corresponding difficulties in prescribing joint working arrangements.

ALLIANCE EVOLUTION AND THE CAPACITY TO LEARN

The notion of learning is particularly difficult to capture across different organizations. We borrow from Senge (1990: p.5) in describing what is meant by a learning philosophy:

> organizations where people continually expand their capacities to create the results they truly desire, where new and expansive patterns of thinking are nurtured, where collective aspiration is set free, and where people are continually learning how to learn.

We operationalize this by concentrating on the notion of mutual and collective benefits (aspirations) emerging and changing over time, on the creation of new responsibilities, and on the seeking for new things to do together. The idea that learning is taking place is indicated by these characteristics.

On this basis we again obtain the same two groups with the one difference that EB becomes a member of the laggard group. The circumstances of EB makes its low capacity unsurprising. The commitment of the partners and top management is somewhat lacking and its lack of true autonomy is significant. Thus EB can be seen as operationally effective, meeting its immediate strategic goals, but lacking in long-term strategic direction—and therefore ranks as a "latent" alliance (viz. "OK but could do better").

The high learners clearly demonstrate this capacity. IF has developed and extended product lines, adjusted its working relationships over time, and has entered new markets sometimes with one and sometimes with the other as lead organization. RBSS developed a major new consortium (IBOS). RH has developed new products, shared technologies, and assisted each other in building and rebuilding factories. It is salutary to note that Rover's parent, British Aerospace (BAe), had long-term objectives inconsistent with those of Honda which led eventually to the sale of Rover to BMW (although Honda did have first refusal). The weakness in this alliance was the construction of the relationship between a principal (Honda) and a subsidiary (Rover) within which true long-term mutual benefit could not be worked out as BAe were not party to any of the alliance activity. CWC has been able to set up a further joint venture and the consortium has achieved market share and revenue gains well beyond its original hopes.

By contrast the laggards have shown little evidence of learning. The lack of true autonomy affects EVC, DS and EB. The divergent interests of the partners affects IP, IW and CN.

SUCCESS AND FAILURE: THE CAUSES?

Three general propositions emerge from this discussion. The first is that any lack of agreement on long-term aims and ambitions and/or the creation of alliance structures without sufficient independence in decision making or control over its value chain will result in an inability to progress beyond initial objectives (cf. IP, EVC, IW, DS, EB and CN). Second, those alliances rated as "dynamic" were very clear about their organizational arrangements and management processes. Third, the most dynamic alliances showed a capacity to learn and an ability to evolve from their initial foundation conditions.

The laggards in this limited sample all had deficiencies in their formative stages and therefore set up legal forms and organizational arrangements which were not conducive for longer-term development. These alliances were predestined *not* to change and develop. The high performers seemed to avoid the legal and organizational traps (although more work needs to be done on the question of any *intent* to avoid such traps). But they did exhibit a quality of organization and management of an appreciably higher order than those in the other group and this seems to be important in their ability to learn and to achieve results beyond the levels originally expected. This degree of success can be expressed in four propositions which emerge from the analysis and which deserve further attention:

1. The most important factors necessary for the development of a successful alliance would seem to be contained in the concept of a close relationship between the partners, such that they demonstrate flexible, trusting and committed attitudes towards each other. In contrast the nature of the motivation for alliance creation, and the choice of form do not seem to be very important factors in the equation leading to a successful outcome for the alliance.
2. Good organizational arrangements, especially in relation to information dissemination, and dispute resolution, e.g. the establishment of "gateways", enable the inevitably difficult problem of managing an enterprise by consensus to be carried out with a good chance of success.
3. The essence of a successful alliance must be to learn from one's partner, and not just to use the partner's skills to substitute for one's own deficiencies. Adoption by both partners of a learning philosophy, but within a situation in which personal and inter-company bonding has taken place is therefore a good sign for a successful alliance.

4. An evolving partnership in which new projects and new responsibilities emerge, often not thought about at the outset, heralds a successful partnership.

Of the factors identified above, by far and away the most important seems to be the commitment, mutual trust and flexibility of the relationship between the partners. Given such positive attitudes, any frictional problems can be resolved. However, in the absence of flexible and trusting relationships any problem encountered places the relationship in jeopardy.

APPENDIX 1

THE CASE STUDIES

The Limited Alliances

Case #1:   ICI Pharma

ICI Pharma is a joint venture set up in 1972 by ICI Pharmaceuticals (60%) and Sumitomo Chemicals (40%) to produce and market certain ICI pharmaceutical products in Japan. ICI provides the product specification. Sumitomo manufactures the product and achieved Japanese registration, and the joint venture ICI Pharma sells and distributes it.

Case Study #2:   EVC

EVC is a joint venture set up in 1986 by ICI and Enichem of Italy to rationalize the production and sales of PVC in Europe. In order to do this it was judged necessary to take up to 1 million tonnes of capacity out of the joint capacity of the two partners. EVC is a 50:50 owned venture company based in Belgium, with the remit to sell PVC and allied products based largely on ICI and Enichem raw material and manufactured in plants still run by ICI and Enichem respectively.

Case Study #3:   Imperial–Wintermans

The collaboration between Imperial and Henri Wintermans in the marketing of Wintermans' cigars in the UK is an alliance that exchanges UK market access provided by Imperial for Wintermans, for technology transfer provided by Wintermans to update Imperial's cigar manufacturing technology. The alliance was formalized in 1989, and has been successful in that Imperial has met its target for sales of Wintermans' cigars, and Wintermans has transferred its technology.

The Latent Alliances

Case Study #4:   Dowty–SEMA

Dowty–Sema was set up as a joint venture in 1982 by the current partners' predecessor companies at the instigation of the Ministry of Defence, in order to provide an alternative tenderer to Ferranti in the specialized market of command and control systems for ships. Until its integration into Bae-Sema in 1992 it was 50:50 owned by Dowty and SEMA.

Case Study #5:   Courtaulds–Nippon Paint

Courtaulds set up a collaborative alliance with Nippon Paint of Japan in 1976, because it needed a reliable Japanese company to service its and its customers' needs in Japan. Nippon for its part wished to rise in the league table of Japanese marine paint companies, and regarded an alliance with Courtaulds, the acknowledged world leader in the area, as a significant step in helping it achieve this aim.

Case Study #6:   Eurobrek

The name Eurobrek is a fictitious one invented to represent the joint venture company set up in 1989 by two major European and American food companies to compete in Europe against Kellogg's in the breakfast cereals market. A confidentiality agreement precludes the use of the real names. The joint venture operates from a base in the UK and, largely as a result of purchasing the cereal interests of another major UK producer, it already has in excess of 10% of the UK market.

Case Study #7:   International Digital Corporation

Cable and Wireless are pursuing a strategy of becoming a global force in the telecommunications market. Given their limited size in global terms, this requires development through strategic alliances. The Japanese market is clearly important for this strategy, and C&W determined in 1986 to attempt to obtain the licence to become the second Japanese international carrier. In order to do this they decided that a consortium company needed to be set up including some major Japanese corporations in order to achieve credibility with the Japanese government. International Digital Corporation was therefore founded, with C&W, Toyota and C Itoh each holding 17% of the equity and about 20 Japanese shareholders sharing the remainder. The consortium was, after a considerable battle with the Japanese government, successful in obtaining the international carrier licence.

The Dynamic Alliances

Case Study #8:   Rover–Honda

The collaboration between Rover and Honda was a very long-lasting one that led to the resurrection of Rover as a quality car maker, and the effective entry of Honda into the European market. It started in 1979 as a simple arm's-length franchise for Rover to assemble a Honda car in the UK, badge it as a Triumph and market it, and subsequently developed into a very extensive alliance including joint manufacturing, joint sourcing, design and R & D. Only marketing and distribution were handled separately in the UK.

Case Study #9:   RBS–Banco Santander

The collaboration alliance between the Royal Bank of Scotland and Banco Santander of Spain set up in 1988, is partial union of two medium-sized national banks in the face of the expected Europeanization of the banking industry. The partners own a small minority of each others' shares. The alliance operates on many fronts, including joint ventures in Germany and Gibraltar, and a consortium for money transfer covering a number of European countries. This consortium, named IBOS, is to date the most successful part of the alliance, and was not foreseen as a significant project at the outset of the alliance, demonstrating the importance of allowing evolutionary forces to develop in successful alliances.

Case Study #10:   ICL–Fujitsu

The collaboration between ICL and Fujitsu came about in stages over a 10-year period. It began as technology co-operation in 1982, and then extended through Fujitsu buying a minority of ICL equity, to the present situation where the Japanese partner owns 80% of ICL, but is pledged to treat it as a partner rather than as a subsidiary, and to place a large part of its shareholding back on the market at an opportune time.

REFERENCES

Achrol, R.S., Scheer, L.K., and Stern, L.W. (1990) "Designing Successful Transorganizational Marketing Alliances," Report No. 90–118, Cambridge Mass.: Marketing Science Institute.

Anderson, J. and Narus, J. (1990) "A Model of Distribution Firm and Manufacturing Firm Working Partnership", *Journal of Marketing Research*, **54**.

Asley, W.G. (1984) "Towards an Appreciation of Collective Strategy", *Academy of Management Review*, **9**(3), 526–535.

Auster, E.R. (1987) "International Corporate Linkages: Dynamic Forms in Changing Environments", *Columbia Journal of World Business*, Summer, **22**, 2, 3–6.

Axelrod, R. (1984), *The Evolution of Cooperation*. New York: Harper Collins.

Bartlett, C.A. and Ghoshal, S. (1989) *Managing across Borders*. London: Hutchinson.

Bertodo, R. (1990) "The Collaboration Vortex: Anatomy of a Euro-Japanese Alliance", *EIU Japanese Motor Business*, Summer, 29–43.

Bleakley, M. and Devlin, G. (1988) "Strategic Alliances—Guidelines for Success", *Long Range Planning* **21**(5), 18–23.

Bleeke, J. and Ernst, D. (1991) "The Way to Win in Cross-Border Alliances", *Harvard Business Review*, Nov/Dec, 127–135.

Bresser, R.K. and Harl, J.E. (1986) "Collective Strategy: Vice or Virtue", *Academy of Management Review*, **11**(2), 408–427.

Brooke, M.Z. and Remmers, H.L. (1970) *The Strategy of the Multinational Enterprise*. London: Longman.

Chandler, A.D. (1986) "The Evolution of Modern Global Competition", in M.E. Porter (ed.) *Competition in Global Industries*, Boston, Mass.: Harvard Business School Press, 405–449.

Chandler, A.D. (1990) *Scale and Scope: The Dynamics of Industrial Capitalism*. Boston, Mass.: Harvard University Press.

Collins, T. and Doorley, T. (1991) *Teaming Up for the 90's*. Illinois: Homewood.

Contractor, F.J. and Lorange, P. (eds) (1988) "Why Should Firms Cooperate?: The Strategy and Economic Basis for Cooperative Ventures" chapter in *Cooperative Strategies in International Business*, Boston, Mass.: Lexington Books, 1–28.

Faulkner, D.O. (1994) *International Strategic Alliances: Cooperating to Compete*. McGraw-Hill, Maidenhead.

Glaister, K.W. and Buckley, P.J. (1994) "UK International Joint Venture: An Analysis of Patterns of Activity and Distribution", *British Journal of Management*, 5, 33–51.

Gupta, A.K. and Singh, H. (1991) "The Governance of Synergy: Inter-SBU Coordination vs External Strategic Alliances", Academy of Management Conference, Miami, unpublished.

Hamel, G. (1991) "Competition for Competence and Inter-partner Learning within International Strategic Alliances", *Strategic Management Journal*, 12, 83–103.

Handy, C. (1992) "Balancing Corporate Power: A New Federalist Paper", *Harvard Business Review*, Nov/Dec, 59–72.

Harrigan, K.R. (1984) "Joint Ventures and Global Strategies", *Columbia Journal of World Business*, 19(2), Summer, 7–16.

Harrigan, K.R. (1987) "Strategic Alliances: Their New Role in Global Competition", *Journal of World Business*, Summer, 22, 2, 67–69.

Hennart, J.F. (1988) "A Transaction Cost Theory of Equity Joint Ventures", *Strategic Management Journal*, 9, 361–374.

Hill, C.W.L. (1990) "Cooperation, Opportunism, and the Invisible Hand: Implications for Transaction Cost Theory", *Academy of Management Review*, 15(3), 500–513.

Hrebiniak, L.G. (1992) "Implementing Global Strategies", *European Management Journal*, 10(4), Dec, 392–403.

Jarillo, J.C. (1988) "On Strategic Networks", *Strategic Management Journal*, 9, 31–41.

Johanson, J. and Mattsson, L-G. (1991) "Interorganisational Relations in Industrial Systems: a Network Approach Compared with the Transaction-Cost Approach", in G. Thompson, J. Frances, R. Levacic and J. Mitchell (eds) *Markets, Hierarchies and Networks*, London: Sage Publications, pp. 256–264.

Kanter, R.M. (1989) *When Giants Learn to Dance*. London: Simon and Schuster.

Kogut, B. (1988) "Joint Ventures: Theoretical and Empirical Perspectives", *Strategic Management Journal*, 9, 319–32.

Levitt, T. (1960) "Marketing Myopia", *Harvard Business Review*, Jul–Aug, nk.

Lorange, P. and Probst, G.J.B. (1987) "Joint Ventures as Self-organizing Systems: a Key to Successful Joint Venture Design and Implementation", *Columbia Journal of World Business*, Summer, 22, 2, 71–78.

Lorange, P. and Roos, J. (1992) *Strategic Alliances: Formation, Implementation and Evolution*. Oxford: Basil Blackwell.

Lynch, R.P. (1990) "Building Alliances to Penetrate European Markets", *Journal of Business Strategy*, March/April, 4–8.

Miles, R.E. and Snow, C.C. (1986) "Organizations: New Concepts for New Forms", *California Management Review*, 28, 62–73.

Morris, D. and Hergert M. (1987) "Trends in International Collaborative Agreements", *Columbia Journal of World Business*, Summer, 22, 2, 15–21.

Nelson, E.R. and Winter, S.G. (1982) *An Evolutionary Theory of Economic Change*. Cambridge, Mass.: Harvard University Press.

Ohmae, K. (1989) "The Global Logic of Strategic Alliances", *Harvard Business Review*, March/April, 143–154.

Osborn, R.N. and Baughn, C.C. (1987) "New Patterns in the Formation of

US/Japanese Cooperative Ventures: The Role of Technology", *Columbia Journal of World Business*, Summer, 57–64.

Paterson, D. (1992) "Cooperation for Competition: The Formation and Growth of 'Strategic' Networks in the International Motor Vehicle Industry 1959–1988", unpublished Ph.D dissertation, University of Illinois.

Pfeffer, J. and Salancik, G. (1978) *The External Control of Organizations*. New York: Harper.

Porter, M.E. (1987) "From Competitive Advantage to Corporate Strategy", *Harvard Business Review*, May/June, 9–25.

Porter, M.E. and Fuller, M.B. (1986) "Coalitions and Global Strategy", in M.E. Porter (ed.) *Competition in Global Industries*, Cambridge, Mass.: Harvard University Press, 315–345.

Prahalad, C.K. and Hamel, G. (1990) "The Core Competence of the Corporation", *Harvard Business Review*, **90**, 79–91.

Pucik, V. (1988) "Strategic Alliances, Organizational Learning, and Competitive Advantage: The HRM Agenda", *Human Resource Management*, **27**(1), Spring, 77–93.

Senge, P.M. (1990) "The Leader's New Work: Building Learning Organizations", *MIT Sloan Management Review*, Fall, **32**, 7–23.

Senge, P.M. (1992), *The 5th Discipline: The Art and Practice of the Learning Organization*. London: Century Business.

Spekman, R.E. and Sawhney K. (1991) *Towards a Conceptual Understanding of the Antecedents of Strategic Alliances*, Management Science Institute, Report No. 90/114, Cambridge, Mass.

Stopford, J.M. and Turner, L. (1985) *Britain and the Multinationals*. Chichester: Wiley.

Stopford, J.M. and Wells, I. (1972) *Managing the Multi-National Enterprise*. London: Longman.

Taucher, G. (1988) "Beyond Alliances", IMD Perspectives for Managers, No. 1.

Teramoto, Y., Kanda, M., and Iwasaki, N. (1991) *The Strategic Alliances between Japanese and European Companies—Cooperative Competition, A Growth Strategy for the 90s*, Research Report No. 91–05, Tokyo.

11

The Unit of Activity: Towards an Alternative to the Theories of the Firm

KNUT HAANES, BENTE R. LOWENDAHL

INTRODUCTION

This chapter discusses limitations of previous theories of the firm, and based on this introduces an alternative unit of analysis—the *unit of activity*. The main characteristics of the unit of activity are introduced and illustrated; namely that people can belong to several activities simultaneously; that organizations consist of several units of activity; that units of activity are established and disappear continually; and that value-creating units of activity can be found inside an organization, between organizations and outside organizations.

Furthermore, we argue that utilizing the unit of activity is more suitable for understanding organizational processes than analyzing the firm. We link the unit of activity to the resource-based perspective. The discussion of the resource-based perspective and of resources *per se* is illustrated with insights from several research projects in knowledge-intensive organizations undertaken by the authors, most notably a case study on the Lillehammer Olympic Organizing Committee, but also on a business school, a biotechnology company, and studies of four engineering consulting firms.

Finally, we link the concept of units of activity back to firms, arguing that a key difference between dynamic and nondynamic firms is their ability to

Strategy, Structure and Style. Edited by H. Thomas, D. O'Neal and M. Ghertman
Copyright © 1997 John Wiley & Sons Ltd.

appropriate value from activities and conversely to stay away from nonvalue-creating activities. Since value-creating activities may be situated inside or outside the firm, the issue of whether or not the key resources in dynamic activities belong formally to the firm becomes rather inconsequential.

THE NEED FOR AN ALTERNATIVE THEORY OF THE FIRM

Today's complex organizations face challenges that are fundamentally different from those driving firm establishment and growth only a few decades ago. These challenges include:

(a) rapid changes in technologies and tastes;
(b) continuously changing political contexts;
(c) gradually more intense international competition;
(d) fast economic changes;
(e) the increasing role of knowledge as a competitive resource.

Still, our theories of why firms exist and why and how they grow are predominantly based on the assumptions and models developed several decades ago (e.g. Coase, 1937; Cyert and March, 1963).

According to Holmstrom and Tirole (1989), a theory of the firm needs to answer two fundamental questions, namely (1) why do firms exist, and (2) what limits their scale and scope? Whereas the first question remains interesting in a postmodern society, we regard the second question as outdated, as the scale and scope of the firm may be redefined in seconds through extensive networks at all stages of the value creation process. Instead, the fundamental question of "What is a firm?" also needs to be raised for a theory of the firm to be meaningful when a large part of the value creation attributed to it does not really belong to the firm's owners.

In a recent extension of the theory of the growth of the firm proposed by Penrose (1959), researchers in the strategy field have returned to a focus on firm resources (Barney, 1991; Conner, 1991; Itami, 1987; Prahalad and Hamel, 1990; Rumelt, 1984; Teece, Pisano, and Shuen, 1990; van de Ven, 1992; Wernerfelt, 1984). The development of this new perspective may be seen as a reaction to the previous emphasis on environmental analysis—on opportunities and threats—which can be exemplified by the work on economies of scale and imperfect factor markets (Bain, 1948) and the Industrial Organization (IO) economics based work on competitive advantage (Porter, 1980).

However, as illustrated in further detail below, the concept of a firm's resources is problematic in complex organizations. Even in the resource-based perspective the issue of how resources are mobilized is not clearly addressed. The value of resources is implicitly treated as given, i.e. if you have them they will perform. We regard this to be directly wrong. While recognizing the importance of analyzing resources, we will argue that the real challenge is to energize the people in the organization to better utilize and build on available resources. We suggest that neither the concept of the firm nor the concept of firm resources is the most appropriate unit of analysis for future studies of strategic processes. Two major challenges lead us to this conclusion.

First, value-creating resources are increasingly intangible, invisible, and hence extremely difficult to define. Such resources are very hard to observe and even more difficult for a firm to control. As a result, the resource as a unit of analysis has proven problematic in empirical research, and it is not surprising that very few researchers have succeeded in operationalizing such concepts as tacit knowledge, capabilities, and core competences.

Second, ownership of such resources is no longer critical to a firm's ability to appropriate value from value-creating activities. As a result, what constitutes the boundaries of a firm becomes increasingly blurred, and the firm as a unit of analysis becomes inappropriate for the study of value creation in complex organizations.

We intend to use the "unit of activity" as our level of analysis for three reasons:

1. Activities are key for understanding knowledge creation (Polanyi, 1962) and the development of routines (Nelson and Winter, 1982), both contributions key for understanding learning and the evolution of organizations;
2. Activities may take into account interfirm cooperation, projects and cross-functional teams, neither of which is well explained through today's
concept of the firm;
3. Each firm might consist of both activities that are dynamic (read mobilized) and activities that are not.

It therefore seems more relevant to look at activities than firms.

In the following, we discuss a number of critical concepts and definitions within the resource-based perspective. Then we propose the unit of activity as an alternative and more appropriate unit of analysis, and finally we elaborate on the implications of this perspective.

EXTENDING THE RESOURCE-BASED PERSPECTIVE

An early challenge to the underlying assumptions of the neoclassical theory of the firm, such as the static nature and the homogeneity of firms, was presented by Penrose (1959). The emphasis on—and attention to—these issues, however, came much later and it is only during the last decade that the resource-based perspective has become one of the main theoretical foci among strategic management researchers. In the resource-based perspective, firms are viewed as basically heterogeneous both with respect to their resources and capabilities (Barney, 1991; Rumelt, 1984; Teece, Pisano, and Shuen, 1990; Wernerfelt, 1984) and with respect to their ability to improve these assets (Itami, 1987; Penrose, 1959; Teece, Pisano, and Shuen, 1990). A number of research streams have had and still have substantial influence on the development of this new theoretical perspective, including, but not limited to, Wernerfelt's (1984), Rumelt's (1984), and Barney's (1986, 1991) work on describing the resource-based perspective of the firm—elaborated by among others: Dierickx and Cool (1989); Mahoney and Pandian (1992), and Peteraf (1993); Quinn's (1980) work on logical incrementalism, Nelson and Winter's (1982) evolutionary theory of the firm, where they focus on skills and routines, and Prahalad and Hamel's (1990) introduction of the concept of core competence. Other relevant work looking at firm resources has focused on topics such as innovation (Burgelman, 1983; Dosi, 1982, van de Ven, 1992), human resources (Kanter, 1983; Pettigrew and Whipp, 1991), the role of technology (Abernathy and Utterback, 1978; Clarck, 1985; Durand, 1993) and strategy processes *per se* (Chakravarthy and Doz, 1992; Lorange et al., 1993; Pettigrew and Whipp, 1993, Van de Ven, 1992). These contributions have in common that they directly or indirectly point to invisible resources such as knowledge and capabilities as a key source of rent for organizations.

Such resources are considered by both Penrose (1959) and Barney (1986, 1991) as key to understanding sources of sustained competitive advantage. Penrose pinpoints unique managerial talent that is inimitable as a resource for obtaining economic rent. In her theory, we are not only dealing with "flesh-and-blood" firms, but also with "flesh-and-blood" managers. The firm is defined as a bundle of human and material resources, where the human beings learn with experience and hence become more productive. Penrose also points out that human resources are different from material resources, in that they are not finite but rather increase with experience and with confidence in other team members. As a result, the experience of the managerial team may contribute to the uniqueness of the opportunities pursued by the firm (1959: p. 53).

FIRM RESOURCES; SUGGESTED DEFINITIONS

The definition of what constitutes a firm resource has received some attention in the literature on the resource-based perspective, but to date no consensus on the key concepts seems to have emerged. It is not even evident that the key concept of the theory is or should be "resources". Whereas some authors use the words "resource" and "asset" synonymously, others have suggested that the definitions need to be different. Barney (1991) uses the term "resources" only, which he defines as: "all assets, capabilities, organizational processes, firm attributes, information, knowledge, etc. controlled by a firm that enable the firm to conceive of and implement strategies that improve its efficiency and effectiveness" (1991: 101). He also defines three different categories of resources, namely: "physical capital resources", "human (individual) capital resources", and "organizational capital resources". Teece, Pisano, and Shuen (1990) build on definitions suggested by Amit and Schoemaker (1990), namely that "assets" be used as the overall term, and that the two basic types of assets are resources and capabilities. "Resources" are defined as "transferable input factors controlled by the firm, that are converted into outputs using a wide range of firm assets and bonding mechanisms such as management information systems, incentive systems, or trust between management and labor" (Teece, Pisano, and Shuen, 1990: 9). "Capabilities", in contrast, are defined as "tangible or intangible (invisible) assets that are firm specific and are created over time through complex interactions among the firm's resources" (Teece, Pisano, and Shuen, 1990: 9).

One problem with the term "asset" is that it has both the connotation of something useful and valuable, and the connotation of a property; something that is owned and controlled by the firm (Nordhaug, 1993). As will be discussed in further detail below, the issue of ownership and control is of fundamental importance, as the firm does not have the ownership of individual competences crucial to firm value creation. In addition, assets are typically accounted for in a firm's balance sheet; competences are invisible even in this respect.

Itami (1987: 12) uses the term "resource" as the overall term, and suggests that a firm's resources consist of on the one hand, the physical, human and monetary resources that "need to be physically present for business operations to take place", and on the other, the information-based resources such as management skills, technology, consumer trust, and corporate culture. These information-based resources are called "invisible assets" and include assets "such as a particular technology, accumulated consumer information, brand name, reputation, and corporate culture" (Itami, 1987: 1).

In the future, it may be more fruitful if the researchers within the resource-based perspective could agree on the use of these terms, and it is hereby suggested that the term *resources* be used as the overall term within this perspective.

CATEGORIES OF RESOURCES

Resources may be said to consist of both *tangible resources*, namely the physical, financial, and labor hours traditionally defined as factors of production in economic models, and *intangible resources*. The term "intangible resources" is similar, but not equal, to what Itami called "invisible assets" since not all intangible resources are information based. Hence intangible resources is a broader term than invisible assets. Intangible resources is a term which may replace the term "capabilities" as it is broadly defined by Amit and Schoemaker (1990: 7):

> Capabilities are often developed in functional areas (e.g. brand management in marketing) or by combining physical, human, and technological resources. As a result, firms may build such corporate capabilities as reputation, culture (or norms and organizational routines), reliable service, repeated process and product innovations, flexibility, responsiveness to market trends, and short product development cycles, etc.

It is suggested here that the term "capability" be limited to the intangible resources which are directly linked to an organization's or an individual's ability to perform a given set of tasks. Tasks should, however, be broadly defined, such that the concept of capabilities may be used for such complex tasks as innovative and flexible service development, rapid response to new client needs, and the ability to adapt to changing environmental demands. The reason for such a more limited definition is that the implications for strategic management are very different when discussing intangible resources such as organizational routines compared to an intangible resource such as firm reputation. Capabilities such as routines affect value creation through activities, whereas the reputation affects customers' (and other stakeholders') *perceptions* of firm value creation.

The concept of "capability" has also been used as synonymous with *organizational competence*. Teece, Pisano, and Shuen (1990: 12) refer to Amit and Schoemaker's concept of capabilities, and state that these capabilities may be increased through a process of business learning, as the "knowledge generated by such activity resides in organizational routines." Prahalad and Hamel (1990: 82), on the other hand, refer to the same kind of learning in their definition of "core competences": "Core competences are the collective learning of the organization, especially how to coordinate diverse production skills and integrate multiple streams of technologies."

In our view it may be more fruitful to distinguish the two concepts of competence and capability. Nordhaug (1993) discusses competences at the individual level, and suggests that *competences* consist of three different, but interdependent, dimensions: knowledge, skills, and aptitudes. Knowledge is based on more specific information, and may be articulable (Winter, 1987) and thus potentially transferable. A skill (Nelson and Winter, 1982: 73) is "a capability for a smooth sequence of coordinated behavior that is ordinarily effective relative to its objectives, given the context in which it normally occurs . . . skills are programmatic, in that they involve a sequence of steps with each successive step triggered by and following closely on the completion of the preceding one". Finally, an aptitude is a relevant talent, and as such very hard to transfer or even develop.

This tri-part definition of competence highlights two important aspects of competences: first, "competence" is a broader term than "knowledge", as it includes both articulable knowledge, tacit knowledge, skills, and innate aptitudes. Skills are largely based on tacit knowledge, and hence there is also a fundamental difference between knowledge and skill. Skills may be seen as knowledge (largely tacit) applied to tasks, where aptitudes may contribute both to the quality (stock) of these skills and to the ability to learn new skills quickly. Similarly, knowledge contributes both to the skills applied and to the ease with which new skills may be learned.

Second, "competence" is a broader term than "capabilities". The term "capability" is frequently used as synonymous with "skill", such as where Nelson and Winter (1982) define organizational routines as organizational skills, and Teece, Pisano, and Shuen (1990) use the term "organizational capabilities" for the knowledge residing in organizational routines. In line with Nordhaug (1993), we suggest that competence includes but is not limited to capabilities or skills. The broader concept of capabilities suggested by Amit and Schoemaker (1993) includes both skills and aptitudes, and is more in line with the definition of capabilities suggested here— namely an intangible resource which enables the firm or individual to perform a task.

On the organizational level, it may be fruitful to extend the tri-part definition of competence: first, what is called knowledge at the individual level closely corresponds to the information accumulated on the collective level, which may be stored in information data bases, such as computerized or manual filing systems. The concept of organizational memory has been discussed among researchers on information systems, and also seems to be of relevance here. Second, what corresponds to skills on the individual level have already been defined as organizational routines and procedures (Nelson and Winter, 1982). Finally, although it is clearly not possible to transfer the concept of an aptitude to the collective level, there is a third factor involved in the competence of organizations, which is neither explained by information and knowledge, nor by skills. The organizational culture may be seen to include such collective competence, e.g. in the form of norms for "the way of doing things".

Intangible resources, then, fall into two fundamentally different categories, namely competence, at both the individual and the collective levels, and other intangible resources such as reputation and client loyalty. We suggest that this latter group of resources may be called *relational resources*, as these relate to the relationship between the firm and external stakeholders. FIGURE 11.1 summarizes the relationship between the key concepts suggested in the present chapter.

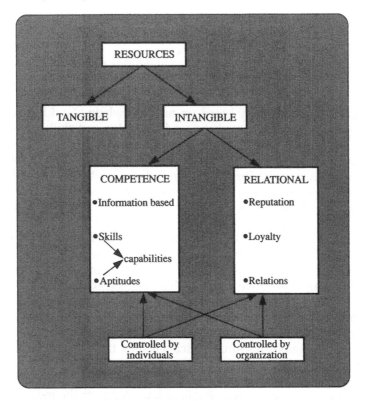

FIGURE 11.1   Strategic resources

RESOURCE OWNERSHP OR CONTROL

We suggest that the firm's competitive position depends on all the value-creating resources that have an impact on the firm's performance. The relevant resources are both tangible and intangible, and include competences, both organizational and individual, as well as relational resources. It is not obvious, however, that the resources which contribute to the firm's value creation actually belong to the firm. Individual competences belong to individuals, and the ownership or control of the relational resources lies more with clients and other external stakeholders than with the firm itself. This challenging control issue is illustrated in FIGURE 11.1 through the arrows reminding us that both competence and reputation are resources that may be controlled by individual employees. Hence, limiting a discussion of intangible resources to organizational capabilities will be highly misleading in situations where value creation depends on individuals more than on firm-level resources.

In addition, many of today's knowledge-intensive firms are experts on the mobilization of resources, especially intangibles, which are associated with other firms. Value-creation based on the mobilization of resources may just as much involve external resources, such as when a firm forms an alliance with Rolls-Royce in order to improve its own value-creation through the association with Rolls-Royce's reputation. As a result, the key issue is not only which bundle of resources the firm possesses, but also which resources the firm is able to mobilize to support their value-creating activities.

THE "UNIT OF ACTIVITY"

Today's organizations face external and internal challenges fundamentally different from those of the industrial era. The external challenges include changes in technologies; consumption patterns; political contexts; economic conditions, and more international competition. Furthermore, firms are both challenged and enhanced by the increasing role of knowledge as a competitive resource. Knowledge is hence a key factor for important changes taking place within and between organizations. More than ever firms cooperate, even with their competitors. Furthermore, they seek to utilize their networks more actively than before. The role of the individual in organizations is also changing in important ways. People increasingly work on several projects simultaneously and are often employed by more than one firm. The outcomes of these changes are manifest on a macro level through firms being forced to organize differently—more through projects, networks, and *ad hoc* teams—and on a micro level by individuals adopting multiple, complex, and changing roles (Hage and Powers, 1992). Both changes are key reasons why we suggest that organizational processes are best understood through analyzing activities. We propose that the unit of activity is a more suitable unit of analysis for understanding key organizational processes, such as resource mobilization, innovation, and the building-up of core competences than the firm or the firm's resources. One reason for this is that the activities encompass important units of economic activity such as projects and alliances. Another reason is that it recognizes the fact that each firm consists of several different types of activities, and that these do not always take place within the boundaries of the firm.

Porter (1991: p.102) also draws attention to activities as the drivers of firms' value creation, stating: "A firm's strategy is its configuration of activities and how they interrelate." Our perception of the unit of activity is an extension of this view, because it incorporates external and cooperative ventures as well as in-firm activites. Related research introduced the notion of communities-of-practice (Brown and Duguid, 1991), where practice is used to understand work, learning, and innovation, and for describing informal organizations (Brunsson, 1985) as learning systems. In fact, Brown and Duguid (1991) conclude by observing that organizations must perceive themselves as "communities-of-communities" in order to foster innovation. These subcommunities are indirectly what we label units of activity. In fact, most firms encompass several such units. However, units of activity may also lie between two or more firms, or entirely outside of the firm. The "unit of activity" is hence distinct from the firm. Consequently the unit of activity should not be defined in terms of ownership but rather in terms of managerial grasp and a joint understanding of a common task. A unit of activity may be distinguished from other units of activity by joint expectations, a common understanding of the objectives, mutual practice, shared motivation, and commitment for the tasks at hand. Spender (1993) argues that collective implicit (tacit) knowledge is built through activities. We will argue that where this building-up of tacit knowledge (Polanyi, 1962) in groups or organizations takes place can be characterized as a unit of activity—as a "body of practice". Other related work includes Weick and Roberts's (1993) introduction of the concept "collective minds" in high risk organizations, where the practice of "collective minds" can be seen as an "activity system". Cassell's (1991) description of the work and knowledge of surgeons, pointing out that some types of learning can only take place through practice is also of interest to the "unit of activity" concept.

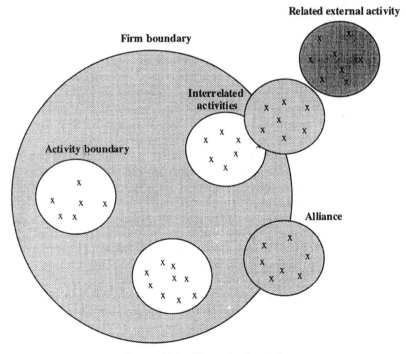

FIGURE 11.2   The unit of activity

FIGURE 11.2 shows (1) that several units of activity can be found within the firm; (2) that they can be found between the firm and other firms ("alliance"), and (3) that related activities can take place outside the firm. Furthermore, (4) it illustrates that each individual can have roles in several activities at the same time.

We emphasize that individuals may "belong" to several activities simultaneously. Conversely, looking at the unit of activity as the unit of analysis corresponds well with Schutz and Luckmann (1973), as well as Hage and Powers (1992), pinpointing individuals' increasing number of roles. In firms this is reflected in employees working on multiple projects and other activities—within the organization, outside of the organization and in cooperation with other organizations. FIGURE 11.3 is meant to illustrate some possible contexts where units of activity can be studied.

In using this concept of the activity—as opposed to the firm—we are able to distinguish dynamic as opposed to static activities in a firm's value-generating processes. There are several reasons for this. The activity will either be mobilized or not, and the firm might consist of both dynamic and

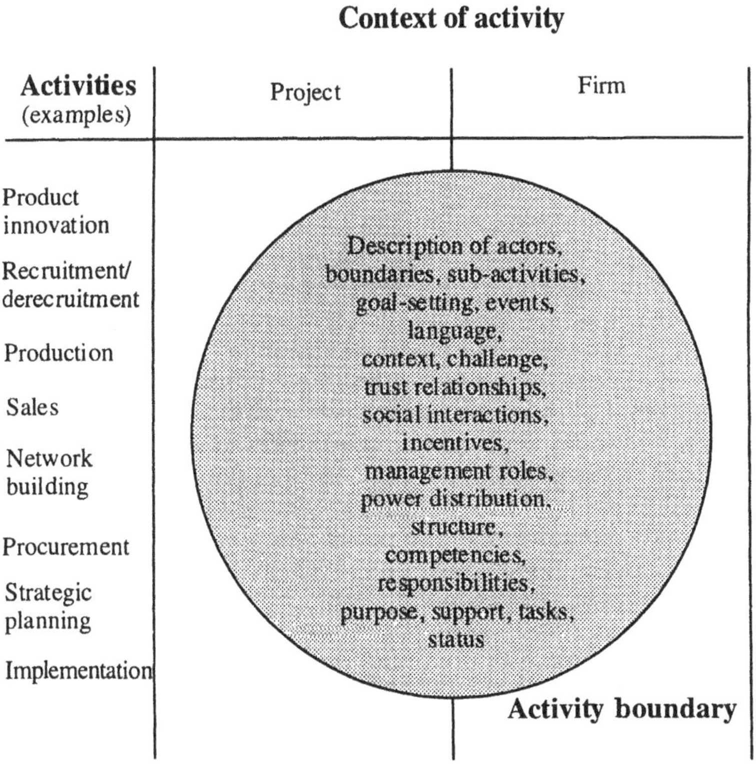

Context of activity

Activities (examples)	Project	Firm

Product innovation

Recruitment/ derecruitment

Production

Sales

Network building

Procurement

Strategic planning

Implementation

Description of actors, boundaries, sub-activities, goal-setting, events, language, context, challenge, trust relationships, social interactions, incentives, management roles, power distribution, structure, competencies, responsibilities, purpose, support, tasks, status

Activity boundary

FIGURE 11.3   Examples of activity contexts

nondynamic activities. Thus, the factors that mobilize the activities will be easier to isolate and study. Furthermore, activities have a clear time dimension, which is an important driver for the mobilization of resources.

ILLUSTRATIONS FROM PREVIOUS STUDIES

In the following illustrations from our previous research, the implications of the unit of activity concept are discussed in further detail. As these illustrations indicate, a focus on activities as the main unit of analysis may help us throw light on the value-creating processes taking place in today's complex and knowledge-intensive organizations.

People Can Belong to Several Activities Simultaneously

The Lillehammer Olympic Organizing Committee (LOOC) was part of a very complex whole which included many stakeholders and contributors, all working with the aim of arranging a successful Olympic Winter Games in 1994 (see e.g. Lowendahl, 1995 for a description of the study). For several years the organization was occupied by preparations, and for a short period when the Games took place it was operational. Hence, LOOC had two organization structures; one for planning and one for undertaking the Games. All employees belonged to both, and during the transition most employees had roles in both planning and operations at the same time. Thus, on a general level the LOOC organization had two main activities, and these influenced the functioning of the organization over time. Moreover, the two organizations were again divided into a set of *ad hoc* groups, projects, etc. We found that some of the critical competences in LOOC were to be able to work across (and outside of) the organization—to be able to initiate activities and to accept continuous change.

Similarly, in engineering consulting firms (e.g. Lowendahl, 1992, 1996) it is common that employees also become owners of firm stock after a number of years' tenure. Typically, senior employees are also promoted to managerial positions, such that one individual engineer may simultaneously be owner, manager, and employee. When (s)he is also elected to the board of directors as an employee representative, the person has four different "hats", and must be very careful in separating out which "hat" (or activity base) (s)he represents in any given discussion.

Organizations Consist of Several Units of Activity

There were a complex set of activities in both the preparations and in the actual Olympics, ranging from construction of arenas to sports and cultural events. Each main activity area consisted of several subareas. Some of the activities were clearly internal, others took the form of cooperative ventures. The configuration of the activities in terms of coordination as well as control was critical, and one of the most important competences required of employees as well as managers was the ability to bridge the interests of multiple functions and activities.

In business schools such as the Norwegian School of Management, the combination of multiple activities is also quite obvious (Lorange and Lowendahl, 1995). A number of programs coexist, such as the undergraduate ("Siviløkonom") program, the graduate MBA program, the graduate M.Sc. program, the Ph.D. program, and the executive programs. Some of these sets of activities are highly interdependent, whereas others could be run almost without any interaction with the other programs. Faculties contribute to different combinations of programs, in addition to their research activities which also typically belong to the bundle of activities of the school. However, some research projects are initiated by other research institutions, and some may be entirely run by a faculty member, outside the "boundaries" of the school.

Units of Activity Are Established and Disappear over Time

In LOOC the planning organization gradually faded away as the Games drew closer. Furthermore, a set of planning activities was terminated and became operationalized. But many kinds of activities changed in character as the Games approached; meetings became shorter and more *ad hoc*, problems were solved on the spot, and the organization grew less formal. Even the "culture" in the organization changed, reflecting the new character of the activities. Even the dress code gradually evolved from "suit and tie" to "winter sports clothing".

Similarly, in engineering design firms the primary organizing unit is the project, and the bundle of projects undertaken at any given point in time represents the major set of activities of the firm. As projects are completed and new project contracts won, the activities of the firm shift over time. Even the size of the firm is a temporary notion, as large projects often lead to the hiring of many new engineers, who then move on to other firms and projects after the completion of their project.

Units of Activity Can Be Found inside an Organization, between Organizations and outside Organizations

The boundaries of LOOC were not only difficult to define, they made no sense. Most of the activities were undertaken by project groups, informally or formally set up, where participants came from different organizations that had an interest in the outcome. These could be sponsors, other contributors, political institutions, athletic organizations, consultants, or LOOC employees. Furthermore, who were actually LOOC employees was not very clear either because of the many consultants drawn in to solve specific tasks, or the amount of volunteers recruited to fill influential positions. The marketing activities of LOOC were successful in a large part due to the contribution of external sponsors and other contributors. Similarly, the success of the television broadcasting was not just the result of successful implementation by LOOC, but even more the outcome of the quality work of external partners such as Norwegian Telecom, and in particular ORTO—the organization set up by the Norwegian Broadcasting Company (NRK) in cooperation with CBS and a large number of other international broadcasting companies. Thus, people and activities did not need to be part of the LOOC organization in order to contribute to it reaching its goals.

The biotech company Dynal (Haanes and Lorange, 1995) commercialized its most important product worldwide to a large extent through an external research team, as the researchers at the hospital first using the product in turn used their international network to introduce the product globally. Strategically this was much more interesting for the company than building up a network by themselves. Thus, the market development was largely initiated by an external party. The company also commercializes a product which is used in many different applications, including food testing, cancer treatment, and AIDS research, where the pharmaceutical uses are found in segments ranging from research to diagnostics and therapeutics. For their strategic work the concept of the industry is not very helpful. Rather an understanding of available competence, reputation, and networks of relationships seems to be the most relevant guide for initiating cross-organizational activities to develop potential applications of their product.

CONCLUSIONS AND IMPLICATIONS

Traditional strategy research has primarily focused on the firm or even the industry as the appropriate level of analysis. The more recently developed resource-based perspective fruitfully shifted the focus to an internal and more micro level of analysis. Yet in our view even this perspective has limitations, in particular when it comes to operationalizations and empirical research. Resources are extremely difficult to define, and as organizations are becoming increasingly dependent on intangible or invisible resources, they are also difficult to observe and control. In addition, resources—whether tangible or intangible—frequently do not belong to the firm. Value creation may happen within, outside, or at the boundary of the organization, and be totally dependent on resources which are not controlled by the owners of the firm. Finally, the value of a resource is dependent on its usage. A value-creating resource must be mobilized in order for its value to manifest itself; latent resources may have value-creation potential, but their true value can only be judged as a result of their application. Hence, in order to study resources, we need to focus on *resources in action*, and in order to do so, we suggest that the *unit of activity* is a more fruitful starting-point for analysis than the resources or the firm.

The implications of such a shift are many, and a few have been mentioned here: the size of the firm is no longer seen as relevant, because the boundaries of the firm have become (even more) blurred. Growth may be positive or negative, but in many cases size is of a temporary nature, as activities shift in and out of the organization. Similarly, ownership is no longer the key to understanding organizational performance, and the authority over activities is no longer vested in managers employed by firm owners. Rather, authority also shifts over time, and follows the bundles of activities which lead to value creation at any given point in time. As a result, time becomes a critical issue in the analysis of organizations, and a comparative static approach may yield very little insight into the actual processes of such complex organizations. Both in terms of management and research, we may need to look at new and different approaches to the study of these activities, including, but not limited to, action research and participant observation.

In our view, the unit of activity offers an improved perspective relative to the traditional resource-based literature as it seems to offer better potential for the development of operationalizable constructs and thus further empirical testing. The insights and strengths of the resource-based view may be kept and further developed as the main shift is the focus: in the key unit of analysis and the basic unit used for theory development.

In terms of implications for managers, we will argue that seeing the firm as a set of past, present, and future activities has many interesting implications. The framework allows for a more open approach to how resources can be activated—and which resources this includes. Resources and activities need not belong to the firm. This goes for human resources, as people can be drawn in when needed, as well as for physical resources, as plant and equipment need not be owned to be utilized for value creation. Hence, we will argue that a key challenge for managers is to provide an interesting basis for attracting and mobilizing internal and external resources. The organizational climate becomes key; one cannot force the mobilization of resources. The real competitive advantage may belong to the firms that provide a nexus for activities (i.e. a "climate" for dynamic, relevant, and value-adding activities), and at the same time have the capabilities required to identify the value-adding activities early.

Excellent firms may be seen as having some "magnetic" force drawing people as well as value-creating activities to the firm and making them "stick" such that the value-creation is appropriable by the firm, regardless of its ownership over the resources in use. Management then becomes concerned with bringing in, overseeing, and mobilizing, rather than directing, controlling, and owning. Major challenges lie ahead in terms of career management, organization, allocation of values to contributors, accounting, and other measurement of value creation, etc. Yet, today's complex organizations are increasingly dealing creatively with such a reality, without having the answers to how these and many other such issues may be solved. A tight cooperation between managers and researchers will be required, in order for these issues to be addressed and potential improvements tried out. Taking one activity at a time, we may jointly improve both our models and theories and the managerial capabilities required in order to manage this new complexity.

REFERENCES

Abernathy, W.J. and Utterback, J.M. (1978) "Patterns of Industrial Innovation", *Technology Review*, **50**, June–July, 41–47.
Amit, R. and Schoemaker, P.J.H. (1990) "Key Success Factors: Their Foundations and Applications", unpublished working paper, University of British Columbia and University of Chicago, June (cited in Teece, Pisano and Schuen, 1990).
Amit, R. and Schoemaker, P.J.H. (1993) "Strategic Assets and Organizational Rent", *Strategic Management Journal*, **14**(1), 33–46.
Bain, J.S. (1948) "Price and Production Policies", in H.S. Ellis (ed.) *A Survey of Contemporary Economics*. Homewood: Irwin, pp. 129–173.
Barney, J. (1986) "Types of Competition and the Theory of Strategy", *Academy of Management Review*, **11**, 1231–1241.
Barney, J. (1991) "Firm Resources and Sustained Competitive Advantage", *Journal of Management*, **17**(1), 99–120.
Brown, J.S. and Duguid, P. (1991) "Organizational Learning and Communities-of-Practice: Toward a Unified View of Working, Learning and Innovation", *Organization Science*, **2**(1), 40–57.
Brunsson, N. (1985) *The Irrational Organization*. Chichester: John Wiley.
Burgelman, R. (1983) "A Process Model of Internal Corporate Venturing in a Major Diversified Firm", *Administrative Science Quarterly*, **28**, 223–244.
Cassell, J. (1991) *Expected Miracles: Surgeons at Work*. Philadelphia, Pa.: Temple University.
Chakravarthy B.S. and Doz, Y. (1992) "Strategy Process Research: Focusing on Corporate Self-renewal", *Strategic Management Journal*, **13**, 5–14.
Clark, K.B. (1985) "The Interaction of Design Hierarchies and Market Concepts in Technological Evolution", *Research Policy*, **4**, 235–251.
Coase, R.H. (1937) "The Nature of the Firm", *Economica*, **4**, 331–351.
Conner, K.E. (1991) "A Historical Comparison of Resource-based Theory and Five Schools of Thought within Industrial Economics: Do We Have a New Theory of the Firm?", *Journal of Management*, **17**(1), 121–154.
Cyert, R.M. and March, J.G. (1963) *A Behavioral Theory of the Firm*. Englewood Cliffs, NJ.: Prentice-Hall.
Dierickx, I. and Cool, K. (1989) "Asset Stock Accumulation and Sustainability of Competitive Advantage", *Management Science*, **35**, 1504–1511.

Dosi, G. (1982) "Technological Paradigms and Technological Trajectories. A Suggested Interpretation of the Determinants and Directions of Technical Change", *Research Policy*, **11**, 147–162.

Durand, T. (1993) "The Dynamics of Cognitive Technological Maps", in P. Lorange et al. (eds) *Implementing Strategic Processes: Change, Learning and Co-Operation*. Oxford: Blackwell Publishers, pp. 165–189.

Haanes, K. and Lorange, P. (1995) *The Dynal Biotech Joint Venture*. IMD case study. GM 593. Lausanne: International Institute for Management Development.

Hage, J. and Powers, C.H. (1992) *Post-Industrial Lives: Roles and Relationships in the 21st Century*. Newbury Park, Calif: Sage.

Holmstrom, B.R. and Tirole, J. (1989) "The Theory of the Firm", in R. Schmalensee and R.D. Willig (eds), *Handbook of Industrial Organizations*, Vol. 1, Amsterdam: North-Holland, pp. 61–133.

Itami, H. (with T. Roehl) (1987) *Mobilizing Invisible Assets*. Cambridge, Mass.: Harvard University Press.

Kanter, R.M. (1983) *The Change Masters*. New York: Simon and Schuster.

Lorange P., Chakravarthy, B., Roos, J. and Van de Ven, A. (1993) *Implementing Strategic Processes: Change, Learning and Co-Operation*. Oxford: Blackwell Publishers.

Lorange, P. and Lowendahl, B.R. (1995) "Organizational Learning in Academic Institutions", in H. Thomas, D. O'Neal and J. Kelly (eds) *Strategic Renaissance and Business Transformation*, Chichester: John Wiley & Sons, pp. 241–260.

Lowendahl, B. (1992) "Global Strategies for Professional Business Service Firms", Unpublished Ph.D. dissertation University of Pennsylvania, the Wharton School.

Lowendahl, B.R. (1995) "Organizing the Lillehammer Olympic Games", *Scandinavian Journal of Management*, Special Issue on Project Management and Temporary Organizations, **11**(4), 347–362.

Lowendahl, B.R. (1996) *Strategic Management of Professional Service Firms*, Copenhagen Business School Press/Blackwell, forthcoming.

Mahoney, J.T. and Pandian, J.R. (1992) "The Resource-based View within the Conversation of Strategic Management", *Strategic Management Journal*, **13**(5), 363–380.

Nelson, R.R. and Winter, S.G. (1982) *An Evolutionary Theory of Economic Change*. Cambridge: Belknap Harvard University Press.

Nordhaug, O. (1993) *Human Capital in Organizations*. Oslo: Scandinavian University Press.

Penrose, E. (1959) *The Theory of the Growth of the Firm*. Oxford: Oxford University Press.

Peteraf, M. (1993) "The Cornerstones of Competitive Advantage: A Resource-based View", *Strategic Management Journal*, **14**(3), 179–191.

Pettigrew, A. and Whipp, R. (1991) *Managing Change for Competitive Success*. Oxford: Basil Blackwell.

Pettigrew, A. and Whipp, R. (1993) "Managing the Twin Processes of Competition and Change", in P. Lorange et al. (eds) *Implementing Strategic Processes*, Oxford: Blackwell, pp. 3–42.

Polanyi, M. (1962) *Personal Knowledge: Towards a Post-critical Philosophy*. Chicago, The University of Chicago Press.

Porter, M.E. (1980) *Competitive Strategy*. New York: The Free Press.

Porter, M.E. (1991) "Towards a Dynamic Theory of Strategy", *Strategic Management Journal*, **12**, Summer Special Issue, 95–117.

Prahalad, C.K. and Hamel, G. (1990) "The Core Competence of the Corporation", *Harvard Business Review*, **68**(3), 79–91.

Quinn, J.B. (1980) *Strategies for Change: Logical Incrementalism*. Homewood, Ill.: Irwin.

Rumelt, R.P. (1984) "Towards a Strategic Theory of the Firm", in B. Lamb (ed.) *Competitive Strategic Management*. Englewood Cliffs, NJ: Prentice-Hall. (First issued as University of Southern California Working Paper, 1981).

Schutz, A. and Luckmann, T. (1973) *The Structure of the Life World*. Evanston, IL: Northwestern University Press.

Spender, J. C. (1993) "Competitive Advantage from Tacit Knowledge? Unpacking the Concept and its Strategic Implications", *Academy of Management Best Paper Proceedings*, pp. 37–41.

Teece, D.J., Pisano, G., and Shuen, A. (1990) "Firm Capabilities, Resources, and the Concept of Strategy", Economic Analysis and Policy Working paper, EAP-38, University of California at Berkeley, September.

Van de Ven, A. (1992) "Suggestions for Studying Strategic Processes", *Strategic Management Journal*, Special Issue, 169–188.

Weick, K.E. and Roberts, K.H. (1993) "Collective Mind in Organizations: Heedful Interrelating on Flight Decks", *Administrative Science Quarterly*, **28**, 357–381.

Wernerfelt, B. (1984) "A Resource-based View of the Firm", *Strategic Management Journal*, **5**(2), 171–180.

Winter, S. (1987) "Knowledge and Competence as Strategic Assets", in D. Teece (ed.) *The Competitive Challenge*. Cambridge: Ballinger, pp. 159–184.

12

Patterns of Strategic Alliance Activity in the Global Steel Industry

RAVINDRANATH MADHAVAN, BALAJI R. KOKA,
JOHN E. PRESCOTT

Interfirm relationships, including joint ventures and other forms of strategic alliances, are acknowledged to represent significant flows of knowledge and other resources between industry players. Building on this insight, and responding to the proliferation of strategic alliances in several key industries, strategic management research has begun to develop a substantial literature on interfirm relationships. The main focus of this research has been at the dyadic level, i.e. relationships between pairs of firms have been studied one at a time. While such an approach has contributed greatly to our understanding of many facets of strategic alliances, it has also left room for a complementary approach that analyzes interfirm relationships at a network level. Multiple dyadic relationships interconnect and bind firms into networks (Nohria, 1992). Analysis at the network level can help us understand the overall patterns of strategic alliance activity in an industry, thereby throwing light on some of the industry-level drivers of the phenomenon. As part of a larger study exploring competitiveness in the global steel industry, this chapter analyzes and interprets the pattern of worldwide strategic alliance activity among steel industry firms.

THE NETWORK PERSPECTIVE OF STRATEGIC ALLIANCE ACTIVITY

A fundamental premise of this study is that interfirm relationships can be considered to be resources in their own right, as they are the channels by which firms access goods and services (Freeman and Barley, 1990). Firms that are well-positioned in their industry network have superior access to industry resources and capabilities. For example, a firm that has a strategeic alliance with another firm that is developing a new technology potentially has an option to access the latter's technological knowledge. Well-connected firms (i.e. those with well-structured networks) have information and control benefits (Burt, 1992) that other firms to not have. Since a favourable network position endows the firm with strategic benefits, managers can be expected to "jockey" for competitive advantage through positioning their firm in the industry network. Thus, the structure of inter-firm networks is a significant influence on firm and industry performance. Building on this logic, the broad objective of our study was to understand how the structure of the strategic alliance network shapes—and is shaped by—competition in an industry.

There are several reasons why it is meaningful to study patterns of strategic alliance activity, as against, say, the structure of interlocking directorates or mergers and acquisitions. First, strategic alliances represent relationships between rivals, and have been acknowledged sources of influence on industry evolution (Porter, 1980). Second, strategic alliances represent flows of knowledge and access to markets, which are key success factors in most industries (e.g. Grant et al., 1995). Finally, there has been a signficant amount of strategic alliance activity in a wide variety of industries, ranging from retail to aluminium (e.g. Madhavan and Prescott, 1995).

The steel industry is an appropriate context in which to empirically examine our research question, for several reasons. First, despite weathering a good deal of turbulence over the last few decades, the steel industry continues to be an important sector of the world economy. While the demand for steel in the West has been steady, the market has witnessed growth in developing countries such as China. In many parts of the world, including Europe and Asia, the steel industry remains an important source of employment. Second, interfirm relationships have been acknowledged as having been a significant influence on the industry's evolution (e.g. Knoedler, 1993). Third, the industry has witnessed significant strategic changes, such as increasing international competition and heightened threat from substitute products, over the last few decades (e.g. Abe and Suzuki, 1991), which makes it a suitable context to observe subsequent structural change as well. Finally, being a mature industry, steel faces significant constraints on strategic flexibility, imposed by high fixed costs and high exit barriers (Harrigan, 1985). One of the ways in which the industry has dealt with the need for strategic flexibility is through the creation of strategic alliances with other industry players, suppliers, and customers (Harrigan, 1986; Madhavan and Prescott, 1995). The extreme constraints on strategic flexibility and the competitive value of strategic alliances combine to make the steel industry an "exemplary case" (Yin, 1989) for our study.

RESEARCH QUESTIONS

Against the backdrop of this broad objective, the specific focus of this chapter is on the following questions.

How Can Understanding the Overall Structure of the Strategic Alliance Network Help Us to Better Understand the Competitive Dynamics of the Global Steel Industry?

While strategic alliances are interfirm arrangements that are usually initiated between pairs of firms, they can be analyzed at different levels. Most strategic management research has been pegged at the level of the dyadic relationship, e.g. dealing with questions of partner learning (e.g. Hamel, 1991). This level of analysis would be most appropriate for researchers interested in issues such as partner motivation and the dynamics of specific interfirm relationships. Another possible unit of analysis is the organization set, focusing on all relationships formed by one firm. This level of analysis is most appropriate for issues such as strategy implementation through networks, as in the establishment of technology standards. A third unit of analysis is the overall network comprising all relationships among the firms of an industry (e.g. Nohria and Garcia-Pont, 1991). This unit of analysis is best suited for research into the industry-level characteristics of strategic alliance activity. For example, both Nohria and Garcia-Pont (1991) and Duysters and Hagedoorn (1995) have employed this approach to investigate how alliance networks are related to strategic group structure. Given our interest in exploring the pattern of strategic alliance activity in the global steel industry, the network level of analysis is most appropriate here.

The network perspective of strategic alliance activity draws upon the influential tradition of network analysis, which in turn is primarily founded upon structural sociology (Wellman, 1988). The distinguishing feature of the network perspective of strategic alliances is the premise that particular alliances need to be viewed in the context of the overall structure of relationships. While the dynamics of each relationship are important, a complete analysis has to take into account the effect of each partner's position in the network. Industries are social networks that represent sets of actors who are connected to each other by sets of relationships. These networks constrain action, as well as being shaped by such action (Nohria, 1992). Thus, strategic action takes place in the context of a complex network of relationships, and the firm's relative position in its network is a key influence both on action and on performance. This logic provides the rationale for our attempt to map the steel industry network—knowledge of the network structure of an industry can potentially help us better understand the competitive dynamics of the industry.

What is the Pattern of Relationships between and among Strategic Groups in the Global Steel Industry?

Strategic groups have been widely used as a means of understanding industry heterogeneity (Thomas and Venkataraman, 1988). In an investigation of the pattern of strategic alliance activity, it is of interest to ask if the interdependence between firms is influenced by their strategic group affiliation (Duysters and Hagedoorn, 1995). Thus, our second research question seeks to understand how theoretically derived strategic groups in the steel industry are connected to each other through alliances.

How Have Key Industry Events Affected the Overall Structure of the Strategic Alliance Network in the Global Steel Industry?

Network analysts usually assume that social structure endures over time (Schott, 1991), although there are significant exceptions (e.g. Burkhardt and Brass, 1990). As a result, most network analysis studies in strategic management have been static rather than dynamic, and have resulted in "snapshot" pictures of industry networks at particular points in time. As a first step towards a more dynamic theory of industry networks, we wanted to explore how specific events tend to reshape networks. Our reasoning was as follows: firms take strategic action in order to defend their positions when key industry events appear to be changing the fundamental competitive forces in their industry (Christensen et al., 1982). One of the forms of such strategic action could be changing the position of the firm in its network. For example, firms could ally with new partners so as to take advantage of the new set of competitive forces. If many firms in the industry take action to "recalibrate" their network to match the new competitive regime, there should be observable change in the network structure consequent to key industry events. Moreover, the extent and nature of structural change will vary with how each industry event affects the competitive forces in the industry. As a prelude to developing a theory of the evolution of industry networks, we proposed to examine how key events in the steel industry have influenced network structure.

DATA AND METHOD

In order to explore the above three research questions dealing with overall structure, strategic group relations, and the structural impact of key industry events, we collected data on strategic alliances initiated in the global steel industry between 1977 and 1993. The data were obtained from the Dow Jones News Retrieval Service, and related to all types of strategic alliances, including joint ventures, joint programs, licensing arrangements, and long-term supply relationships. There were 130 firms participating in the network, comprising integrated, minimill, and specialty producers, as well as upstream partners (e.g. a coal mining company) and downstream partners (e.g. an automobile manufacturer). Overall, 130 strategic alliances were reported during this time period, of which 8% were technical training arrangements, 10% were patent licensing agreements, 3% were production/buy-back agreements, 3% were "know-how" licensing agreements, 1% were service agreements, 6% were nonequity alliances, 5% were joint ventures in existing operations, and 64% were greenfield joint ventures.

IDENTIFICATION OF STRATEGIC GROUPS

Consistent with the recommendation of Thomas and Venkataraman (1988), we developed the strategic groups *a priori*, based on the dimensions of technology group (integrated, minimill, specialty, other), and nationality (North America, Europe, Japan, other). Expert commentary on the steel industry has consistently treated both technology (e.g. Hogan, 1991; Ghemawat, 1993) and nationality (e.g. Abe and Suzuki, 1991) as key competitive dimensions. This process should have resulted in 16 strategic groups; however, some groups were empty, or were so sparsely populated that they were combined with contiguous groups to facilitate analysis. We felt that using very sparsely populated groups for network analysis would give a distorted picture of the overall pattern of relationships. Another reason for combining some groups was to make possible more meaningful analysis and interpretation. Thus, we were left with 10 strategic groups (American–Integrated, American–minimill, American–specialty, American–other, Japan–integrated, Japan–other, Europe–integrated, Europe–other, other–integrated, other–other).

DETERMINATION OF KEY INDUSTRY EVENTS

Based on an extensive survey of the steel industry literature, we concluded that the two key industry events in the recent past have been the "regulatory shock" of 1984 and the "technology shock" of 1987. The literature suggests that both events had a demonstrable impact on the industry's evolution. The year 1984 witnessed several key regulatory changes that appeared to have impelled strategic alliance activity. These regulatory changes included the institution of voluntary restraint agreements in the USA, the decision of the US Department of Justice to block the LTV–Republic Steel merger while leaving open the possibility of smaller-scale joint ventures, the relaxation of antitrust provisions for R&D-related cooperative activity, and the initiation of a major US–Japanese steel venture (National–NKK). Cumulatively, these developments appeared to signal both a lowering of the traditional institutional barriers to cooperative strategy, and some added impetus to the cooperative production of steel (e.g. *Wall Street Journal*, 1984; Hogan, 1991). Since the announcement of the National/NKK joint venture was one of the better-known milestones in this context, we label this event "National/NKK". The 1987 technological event was the decision by Nucor to adopt the compact strip production technology for thin slab casting in its Crawfordsville, Indiana, plant. This decision had two major implications: (1) a potential threat to the integrated players who had hitherto enjoyed a monopoly of the high-margin sheet steel market, and (2) an acceptance of the compact strip production technology as the apparent winner over other technologies such as the Hazelett process. The literature on the steel industry suggests that this event was widely perceived as a turning point in the recent history of the industry (e.g. Ghemawat, 1993). In our analysis, we refer to this event as "thin slab casting". Our assessment was that both the regulatory change in 1984 and the technology change in 1987 had the potential to change the network structure of strategic alliances in the industry. Accordingly, we used 1984 and 1987 as the "cut points" for our analysis. As discussed further in the section, "Results and discussion", both 1984 and 1987 witnessed significant shifts in the number of strategic alliances formed, validating our choice of key industry events.

ANALYSIS

Adapting the approach suggested by Contractor and Lorange (1988) and used by Nohria and Garcia-Pont (1991), we assigned each alliance a numerical code indicating its "intensity", ranging from 1 for technical training to 9 for a greenfield joint venture. If a pair of partners had more than one alliance, the scores for all alliances were added to form a composite index. The resulting symmetric matrix included all alliances initiated during the entire period of the study, i.e. 1977–93. This matrix was used as input for the visual analysis of overall structure using the network graphics program KrackPlot 3.0 (Krackhardt, Blythe, and McGrath, 1994) as well as of alliances between strategic groups using the COLLAPSE function of UCINET IV (Borgatti, Everett, and Freeman, 1992). In this chapter, we focus on a *graphic* analysis of network structure; in the interests of conserving space, we do not describe network properties such as centralization.

In order to facilitate analysis of structural change "around" each event, four separate matrices were also constructed. These matrices consisted of alliances announced in the time periods 1977–83 (i.e. pre-National/NKK), 1984–93 (i.e. post-National/NKK), 1977–86 (i.e. pre-thin slab casting), and 1987–93 (i.e. post-thin slab casting). Comparing the pre-and post-National/NKK networks would allow us to assess the structural impact of the regulatory change in 1984. Comparing the pre- and post-thin slab casting networks would allow us to assess the structural impact of the technology event of 1987.

The method used to analyze structural change was positional analysis, in which network actors are clustered together on the basis of similarity of patterns of relations. Using the network analysis program STRUCTURE (Burt, 1991), we did a positional analysis of the 1993 network. A position is a set of structurally equivalent actors, i.e. those actors with very similar patterns of relationship will be classified together in one position. In STRUCTURE, subsets of equivalent actors within the network are identified using hierarchical cluster analyses. Further, STRUCTURE also provides methods (based on covariance matrix distances and reliability criteria) for assessing the adequacy of the hypothesis that a given set of actors do comprise a position. Using this method, we identified eight positions. Since these positions represented the current structure of the network, our analysis centered on how relations between these eight positions had changed "around" each event. In other words, having determined the eight positions that were most recent, we superimposed the same eight positions on the earlier networks and investigated the relationships between them. For example, position eight consisted of the Canadian steel firms Dofasco, Sidbec, Ipsco, Ivaco, Algoma, and Stelco in all four time periods. Keeping the positions fixed in this manner allowed us to understand how the pattern of relationships had changed over the years.

RESULTS AND DISCUSSION

We began the analysis by examining the overall trends in steel industry strategic alliance activity over the years. FIGURES 12.1(a) and (b) present the number of alliances in the global steel industry between 1980 and 1993. (The period 1977–80 has been collapsed into 1980 for ease of depiction.) While the data show a steady increase in the cumulative number of strategic alliances announced, there was a sharp rise in the number of new alliances in 1984, i.e. immediately after the National/NKK alliance. On the other hand, there was a drop in the number of new alliances after the thin slab casting event in 1987. Thus, there appears to be prima facie evidence

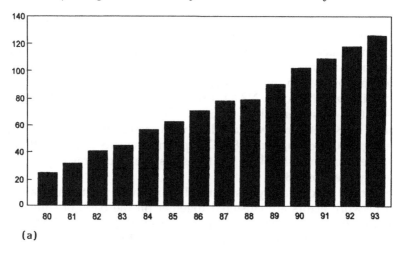

(a)

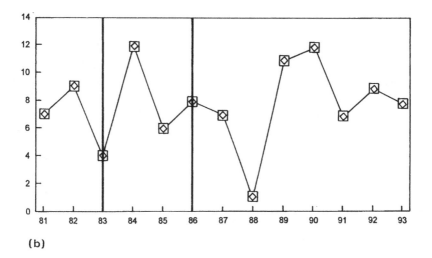

(b)

FIGURE 12.1   (a) Cumulative number of strategic alliances from 1980 to 1993;
(b) number of new alliances each year from 1981 to 1993

that both events had a significant impact on strategic alliance activity in the steel industry. The utility of network analysis is that it enables us to understand the overall structure of the network, as well as the nature of the events' impact, as demonstrated below.

In order to address our first research question dealing with network structure and competitive dynamics, FIGURE 12.2 is a visual representation of the overall structure of the steel industry strategic alliance network. The

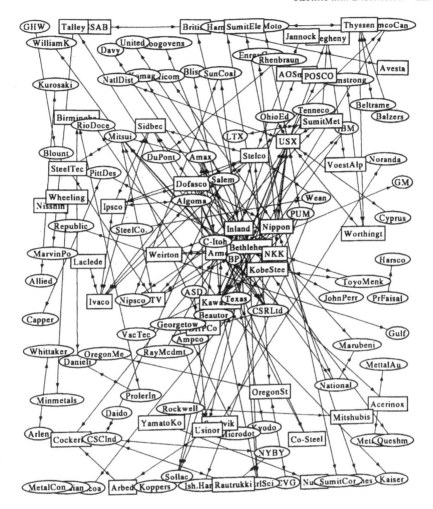

FIGURE 12.2   The strategic alliance network in the global steel industry

ellipses represent steel producers (45 in number), and the boxes represent
other players (85 in number), such as coal mines or major steel users. The
lines represent strategic alliances, with the arrows signifying the direction
of relationship. (Since strategic alliances are bidirectional by definition, all
the lines have dual arrows.) Because of the number of players and relationships, the diagram appears very complex. However, an analysis of the
network leads to three conclusions: first, the industry has witnessed a substantial amount of strategic alliance activity during the period under study.
Second, steel producers have engaged in strategic alliances not only with

each other, but also with downstream and upstream partners. Third, large integrated steel producers have been among the most prolific participants in the network. The American integrated steel producers Armco, USX, and Bethlehem are among the most well-connected in the network. Japanese integrated steel producers such as NKK and Kawasaki are also reasonably well-connected.

In order to further clarify the structure of the network and identify some consequences for competitive dynamics, FIGURE 12.3 presents a simplified diagram of the network, showing only the steel producers and their

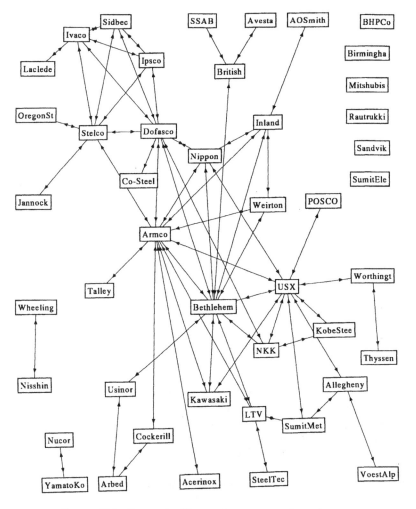

FIGURE 12.3   Strategic alliances between steel producers

relationships with each other. In the central region of the diagram are well-connected players such as Armco, Bethlehem, and USX—all American integrated players. While the diagram does not reveal this, most of Bethlehem's relationships were technology licensing arrangements established during the early 1980s. USX and Armco, on the other hand, had several joint ventures established during the late 1980s and later. In the top left quadrant of the diagram we see a group of Canadian firms (Dofasco, Stelco, Ivaco, Sidbec, and IPSCO), who are well-connected with each other, by virtue of a technology development consortium in which they participated. Several Japanese integrated steel producers (Kawasaki, NKK, Kobe Steel, and Nippon) have close ties to the central American integrated steel producers. This set of relationships is mainly the consequence of the increase in Japanese transplant auto production in the USA. Japanese and American steel companies have been entering into joint ventures so that they could service the demands of the transplant steel producers. Simultaneously, the Japanese partners in these ventures may have seen them as a way to supply steel to American auto producers as well. European steel producers have been relatively less active in the network, though firms such as British Steel, Usinor-Sacilor, and Thyssen have established alliances both with other European partners and with US steel producers. In general, minimill players have not been very active in the strategic alliance network during the period under study, though recent reports suggest this might be changing (*Business Week*, November 7, 1994).

RELATIONS BETWEEN STRATEGIC GROUPS

Our second research question dealt with the pattern of relationships within and across strategic groups. FIGURE 12.4 presents a diagram of the relationships between the 10 strategic groups identified on the basis of technology and nationality. The thickness of lines represents the strength of relationship between the groups. The conclusions parallel those from the previous analysis. The American integrateds (USA and Canada) are the best-connected, having established strong relationships among themselves as well as with Japanese and European integrateds. The Japanese integrateds are relatively well-connected among themselves, as well as with American integrateds and other integrateds. The European integrateds are also well-connected among themselves, and less strongly with American integrateds. The strongest cross-group relations are between American and Japanese integrateds, further evidence of the significance of Japanese transplant auto production as a driver of network activity. Relationships between Japanese and European integrated producers are notable by their absence, perhaps suggesting the differences in regulatory climate in the USA and Europe. The Japanese integrateds also appear to have strong relations with both

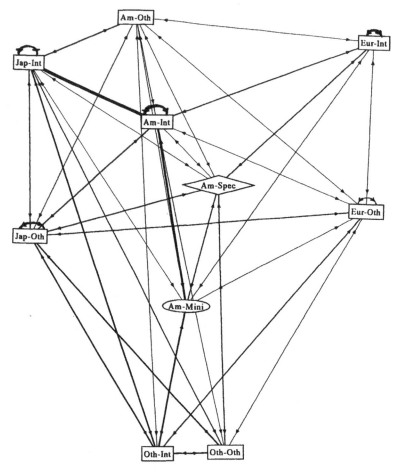

FIGURE 12.4   Strategic alliances between members of strategic groups

integrated steel producers and others in other parts of the world, unlike the American and European players. An implication of this may be that Japanese steel firms are much better positioned for a world in which the only real growth in steel demand may be in developing countries. Clearly, despite their lesser number of relationships, the Japanese steel firms are the most broadly diversified group both geographically and technologically. They have established relationships with steel producers in Japan, USA, and other areas, as well as with downstream and upstream partners in Japan, USA, Europe, and other areas. While integrateds have been the more active players, American minimill and specialty steel producers have been participating in the network as well.

Overall, the extent of strategic alliance interaction is high both between members of the same strategic group and between members of different strategic groups. In conjunction with Nohria and Garcia-Pont (1991) and Duysters and Hagedoorn (1995), this finding underscores the value of applying a network perspective to the strategic group literature. The extent of within-group and cross-group interaction suggests a higher degree of resource flows and strategic interplay than may have been identified before.

IMPACT OF INDUSTRY EVENTS

Our final research question dealt with how industry events impact the structure of industry networks. In order to visually explore the impact of the 1984 and 1987 industry events, we present, in FIGURES 12.5 and 12.6, the relations between identified positions before and after each event. The lines connecting the various groups represent the density of relations between the groups. Density is calculated as the total value of all ties divided by the number of possible ties and represents the overall level of network activity. FIGURE 12.5 shows the results of the position analysis before and after the National/NKK alliance. There was a significant increase in density from 0.05 to 0.105. Positions two and three, isolates before 1984, became active after National/NKK. Only two positions had relations with themselves (i.e. between members of the same position) before 1984; after 1984, seven positions did. While there were seven inter-position relationships before 1984, there were 12 after 1984. Thus, the impact of the 1984 event appears to have been dramatic.

On the other hand, the 1987 event appears not to have had such a major impact. There was one isolate position before 1987, and there was one after 1987. The increase in density, from 0.082 to 0.091, was very small. Four positions had relations with themselves before 1987; after 1987, seven did. There were 10 inter-position relationships before 1987, and there were 10 afterwards. Overall, the impact of the technology event appears to have been quite modest within the time frame of the study.

Complementing the network-level analysis of the impact of the two events, we also investigated their impact on selected firms. FIGURE 12.7 further confirms the impact of the 1984 regulatory event through examining the change at firm level for two firms chosen as illustrations. Both Dofasco and Armco appears to have undergone dramatic change in their network structures. Prior to the National/NKK alliance in 1984, Dofasco had only one relationship. After 1984, it is not only part of a consortium of Canadian steel producers, but also has five other alliances. The numbers in parentheses next to the partners' names indicates which structural position the partner belonged to. Dofasco's partnerships provide it with linkages to positions six, three, and seven—there is no redundancy in positions reached through

232

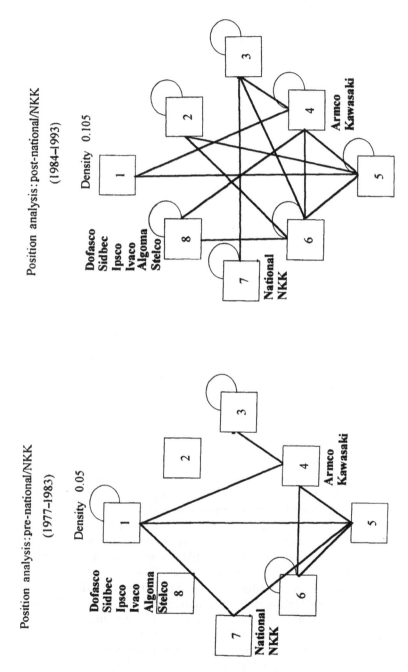

FIGURE 12.5   Structural change following the 1984 regulatory change

233

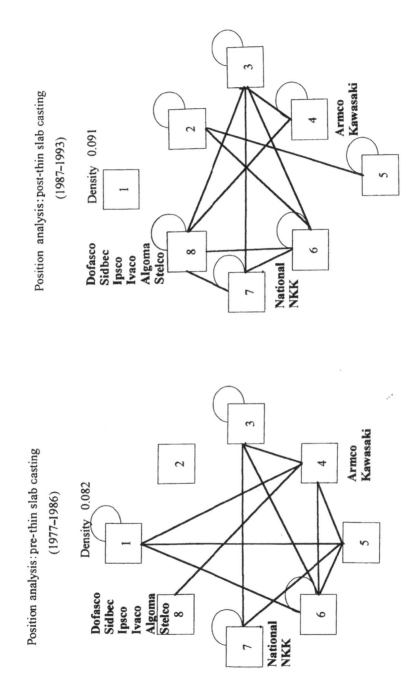

Position analysis: pre-thin slab casting
(1977–1986)

Density 0.082

Position analysis: post-thin slab casting
(1987–1993)

Density 0.091

Dofasco
Sidbec
Ipsco
Ivaco
Algoma
Stelco

National
NKK

Armco
Kawasaki

FIGURE 12.6   Structural change following the 1987 technology change

234

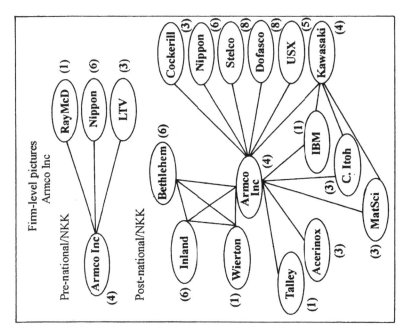

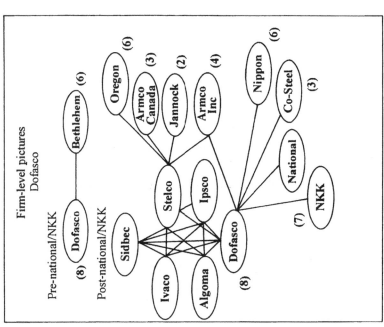

FIGURE 12.7 Structural change at the firm level: two examples

alliances. Since each position is structurally different, potentially providing access to different sets of resources (Freeman and Barley, 1990), this may be interpreted as being an efficient network design (Burt, 1992). The structural change in Armco's case is equally dramatic. However, Armco's network appears to have much greater redundancy in terms of positions reached—there are four linkages to position three, two to position one, and two to position eight. One may speculate as to whether this redundancy is deliberate (e.g. in order to compensate for unreliable relationships with each partner), or merely circumstantial.

Limitations

A few limitations must be kept in mind while interpreting our conclusion that the regulatory event of 1984 had a greater structural impact than the technology event of 1987. While this study focused on the magnitude of the impact, studying the nature and direction of the impact may lead us to a different conclusion. Another issue is that the two events took place within three years of each other, and some of their effects may have been difficult to separate. Further, the time frame of six years after 1987 (our data ended in 1993) may not have been sufficient for all the effects to have become manifest in the network.

IMPLICATIONS AND CONCLUSIONS

The results of our analysis suggest several interesting conclusions. First, the analysis demonstrates some important structural features of the strategic alliance network in the global steel industry and brings out the competitive factors that either drive or result from those features. The industry network is clearly very active, with a substantial number of relationships established across industry borders (i.e. between steel producers and upstream and downstream partners), and national borders. While American integrated steel producers are evidently the dominant players in the network, Japanese integrated steel producers are the most diversified in terms of their geographical and technological reach. The networking activity of American integrateds may have been driven by the circumstances of the US steel market (specifically Japanese auto transplants), as evidenced by their relatively low level of relations with partners other than American and Japanese firms. The Japanese steel producers appear to be the most outward-looking and best positioned, especially with respect to the part of the world outside the triad of the USA, Europe and Japan Minimills and specialty steel producers, while not as dominant as the integrateds, are significant players in the network.

Second, strategic alliances have been established both between members of the same strategic group and between members of different strategic groups. Group-level analysis confirms the dominant role of American integrateds, as well as the technological and geographical diversity of Japanese steel producers. As suggested earlier, the pattern of strategic alliance activity provides evidence of substantial strategic interaction within strategic groups as well as across strategic groups.

Third, the regulatory shock of 1984 appears to have had a much more significant impact on the structure of the industry network than the technology shock of 1987. Removing the regulatory barriers to interfirm cooperation resulted in a dramatic increase in strategic alliance activity, as well as observable changes in the pattern of such activity. On the other hand, the technology shock of 1987 was not followed by a comparable change either in the quantity or the structure of alliance activity. This result is not entirely consistent with the predictions in the literature as regards the effect of major technology shocks. For example, Piore and Sabel (1984) have argued that changes in production technology underlie radical shifts in the institutional structure of industries. Given the assessment of the 1987 event as a major turning point in the history of the steel industry (e.g. Ghemawat, 1993), a more radical realignment could have been expected. This inconsistency appears to point the way toward a more fine-grained analysis of the structural impact of industry events.

Apart from mapping the structure of the alliance network in the steel industry, the present study has provided a point of departure for a research program aimed at developing a theory of structural evolution in industry networks. Such a theory would begin by classifying ways in which industry events impact the underlying competitive forces of an industry, and propose how events in each category would change the structure of industry relationships. A conceptually rigorous and empirically valid theory of structural evolution in industry networks would be the necessary first step toward specifying how managers may use industry networks in their search for strategic competitiveness.

MANAGERIAL IMPLICATIONS

There are several managerial implications embedded in the context of this study. Our study illustrated the network of alliances in the global steel industry and how it evolved over time. Managers can use the framework developed in this chapter to examine their own networks. This process will shed light on both the flexibility and constraints facing their firm as a result of their network position.

One of the key managerial implications of adopting a network perspective is that it focuses on relationships between a set of partners rather than on the attributes of firms. That is, often managers develop profiles of competitors and examine their financial structure, market position, product offerings, and R&D orientation (i.e. attributes). This information is then used to develop action plans to address competitive threats. A network perspective suggests that the attributes of a firm are often derived or influenced from the set of relationships that the firm develops with suppliers, customers, and even competitors. Thus, action plans are often constrained by the set of relationships developed over time. Sometimes a firm cannot initiate a set of actions because it might violate an explicit or implicit contract, harm a current partner, or require additional resources that are not part of the current network. An important principle of the network perspective is the following: "Who you associate with matters."

A second implication relates to resource allocation. In today's economy where total quality management, outsourcing, alliances, and virtual corporations are the norm, the choice of partners is critical. The network perspective focuses on the flows of resources (e.g. knowledge, financial, managerial, physical) across organizational boundaries. In this setting, an appreciation of the amount and type of key resources that flow between organizations can have important competitiveness consequences. Further, how partners absorb and internalize the flow of resources over time can be a key component of industry evolution. Forward integration by a supplier can be the result of partnering with a customer and the customer's customer.

A third managerial implication is that a methodology exists for conducting a network analysis. We suggest that firms begin a network analysis in an area that is key to the organization. For example, in the multimedia industry, there is a diverse set of companies trying to establish a technological presence. A network analysis focusing on the technological relationships between partners can show which sets of firms are concentrating on particular technologies. Armed with this knowledge, your firm can assess the information and control benefits arising from your position in the network. Action plans can then be developed which focus on neutralizing competitor networks and enhancing the position of your network.

Adopting a network perspective complements the attribute perspective that currently dominates strategic management. Networks focus on relationships, how they are established, how they evolve and the benefits and constraints they place on organizations. Managers intuitively know that networks matter. However, intuition suffers from problems related to inconsistency and bias. We feel that the network perspective and its associated methodologies provide a mechanism for approaching fundamental business issues that addresses the inherent problems with intuitive decision making.

ACKNOWLEDGEMENT:

Research support from the Alfred P. Sloan Foundation program "Competitiveness in the Global Steel Industry" is gratefully acknowledged.

REFERENCES

Abe, E., and Suzuki, Y. (1991). *Changing Patterns of International Rivalry: Some Lessons from the Steel Industry*. Tokyo: University of Tokyo Press.

Borgatti, S.P., Everett, D., and Freeman, L.C. (1992). *UCINET IV Network Analysis Software*, Version 1.00. Columbia, SC: Analytic Technologies.

Burkhardt, M.E. and Brass, D.J. (1990). "Changing Patterns or Patterns of Change: The Effect of a Change in Technology on Social Network Structure and Power", *Administrative Science Quarterly*, 35, 104–127.

Burt, R.S. (1991). *Structure: A General Purpose Network Analysis Program*, Version 4.2. New York: Columbia University.

Burt, R.S. (1992). *Structural Holes: The Social Structure of Competition*. Cambridge, Mass.: Harvard University Press.

Business Week (1994). "The Odd Couple of Steel", 7 Nov., 106–108.

Christensen, C.R., Andrews, K.R., Bower, J.L., Hamermesh, R.G., and Porter, M.E. (1982). *Business Policy: Text and Cases*. Homewood, Ill.: Irwin.

Contractor, F. and Lorange, P. (1988). "Competition vs. Cooperation: A Benefit/cost Framework for Choosing between Fully-owned Investments and Cooperative Relationships", *Management International Review*, Special Issue, 5–18.

Duysters, G. and Hagedoorn, J. (1995). "Strategic Groups and Inter-firm Networks in International High-tech Industries", *Journal of Management Studies*, 32(3), 359–381.

Freeman, J. and Barley, S.R. (1990). "The Strategic Analysis of Inter-organizational Relations in Biotechnology", in R. Loveridge and M. Pitt (eds), *The Strategic Management of Technological Innovation*. Chichester: John Wiley & Sons.

Ghemawat, P. (1993). "Commitment to a Process Innovation: Nucor, USX and Thin Slab Casting", *Journal of Economics and Management Strategy*, 2(1), 135–161.

Grant, J.H., Ahlbrandt, R., Giarratani, F., and Prescott, J.E. (1995). "Restructuring for Competition in the Global Steel Industry", *Long Range Planning*, forthcoming.

Hamel, G. (1991). "Competition for Competence and Inter-partner Learning within International Strategic Alliances", *Strategic Management Journal*, 12, 83–103.

Harrigan, K.R. (1985). *Strategic Flexibility*. Lexington, Mass.: Lexington Books.

Harrigan, K.R. (1986). *Managing for Joint Venture Success*. Lexington, Mass.: Lexington Books.

Hogan, T. (1991). *Global Steel in the 1990s: Growth and Decline?* Lexington, Mass.: Lexington Books.

Knoedler, J.T. (1993). "Market Structure, Industrial Research, and Consumers of Innovation: Forging Backward Linkages to Research in the Turn-of-the-century U.S. Steel Industry", *Business History Review*, 67, Spring, 98–139.

Krackhardt, D., Blythe, J., and McGrath, C. (1994). "KrackPlot 3.0: An Improved Network Drawing Program", *Connections*, 17(2), 53–55.

Madhavan, R. and Prescott, J.E. (1995). "Market Value Impact of Joint Ventures: The Effect of Industry Information Processing Load", *Academy of Management Journal*, 38(3), 900–915.

Nohria, N. (1992). "Introduction: Is the Network Perspective a Useful Way of Studying Organizations?", in N. Nohria and R.G. Eccles (eds), *Networks and Organizations: Structure, Form and Action.* Boston, Mass.: Harvard University Press.

Nohria, N. and Garcia-Pont, C. (1991). "Global Strategic Linkages and Industry Structure", *Strategic Management Journal,* **12** Summer special issue, 105–124.

Piore, M. and Sabel, C.F. (1984). *The Second Industrial Divide.* New York: Basic Books.

Porter, M.E. (1980). *Competitive Strategy: Techniques for Analyzing Industries and Competitors.* New York: Free Press.

Schott, T. (1991). "Network Models", in R.S. Burt (ed.), *Structure: A General Purpose Network Analysis Program,* Version 4.2. New York: Columbia University, pp. 107–206.

Thomas, H. and Venkataraman, N. (1988). "Research on Strategic Groups: Progress and Prognosis", *Journal of Management Studies,* **25**, 537–555.

Wall Street Journal (1984). "Ruling on Steel Merger Hurts Industry Consolidation Plans", 16 Jan.

Wellman, B. (1988). "Structural Analysis: From Method and Metaphor to Theory and Substance", in B. Wellman and S.D. Berkowitz (eds), *Social Structures: A Network Approach,* New York: Cambridge University Press, pp. 19–61.

Yin, R.K. (1989). *Case Study Research: Design and Methods.* Newbury Park, Calif.: Sage.

13

Beyond or Behind the M-form? The Structures of European Business

RICHARD WHITTINGTON, MICHAEL MAYER

THE DOUBTFUL PROGRESS OF THE M-FORM

For the second time in the post-war period, European business is being promised an organizational revolution. The first revolution was that embodied in the decentralized multidivisional structure, the so-called M-form. Developed by the likes of General Motors and DuPont in the United States before the war (Chandler, 1962), the multidivisional structure was supposed to sweep the world, driving out earlier functional and holding company forms. Already by 1969, three-quarters of large American industrials had divisionalized (Rumelt, 1974). European business seemed to be lagging, but the trend was the same: by the beginning of the 1970s, the proportion of large industrial companies that had adopted the multidivisional structure was approaching half (Scott, 1973). In an influential *Harvard Business Review* article, Bruce Scott (1973: 141) summarized research by Harvard on the major European economies to say: "Overall, both in strategy and structure, European companies appear headed the same way as their US counterparts." Europe's future lay with the M-form of America.

Today's organizational revolution challenges the traditional multidivisional itself. The *keiretsu* structures of Japan (Fruin, 1992) and the loose networks of Chinese family businesses (Whitley, 1991) have shown that there is more than one way to organize successfully. The multidivisional's tendencies to exaggerated hierarchy, quantification and fragmentation have become manifest. The traditional multidivisional is now accused of excessive separation of strategy formulation from implementation (Mintzberg, 1994), an emphasis on financial performance at the expense of operations (Hayes and Abernathy, 1980) and a dangerous compartmentalization of innovation in separate divisions (Pavitt, 1991). At the end of the century, the structure developed in pre-war Dupont and General Motors may now be anachronistic, superseded by new, highly decentralized "network" or "federal" forms of organization (Miles and Snow, 1992; Bartlett and Ghoshal, 1993; Hedlund, 1994; Hamel and Prahalad, 1996). According to Bartlett and Ghoshal (1993), organizations today are going "beyond the M-form". Now is the time for the "N-form" (Hedlund, 1994). ABB replaces General Motors as the model (Taylor, 1992).

So the M-form is in doubt. This chapter reports research on its progress in two European countries, France and Germany, during the 1980s and early 1990s. Its context is the earlier Harvard research on the spread of the multidivisional form during the immediate post-war period.

According to Harvard, Europe at the beginning of the 1970s was still emphatically "behind", clinging on to the loosely organized "holding company" form and only slowly accepting the superior logic of the American multidivisional. While the research we report on here replicates and updates this Harvard research, our argument diverges. The traditional European holding company is not at an overwhelming disadvantage to the multidivisional. Examples from France and Germany suggest that this older form still has a place in advanced European economies. On the one hand, the holding company can be a highly dynamic and effective adaptation to the institutional constraints that derive from Europe's particular economic history. On the other, especially in its abhorrence of bureaucracy, the traditional holding company style echoes many of the virtues of the new network and federal models preached today. Either way, the holding company survives.

If the conventional M-form has only incompletely triumphed over this older form, how is it faring against the new network forms? Here we shall argue that, in Europe at least, there is still little evidence for a fundamental change in the structure of contemporary big business. Indeed, drawing on the example of French chemicals giant Rhône-Poulenc, we shall emphasize the continuities between the Chandlerian multidivisional and the new organizational forms. The M-form is adapting, not dying.

Thus our argument is a pluralistic and Fabian one. The multidivisional has not devoured all its predecessors; it coexists with them today and will probably continue to do so in the future. Over time, moreover, the multidivisional is itself gradually changing. The new form is not a radical break; it is just the third generation of the highly robust—but still not universal— multidivisional structure born in the 1920s.

RESEARCHING STRATEGY AND STRUCTURE IN EUROPE

This chapter draws upon findings from a study intended to update to the 1990s the original Harvard research on the spread of the diversified, multidivisional firm in Britain, France and Germany during the post-war period (Channon, 1973; Dyas and Thanheiser, 1976). We cannot present national statistics at this stage. Instead, we shall consider qualitative and case-based data drawn from a combination of documentary sources on the largest industrial firms in France and Germany and over 70 interviews with senior managers from 59 of these firms. These data give a broad overview of contemporary European organization, as well as allowing us to use mini-cases to explore particular aspects of organizational forms as they exist in Europe today.

Before going on, we need to define the basic organizational forms carefully. Harvard traditionally distinguishes between functional, holding and multidivisional forms (Channon, 1973; Rumelt, 1974). The distinction between the functional form and the multidivisional is easy, the former being highly centralized around key functions, the latter decentralized into business units. More difficult will be to distinguish the multidivisional from the other decentralized forms, the supposedly anachronistic holding company on the one hand, the new network organizations on the other.

Classically, the essential characteristic of the multidivisional is the separation of operating and strategic decisions (Chandler, 1962; Williamson, 1975: 288). Operating matters are decentralized to divisions ("quasi-firms" in Williamson's terms), while the centre retains firm strategic control over the portfolio as a whole. By equipping itself with an elite staff and rigorous reporting systems, and by detaching itself from operational responsibilities, the multidivisional head office is supposed to suppress operating management opportunism and to decide strategy and control performance rationally and objectively (Williamson, 1985). The multidivisional is decentralized operationally, centralized strategically. As is clear from Chandler's (1977) very title *The Visible Hand*, Williamson's (1985: 284) conception of the M-form as an internal capital market, and Scott's (1973) insistence on the internalization of market mechanisms, these authors tend to attribute to the multidivisional form the same frictionless, transparent rationality as claimed for the invisible hand of the market itself.

It is this capacity for top-down strategic control over the corporate whole that is the essence of the multidivisional. The characteristic of the holding company, however, is that the strategic control of the centre is often only partial or unsystematic. In their accounts of European holding companies 30 years ago, the Harvard researchers stressed how small headquarters, minority participations and top managers' involvement in operating businesses all combined to compromise the detached, rational and hierarchical control imputed to the multidivisional (Channon, 1973; Dyas and

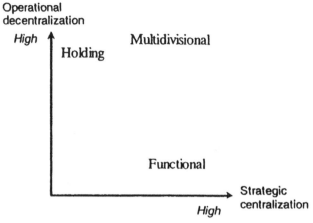

FIGURE 13.1   Basic organizational forms

Thanheiser, 1976). The holding company, then, was decentralized operationally, but without the centralized strategic control of the multidivisional.

FIGURE 13.1 provides a schematic representation of the three basic organizational forms identified by Harvard. The figure makes clear that the transition from either functional or holding types of organization involves a fundamental change in organizing principles—a decentralization of operations in the functional case, a centralization of corporate strategy in the holding. FIGURE 13.1 gives no space to the new network forms, however. As we shall argue later, this new generation of organizations involves no radical break equivalent to that between functional and multidivisional or holding and multidivisional. As we map the new form on to FIGURE 13.1, we shall see that it is merely a development of the multidivisional principle—decentralized operationally, centralized strategically. First, though, we shall consider the continued vitality of the European holding company.

THE EUROPEAN HOLDING COMPANY

For the original Harvard researchers, the problem of the holding company was the lack of independent central control over the various decentralized operational units. This did not exclude the possibility of operational excellence within subsidiary units; what was at stake was the capacity to manage the corporate whole. Without adequate headquarters staff, senior management detachment from operations or complete ownership of subsidiaries, strategic control could never be certain and systematic. The use of capital could not be effectively monitored, cash could not freely circulate, operations could not be objectively rationalized and poor performance could not be independently sanctioned (Channon, 1973; cf. Williamson, 1975). In these conditions, theory said, the holding company would be chronically inefficient.

At the beginning of the 1970s, between around a quarter and a third of British, French and German top industrial firms were still clinging to this apparently irrational and anachronistic form of organization (Channon, 1973; Dyas and Thanheiser, 1976: see TABLE 13.1). In the United States, by contrast, less than 3% of leading companies were still pure holding companies (Rumelt, 1974). In the era of the "American challenge" (Servan-Schreiber, 1969), Europe seemed distinctly "behind". Unless the European holdings changed, it was plain to the Harvard researchers that the competition from M-form American multinationals would soon sweep these unprofessional anachronisms away. Summarizing the findings of the Harvard research, Scott (1973: 142) made a direct Darwinian analogy, comparing the arrival of the American multidivisional in Europe to the introduction of the weasel in New Zealand: in the face of this new import, uncompetitive European forms of organization, such as the holding company, were as doomed to extinction as the kiwi.

A generation later, we can see that Harvard was too bold. There have been a surprising number of recent sightings of this supposedly extinct organizational form, the holding company. TABLE 13.1 compares the proportions found in various recent studies of large industrial firms in France, Germany and the UK. The pattern is considerably confused by the different definitions, methodologies and samples used in these studies, with some probably less sensitive to holding companies than others. However, it does seem safe to conclude from this table that something looking remarkably like the holding company is still at large in Western Europe.

What explains this incomplete triumph of the weasel-like M-form over

TABLE 13.1   Proportions of holding or functional/holding companies in various studies of large European industrial firms (%)

	Year	France	Germany	UK
Channon (1973)	1970			23
Dyas and Thanheiser (1976)	1970	33	27	
Cable and Dirrheimer (1983)	1980		31	
Hill and Pickering (1986)	1981?			16
Hill (1988)	1984/85?			23
Schmitz (1989)	1965–85		13	
Ezzamel and Watson (1993)	1985/86?			31
Pugh et al. (1993)	1988/90	20	8	0
Geroski and Gregg (1994)	1993			18

(Source: Mayer and Whittington, 1996, The Survival of the European Holding Company in R. Whitely and P. H. Kristensen (eds), *The Changing European Firm*, Routledge. Reproduced with permission).

the European kiwi? The answer is twofold. In this section, we shall emphasize the holding's fit with certain institutional peculiarities of the European environment. Later, though, we shall suggest that the classic M-form's competitive superiority over the holding has been much exaggerated, and that the new principles of organization emerging in the 1990s in some ways simply rediscover many of the traditional advantages of the European holding company. The kiwi can compete with the weasel.

It is today's increasing understanding of socio-economic institutions that saps old faiths in the universalistic one-best-way approaches embodied in claims such as Scott's (1973). The success of the Japanese and other Asian economies in recent years has brought much greater appreciation of the robustness of institutional differences between countries and therefore the variety of effective ways of competing locally (Whitley, 1994). Even Williamson (1993), once a convinced advocate of the universal superiority of the M-form, now concedes the importance of institutional context as providing "shift parameters" determining the local effectiveness of different forms of organization. This institutional sensitivity focuses attention on key parameters whose variation in different societies may alter the relative advantage of particular modes of operation, here particularly that of the multidivisional.

The key parameter shaping the origins of the multidivisional is well-developed capital markets. In the United States, capital is easily raised, shareholdings have become diffuse and there is an active market for corporate control (Fligstein and Brantley, 1992; Demsetz and Lehn, 1988). Families have withdrawn from management and large companies are run by a new, well-trained and abundant class of professional managers (Chandler, 1990; Fligstein, 1990). For the multidivisional—hungry for capital as it diversifies, demanding complete ownership of operations and dependent upon ranks of professional managers—these are fertile conditions. But such conditions are far from the rule in continental Europe.

The institutional context of Europe is very different from that of the United States. Stock markets are less efficient, ownership and control are closely connected, and professional management still an emergent phenomenon. In France at the end of the 1980s, 28% of the top 180 industrial and commercial corporations were under "active" family control, in the sense of owning families being directly involved in management, with a further 16% under "passive" family control, simply with large ownership stakes (Leser and Vidalie, 1991). In Germany, Ziegler (1984) estimated that 37% of the 259 largest firms in the late 1970s were still privately owned and controlled, with a further 21% state-owned. According to Bauer and Bertin-Mourot's (1992) analysis of the top 100 firms in each of France and Germany, 34% of French chairmen/chief executives, and 27% of German, had significant ownership connections, either as founders of their firms or as members of shareholding families. Thus European families and entrepreneurs seem much more closely involved in big business than in America, clinging on to managerial control and constraining free access to external capital. The total ownership of subsidiaries and reliance on professional management characteristics of the multidivisional are not likely to be attractive or universally available options.

Under these institutional constraints, reliance on family managers or partial ownership of new ventures is often the most practical way forward for ambitious enterprises, even if second-best in theory. Particularly in the food industry, family holding companies such as Tchibo and Oetker in Germany, or the private empire of Bongrain in France, have achieved rapid growth and diversification in the last 20 years, more than resisting the challenge of professionally managed multinationals such as Nestlé and Unilever. But perhaps the most spectacular example of turning institutional constraints to advantage is the case of Financière Agache, the French luxury goods conglomerate created by Bernard Arnault.

During the 1980s, this typical French holding has been transformed by Bernard Arnault into the leading luxury goods company in the world. This was despite breaking all the rules of multidivisional organization (see next section, below). Arnault has not detached himself from strategy, but is closely involved in subsidiary management at various levels. He is supported by the smallest of head office staffs, he continues to depend heavily on original families for management and he has not yet integrated related subsidiaries into coherent divisions. He does not even have majority ownership of his largest business—LVMH—a company that is quoted in its own right and operates its own reporting system independent of the rest of the group's. Guinness has a "minorité de blocage" over the crucial drinks activities of Moët-Hennessy, while the Guerlain family sits on the board of Dior, controller of their own parent company. Without the staff, systems or share-ownership that would allow unambiguous command, Arnault must rely on informal, spontaneous cooperation for the creation of group synergies.

Financière Agache

Financière Agache is the highest level managerial unit in a cascade of financial holdings and sub-holdings that include such famous names as Christian Dior, Bon Marché, and the various components of the LVMH group (including Louis Vuitton, Givenchy, Christian Lacroix, Moët et Chandon and Hennessy). In 1994, Financière Agache was the fifth largest group in France by market capitalization, only 10 years after its creation in its present form.

Bernard Arnault had created the group by a series of daring acquisitions during the 1980s, most notably of Agache Willot, a failing textiles holding company in 1984, and the family luxury goods company LVMH in 1988. Ultimate control of the group rests with Arnault's family investment company SEBP, although several parts are independently quoted and ownership is partial at nearly every stage in the cascade. Indeed, the largest part of the empire, LVMH, is only 45% owned by a sub-holding far removed from Arnault's own

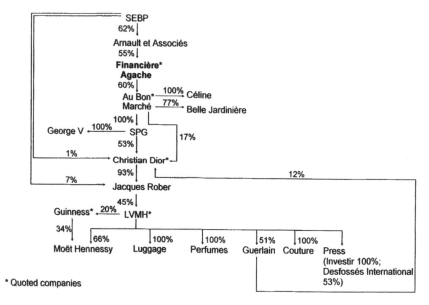

FIGURE 13.2   Simplified organigram of Financière Agache, 1994

ultimate holding (see FIGURE 13.2). At various levels, Arnault has deliberately brought in various external shareholders to help support his newly constructed empire—especially British drinks group Guinness, the private Banque Worms and state-owned Crédit Lyonnais.

Financière Agache is not managed along conventional multidivisional lines. The company describes itself as "a federation of small and medium-sized enterprises", with operations having a great deal of autonomy and few central constraints. The main functional coherence is provided by a human resources department at the level of Financière Agache, which oversees personnel policy, especially management development, for the group as a whole. Financial reporting and treasury functions are not integrated, however, with LVMH for instance operating independently as a quoted company in its own right. Within LVMH itself, clusters of subsidiaries are only gradually being coordinated within *secteurs* (not divisions): the seven main champagne brands were not merged under a common *Directeur Général* until 1994; on the couture side, Céline and Christian Dior were independent of LVMH's own couture sector. Members of the original owning families are still prominent in management positions and retain considerable shareholder rights. Thus when in 1994 Arnault brought the perfume company Guerlain into the group, the Guerlain family was left with a slight majority of the voting shares in the new subsidiary, management control and a 12% share of Christian Dior.

Financière Agache has only 30 head office staff; there are no distinct headquarters for sectors. Control and coordination are typically direct and informal, relying largely upon Bernard Arnault himself. Arnault is *Président-Directeur Général* (PDG) not only of the financial holding company Arnault et Associés, but of the two most important operating companies, Christian Dior and LVMH, as well. Every two months, Arnault presides personally over the Comité d'Information et Renseignements Généraux, bringing together all subsidiary PDGs or DGs. Arnault also presides over the bimonthly meetings of each sector. Synergies are negotiated voluntarily between subsidiaries, according to the opportunities that come to the attention of either Arnault or subsidiary presidents at any of their formal or informal interactions.

The success of Financière Agache's holding structure lies in its resolution of the French institutional problem of a weak stock market. Arnault was able to construct a world-wide group so quickly precisely because he had not insisted on total ownership of integrated divisions, but had instead brought in outside capital and managers through his complex pyramid of holdings and sub-holdings. Financière Agache's effectiveness as a holding derives not from administrative efficiency, but from entrepreneurial efficiency within a French context. Part of the answer to the puzzle of the holding company's survival lies, therefore, not in the sleepy traditionalism of European management, but in how institutional differences in Europe alter the relative advantage of the multidivisional. In the absence of well-developed stock markets, the multidivisional is not clearly a superior organizing vehicle for acquisitive expansion by capital-starved ambitious entrepreneurs such as Arnault. In other words, the relative advantage of organizational forms still depends on institutional context.

Today, however, the comparative advantage of the traditional multidivisional is under general attack. Its detachment from operations, its liability to short-term financial biases and its inherent divisiveness are criticized from nearly every side (Mintzberg, 1994; Fligstein, 1990; Bartlett and Ghoshal, 1993). Now, it is claimed, is the turn for the "N-form".

BEYOND THE M-FORM?

As it turns out, the European holding company has not shared the fate of the New Zealand kiwi. Indeed, if we are to credit recent modish talk about new "federal" (Handy, 1992), "flatter" (Drucker, 1988), "network" (Miles and Snow, 1992), "internal market" (Halal, 1993), or "management holding" (Bühner, 1992) types of organization, then the multidivisional form itself is about to become as extinct as—well—the dodo. Bettis (1991) buries it even deeper, labelling the multidivisional an "organisational fossil". Times have certainly moved on since the birth of the original M-form in pre-war corporate America. All the same, we think there are good grounds for treating these claims cautiously.

The essence of the new form appears to be the supersession of hierarchies by "networks" of alliances and subcontracting relationships (Miles and Snow, 1992). Instead of by command down an ultimately centralized hierarchy, business activities are coordinated by systems of market or market-like contracts between decentralized business units, internal or external to the firm. These networks appear to challenge the notion of the multidivisional enterprise from at least two directions. Briefly, internal networks overturn the traditional bureaucratic hierarchies of the multidivisional, while external networks undermine the firm's very boundaries (Hamel and Pralahad, 1996). Here we shall focus on the first of these challenges.

The most frequently cited model for the new internal network form appears to be the Swedish engineering multinational ABB (Handy, 1992; Miles and Snow, 1992; Bartlett and Ghoshal, 1993; Halal, 1993). In the most careful analysis, Bartlett and Ghoshal (1993) acknowledge continuities between ABB and the traditional M-form, particularly in the strategic role of the company's head office, its decentralization of operations and its rigorous reporting system. However, according to these two researchers, what qualifies ABB as "beyond the M-form" is a series of both structural and processual characteristics that together add up to something distinctly new.

On the structural side, Bartlett and Ghoshal (1993) highlight a number of ABB's characteristics, particularly: the company's business–geographic matrix, replacing unidimensional divisions; the extreme decentralization, creating a "federation" of 1300 companies; the leanness of the structure, with only one intermediate level; the thinness of central staffs, working usually as contractors in an internal market; and finally the financial responsibility of front-line companies, each with their own balance sheets, the capacity to retain a third of their profits, and their own treasury management. Important to holding together and maximizing the value of this highly decentralized structure are two key processes, vertical and horizontal. In an environment where knowledge has become as important a resource as capital, horizontal processes of networking and learning emerge through functional councils or *ad hoc* task forces exchanging experience between decentralized units. These horizontal processes are encouraged by the vertical process of creating and communicating a shared mission and sense of corporate unity, led by the highly visible personality of CEO Percy Barnevik. As Bartlett and Ghoshal (1993: 42) sum up, ABB is "based on a principle of *proliferation and subsequent aggregation* of small independent entrepreneurial units from the bottom up, rather than one of *division and devolution* of resources and responsibilities from the top. . . . In contrast to the classic M-form, where control over most resources is held at the corporate level, in the new model resources are decentralized to the front-line units which operate with limited dependence on the corporate parent for technological, financial or human resources, but with considerable interdependence among themselves" (emphases in the original).

How important and how radical is the oft-cited ABB example? It is easy to carp. The matrix dates from the 1960s at least (Knight, 1976), Chandler (1962) remarked on an equivalent tendency towards ever smaller business units at General Electric, with already more than 100 in the 1950s, and

Barnard (1938) wrote of the importance of corporate leaders instilling business purpose at exactly the same epoch as the emergence of the multidivisional itself. Although Miles and Snow (1992) and Bartlett and Ghoshal (1993) emphasize the emergent nature of this new form, it is still remarkable how few other in-depth examples have so far been put alongside ABB.

Yet ABB is not quite alone and it certainly does not look very much like previous models, either pre-war DuPont or pre-Welch General Electric. The recent initiatives of companies such as BP in the UK, Vorwerk in Germany and Rhône-Poulenc in France do seem to stretch the limits of traditional multidivisional thinking. New things are being done. Our perception, however, is that this new form of organization represents an extension rather than a supersession of the older types of multidivisional. The fundamental continuities in structural principles become evident if seen in the context of previous evolutions in the multidivisional. There has been no great step comparable to that between the functional and the multidivisional. In the remainder of this section, we shall propose a simple schema for understanding the evolving multidivisional, and explore the latest generation through an analysis of both the well-known case of ABB and another firm from our sample that seems to be experimenting in a similar fashion—Rhône-Poulenc (see next section, below).

Rhône-Poulenc

Rhône-Poulenc is France's largest chemicals company, with a turnover of over FF86 000m. State-owned, it expanded rapidly overseas during the 1980s through a series of acquisitions, especially in the United States. Since 1969, the company had been based on a classic multidivisional structure, introduced by McKinsey itself and with eight main divisions. However, as it began to digest its acquisitions during the early 1990s, the company began a radical decentralization.

Jean-René Fourtou, PDG since 1986 and an ex-consultant himself (from Bossard, France's leading firm), reorganized Rhône-Poulenc around five sectors, split into a total of 50 strategic business units. These SBUs were themselves broken down into typically three or more *entreprises*, each focused on a particular activity and market. It is these *entreprises*—about 300 in all—that are now the effective profit centres. The SBUs themselves exist less as managerial sub-units than as groupings to bring together related *enterprises* for common strategic coordination and reflection. "Country delegates" provide some lateral coordination as well, representing Rhône-Poulenc locally.

This decentralization to *entreprises* has been reinforced by substantial changes at the centre. The headquarters staff has been cut from 900 to 250. Central planning has fallen from 30 to 3 professional staff: the company no longer produces consolidated plans for Rhône-Poulenc as a whole. Formerly central functions have been either decentralized towards sectors, as was R&D, or constituted as internally contracting central services, as was engineering. Remaining central functional staffs now define and audit central policies—of which there are very few—and have the responsibility for cultivating professional networks between decentralized operating units (for instance the finance and R&D staff networks).

The top *comité exécutif* is now smaller (seven against nine members) and includes only three of the five sectoral chiefs. Meeting two days a month, it has a simplified agenda: overall group performance, with basic sectoral (rather than SBU or *entreprise*) figures; strategic items, for instance adjustments to the portfolio; and human resources. Human resources is a regular agenda item because the effectiveness of decentralization depends on the quality of its managers. The *comité exécutif* only reviews sector investment decisions exceptionally. It considers its role as primarily allocating broad capital totals to sectors at the beginning of the year, the sectors themselves deciding how to spend them. Some oversight is maintained by the five *conseils de secteur*, typically including two or three members of the *comité exécutif* as well as representatives of central functions and meeting three times a year. It is up to the *conseils* and the sectoral presidents to decide whether to refer anything up to the *comité exécutif*—there are few compulsory rules. Treasury functions are however centralized and all sectors conform to common reporting systems.

Although the *comité exécutif* diffuses clear statements of corporate vision, values and management principles, it does not directly enforce internal cooperation from the top. In the words of a senior manager: "The synergies must appear of their own accord; if they don't appear, they're not true synergies". Within sectors, synergy is facilitated by the loosely structured SBUs and through interventions by sectoral management. Between sectors, synergy and other corporate strategic issues can be addressed through the professional networks, internally contracted central services and the *comité d'orientation*, a group of 60 top managers from around the world who meet three times a year for two-day seminars on key corporate themes. Common managerial training policies and extensive transfers between sectors, *entreprises* and countries reinforce personal networks. According to one senior manager, "The problem of decentralization is not a problem of organigrams. It is a problem of behaviour. . . . Decentralization is not a design. It lies in the principles of management and the sort of people who go with it".

As TABLE 13.2 indicates, the structure described by Alfred Chandler (1962) is just one early type of multidivisional. The multidivisional structures developed by DuPont and General Motors before the Second World War achieved the separation of operations from strategy primarily by introducing for the first time financial systems. The problem for these companies was the allocation of capital between competing alternatives within these newly diversified corporations. Their new tool was the famous pyramid of ratios culminating in the return on investment criterion developed by Du Pont. This pyramid of financial ratios was mirrored by the organizational shape, with the hierarchy cascading down towards an ever-wider base of more and more disaggregated profit centres. These new financial methods lent themselves later to the development of the conglomerate, a form that Chandler (1990) regards with suspicion but Williamson (1985) takes as a perfectly natural extension of the idea of internal capital markets.

The model that Harvard preferred in the 1970s was the second generation

TABLE 13.2   The evolving multidivisional

	Investor	Managerial	Network
Emergence	1920s–1950s	1960s–1970s	1980s–
Key resource	Capital	Scale and scope	Knowledge
Key technique	Financial controls	Planning	Exchange
Key function	Finance	Corporate planning	Human resources
Structure shape	Pyramid	Pear	Pancake
Examples	Du Pont	General Electric	ABB, Rhône-Poulenc

of multidivisional, the "managerial", relying on a new technology, corporate planning. Here too, strategy was rigorously separated from operations, but now the focus was on the search for advantages of scale and scope. The ideal type is General Electric during the 1960s and 1970s, when its 200 corporate planners were at the lead in creating the technological apparatus of modern planning (Pascale, 1990). Companies like General Electric began to acquire rather pear-like profiles as their middles swelled with corporate staff and second- and third-level managers struggling to analyse and control.

Since the 1980s, the "managerial multidivisional" has been widely challenged, as the example of "neutron Jack" Welch at General Electric most famously illustrates (Pascale, 1990). This challenge, we argue, has not resulted in the complete supersession of the basic multidivisional structure, but the emergence of a new flatter version, what we term here the "network" multidivisional. Here the emphasis is on the horizontal, rather than the vertical, exchange rather than command and control, self-organizing instead of bureaucracy, and networking instead of managerialism.

With the label "network multidivisional", we acknowledge the proponents of new forms of organization and incorporate key elements of their analysis into our model. But we also stress substantial continuities with the multidivisional on critical organizational dimensions. The recent rejection of planning, and the resorting to internal network forms of coordination, do not alter the fundamental centralization of strategy and decentralization of operations. Indeed, the extreme decentralization of ABB or Rhône-Poulenc has if anything accentuated the divide. The purging of corporate staffs at ABB and Rhône-Poulenc, as at many other companies recently, has removed even the means by which senior management might get involved in operating decisions. They have neither the staff nor the time to meddle. Moreover, reliance on market mechanisms for the control of remaining central services (as for engineering at Rhône-Poulenc, for example) represents merely an extension of the internal market principle so emphasized by the early theorists of the multidivisional. At the same time, the rigorous reporting systems installed at both ABB and Rhône-Poulenc work effectively to increase the transparency of the internal capital market. Even the partial retention of profits allowed to subsidiaries in ABB, although apparently a flagrant contravention of the internal allocative efficiency of the multidivisional, is finally provisional: it has not inhibited the closure and sale of many businesses within the company's extensive empire. The centre retains clear overall control of the corporate portfolio, and, as the stream-lined top-management agenda of Rhône-Poulenc indicates, is possibly more than ever focused on the strategy and performance of the corporation as a whole. In short, in the "network multidivisional" accountability for operations is more transparent, and top management more objectively detached, than ever in the older "managerial" model. Returning to Figure 13.1, the network multidivisional occupies the same corner as earlier generations.

More innovative, however, are the ways in which the network multidivisional strives to maintain coherence between its decentralized operations. A stripped-down headquarters, combined with the transfer of responsibility to a decentralized mass of operating units (1300 in ABB, 300 in Rhône-Poulenc), creates an organization which is more than flat. The pancake image also puts the accent on circular interaction between these fragmented units. With so many decentralized business units (effectively Williamsonian quasi-firms), this interaction cannot be managed top-down, but relies on self-organizing, personal and informal networks. Core shared values become important. Thus we have in the network model not just the inter-change of internal contracting, but the heavy emphasis on corporate visions and philosophies now evident at both ABB, Rhône-Poulenc and much more widely. The two companies go to great lengths to reinforce informal ties between management—through Barnevik's famous travelling slide-shows (Bartlett and Ghoshal, 1993), or through Rhône-Poulenc's regular assem-blies at its *comité d'orientation*. The French company, especially, reinforces these linkages by its policies on managerial mobility and the *comité exécu-tif*'s attention to human resource issues. The functional networks and coun-cils at both companies again create opportunities for horizontal exchange.

In these interactions, the new critical resource is knowledge (Bartlett and Ghoshal, 1993; Hedlund, 1994)—knowledge of internal best practice, knowledge of market opportunities, knowledge of competitor moves around the globe. Here the search for synergy is not managed top-down, but is spontaneous and bottom-up. Critical is the creation of a corporate human resource with the mutual trust and common identity that is able and prepared to exchange knowledge in these informal ways. The network multidivisional needs the visible handshake of enduring relationships as much as the invisible hand of internal markets. But the development of this human resource is not simply compartmentalized within the human resource function at head office; it becomes a diffused responsibility. At Rhône-Poulenc, all chiefs—at group, sectoral, SBU and functional levels—have the task of ensuring coaching and learning.

Informal exchanges have always existed within organizations. The difference of the network multidivisional is both that it is so much more reliant on these unmanaged exchanges and that it is much more deliberate in creating the framework in which they can take place. Our conclusion, then, is that the new form does not go "beyond" the multidivisional; it simply extends and develops certain principles that were always more or less latent within either the ideal or the practice of previous generations of multidivisional. Moreover, new features of this network-model multidivisional do not make redundant those of previous generations: old considerations for capital allocation or scale and scope are not displaced, simply complemented by a more explicit concern for knowledge. In the same vein, the network model is no more likely to become a universally triumphant model than its predecessors. Just as the managerial model never extinguished the investor model, and the multidivisional as a whole has failed to drive out the holding, so can we expect the network model finally to exist alongside other forms of organization, not to supersede them entirely. The appropriate model will depend, as ever, on contingency factors such as scale, scope, knowledge intensity and both competitive and institutional environments. We should abandon the language of "beyond" and "behind", with its teleological undertones, and talk more of "beside".

This conservative message should reassure managers, even if it disappoints consultants. Managers do not universally face a need for wholesale organizational transformation. For many firms, earlier generations of the multidivisional structure will remain essentially adequate, especially where there are either few real linkages between divisions or where brute capital intensity dictates the pursuit of scale economies rather than the "depth" economies of knowledge-intensive sectors. Even for those firms where networking needs do press, the transformation will demand in many respects simply the extension and facilitation of practices that are already established. As they move to the network multidivisional, managers will be doing many things that they have done before, only more. They will be decentralizing still further, learning more actively and interacting more intensely. Indeed, managers themselves will become more important, as their knowledge and their interrelationships overtake capital, scale and scope as the key competitive resource.

CONCLUSIONS

This chapter has addressed two organizational models, Harvard's multidivisional of the 1970s and the new network organization of the 1990s. The record of the Harvard multidivisional looks distinctly tarnished now. It has failed to drive out the traditional holding company, while being overtaken by the latest generation of organizational innovations. The claims for its superiority were exaggerated, its institutional specificity neglected. This understanding of the previous model makes us cautious about the new. Our argument has been that the new network organization does not represent a radical break in organizing principles, and that it is as unlikely to supersede earlier forms as the earlier multidivisional failed to crush the holding.

Claims for the classic multidivisional have been disappointed because they underestimated the strengths of the old forms and failed to anticipate the innovations of the new. In reserving too exclusively the strategy-making process for the centre, and in smothering horizontal collaboration with vertical control, the multidivisional has often extinguished its competitive advantages in accountability and system. Today's conditions seem increasingly to demand a closeness of decision to action, lateral as well as hierarchical interaction, and self-organizing rather than bureaucratic coordination. In the light of these demands, the holding company may not be as bad as it once looked. Indeed, the decentralization, spontaneity and direct involvement of the holding company seem now to provide the link between recent trends in managerial fashion and enduring features of European organization. In its continued attachment to the holding, Europe has not necessarily been "behind".

The claim that advanced economies are actually going beyond the M-form is no more certain. This chapter does suggest that there has been some change, but within quite strict limits. We would not want to confuse some prominent recent experiments with a fundamental revolution in corporate organization. By comparison with previous innovations in organizational design, the emerging ABB-style organization appears essentially conservative, leaving intact the key properties of the multidivisional—decentralization of operations, centralization of strategy. Indeed, in taking as their exemplars for the new network corporation not only ABB but also Electrolux, Bartlett and Ghoshal (1993) have missed one very traditional aspect of their organization, their ownership. Ironically enough, both companies are embedded in a very old form of network—the Wallenberg family's personal empire in Sweden, dating from before the Second World War. At this higher level of analysis, these "new form" companies are throwbacks to a very ancient type of familial capitalism, one more reminiscent of the much-maligned holding than any of the subsequent forms preached in business school theory. Plus ça change, plus c'est la même chose.

ACKNOWLEDGEMENTS

The authors would like to thank the Nuffield Foundation, Warwick Business School and Groupe HEC, France, for their support in the course of this research.

REFERENCES

Barnard, C. (1938) *The Functions of the Executive.* Boston: Harvard University Press.

Bartlett, C. and Ghoshal, S. (1993) "Beyond the M-Form, Towards a Managerial Theory of the Firm", *Strategic Management Journal,* **14,** Special Issue, 23–46.

Bauer, M. and Bertin-Mourot, B. (1992) *Les 200 en France et Allemagne.* Paris: CNRS/Heidrich and Struggles.

Bettis, R.A. (1991) "Strategic Management and the Straight-Jacket: an Editorial Essay", *Organization Science,* **2**(3), 315–319.

Bühner, R. (1992) *Management Holding: Unternehmensstruktur der Zukunft.* Landberg am Lech: Verlag Moderne Industrie.

Cable, J. and Dirrheimer, M.J. (1983) "Markets and Hierarchies: an Empirical Test of the Multidivisional Hypothesis in Germany", *International Journal of Industrial Organization,* **1,** 43–62.

Chandler, A.D. (1962) *Strategy and Structure: Chapters in the History of American Enterprise.* Cambridge, Mass.: MIT Press.

Chandler, A.D. (1977) *The Visible Hand: the Managerial Revolution in American Business.* Cambridge, Mass.: Harvard University Press.

Chandler, A.D. (1990) *Scale and Scope: the Dynamics of Industrial Capitalism.* Cambridge, Mass.: Harvard University Press.

Channon, D. (1973) *The Strategy and Structure of British Enterprise.* Cambridge, Mass.: Harvard University Press.

Demsetz, H. and Lehn, K. (1988) "The Structure of Corporate Ownership: Causes and Consequences", in H. Demsetz (ed.), *Ownership, Control and the Firm,* Oxford: Blackwell.

Drucker, P.F. (1988) "The Coming of the New Organization", *Harvard Business Review,* Jan–Feb, 45–53.

Dyas, G. and Thanheiser, H. (1976) *The Emerging European Enterprise.* London: Macmillan.

Ezzamel, M. and Watson, R. (1993) "Organisational Form, Ownership Structure, and Corporate Performance: a Contextual Analysis of UK Companies", *British Journal of Management,* **4,** 161–176.

Fligstein, N. (1990) *The Transformation of Corporate Control.* Cambridge, Mass.: Harvard University Press.

Fligstein, N. and Brantley, P. (1992) "Bank Control, Owner Control or Organisational Dynamics: Who Controls the Large Modern Corporation", *American Journal of Sociology,* **98**(2), 280–307.

Fruin, W.M. (1992) *The Japanese Enterprise System: Competitive Strategies and Co-operative Structures.* Oxford: Clarendon Paperbacks.

Geroski, P. and Gregg, P. (1994) "Corporate Restructuring in the UK during the Recession", *Business Strategy Review,* **5**(2), 1–19.

Halal, W. (1993) "The Transition from Hierarchy to ... What?" in W.E. Halal, A. Geranmayeh, and J. Pourdehnad (eds), *Internal Markets,* New York: Wiley, pp. 27–51.

Hamel, G. and Prahalad, C.K. (1996) "Competing in the New Economy", *Strategic Management Journal,* **17,** 237–242.

Handy, C. (1992) "Balancing Corporate Power: a New Federalist Paper", *Harvard Business Review,* Nov–Dec, 59–72.

Hayes, R.H. and Abernathy, W. (1980) "Managing our Way to Economic Decline", *Harvard Business Review,* July–August, 67–85.

Hedlund, G. (1994) "A Model of Knowledge Management and the N-Form Corporation", *Strategic Management Journal*, **15**, 73–90.

Hill, C.W.L. (1988) "Corporate Control Type, Strategy, Size and Financial Performance", *Journal of Management Studies*, **25**(5), 403–417.

Hill, C.W.L. and Pickering, J.F. (1986) "Divisionalization, Decentralization and Performance of Large United Kingdom Companies", *Journal of Management Studies*, **23**(1), 26–50.

Knight, K. (1976) "Matrix Organization: a Review", *Journal of Management Studies*, **12**(2), 111–130.

Leser, E. and Vidalie, A. (1991) "Le Capital des 200 Premières Entreprises Françaises", *Sciences et Vie Economique*, **76**, October, 46–57.

Mayer, M. and Whittington, R. (1996) "The Survival of the European Holding Company", in R. Whitely and P.H. Kristensen (eds), *The Changing European Firm*, London: Routledge, pp. 87–109.

Miles, R. and Snow, C. (1992) "Causes of Failure in Network Organizations", *California Management Review* Summer, 53–72.

Mintzberg, H. (1994) *The Rise and Fall of Strategic Planning*. Englewood Cliffs, NJ: Prentice-Hall.

Pascale, R. (1990) *Managing on the Edge*. New York: Simon and Schuster.

Pavitt, K. (1991) "Key Characteristics of the Large Innovating Firm", *British Journal of Management*, **2**, 41–50.

Pugh, D., Mallory, G. and Clarke, T.A. (1993) "Organisational Structure and Structural Change in European Manufacturing Organisations". Paper given at *British Academy of Management Conference*, Milton Keynes.

Rumelt, R. (1974) *Strategy, Structure and Economic Performance*. Boston: Harvard Business School.

Schmitz, R. (1989) "Zur Erfolgsrelevanz der internen Organisation börsennotierter Industrieaktiengesellschaftenn, in H. Albach (ed.), *Organisation*, Wiesbaden: Gubler, pp. 173–208.

Scott, B. (1973) "The New Industrial Estate: Old Myths and New Realities", *Harvard Business Review*, March–April, 133–148.

Servan-Schreiber, J. (1969) *The American Challenge*. London: Penguin.

Taylor, W. (1992) "The Logic of a Global Business: an Interview with ABB's Percy Barnevick", *Harvard Business Review*, March–April, 91–105.

Whitley, R.D. (1991) "The Social Construction of Business Systems in East Asia", *Organization Studies*, **12**(1), 1–28.

Whitley, R. (1994) "Dominant Forms of Economic Organization in Market Economies", *Organization Studies*, **15**(2), 153–182.

Williamson, O.E. (1975) *Markets and Hierarchies: Analysis and Anti-Trust Implications*. New York: Free Press.

Williamson, O.E. (1985) *The Economic Institutions of Capitalism*. New York: Free Press.

Williamson, O.E. (1993) "Transaction Costs and Organizational Theory", *Journal of Industrial and Corporate Change*, **2**(2), 107–156.

Ziegler, R. (1984) "Das Netz der Personen und Kapitalverflechtungen Deutscher und Osterreichischer Unternehmen", *Kölner Zeitschrift für Soziologie und Sozialpsychologie*, **36**, 585–614.

Section III

Style

In 1966, convinced that the most significant developments of the next quarter-century would be in the social sciences rather than the physical sciences, Douglas McGregor added significantly to discussions of how to make human organizations more effective. In *The Human Side of Enterprise* he compared two views of the tasks of management. The "conventional view" had management perceiving the workforce as indolent, lacking in ambition, indifferent to organizational needs, resistant to change, gullible, and unwilling to accept responsibility. He labeled this view "Theory X". McGregor suggested that people are not, by nature, as the conventional view portrayed them, but may have become so as a result of their experience in organizations. He then proposed an alternative management philosophy, in which an organizational environment is provided in which workers are encouraged to achieve their own, as well as organizational goals, to direct their own efforts, to assume more responsibility, and to recognize and develop their own capabilities. This view he called "Theory Y".

Now, well past the end of McGregor's quarter-century, his philosophies of management have become well known throughout the world, and have become the basis of the management philosophy for countless organizations. In the process, management style has gained recognition as an important element in corporate effectiveness, as corroborated by the chapters in this section.

Craig and Yetton examine international management skills of Australian firms competing successfully overseas. The authors describe their findings as contrary to the commonly held belief that the future belongs to those firms that are best at integrating globally while remaining locally responsive. They utilize two mini case studies to illustrate this proposition.

Delmas, Ghertman, and Heiman utilize transaction cost economics to explain the wide difference in credibility between US and French government policies for their nuclear power industries. They find that France, with its well-insulated institutional setup, has avoided the US problems that stem from a system that is open to inputs from virtually all interested parties. Their evidence supports the hypothesis that transaction costs are higher in the USA than in France for nuclear power.

Gilbert and Lorange look at how the business community and business schools have responded to the need for producing business executives who are visionaries, strategists, multiple-culture oriented, charismatic leaders, fast decision-makers and flexible, innovative, rigorous managers. They conclude that, while corporations would like to establish learning partnerships, business schools, who should be their natural partners, are having difficulty responding to the challenge.

Hafsi and Martin de Holan offer an approach to studying strategic management in leading nations—an area that they feel has been avoided by researchers as either nonexistent or too complex to study. Using a framework for the strategy-making process, and a study of the economic development of Taiwan over the past 100 years, the authors argue that the processes that determine behavior in large complex private-sector organizations are not all that different from those in large, complex organizations (e.g. national governments) in the public sector.

Thiétart and Xuereb propose that organizations attempt to confine complex and uncertain systems into "islands of rationality", in order to enhance project managers' ability to make decisions and take actions. The authors examine the effectiveness of the different means used by organizations to reduce managers' perceptions of uncertainty and complexity. They find that, in highly uncertain and complex situations, formal tools do not allow managers to react rapidly enough, but an innovative culture or a project management process tends to reinforce managers' feelings of certainty and good management.

Wooldridge and Floyd discuss two forms of consensus associated with organizational performance: (1) consensus on goals and means (e.g. deliberate strategies), and (2) top management team agreement on organizational capabilities (e.g. emergent decisions). Based on their integrative model, the authors suggest that the presence of both forms of consensus is more consistently associated with high levels of organizational performance.

Following are additional readings relating to style:

- In *Scientific Management* (1912) Frederick Taylor described four principles of scientific management: (1) development of a science to replace the old rule-of-thumb methods; (2) scientific selection and progressive teaching/development of the workmen; (3) bringing together the scientifically selected workmen and science; and (4) division of work between management and labor. This would result, he suggested, in managers becoming more the servants of the workers than the workers being servants of the managers—a concept that must have been quite revolutionary at that time.

- Reminding us that the concept of management was relatively unknown before the mid-nineteenth century, Peter Drucker suggests that, in all of human history, no institution has emerged as fast, or had a greater impact in such a relatively short time, as has management (*The New Realities*, 1989). Drucker describes management as both a social function and a liberal art, and that it consists of a very few, essential principles, which he describes.
- In *The New Competitors* (1985) D. Quinn Mills describes a changing business environment that requires managers to rethink both their values and the way they manage. Mills suggests several values that are becoming essential for companies competing in a world in which change is the norm, including a genuine people-orientation.
- Jerry Harvey offers a number of interesting perspectives on management style in *The Abilene Paradox—And Other Meditations on Management* (1988).
- Peter Block argues that, despite voluminous discussion of such managerial concepts as continuous improvement, visionary leadership, and customer-focus, real change has been limited. In *Stewardship* (1993) he suggests that organizations encourage partnership between customers and their suppliers at all levels within organizations, as well as with outside customers.

14

The Myth of the Global Renaissance Manager

JANE F. CRAIG, PHILIP W. YETTON

This chapter is an empirical and theoretical piece that examines the international management skills of Australian firms competing successfully overseas. The perspective generated by this analysis of successful firms from a small economy sheds a different light on the question of how best to manage multinational corporations (MNCs).

It is almost a truism that in increasingly global and dynamic competitive environments, international firms need "global managers" (Adler and Bartholomew, 1992; Bartlett and Ghoshal, 1992). Identifying and developing these resources have become a central issue for international firms. The focus of the study reported here was on identifying what key Australian firms consider critical to pursuing their international strategies, as a basis for determining appropriate training and other policy responses. There was an expectation, grounded in recent research on how Australian firms compete successfully in international markets, that locally domiciled firms would have some distinctive characteristics as a function of their home-base imprinting (Kogut, 1993).

The research has an advantage of tractability that stems from two factors. First, the small scale of the Australian economy makes it possible to conduct what is effectively a case study at the national level—there were fewer than 20 manufacturing firms with sales of over $1 billion in 1988/89. Second, the national portfolio of successful firms is distinctive and focused, with only two dominant forms of international competition. One is firms that compete globally by operating small- to medium-scale production facilities across multiple locations and selling locally rather than exporting (PCEK/Telesis, 1990). The other is extremely small global exporters, mostly

Strategy, Structure and Style. Edited by H. Thomas, D. O'Neal and M. Ghertman
Copyright © 1997 Jane Craig and Philip W. Yetton. Published 1996 by John Wiley & Sons Ltd.

high growth firms, in high technology markets, for whom exports are a major source of sales from their earliest years. There are no traditional MNCs which both export from the home base and have a substantial level of foreign production. These two factors give this study a unique focus, and bring into sharp relief a set of issues that would rarely if ever be apparent in a larger and more diverse economy.

The findings were counter-intuitive. To provide an interpretation of them, the chapter departs from the traditional form. Conventional background, methodology and results sections are followed by a discussion section that takes the form of a dialogue between the current emphasis on global managers, and this study's empirical results, and provides a resolution to the apparent paradox by reframing the question.

BACKGROUND

The study is grounded in two streams of literature: international human resource management (HRM), and international competitiveness of Australian firms.

The current international HRM field emphasizes "global managers" as a crucial resource for all firms wanting to be globally competitive in the 1990s (Hambrick et al., 1989; Bartlett and Ghoshal, 1992; Adler, 1992). Such individuals have a strong interest in, and tolerance for, other cultures as well as a sound understanding of how a particular decision might affect a company's many competitors and markets around the world. They can "think globally and act locally". Consequently, many multinational firms identify building a globally oriented staff as a top priority (Ely and McCormick, 1994). However, most firms have only recently embarked on programmes designed to foster this (Odenwald, 1993) and face continuing problems (Weeks, 1992; Ely and McCormack, 1994).

Although global managers are currently emphasized, the international HRM literature fundamentally takes a contingency approach, arguing that skills should be tailored to a firm's particular circumstances (Miles and Snow, 1984; Tichy, Fombrun, and Devanna, 1982). This contingent view is embedded in a stages model (Cavusgil, 1980) of internationalization. Each stage a firm passes through requires different skills (Adler, 1992; Dowling and Schuler, 1990). Dowling and Schuler's (1990) schema, summarized below, is representative.

Firms in the first stage have a domestic focus. Initial exports tend to be opportunistic (Williamson, 1990), typically handled by an agent or distributor in the foreign market. As export sales increase, an export manager may be appointed to control sales offshore and identify new markets. When exporting becomes a strategic activity, a major commitment is made in the form of setting up an export department at the same level as the domestic sales department. The export manager tends to travel extensively. This stage has few special HRM or skill implications.

As it continues to grow, and exhausts opportunities for growth in the local market, the firm becomes a strategic exporter, producing specifically to service overseas, as well as domestic, markets. In this second stage, sales subsidiaries or branch offices in the foreign market replace the agents or distributors. Most firms choose to staff the subsidiary with host country nationals, reflecting a judgement that country-specific factors are important. The corporate HR issues for firms that choose to send parent country nationals (PCNs), are limited to monitoring the selection and compensation of staff for the sales subsidiary and export department.

Moving to foreign production constitutes the third stage of internationalization and often involves creating a separate international division with responsibility for all international activities. Historically, most firms in this phase have emphasized control of the foreign subsidiaries, and staffed the new facilities with PCNs. Selecting, compensating and managing expatriates, and their conditions of service while overseas, are the main HR issues (Pucik, 1985). Training for expatriates and their families is culturally specific, focused on a single country. However, in some industries, national responsiveness was considered the key strategic demand of this phase (Bartlett and Ghoshal, 1989), and each subsidiary was treated as a distinct national entity, with some decision-making autonomy. Local nationals usually managed the subsidiaries, but were rarely promoted to head office positions. Any corporate coordination of HR policies was loose and informal. The subsidiary's manager and staff made the adaptations not only to local product market conditions, but also to local sociocultural circumstances (Evans, 1986). Most US manufacturing firms moved to this third stage of foreign production in a haphazard fashion (Dowling and Schuler, 1990). The decisions were often defensive reactions to the possibility of losing markets that had been acquired almost by accident (Stopford and Wells, 1972).

In the fourth stage, the organization moves towards product standardization and diversification. The size and diversity of operations create communication and efficiency problems. Subsidiaries face pressure to be responsive to local conditions, because of factors such as customer needs, differences in market structures, distribution channels, pressure from local governments and local culture. At the same time, the corporation's headquarters faces pressure to centralize and integrate the separate national operations. Inevitably, tensions arise around these conflicting needs for the subsidiary to be responsive to local conditions, and the pressures from headquarters for global integration.

Importantly, this phase, in which top managers recognize that strategic planning and major policy decisions need to be made in the central headquarters to ensure that a world-wide perspective on the interests of the organization can be maintained, is considered to be the coming of age for a multinational. The fifth and final stage is essentially an acceleration of this trend towards taking a global perspective. In response to a highly complex environment, in which a range of forces such as global customers and competitors, world-scale factories and universal products provide pressure for global integration, and local responsiveness is still required by local markets and governments, many firms are seeking to become transnationals (Bartlett and Ghoshal, 1989).

It is this transnational firm, found in the final of Dowling and Schuler's (1990) stages, that calls for global managers, and is considered to be the most highly evolved form for an MNC. Much of the international HRM literature, with its stages model basis, infers that all firms that wish to compete effectively will need to be transnationals, and thus, will need global managers, and should be working towards developing a cadre of such staff. The best way to achieve this remains unclear.

Building on this background, this study set out to identify how key Australian firms were solving the problem, by examining what a sample of successful international players currently saw as the critical elements they require to pursue their international strategies. This knowledge would then provide a basis for developing priorities for policy about the development of skills for international operations. Thus, our first working hypothesis for the research, deriving from this stream of literature, was that operating internationally requires a firm to have specific skills, many of which would be HRM-related.

Since the context was a wider research agenda for a government task force, the study specifically researched the skills for international operations of Australian firms that are already competing successfully overseas, with the intent of maximizing the relevance for Australian firms and managers. In taking this approach, the study also drew on an emerging literature, about how Australian firms compete and win internationally.

Recent analysis and research (PCEK/Telesis, 1990; Yetton, Davis, and Swan, 1992; McKinsey, 1993), suggest that Australian firms must compete and will win differently in some crucial respects from the traditional models of internationalization, derived exclusively from US and European experience. The findings of these studies suggest that the future for locally based manufacturing firms lies primarily in one of two dominant organization forms. The first is the multi-domestic, which is the form adopted by Australia's large and successful manufacturing firms. They compete internationally by operating small- to medium-scale production facilities across multiple locations and selling locally, rather than exporting (Yetton, Davis, and Swan, 1992). The other form are global exporters which, as yet, exist only in emergent form in Australia. These are small, high growth firms, typically in high technology production markets, for whom exports are a major source of sales from their earliest years (McKinsey, 1993).

Significantly, as FIGURE 14.1 shows, none of Australia's large manufacturing firms are MNCs—firms which have both a high proportion of exports from home base and whose foreign production accounts for a high percentage of their total sales. In this graph, the vertical axis represents the proportion of home-base production that is exported, while the horizontal axis shows the proportion of total sales that comes from foreign production. Australia's emerging global exporters have such low sales volumes that they would not be visible on this graph, which depicts firms with total sales of more than $1 billion in 1988/89. The largest of the emerging exporters are smaller than that amount by a factor of 50.

Related analysis of Porter's view about the competitive advantage of nations (Porter, 1990) also indicates that, just as the population of Australian-based successful international firms is distinctive, so too are the environmental and other factors that determine the competitive capabilities of local firms (Yetton et al., 1992). In other words, the competitive environ-

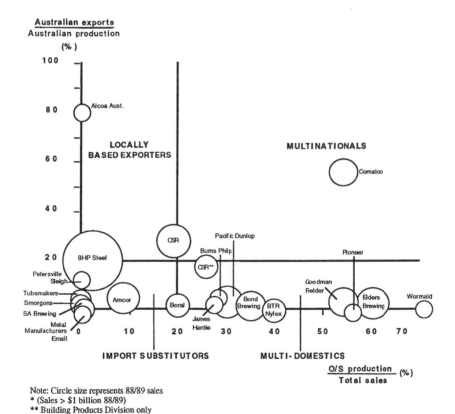

Note: Circle size represents 88/89 sales
* (Sales > $1 billion 88/89)
** Building Products Division only

FIGURE 14.1   International exposure of Australia's large, locally-based manufacturers (Source: PCEK/Telesis 1990, Exhibit 7F, reproduced with permission)

ment faced by Australian firms is not the same as that in North America or Europe in some key respects.

This research suggests then that successful Australian firms in the global arena have some distinctive elements to their strategies which result directly from the domestic competitive environment, that their configuration and growth paths are not consistent with the popular models of internationalization, and that Porter's model for competitive firms is not appropriate for Australia. While these findings emerged from research undertaken on the manufacturing sector, we judged that it would not be difficult to extend the argument that most service organizations will also be run in either of these two ways, with a high probability that multi-domestics will be the dominant form.

This second body of literature generated our second working hypothesis: Australian firms would have developed unique solutions to the question of skills for international operations, because of the distinctive nature of their home-base environment. Understanding the nature of the international operations of the firms that predominate in the manufacturing and service sectors in Australia was considered crucial to evaluating their skill needs, given the contingency approach of the international HRM literature.

METHODOLOGY

A qualitative research methodology was chosen in light of the incomplete understanding that currently exists (Yin, 1994; Eisenhardt, 1989) in relation to both the development and management of global managers, and the successful international operations of Australian firms. Over 40 hours of extensive in-depth unstructured interviews were conducted with more than 20 senior managers in those 17 companies. The aim was to elicit their views about which issues were crucial to their firms, rather than to gather information about issues already determined to be important. Transcripts of these meetings formed the basis for detailed analysis. Specifically, the CEOs and other senior managers were asked about how they competed and won internationally, what skills they thought mattered most, and how easy they were to come by. Publicly available documentation (e.g. annual reports, business press commentary) on the companies studied was also reviewed. Where available, documents covering policies and procedures for the selection, training, evaluation and rewards for managers responsible for overseas activities were also studied.

The selection of firms to be studied reflected our second working hypothesis—that Australian-domiciled firms, which predominantly take one of two forms (multi-domestic or global exporters) have found distinctive solutions to the problems of operating internationally. Three large multi-domestic manufacturing firms (from Yetton et al., 1992), were selected for analysis, along with 10 emerging exporters (from McKinsey, 1993), five from each of the two main cities, Sydney and Melbourne, and three large service firms. As expected, the service firms competed in a fashion similar to the multi-domestics. One medium-sized multi-domestic manufacturing firm was also studied to explore whether size was a critical factor—it was not. Mining and agricultural houses were not included because, for the most part, they do not export high value added goods.

Two characteristics of this methodology—representativeness of the sample, and the fact that it is a success sample—were not an issue in the original design. It was assumed that the firms studied would have a set of skills for international operations, would define how to acquire and develop them, and that this would provide a guide to developing training policies. But, as the following section that outlines the findings shows, the actual results are different from those originally anticipated. So the questions of whether the firms studied are representative of other firms, and the characteristics of the marginally successful and unsuccessful firm become relevant. We address these issues in the discussion section.

FINDINGS

The findings from this research were surprising against the background of existing literature. Specifically, identifying and developing managers who can think globally and act locally was not raised as an issue. There was a high degree of consistency across interviews. Not only were the issues from the mainstream literature and discussion about skills for international operations not raised, but across the sample of 17 firms, executives talked consistently (and unprompted) about the same set of alternate, more business-focused issues as being important. The findings are reported in summary form only, in order to protect the confidentiality of the firms studied. Points made by the majority of executives interviewed and representative quotes are reported.

The skills identified by interviewees can be grouped into four categories, identified in TABLE 14.1, which reflect the key elements of operating internationally. The first deals with the set of skills and competences that are simply taken as given, if a firm is to compete offshore. The second relates to the decision to go international. The third concerns entering foreign markets, and the fourth is about operating on a continuing basis in those foreign markets.

It was taken as given by all firms that they offered high quality products/ services at the right price, understood what their customers want, and were successful in the Australian market:

> People buy any product because they see the perception of value. That's the reason why anybody buys anything.

The second issue on which there was consensus was that the firms *had* to go to overseas markets because they had exhausted the opportunities in Australia. It was not a choice, or a matter of will, but a necessity for continued growth or even survival.

> The export thing came along not as a conscious decision to export, but as an imperative. When I discovered that there wasn't enough business in Australia for xxx to be successful, export became a necessity. And it very soon became obvious it wasn't difficult and it enables a high tech company in a small country like Australia to actually become quite large.

The third main set of points related to entering foreign markets. This involved several issues. First, all agreed that it is vital to understand the market being entered.

> Well, the first step was to define the market, the approach to the market and make sales before recruiting anybody.

> We now buy formal market research whereas before, it someone had come in and said, I'll tell you about the United States market, all you have to do is pay me $5,000, I wouldn't have spent it. I would rather ring up some people I knew over there. But now it's different. Again, as the company grows you have to do things differently.

> Market research is critical, absolutely critical.

Almost all identified finding someone they trust to guide them around a new foreign market as a crucial issue:

> We have found partnerships by and large are difficult, but they have worked. We have used them when we are entering a market that we don't know much about. When you get into European markets, it is very sophisticated. In fact, that is the problem—there is so much unsaid, unwritten, but only implied once you get there. . . . So that is why the partnerships we think have been a good avenue for us. But we always must have a route to control at the end of the day.

> Someone approached us for some work, and we ended up with the one representative/agent to start with and that was a set back. We spent the first two to three years trying to get rid of him, and we unwisely made an agency arrangement, which we shouldn't have. We are much more careful now about that sort of thing.

While most firms thought their ability to identify and work with partners had improved with experience, they did not consider that the critical agendas and issues in one location were ones that even they could specifically use again. In general, they seem to have learnt to move carefully.

There was also agreement that persistence often mattered:

> Are you prepared to stay in there for four or five years in that market-place and not score, and still keep knocking on that door?

Another frequently made point was that the firms face many more market opportunities than they can fulfil. The dilemma is choice, rather than scarcity.

> Our biggest problem at the moment is selecting joint venturers. We would have 10 companies overseas at the moment who want to do some sort of deal or other.

Finally, all those interviewed pointed out that, in most instances, their customers are sophisticated and informed purchasers, who are just as willing to invest in search processes as are the firms wishing to sell. This may partly account for the fact that even when asked specific questions about cross-cultural and other skills, all said that those issues were not problems. Some even directly commented that they were peripheral.

> I don't think it is a particularly Asian thing. Turn it around. People roar into Australia. You know, they come in from France, England or America and they want to see you, and you see them, and you think "who on earth was he?", and you never see them again. But if they come back and come back, you think "this guy must be serious". I think we react in almost the same way.

> A lot of the myths that are out there about the fact that it's more competitive, that you've got to be cheaper in price, the cost of freight will kill you, you have to understand the culture of the people, it's all rubbish. At the end of the day, if your product will work as well as or better than the other product, and will save them or make them more money than any other product, regardless of your religion, what country you come from, your colour, or anything else, they deal. That's the bottom line. It helps you to understand that you shouldn't point your foot in Thailand, and so on. But I mean, they're pretty basic things, and you don't do anything to offend people in that way. But if you've got what they want, and they want to do business, then it's fine by them.

There is no intention to say here that understanding a foreign market and its characteristics, particularly its cultural characteristics, is not important. Indeed, all those interviewed said it was, but did not invest in internalizing that understanding. Instead, they outsourced this to a third party. To an extent, this mimics best practice within their domestic market.

> I don't think we could open our doors in Queensland without having had a presence up there and knowing a little bit about Queensland and be success-ful. . . . Our success there is because we acquired xxx, which was a household

name in this field in that state. What we did was to purchase the networks, we purchased an order book and we purchased people who knew their way around, and we have been successful.

The fourth and final category of findings related to managing the international operations once they were in place. Foreign subsidiaries were routinely staffed on a permanent basis by host country nationals, but with a slightly different flavour for the two main types of firms. The multi-domestics had technical experts from the home base oversee the adjustment of acquired, or commissioning of new, plants. Continued operation, however, was in the hands of subsequently appointed local managers.

> Another recipe for our success, from our point of view, is that we have been prepared to leave a local person in charge of every business.

Performance data, either financial or technical, were continuously monitored; problems surfaced at early stages. Subsidiaries were expected to explain/ rectify shortfalls, and were given technical assistance if a production process problem turned out to be difficult or unusual. This new knowledge would often be transferred to all plants through the central technical teams.

> We just put a new piece of equipment into one of our plants in England, and it has been terrific. So there is a team of people from all over the rest of the world going across to look at it, and if we think it is good, then we'll put that piece of equipment elsewhere.

For their part, the emerging exporters staffed sales and service subsidiaries with host country nationals. A crucial first step on market entry was identifying those individuals, with the CEO, or a key individual putting in a substantial effort.

> If you want to sell anywhere, the best guy to do it is a local. The problem is to make that local want to work for you. The hardest thing was to find the right first few people, with the right attitude, aptitudes and skills to face an unknown market as a subsidiary of an unknown company.

All firms in the sample maintained close communication with their local managers of either sales and service subsidiaries (for emergents) and of production facilities (for multi-domestics).

> We have a very short line from them (overseas investments) to home—they don't go through local filters or bean counters or something. All the country chief executives are on the board, so that gives them a feeling of belonging. And we get them together about five or six times a year at the board. Four of the meetings are usually here and we will have two somewhere else. We get monthly reports and they are vitally important—they are consolidated and analysed, etc., but if you are not there face to face, then you are on the phone, and you are getting a feel of what is going on.

In the emergents, overseas operations imposed a heavy burden on the owner/CEO, who was constantly travelling:

> I travelled overseas 12 or 13 times last year.

The strains imposed by continuing rapid growth are also a problem. Emerging exporters in particular face constraints from the lack of financial resources to go to the next stage of growth, particularly given the post-1980s reluctance of banks to lend against cash flow rather than assets. They also have limited succession capacity.

> We believe we need to bring someone else in to train. The problem is to find someone who also has that commitment to the company.

Finally, technical skills are crucial to continued success of most of the firms, but are not generally in short supply.

These findings, based on our detailed analysis of the meeting transcripts, are summarized in TABLE 14.1, which lists the main issues identified by interviewees, and reports the proportion of the 17 firms studied for which these points were raised unprompted.

As the preceding summary of the main themes that pervaded the interviews shows, these firms do not place finding and managing global managers high on the list of key factors required for international operations. There was a high level of consistency across all interviewees about what did matter—having a good product/price/service, deep mastery of your own business and knowledge of your industry, knowing the market, meeting customer needs, etc. Cultural and language skills were secondary. The firms did all recognize that various national, and often regional, markets operate differently. However, instead of developing the local understand-

TABLE 14.1 Skills for international operations: summary of findings

Category	Issue raised	% of firms ($n = 17$)
Taken as given	Subjectively benchmarked as top 20% in Australia	94
Decision to go international	Had to go offshore	94
Entering foreign markets	Need to understand market	100
	Find local expert—partner/friend/guide	94
	Persistent	100
	Sophisticated buyers	100
Continuing operations	Run it with a local	100
	Constant communication	100

ing themselves, their solution was for a "local" to manage those elements of the business. They did not talk about finding or developing managers who can think globally and act locally, and when specifically asked, all but one replied that they did not fundamentally matter. It is worth recalling here that an unstructured, open-ended interview technique was used, so the flow and content of the interviews reflected the priorities and concerns of the managers.

The strong assumption that Australia's large organizations, mainly multi-domestics, had some skills, such as cultural awareness, that were critical for their international success was implicit in designing this research study and in asking the successful firms what skills they needed for international operations. So the findings were unexpected. The following discussion section attempts to reconcile both the findings and the existing literature on skills for international operations.

DISCUSSION

The results reported here appear to be inconsistent with the current emphasis on "global managers". In this section, we integrate these findings within a framework that takes account of both the literature and the portfolio of Australian international firms. We resolve the apparent contradiction by showing that the conventional view does not apply to the Australian multi-domestics, service firms and emerging exporters. The integration we propose suggests that the mainstream literature is not relevant for Australian-based firms, by showing that the two types of Australian firms which compete internationally are not those studied in the mainstream literature. So while the conventional view applies to and is useful for many foreign multinationals, it is less relevant for Australian firms competing overseas.

The starting point for understanding these somewhat counter-intuitive findings, is to return to the literature on international HRM, particularly its contingency perspective that links the stage of an international firm's development to skill needs.

The three stages that an international firm is assumed to pass through as it grows over time: domestic, strategic exporter and MNC, can be shown as a curved trajectory, depicted in FIGURE 14.2, which uses the same axes as FIGURE 14.1. The vertical axis represents the proportion of home-base production that is exported, while the horizontal axis shows the proportion of total sales that comes from foreign production.

Conceptualizing the internationalization process in this way reveals how firms have experimented with several structural solutions to the "problem" of being an MNC. This problem revolves primarily around the complexity generated by multiple markets, cultural environments and governmental

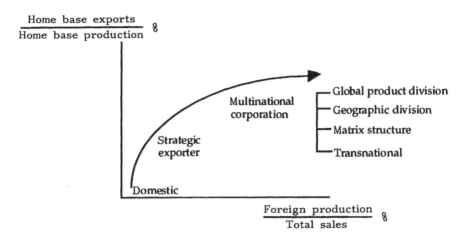

FIGURE 14.2   Conventional stages of internationalization

regimes, often for multiple products. The international business literature takes this inherent complexity, which makes competing internationally difficult, as given (Ghoshal and Westney, 1993). It is also often implicitly assumed that firms competing in world markets will be MNCs, who do both exporting and foreign production.

We suggest that the problem created by this complexity centres around two fundamental issues: control, and degree of centralization. Centralization is typically associated with high efficiency and low cost, but at the expense of flexibility and responsiveness. Conversely, decentralization allows the organization to be responsive, but at a high cost. Whereas once these were regarded as trade-offs, they are now goals that firms must achieve simultaneously. The extent to which local managers are required to conform to centrally determined practices in turn influences the degree and nature of control that would be exerted by the headquarters over the subsidiary unit. Over time MNCs have grappled with different aspects of this dilemma, through varied structural responses, depicted in FIGURE 14.2. Each has carried different international HRM implications.

The global product and geographic divisional structures represent attempts to reduce complexity: a product-based global structure emphasizes centrally managing products on a global basis, while an area-based structure emphasizes responsiveness to local conditions. In both cases, corporate management of human resources across the organization is strategically important. Managerial expertise is needed to coordinate activities and form strategies for world-wide markets, and oversee contracts between the parent and its foreign affiliates. The need to develop cross-cultural sensitivity as a prerequisite for devising effective management practices for different subsidiaries often becomes apparent (Desatnick and Bennett, 1988).

By contrast, the matrix or mixed structure, with authority shared jointly by the product and geographic divisions, makes conflicts of interest explicit, and ensures that priority issues are not neglected by allocating top management champions. Some suggest that this structure was an intuitive response for firms pursuing multiple business dimensions simultaneously (Galbraith and Kazanjian, 1986). The popularity of this matrix structure has declined since the 1970s when it was first developed, largely because it is an expensive method of organization.

The currently favoured solution to the problem of the diversified MNC is the transnational (Bartlett and Ghoshal, 1989). The goal of these organizations is "the ability to manage across national boundaries, retaining local flexibility while achieving global integration". Instead of trying to solve the centralization/decentralization dilemma structurally, these firms effectively internalize the solution in their managers, by focusing on developing "truly global" executive managers. The assumption is that the skills of the managers will solve the decentralization/centralization and control dilemmas facing those firms. Consequently, many multinational firms identify building a globally oriented staff as a top priority. However, this latest resolution to the dilemma of being an MNC remains more a vision, and a hope, than a reality (Weeks, 1992; Odenwald, 1993; Ely and McCormick, 1994).

It is useful to recall that "global managers" are put forward as the current solution for MNCs, firms with high levels of both exports and foreign production, and to recall that this currently advocated solution internalizes in individual managers the solving of dilemmas that various structural responses have failed to resolve. In other words, it is only these firms that need "global managers", and the attendant development of an executive cadre with the requisite skills.

With this contingency perspective in mind, we then turn to consider Australian-domiciled firms that are competing internationally, and find that there are no MNCs. Earlier research, illustrated in Figure 14.1, shows that such firms are missing from the portfolio of large Australian manufacturing firms (PCEK/Telesis, 1990). Nor do they occur in large numbers among the smaller manufacturing firms that export from Australia (McKinsey, 1993). A simplified representation of the axes used in Figures 14.1 and 14.2 can be used to create a matrix of firms operating internationally, shown in Figure 14.3, that highlights the different types of firm. Australia's large manufacturing firms are primarily multi-domestics, and the emerging exporters operate as global exporters. Both these sets of firms are able to partition the two issues of local responsiveness and global integration. Consequently they do not face the systemic conflict that the literature on MNCs is

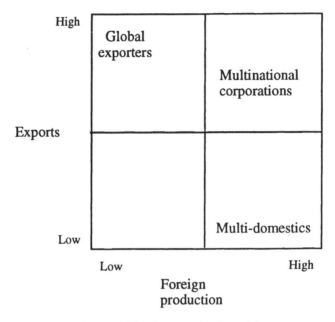

High

Exports

Low

Low   High

Foreign
production

FIGURE 14.3 A categorization of firms

grappling with, and therefore do not need "global" managers with the skills and the organizational capabilities to mediate those tensions continually.

Instead, we conceptualize the approach both sets of firms take as a partitioning of issues, with some to be managed globally, and some to be managed locally. In effect, the firms studied were acting as though there were two sets of skills for internationalization. The first were business and industry skills, related to product, process and management, which form the basis of a firm's core competences and competitive advantage. The second were those skills relating to country-specific resources and knowledge, that allow a firm to leverage its competitive advantage in foreign markets. These include market characteristics (e.g. level of economic sophistication), government, banking and financing sources, and workforce characteristics and conditions. Responsibility for these two sets of skills was partitioned. The core business skills were managed centrally for the entire scope of the firm's operations, while the country-specific skills were acquired in each national market-place. Whether this took the form of agents, joint ventures or subsidiaries varied, depending on whether the firm was an emergent manufacturing exporter, or a multi-domestic manufacturer or service firm, as well as on industry characteristics. In effect, the core business skills were managed for "world-wide operations" in-house, and the country-specific ones were outsourced locally.

This plays out in different ways for emerging exporters and multi-domestics. The former handle production and R&D centrally, in Australia. Sales and service activities are the primary responsibility of local managers in local markets. In other words, production and product are managed globally, and sales and service are managed locally. This is consistent with the conventional international HRM literature.

For their part, the Australian multi-domestics operate within industries where the efficient plant scale is small to medium-sized (Yetton et al., 1992). Consequently, operating multiple plants in multiple locations does not destroy economies of scale. Nor has being locally responsive damaged their capacity to capture global learning or operate global strategies. Elsewhere, we suggest (Yetton, Davis, and Craig, 1995) that this is because the product and its characteristics are uncoupled from the production process. The global component for these firms is the process technology, and not, as commonly assumed, product characteristics. The introduction, maintenance and development of processes are coordinated and regulated on a global basis, and various mechanisms ensure that the learning that occurs in one location is transferred throughout the network of plants. Economies of scale are across the network and not at the plant level. Individual plant or country managers do not have the choice to depart from existing best internal practice for the process technology in significant ways. They also generally have the opportunity and some incentive to contribute to that development process. The multi-domestics then, manage processes globally across multiple plant locations, and allow other issues, including product characteristic variations that do not prejudice the global processes, to be managed locally. In this fashion, the multi-domestics can be simultaneously globally integrated and locally responsive. As the findings and this description indicate, however, this outcome is achieved by very different means than those advocated for the transnational, which also has these performance characteristics as goals, and for which "global managers" are considered to be the primary delivery mechanism for thinking globally and acting locally.

In summary then, we propose that the lack of MNCs in the Australian portfolio of manufacturing and service firms explains why none of the firms studied raised the issues that predominate in the management literature on skills for international operations originating from the USA and Europe.

Given the findings, an issue arises about the representativeness of the sample of firms studied here. In terms of the emerging exporters, 10 firms were selected from the 40 originally in McKinsey's (1993) study of emerging exporters who agreed to be named in that report, with the constraint that firms were drawn equally from the two largest cities and commercial centres in Australia. Since the sample of emergents is therefore random to an extent, it is likely that what we found is typical of that class of firm. Nor was there anything different about the way we selected the multi-domestics for study. Again, one would expect them to be typical of such firms, which have been extensively studied elsewhere (Yetton et al., 1992). There were no reasons to believe, *ex ante*, or *ex post*, that those selected were not representative. The only remaining question is whether there are other firms that do not fall into either category. Recent analysis of emerging exporters, by the authors, for the Australian Manufacturing Council shows no trend to becoming an MNC among the small and growing Australian manufacturing firms.

The findings also implicitly call into question the assumption in the international HRM literature that international firms will naturally evolve into MNCs, and inevitably become transnationals. We speculate that the prevailing focus in the literature on the transnational form derives from problem-driven analyses. The dispersed production locations of many MNCs have been described as reflecting historical accident rather than optimal strategic considerations (Porter, 1990a; Stopford and Wells, 1972). Porter (1990a: p.58), for instance, makes it clear that being forced into such configurations can be a competitive liability:

> ... many Swedish, Swiss, and American multinationals moved abroad before World War II when trade barriers as well as transport costs were more significant, one reason they often have widely dispersed activities compared to Japanese or German firms in the same industry. A dispersed configuration is frequently hard to integrate and consolidate in one place, because local country managers desire to retain power and autonomy. The inability to shift to more concentrated and coordinated strategies necessary for competitive advantage is one reason why firms lose advantage in some industries.

This is in part a function of history, and Japanese firms have followed a different path. Those in global industries have tended to remain exporters for as long as possible. Where they have established foreign production locations, the preference has been to locate only one or two large plants in each of the major triad markets. Nevertheless, perhaps because the diversified multinational corporation is complex, it is assumed to be the most sophisticated evolutionary stage.

CONCLUSION

The prevailing view of international competition is that firms must simultaneously be able to capture global economies of scale, be flexible and responsive to local market conditions, and leverage learning on a world-wide basis. The transnational (Bartlett and Ghoshal, 1989) solution endeavours to resolve the issues by locating them within individual executives who can think globally and act locally—global managers. In this context, it then becomes natural to ask whether European, US or Japanese cultures give their managers a competitive advantage in such an environment. Here, we argue that these are the wrong questions and the answers potentially misleading and dangerous. This is not to deny that many organizations have concluded that a "super-manager" is the answer to the problem they currently cannot resolve—global integration combined with local responsiveness. Most well-known MNCs have come to this potential solution after trying several types of structure in response to the complexity involved in operating in a diversity of markets and cultural environments.

Indeed, the study reported here initially accepted, as the right one, the question that we are now rejecting. The methodology devised for this project was specifically designed to identify how successful Australian firms managed the factors that dominate the current literature. It was assumed that they would have a set of skills around identifying the dimensions of cultural differences, the nature of global as distinct from domestic markets, and the type of skills managers need to operate in other countries. What the research revealed, however, is that, without exception, none of the sample of Australian firms that are successful internationally identified these particular issues as problematic for them.

The conventional assumption would be that the Australian firms are in an earlier phase of development and would move at some stage in the future to become MNCs, and have to solve the same problem. The alternative view would be that the simpler forms—the multi-domestic as represented by the Australian firms, and the strategic exporter form preferred by many Japanese firms—are the dominant ones, and that it is the MNCs which will move to one of those two configurations over time.

History and heightened international competition have led us to ask who competes best, and to focus on cultural factors. This study reminds us that a more important question is how to compete best, in which cultural factors play a small role, and furthermore, a role that can be outsourced to local experts.

REFERENCES

Adler, N.J. (1992) *Human Resource Management in the Global Economy*, Don Wood Lecture Series, Kingston, Ontario: Industrial Relations Centre, Queen's University.

Adler, N.J. and Bartholomew, S. (1992) "Managing Globally Competent People", *Academy of Management Executive*, 6(3), 52–65.

Bartlett, C.A. and Ghoshal, S. (1989) *Managing across Borders*, Boston, Mass.: Harvard Business School Press.

Bartlett, C.A. and Ghoshal, S. (1992) "What Is a Global Manager?" *Harvard Business Review*, Sept–Oct, 124–132.

Cavusgil, S.T. (1980) "On the Internationalisation Process of Firms", *European Research*, Nov, 273–281.

Desatnick, C. and Bennett, G. (1988) *Human Resource Management*, **27**(1), Symposium on human resource management in the multinational corporation issue.

Dowling, P.J. and Schuler, R.S. (1990) *International Dimensions of Human Resource Management*, Boston: PWS Kent.

Eisenhardt, K. (1989) "Building Theories from Case Study Research", *Academy of Management Review*, **14**(4), 532–550.

Ely, R. and McCormick, J. (1994) *The New International Executive: Business Leadership for the 21st Century*, New York: Amrop International.

Evans, P. (1986) "The Context of Strategic Human Resource Management Policy in Complex Firms", *Management Forum*, **6**, 105–117.

Galbraith, J.R. and Kazanjian, R.K. (1986) "Organizing to Implement Strategies of Diversity and Globalization: The Role of Matrix Designs", *Human Resource Management*, **25**(1), 37–54.

Ghoshal, S. and Westney, D.E. (eds) (1993) *Organization Theory and the Multinational Corporation*, New York: St Martin's Press.

Hambrick, D.C., Korn, L.B., Fredrickson, J.W. and Ferry, R. (1989) *21st Century Report: Reinventing the CEO*, New York: Korn/Ferry and Columbia University's Graduate School of Business, pp. 1–94.

Kogut, Bruce (1993) "Learning, or the Importance of Being Inert: Country Imprinting and International Competition", in S. Ghoshal and D.E. Westney (eds), *Organisational Theory and the Multinational Corporation*, New York: St Martin's Press, pp. 136–154.

McKinsey and Company (1993) *The Challenge of Leadership: Australia's Emerging High Value-Added Manufacturing Exporters*, Melbourne: Australian Manufacturing Council.

Miles, R.E. and Snow, C.C. (1984) "Fit, Failure and the Hall of Fame", *California Management Review*, **26**(3) 10–28.

Odenwald, S. (1993) *Global Training: How to Design a Program for the Multinational Corporation*, Homewood Ill.: Richard D. Irwin.

PCEK (Pappas, Carter, Evans, and Koop)/Telesis (1990) *The Global Challenge: Australian Manufacturing in the 1990s*, Melbourne: Australian Manufacturing Council.

Porter, M. (1990a) The *Competitive Advantage of Nations*, London: Free Press.

Porter, M. (1990b) "The Competitive Advantage of Nations", *Harvard Business Review*, **68**(2) 73–93.

Pucik, V. (1985) "Strategic Human Resource Management in a Multinational Firm", in H.V. Wortzel and L.H. Wortzel (eds), *Strategic Management of Multinational Corporations: The Essentials*, New York: John Wiley.

Stopford, J. and Wells, L. (1972) *Managing the Multinational*, London: Longman.

Tichy, N.M., Fombrun, C.J., and Devanna, M.A. (1982) "Strategic Human Resource Management", *Sloan Management Review*, Winter, 42–56.

Weeks, D.A. (1992) *Recruiting and Selecting International Managers*, Report No. 998, Washington: The Conference Board.

Williamson, P.J. (1990) "Winning the Export War: British, Japanese and West German Exporters' Strategy Compared", *British Journal of Management*, **1**, 215–230.

Yetton, P., Craig, J., Davis J., and Hilmer, F. (1992) "Are Diamonds a Country's Best Friend? A Critique of Porter's Theory of National Competition as Applied to Canada, New Zealand and Australia", *Australian Journal of Management*, **17**(1), 89–119.

Yetton, P., Davis, J. and Craig, J.C. (1995) "Redefining the Multi-domestic: A New Ideal Type", MNC 96-016, Australian Graduate School of Management Working Paper Series, Sydney.
Yetton, P., Davis, J., and Swan, P.L. (1992) *Going International: Export Myths and Strategic Realities*, Melbourne: Australian Manufacturing Council.
Yin, R. (1994) *Case Study Research: Design and Methods*, 2nd edn., Newbury Park, CA: Sage.

15

Institutional Environment Effects on Transaction Costs: A Comparative Analysis of the US and French Nuclear Power Industries

MAGALI DELMAS, MICHEL GHERTMAN, BRUCE HEIMAN

INTRODUCTION

Backlash against nuclear power, although widespread, had differential impacts on nuclear power programs in the United States and France owing to differing institutional setups. This chapter utilizes a transaction costs economics approach to explain the contrasting results of the credibility of government policies in the French and American nuclear power industries.

What best explains the rapid decline of the American nuclear power industry beginning approximately in 1971 and culminating after the Three Mile Island (TMI) accident on 28 March 1979? The nuclear power industry in the USA planned to build the largest number of nuclear power plants of any country in the world from the mid-1950s to the mid-1970s. US utilities ordered 231 nuclear plants through 1974, but only 15 after that and none after 1977 (Campbell, 1988; OTA, 1984). From 1970 to 1989, 134 nuclear

Strategy, Structure and Style. Edited by H. Thomas, D. O'Neal and M. Ghertman
Copyright © 1997 John Wiley & Sons Ltd.

units were canceled by electric utilities (see FIGURE 15.1). In 1994, 112 reactors were in operation. These cancellations represented over one-half of the previously ordered nuclear generating capacity. Over $15 billion had been spent on these units (Itteilag and Pavle, 1985).* In France, on the other hand, nuclear power prospered for many years before and after TMI. Only two French plants have ever been canceled. France arguably boasts the most successful nuclear power implementation in the world, with over 75% of its electricity generated with nuclear power, while in the USA this fraction has never exceeded 20%.

How might one best account for this substantial variance in outcomes across the two countries? As is generally accepted, high construction costs and declining electricity demand contributed to the decline of nuclear power in the United States between 1972 and 1982 (USDOE, 1983). Is there an important link between nuclear industry decline and the rise of antinuclear public opinion? How does public opinion interact with government structure to affect the ability of government to credibly commit to certain industries? What, if any, special aspects of the US nuclear experience turned the tide against industry when similar opposition was present in many other countries promoting nuclear power, including Japan, Sweden, France, the United Kingdom and Germany? Scholars (Hatch, 1986; Jasper, 1990; Joppke, 1993; Price, 1990; Schrader-Frechette, 1980) agree on the importance of public opinion's role in impeding nuclear power, but with few exceptions (see Campbell, 1988, 1991), little explanation is offered of the mechanics through which public opinion affects policy and outcomes for the industry. No attempt has been made to fit these outcomes into a systemic body of theory. While the standard institutionalist treatment offers the important insight that institutional details matter, little in the way of coherent theory accompanies these observations (Barkenbus, 1984; Campbell, 1987, 1988; Rochlin and von Meier, 1994).

This chapter asserts that licensing and construction costs in the nuclear industry may best be explained in terms of the respective governments' ability to credibly commit to industry. The transaction of getting the licenses for constructing the nuclear power plant is undertaken between the utility and regulatory bodies. Investment decisions that require huge sunk costs have to be made several years before starting the plant. Utilities are very sensitive to a regulatory body which can ease or complicate the process. In the USA, the government's credible commitment was initially strong and has been deteriorating over time, while in France the credibility has persisted.

---

* More recently these costs have run even higher. For example, the Public Service Company of Indiana spent $2.7 billion on its two-unit Marble Hill Nuclear Project but canceled it in 1984 before finishing construction. As the trend continued, experts estimated that utilities would suffer another $25 billion in abandonment costs by 1990 (Itteilag and Pavle, 1985).

We contend that an analysis of the differences in institutional environment attributes can help understand government credibility to the industry. This chapter tentatively extends transaction costs economics (Williamson, 1985) to build comprehension of how differences between institutional environments induce shifts in transaction costs.

This chapter proceeds as follows: first, a model explains why one should expect shift parameters to affect the costs of transacting in the nuclear power industry. Second, empirical evidence is presented supporting the theoretical model. Third, conclusions are drawn.

THEORY: MODELING CREDIBLE COMMITMENT

According to Williamson (1994) each national institutional environment originates "shift parameters" which affect the set of possible organization structures. We demonstrate how these shift parameters affect attributes of transactions in the nuclear power industries. We will focus on the uncertainty of government behavior toward industry. In the case of nuclear

TABLE 15.1   Caseloads and regulations in the USA

Year	Judicial cases/year[a]	New rules and regulations—cumulative[b]
1975	15	20
1976	34	62
1977	41[c]	127
1978	50	187
1979	57	240
1980	59	312
1981	70	392
1982	83	474[d]
1983	21	535

[a] Suits brought against NRC, mostly for failing to follow procedural requirements regarding safety and siting decisions (NRC, 1975–82). Includes pending cases.

[b] Proposed rules are counted in these totals because the industry had to expend resources in evaluating and commenting on rules. Cumulativity of rules is also important because compliance with previous years' rules in the current year is mandatory.

[c] Case consolidation becomes common at this time, suggesting that numbers are understated from here onwards.

[d] Requirement instituted for advance notice of proposed rules. This may be construed as the formalization of "fire alarms" for the Congress, which introduced more costs to the regulators, which detracted from their ability to perform their work, especially in view of increased demand for regulation following TMI. Regulators were now not only constrained from providing industry groups with demand-based regulations in a timely fashion, but the types of regulation that were now in demand (in the Stigler/Peltzman sense) were decidedly antinuclear in leaning. Industry efforts to understand and fight these demands from the environment sector introduced further uncertainty and delays that increased transaction costs associated with building/completing/operating plants.

(Source: NRC, 1975–83, reproduced with permission)

power, a transaction is undertaken between a utility and a government regulatory body. This transaction should result in the utility eventually constructing and operating nuclear power plants under guidelines originated by the regulatory body. This discussion focuses mainly on transactions pertaining to construction and operating permit issuance in the nuclear power industry.

For nuclear power, the transaction is highly asset specific. Once the utility has decided to invest in a nuclear power plant, it may not shift to another regulatory body to modify the contents of the permit. Further, a plant cannot easily be sold to another utility; nor can it be converted for another use. Operating licenses and construction permits are given to a utility which has specific rights and responsibilities that may not be transferred to another company. Sunk costs comprise a high fraction of total investment. Specificity manifests mainly in the construction time (from 4 to 16 years) of a plant. During this lengthy period, regulatory changes can be sudden and/or retroactive. The credibility of a government's commitment to nuclear power projects is thus uncertain.

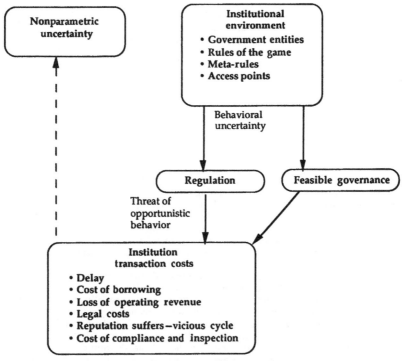

FIGURE 15.1   A model incorporating the effects of nonparametric uncertainty on transaction costs

TABLE 15.2 Average estimated and realized overnight construction costs[a] and lead times (by year of construction start, 1966–77 in 1982 dollars/kW of capacity)

Year of construction start	Estimated costs at various stages of completion					Realized costs	Estimated lead times at various stages of completion					Realized lead times
	0%	25%	50%	75%	90%		0%	25%	50%	75%	90%	
1966–67	298	377	414	560	583	623	52	56	67	76	82	91
1968–69	351	484	552	781	895	1067	56	63	72	83	91	107
1970–71	404	554	683	986	1106	1483	59	77	92	100	111	135
1972–73	569	604	734	1339	1511	1656	66	80	88	100	115	132
1974–75	590	914	1177	1760	2077	2316	71	96	113	124	132	142
1976–77	748	892	1018	1697	1850	2017	82	97	99	102	105	118

[a] Construction costs, with inflation in the input prices and allowance for funds used for construction (AFUDC) removed, are often referred to as overnight costs. Overnight costs measure the quantities of land, labor, and material used to build a nuclear power plant. AFUDC is the cost to the utility to finance the annual expenditures of the plant.
(Source: Hewlett (1994: p. 122). Computations based on data from US, Department of Energy, Energy Information Administration, Form EIA 254, "Semiannual Progress Report on Status of Reactor Construction", reproduced with permission).

Credibility of government actions is vital to support nonredeployable assets. Uncertainty concerning these actions increases transaction costs to the industry (see FIGURE 15.1). If regulations change rapidly and unpredictably, construction is delayed, legal costs and financial costs increase (see Table 15.2). Our formal model unpacks the "Institutional environment" box shown in FIGURE 15.1.

Levy and Spiller (1994) highlight how the credibility and effectiveness of a regulatory framework—and hence its ability to facilitate private investment—vary with a country's political and social institutions. They conclude that commitment is most credible in a democracy with a division of power between the executive and legislative branches of government and an independent judiciary, as opposed to the same kind of democracy with a weak judiciary. Further, a strong government administration helps stability and credibility. Our conclusions differ for the nuclear industry as we find in the French case that credible government commitment to utilities may be enhanced by a weak judiciary as well as a lack of division of power between the executive and legislative.

FIGURE 15.2 illustrates how the Levy and Spiller framework may be used to include opposing interest groups. Starting at the top of the figure, the differences between the USA and France are shown along Levy and Spiller's three critical dimensions:

- There is no real division of power in France, especially compared to the USA.
- Judicial independence in France is rare (David, 1972; Abraham, 1980), even

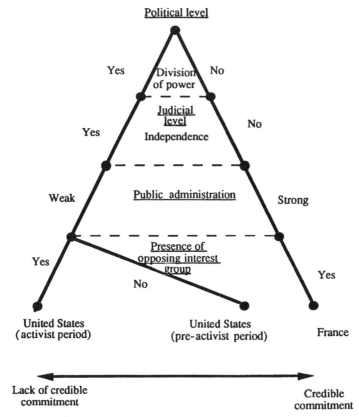

FIGURE 15.2   Attributes of the institutional environment of the French and US nuclear industries. (This is an adaptation of work originally done by Levy and Spiller (1994) building on North (1990). The main difference is that under our framework, the effects of an independent judiciary may not contribute to fostering credible government commitment if there are strong opposition interest groups who have access to courts.)

more so over nuclear power (Nelkin and Pollack, 1981; Carmay, 1982; Dac 1994) issues compared to the USA, where courts have a history of independence (Walker, 1981).

• In France, reliance on the expertise of civil servants of the administration concerning the technical issues of nuclear power is substantial. In the USA, input from multiple politically motivated sources is considered before technical decisions are made (Bupp, 1979; Chubb and Peterson, 1989; US Senate, 1974; Strudness, 1992).

These relationships within the components of the institutional environment explain why credible commitment was stronger in the USA than in France prior to the rise of antinuclear activism in the USA. Prior to the 1970s, however, the US system had the potential to let activists enter the game.* When a branch of FIGURE 15.2 is added to represent the presence of antinuclear activists, the model explains the decrease of credible commitment of the US government to the industry. Antinuclear activists use the court system to challenge government-granted licenses to utilities (Mitchell, 1981), raising their transaction costs (see Table 15.1). Court decisions and lobbying in the US Congress end up in a perception by utilities of a lower government commitment to nuclear power plants.[†] In France, despite the substantial presence of antinuclear interest groups, the imperviousness of the institutional setup (no division of power, weak judiciary, and strong bureaucracy) effectively shut out activists influencing policy outcomes.

In the USA, the TMI incident in 1979 accelerated the decline of the nuclear industry. What if an incident like TMI had happened in France? The model suggests that the public would never have been informed; the strong bureaucracy and unified executive/legislative branches kept the public ignorant. What then, if a Chernobyl were to happen in France? As the media would play its role, asymmetry of information between government officials and public opinion would be much lower. The model suggests that the system would collapse completely and rapidly, instead of incrementally as in the USA.

The above model concludes that transaction costs in the US nuclear industry are higher than in France, where antinuclear activists step in while they were lower before. Let us now turn to the available data to see if they fit the conclusions of the model.

DIFFERENCES IN TRANSACTION COSTS IN THE US AND FRENCH NUCLEAR POWER INDUSTRY

In the words of Weingast (1980: 241), "Lengthening the regulatory process increases the capital costs of the plant by pushing the revenue received from operation further into the future and by adding to the total interest payments on construction loans." Weingast estimates that the cost per kW for US plants increased as shown in TABLE 15.3. Although inflation and the competitive

---

* Although the date of TMI (March 1979) is a convenient marker for denoting the demise of nuclear power in the USA, it is important to note that the decline of the nuclear industry actually began around 1971, when orders for plants fell and the use of delaying tactics by environmental groups became popular (a landmark lawsuit involved the Calvert Cliffs nuclear plant and the failure of its builders to consider the mandate of NEPA). The nuclear industry suffered a gradual decline leading up to the TMI accident. In this sense, one might argue that the transition point from the initial institutional environment to another actually occurred gradually during the period 1971–80.
† For a detailed account of the changes in the US institutional environment of electric utilities, see Delmas Heiman, and Ghertman (1995).

TABLE 15.3   Estimated versus actual costs per kW: US nuclear energy

Year	Estimated cost per kW	Actual cost per kW
1965	$120	$240
1968	$155	$460
1970	$200	—
1975	$700	—

(Source: Weingast (1981) reproduced with permission).

TABLE 15.4   Average delays in nuclear power plant construction (months)

Year	United States	France
1974	20.0	0.7
1977	35.9	3.6
1980	49.4	7.1
1984	53.1	11.3

(Source: Adapted from Campbell, 1988: p.41).

cost of coal are certainly partially responsible for the rise in costs of nuclear power, these elements do not present the complete picture. Procedural delay often caused by the action of public interest groups and increasing costs of compliance with safety and environmental standards played a significant role in increasing transaction costs associated with new plant construction.

In the USA, from 1966 to 1970, the time required to complete the regulatory process rose from 86 months (on average) to 122 months, an increase of 42% (Weingast, 1980). This early escalation of delays resulted in substantially higher costs for utilities in the form of the cost of capital. This trend was to continue well into the 1970s and become exacerbated by the effects of increased public doubt about the appropriateness of nuclear power. TABLE 15.4, adapted from Campbell (1988: 158) gives a comparative look at average construction delays across a 10-year period. FIGURE 15.3 presents the increases in review time for issuing construction and operating permits for the USA. FIGURE 15.4 presents the average lead times for plants (from order to commercial operation) in both France and the USA. The French program is characterized by stability in lead times when compared to the USA. FIGURE 15.5, which presents comparative information regarding the time elapsed from the order of nuclear steam supply systems to the beginning of construction, tells a similar tale; delays in the USA increase over time while the French situation remains comparatively stable.

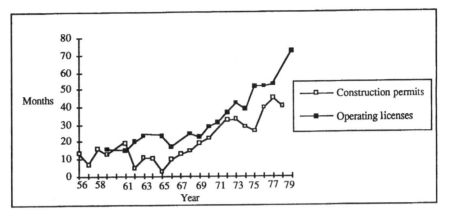

FIGURE 15.3 Average review time for construction permits and operating licenses, USA, 1956–80 (Source: adapted from *Les centrales nucléaires dans le monde* (1994), Commissariat à l'Energie Atomique)

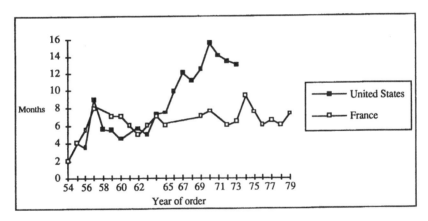

FIGURE 15.4 Average leadtime for nuclear power plant (from first order to commercial operation in the United States and France) (Source: adapted from *Les centrales nucléaires dans le monde* (1994), Commissariat à l'Energie Atomique)

The industry's heyday as the preeminent purchaser of regulation from Congress was clearly over; antinuclear groups were in the ascendancy. One possibility for industry salvation might have been consolidation and subsequent plant standardization. The utilities were not able to achieve sector integration because of a legal framework in the USA that mandated antitrust review. They tried, however, to reduce safety monitoring costs

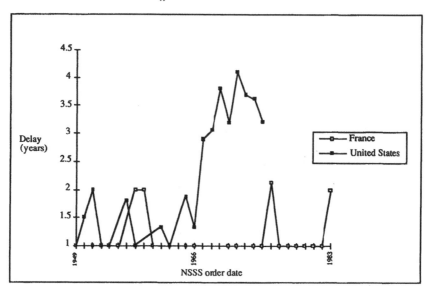

FIGURE 15.5   Time elapsed from order of nuclear steam supply system to start of construction: USA and France (Source: *Les centrales nucléaires dans le monde* (1994), Commissariat à l'Energie Atomique, reproduced with permission)

and to coordinate their knowledge through different associations. The Institute for Nuclear Operations (INPO), an association of all nuclear utilities and some suppliers, was formed to correct problems in utility management, construction, and quality practices. INPO formed a monitoring arrangement with the NRC, through a formal "memorandum of understanding" where they coordinated research efforts and exchanged information with each other (Campbell, 1991). This can be viewed as an industry attempt to self-regulate. The infeasibility of adjusting governance of the industry under the US institutional environment also played a role in the decline of the industry. Governance adaptation was effectively frozen between antitrust law and activist court actions, which seemed to be sensitized to any action the industry might take to help foster a recovery.

Empirically, the evidence suggests that higher transaction costs for nuclear power are strongly correlated with the decline of the industry in the USA. Melicher et al. (1987) find evidence that total stock returns were lower in recent years for nuclear utilities, when compared to nonnuclear utilities. Chen et al. (1987) find an association between US nuclear power plant cancellations and positive share price reaction. The most direct estimate of transaction costs is given by the NEA (1984: 46) which asserts that in 1987, the cost in constant dollars per kW in interest charges in the USA was $296,

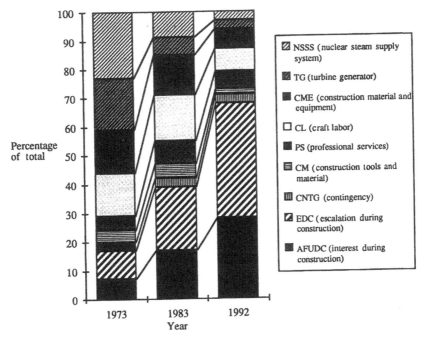

FIGURE 15.6   Composition of nuclear power capital costs in the United States, 1973–92 (Source: NRC Annual Reports, 1973, 1983, 1992, reproduced with permission)

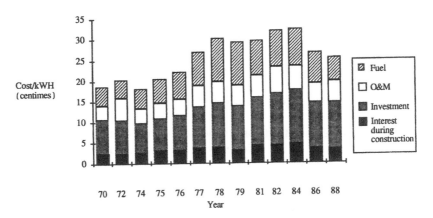

FIGURE 15.7   French reference nuclear costs during construction, 1970–88. (Source: J-M. Capron, "Les coûts de référence de la production d'électricité," November 1993, reproduced with permission). EDF does not publish data on costs for individual stations (or even groups of stations). However, they do publish slightly stylized data for reference nuclear stations. These are all forecasts of future costs, but they are clearly informed by experience of costs experienced over time. Such data for reference plants are available from studies conducted between 1974 and 1990.)

while in France the same cost was $171 or 42% lower.* As shown in FIGURE 15.6, interest costs during construction have been rising continuously in the United States, from less than 10% of the investment costs in 1973, to 30% in 1992. In France, on the contrary, interest during construction as a fraction of entire investment has remained constant during 1970–76 at less than 25% of the total investment cost and has even subsequently decreased (FIGURE 15.7). Compelling evidence for the assertion that the French approach to capital provision is comparatively more efficient is found in the fact that EDF (Electricité de France, the state-owned monopoly utility) recently signed a deal with the French government to reduce its prices and reduce its debt, while investing 20% more in its distribution systems (*Energy Economist*, 1993). In contrast, US utilities have often raised prices and defaulted on debt.

Delay engendered by the open nature of the state and federal regulatory systems in the USA increased transaction costs by raising the amount of interest owed on borrowed capital, decreasing operating revenues, and increasing the costs of compliance with arrays of new rules and regulations. Huge indirect costs have been incurred by the US nuclear industry (and avoided by France) in the area of legal expenses, including defending proposals and analyzing and commenting on new and proposed regulations.

CONCLUSION

The general assertion that "institutional details matter" in the realm of institutional environment appears to have been borne out by this chapter. It has presented arguments asserting that the effects of nonparametric uncertainty on an institutional environment may be felt at the level of trans-actions within particular industrial sectors of an economy. France, with its well-insulated institutional setup, has avoided the problems encountered by the United States, largely opened to inputs from virtually all interested parties.

Taken as a whole, the effects of division of power, weak bureaucracy, and especially easy access to an independent judiciary spelled trouble for the industry in America. US utilities were unable to act to stem regulatory changes, especially under the post-TMI regulatory institutional environ-ment. The effect of unanticipated changes in uncertainty surrounding regu-latory practice caused an escalation in costs and lead times which was

---

* Interest costs are for the entire construction period. NEA (1984: 46) further asserts that "Depending on the phasing of expenditure and construction time, [interest costs during con-struction] can range from as little as 14% of investment cost for plants built within five years to as much as 30% or more for plants taking twice as long (with interest rates of 5% per annum)." Delay can clearly play a major role in increasing transaction costs incurred by utilities in plant construction.

unforeseen by utilities (see TABLE 15.2). For example, for plants entering construction in the mid-1960s, forecast errors in interest costs were about 110%. These increased to about 170% for units entering construction 10 years later (Hewlett, 1994). The French institutional environment, on the other hand, is characterized by important protective attributes for nuclear utilities: concentrated power in the executive and the ministries, a strong administration and no access for citizens to an independent court system. The French political structure seems to be able to carry out a long-term policy while ignoring the fluctuations of public opinion. The disadvantage of the French institutions is the alienation that can result between the public and the government when a large segment of the population's concerns is not incorporated into policy. Powerless courts and the independent nature of bureaucracies such as the Ministry of Industry coupled with the power of the ruling party to enforce party preferences served to insulate French nuclear programs from public opinion. Nuclear power costs are thus expected to be comparatively more stable over time for France than for the United States.

When nonparametric uncertainty impinges on an industry, behavioral uncertainty is also affected, in turn affecting transaction costs. The sequence of our model is presented in the context of France and the USA (in pre-activist and activist periods for the USA) in TABLE 15.5. Differences in governance efficiency are amplified by the impact of distorting behavioral uncertainty via nonparametric uncertainty. Note, however, that *none* of government structures discussed meet all the ostensible "goals" of a democratic system. In this sense and speaking broadly, governance may be said to be "misaligned" with transaction attributes in *both* countries: French government fails to credibly commit to its constituents, who have no voice in nuclear policy and US government commitment to industry is similarly noncredible. The American system leads to nuclear industry decline and the French system seems impervious to public opinion. This chapter does not advocate technocratic, antidemocratic forms of policy planning, nor does it make recommendations about whether or not the USA should try to revive the nuclear sector, and how best to proceed in this endeavour.

The above conclusions are aligned with those of Levy and Spiller (1994): the credibility of the institutional environment strongly impacts the strategies of firms and the comparative efficiencies of industries in different countries.

This chapter adds that, in some circumstances, an independent court system may not always improve the credibility of government commitments, when opposing interest groups become strong players. Evidence was presented that supports the idea that transaction costs are higher in the USA than France for nuclear power. This evidence, however, has limited scope. As the main focus of this chapter was on transaction costs associated with the construction of nuclear power plants, transaction costs associated with operation and decommissioning nuclear plants were not taken into

TABLE 15.5   Comparative transaction costs

	France	USA (pre-activist)	USA (activist)
Facets of the institutional environment:			
Division of power	Centralized: executive, bureaucracy (PEON and Ministry of Industry), utility (EDF)	Centralized: AEC, JCAE	Fragmented: Congress multiple committees, states (PUCs), judiciary
Strength of the bureaucracy	Very strong	Strong	Weak
Judiciary	Nonindependent	Independent, but not engaged by activists	Independent and engaged by activists
Cultural norms	Strong	Weak	Weak
Resulting access points to foment nonparametric uncertainty	Few	Few	Many
Nonparametric uncertainty	Low	Low	High
Transaction attributes:			
Behavioural uncertainty resulting from exogenous nonparametric uncertainty	Low	Low	High
Asset specificity	High	High	High
Frequency	High	High	High
Transaction costs:			
Capital, safety, monitoring, legal	Low	Low	High

account. These have also played an important role in the problems of the nuclear industry.*

Nuclear power in the USA today remains under similar (though presently more dormant) pressure to that experienced during the 1970s and 1980s. The pressure does not seem so intense today because the antinuclear

* An analysis prepared by the Electric Power Research Institute shows that, from 1981 to 1988, operations and maintenance costs increased by 80% (adjusted for inflation) and the average plant staff doubled. The EPRI study found that 30–60% of O&M costs were attributable to NRC requirements (Byus, 1990).

movement in the USA has apparently managed to "impose delay to increase transaction costs" strategy. Estimates, however, projecting the potential costs of nuclear energy in all participating countries for the future consistently fail to take transaction costs as a function of institutional environment into account. "Nuclear generation costs are conventionally split into three main components: capital investment, fuel and nonfuel operation and maintenance costs" (NEA, 1984: 45). These findings suggest that other regulated industries which experience significant controversy may be suitable for analysis using this approach.

ACKNOWLEDGEMENTS

The authors gratefully acknowledge the insights and advice of Severin Borenstein, John Defiguereido, Nicolas Jabko, David Mowery, Jackson Nickerson, Greg Noble, Gene Rochlin, Pablo Spiller, and Oliver Williamson. Remaining inconsistencies or errors are solely attributable to us. Severin Borenstein and the UC Energy Institute are gratefully acknowledged for their support of this project.

BIBLIOGRAPHY

Abraham, H.J. (1980) "Courts Abroad", *The Judicial Process*. New York: Oxford Press, p. 272.

Barkenbus, J.N. (1984) "Nuclear Power and Government Structure: The Divergent Paths of the United States and France", *Social Science Quarterly*, **65**(1), 37–47.

Bupp, I. (1979) "Nuclear Stalemate", in R.Y. Stobaugh Daniel (ed.), *Energy Future: Report of the Energy Project at the Harvard Business School*, New York: Ballantine.

Byus, L. (1990) "O&M Costs and the Investment Community", *Nuclear News*, October, 31.

Campbell, J.L. (1987) "The State and the Nuclear Waste Crisis: An Institutional Analysis of Policy Constraints", *Social Problems*, **34**(1), 18–33.

Campbell, J.L. (1988) *Nuclear Power and the Contradiction of U.S. Policy*. Ithaca and London: Cornell University Press.

Campbell, J.L. (1991) "Contradictions of Governance in the Nuclear Energy Sector", in J.L. Campbell, J.R. Hollingsworth, and L.N. Lindberg (eds), *Governance of the American Economy*, Cambridge, UK and New York: Cambridge University Press.

Carmoy de, H. (1982) "The French Energy Policy", *Energy Policy*, **10**, Sept, 186.

Chen, C. et al. (1987) "Abandonment Decisions and the Market Value of the Firm: The Case of Nuclear Power Project Abandonment", *Journal of Accounting and Public Policy*, **6** Winter, 285–297.

Chubb, J.E. and Peterson, P.E. (1989) *Can the Government Govern?* Washington DC: Brookings Institution.

Dac, H. (1994) *Droit et Politiques Nucléaires*. Paris: Presses Universitaires de France.

David, R. (1972) *French Law: Its Structure, Sources, and Methodology*. Baton Rouge: Louisiana State University Press.

Delmas, M., Heiman, B., and Ghertman, M. (1995) *Government Credible Commitment in the French and American Nuclear Power Industries,* Working paper, Hautes Études Commerciales, Jouy-en-Josas, FOE, p. 546.
Energy Economist (1993) "Energy Market Report: Electricity", **135**, January, 30–31.
Gandara, A. (1977) *Electric Utility Decisionmaking and the Nuclear Option.* Santa Monica: Rand Corporation.
Hatch, M.T. (1986) *Politics and Nuclear Power.* Lexington: University Press of Kentucky.
Hewlett, J.G. (1994) "Why Were the U.S. Nuclear Power Plant Construction Costs and Lead-Time Estimates So Wrong? in T.C. and G.W.H. Lowinger (eds), *Nuclear Power at the Crossroads: Challenges and Prospects for the Twenty-First Century* ICEED, p. 122.
Itteilag, R.L. and Pavle, J. (1985) "Nuclear Power Plants' Anticipated Costs and Their Impact on Future Electric Rates", *Public Utility Fortnightly,* **115**(6), 35–40.
Jasper, J.M. (1990) *Nuclear Politics: Energy and the State in the United States, Sweden and France.* New Jersey: Princeton University Press.
Joppke, C. (1993) *Mobilizing against Nuclear Power: A Comparison of Germany and the United States.* Berkeley: University of California Press, Inc.
Levy, B. and Spiller, Pablo (1994) "The Institutional Foundations of Regulatory Commitment: A Comparative Analysis of Telecommunication Regulation", *Journal of Law, Economics and Organization.*
Melicher, R.W. et al. (1987) "Nuclear Risk Exposure, Stockholder Returns and Costs of Capital Implications", *Electric Potential,* **3** March–April, 36–42.
Mitchell, W. (1981) "From Elite Quarrel to Mass Movement", *Society,* **18**(5), 76–84.
Nuclear Energy Agency (NEA) (1984) *Nuclear Power and Public Opinion.* Paris: OECD.
Nelkin, D. and Pollak, M. (1981) *The Atom Besieged: Extraparliamentary Dissent in France and Germany.* Cambridge, Mass.: MIT Press.
North, D. (1990) *Institutions, Institutional Change, and Economic Performance.* New York: Cambridge University Press.
Nuclear Regulatory Commission (NRC) (1975–82) *Annual Reports.* Washington DC: US Government Printing Office.
Oleszek, W.J. (1984) "Congressional Procedures and the Policy Process", *Congressional Quarterly.*
OTA (US) (1984) *Nuclear Power in an Age of Uncertainty.* Washington DC: GPO. United States, President's Commission on the Accident at Three Mile Island.
Rochlin, G.I. and von Meier, A. (1994) "Nuclear Power Operations—A Cross Cultural Perspective", *Annual Review of Energy and The Environment,* **19**, 153–187.
Schrader-Frechette, K.S. (1980) *Nuclear Power and Public Policy.* Dordrecht: D. Reidel Publishing.
Shonfield, A. (1965) *Modern Capitalism.* New York, Oxford University Press.
Studness, C.M. (1992) "The U.S. Supreme Court and Utility Imprudence", *Public Utilities Fortnightly,* 15 January, 28.
US Department of Energy (USDOE) (1983) *Nuclear Plant Cancellation: Causes and Consequences.* Washington DC.
US Senate (1974) *Financial Problems of the Electric Utilities: Hearings.* Committee on Interior and Insular Affairs.
Walker, D. (1981) *Toward a Functioning Federalism.* Cambridge, Mass.: Winthrop.
Weingast, B.R. (1981). "Regulation, Reregulation and Deregulation: The Political Foundations of Agency Clientele Relationships", *Law and Contemporary Problems,* **44**(1), 149–177.

Weingast, B.R. (1980) "Congress, Regulation and the Decline of Nuclear Power", *Public Policy*, **28**(2), 232.

Williamson, O.E. (1985) Economic Institutions of Capitalism. New York: Free Press.

Williamson, O.E. (1994) "The Politics and Economics of Redistribution and Inefficiency", Working Paper, University of California, Berkeley.

16

A Strategy for More Effective Executive Development

XAVIER GILBERT, PETER LORANGE

The demands placed on business executives by the current strategic challenges facing their organizations are multiple: they are expected to be visionaries, wise strategists, charismatic leaders, fast decision makers, able to operate in and with any culture and, of course, flexible, innovative, rigorous managers. The onus is on executive development to produce these prodigies. The challenge is real; the responses, however, have been very superficially thought out.

Both the business community and the business schools should share the responsibility for making executive development more effective, the former by being more demanding, the latter by being more responsive and both by taking more initiative.

EXECUTIVE LEARNING

Perhaps all parties forget that executive development is, in fact, the enhancement and acceleration of executive learning, with the focus on the "learner" rather than on the "teacher". Learning, although a natural human activity, is also profoundly misunderstood by both the business community and by the business schools, among many others.

The purpose of executive learning can be, and often is, limited to the delivery of high quality factual information which should allow more

Strategy, Structure and Style. Edited by H. Thomas, D. O'Neal and M. Ghertman
Copyright © 1997 John Wiley & Sons Ltd.

effective job execution. In itself this is useful, but in an action-oriented profession, one should expect more from learning. More ambitiously, the purpose of executive learning can also be more effective action-taking, as a result of more effective thinking *and* of more effective approaches and behaviors. The ambitions of executive development, however, seem limited mostly to the information delivery side with a focus on memorization, although often it is only the speaker who is memorable. Behavior changes to the executive's own devices.

In our opinion, three critical learning steps are left out, perhaps even ignored. The first, after new information has been absorbed, is *conceptualization*:

- Where does this piece of information fit in my conceptual models of the world?
- Can it improve one of the conceptual frameworks I use to understand the issues I have to deal with and take action?
- How does it add to the whole picture?

Conceptualization is facilitated by interaction, discussion, and confrontation of different perspectives because it is an integrative, synthesis-seeking cognitive activity. The Socratic learning approach helps conceptualization.

The next critical step in a learning process is *reality testing*:

- What should I do differently given how I now picture the situation?
- Does this new approach or behavior work?
- What feedback do I get when I try it out?
- Is it effective, not effective?
- What are the results?

The purpose of reality testing is feedback on the impact, effectiveness, and consequences of the new approach or behavior. So, like a business, reality testing requires at least some of the elements of reality, issue, co-workers, customers, etc., not just someone else's business problems and observations. Reality testing implies that learning should not be artificially separated from the job context, as is most often the case with "formal" learning, so possible approaches to it are on-the-job learning, projects, and job assignments.

In fact, learning, or rather the ability to relearn autonomously, really starts with the next step: *debriefing*. Learning is not an end in itself: if learning does not create the need for more learning, it quickly becomes obsolete, and it is debriefing that primes the "learning pump". Debriefing addresses the questions that aim at making the learning reusable and thus points to the need for more learning: why did this approach or behavior work? Why not? What should I pay more attention to next time? What else do I need to

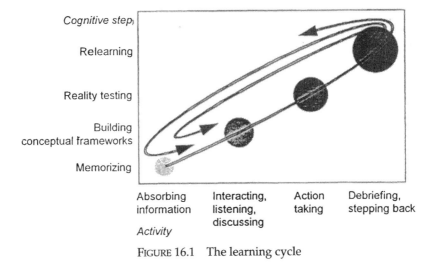

FIGURE 16.1   The learning cycle

know? In what ways should I review my conceptual models? Debriefing is very rarely done; there is generally an urge to get on with the next task, rather than step back and take stock of what has been learned, what more needs to be learned. So approaches to debriefing need to be quite formal to ensure that it does take place, and interactive to stretch one's reflection.

But this is only the beginning of learning, the "initiation", not the "graduation". Learning is an ongoing, self-renewing process, and executive learning is no exception. Yet, enhancing the ability to learn as a basis for effective action-taking is rarely seen as the purpose of executive development.

THE APPROACH: CLOSENESS TO THE BUSINESS COMMUNITY

The potential of executive development is rarely reached, and the responsibility for it must be shared by the business community and by the business schools. There are two reasons why the business community does not live up to this potential: first, executive development is generally approached with low learning ambition and second, it lacks serious management commitment.

The official, stated intentions of executive development give only a limited insight into the learning objectives. If output measurement, however, is any indication of the real priorities, these seem to be only moderately related to learning. Indeed, the extent to which approaches and behavior have changed as a result of an executive development initiative, which, as we have seen, should be the ultimate purpose of such an initiative, is almost never measured.

What is always measured, on the other hand, is the level of immediate satisfaction with the delivery and with the content, although these two dimensions are often not separated. Yet, measuring immediate satisfaction can clearly not be a proxy for measuring learning; the two are not even correlated. In fact, because this is less of a challenge for all parties, immediate satisfaction is easily achieved through low cognitive dissonance, mental or emotional gratification, effortless exposure, which typically are not conducive to learning and change. The exorbitant fees commanded by risk-free speakers, as well as the basis on which human resources development managers often are or feel assessed, provide further evidence that immediate satisfaction is a high priority in many executive development initiatives.

In fact, for adults, learning is an emotional activity, perhaps because it reminds us so much of childhood. A need to learn can be interpreted in a somewhat idealized corporate context as an inadequacy that needs to be remedied. Nonlearning benefits will thus often be sought to compensate for, or hide, this weakness: feeling part of a select group, feeling the object of care and attention, rubbing shoulders with peers, for example. In reasonable doses, these benefits can be helpful. However, if they become the focus of immediate satisfaction, to the point of hijacking the learning initiative, learning is no longer on the agenda.

But perhaps, even if the wrong metrics are used, and even if there are other by-products from a learning initative, the learning ambitions are still high. But, in fact, this is not the case. The articulation of needs developed by corporations for learning initiatives, the learning mandates, also reveal very low learning ambitions. First, these mandates are rarely explicitly related to the strategic priorities and corresponding capabilities of the corporation, be it implementation priorities or renewal priorities. As a result, they are generic, and management-topic oriented, as opposed to issue oriented: in the absence of a strong anchoring into strategic priorities and corresponding capabilities, the thinking behind the articulated learning needs is necessarily superficial.

Second, because the specifications tend to be developed in a vacuum, they easily reflect the current fads and "flavors of the day". The constant renewal of the management vocabulary, giving new names to old concepts, and the overuse of loaded words—value creation, empowerment—also contribute to a potential fear of being associated with outdated semantics. There is often a disturbing lack of selectivity in the use of buzzwords in filling learning specifications. Overall, thus, there is rarely a tight, well thought out connection between the strategic agenda of the firm and the learning agenda of executive development.

The fact that executive development is seen as an off-the-job, "accessory" activity is confirmed by the lack of line-management commitment to this activity. Even though it is potentially an important piece of strategy implementation, and the major ingredient of corporate renewal, senior management rarely give it even a fraction of the attention they give to any physical investment decision. Executive development is delegated to human resource development managers, and all hope for the best.

Executive development also does not receive the "organization room" it requires. It is kept separate from the job, to avoid any interference with the "normal" conduct of business, as if it was not expected to have any effect. The executive time needed for learning guidance, project coaching, debriefing, is rarely available, even though, in a fast changing environment, learning capabilities should be an essential skill. Interestingly, one is expected to know, rather than to learn, act, and relearn.

But the writing is on the wall; the growing awareness of the fleeting nature of knowledge and of the need to relearn quickly will eventually reach executive development and will force it into the strategic agenda. In the competitive context that will prevail, this will have several radical consequences.

RENEWAL CAPABILITIES

The first of these consequences reflects the realization that, in a competitive formula, renewal capabilities are the only really sustainable advantage. In executive development terms, this will lead to shifting the emphasis from delivering discrete pieces of knowledge to developing learning capabilities. There are two ingredients to such capabilities. The first is a constant stream of new insights into business issues. To meet this need, the business community will rely on partners who contribute intellectual integrity, rather than anecdotal support, to the research process. Not only is it in the best long-term interest of the business community to be a partner in this value creation process, but those corporations that will do so will not allow nonpartners to benefit from it. For example, they may prevent the faculty of their partner business schools from being cherry-picked by nonpartners.

The second ingredient in developing learning capabilities is the engineering of the learning process. This calls for highly interactive learning processes that can be used as continuous learning models by executives. It also calls for thoroughly integrated learning processes that stimulate the synthesis capabilities of executives, another critical ingredient of continuous learning. Such learning approaches do not rely on brilliant speakers, but on a rare learning engineering know-how; they do not rely on individuals but on teams. Corporations will be seeking to partner with teams that have a distinctive ability to engineer learning activities.

By the same token, corporations will develop new ways to measure the effectiveness of executive development. In the future, it is the change in behavior that will be sought as evidence of the effectiveness of executive development, a healthy departure from the current "showbiz" inclinations.

STRATEGIC PRIORITIES

In the prevailing competitive context, strategic agendas bring many dimensions of the business together, making division of labor an archaic mode of operation. The consequences for executive development will be important. Rather than being structured along functional areas, as has traditionally been the case, executive development must now become issue-oriented, related to the specific strategic priorities of a corporation, and focused on the mindsets and behaviors required to tackle these.

These strategic priorities are, by definition, idiosyncratic in their genesis, in their corporate culture roots, and in the mindsets and behaviors they call for. The provider of the design, implementation and follow-up of learning activities cannot be a remote academic body in pursuit of its own agenda; it must be a partner with a profound understanding of the company's mode of operation and priorities. The requirement is not to spot the best speakers, but to partner with a team with whom, in addition to developing unique insights on the situation at hand and designing a unique learning process, strategic priorities can be addressed. The same approaches that are applied to procurement should also prevail here, rather than the game of playing business schools against each other.

These strategic priorities are also, by definition, multidimensional. In other words, they do not fit neatly with traditional business functions, and even less with business school departments. Corporations will thus look for partners who are not bound by archaic ways of structuring issues, and can thus assemble flexible and evolving teams capable of relating to complex strategic agenda.

BOTTOM-LINE IMPACT

In today's competitive environment any activity of a corporation will be assessed against its impact on the bottom line. The consequences for executive development are again considerable. Learning cannot remain generic; it must directly enhance actual business processes with measurable value creation.

A first implication is that executive development cannot be subcontracted; it is a line responsibility like any other aspect of strategy formulation and implementation. Learning must rely on a partnership between those who own the business priorities and those who have developed reliable insights into these issues and can engineer an effective learning process to bring it all together. To enhance the effectiveness of the business processes, learning will typically require a mix of inputs from both sides.

A second implication is that executive development must become part of the change process that pervades excellent firms. Corporations will realize that executive development treated as a stand-alone activity can only make a limited contribution to the bottom line. Through partnerships, they will seek more integration between the change process and the accompanying learning process.

Finally, an increased emphasis on cost effectiveness will force the learning partner to look for alternatives to the length of learning events as the main source of their effectiveness; length becomes unnecessary if learning is imbedded in and extended through the value creation process of the firm. More sophisticated designs of learning activities will thus call for partnerships in designing, implementing, and following up the learning process associated with the pursuit of strategic priorities.

In summary, corporations will seek to establish learning partnerships to:

- develop generalizable insights into current and future business issues
- bridge the gap between strategic priorities and learning priorities
- deliver the cross-organization teamwork associated with learning
- monitor the continuous learning process, thus allowing the adaptation of behavior to changing strategic challenges.

THE RESPONSES FROM THE BUSINESS SCHOOLS

Business schools should be natural partners in these learning partnerships. Unfortunately, they have difficulty seeing the signals, not to mention responding to the challenge. There are three main reasons for this lack of responsiveness.

THE ACADEMIC LIFESTYLE

Business schools are entangled in a set of habits developed to protect private faculty agendas. In particular, executive development is often viewed as an adjunct or peripheral activity within the typical business school. The latter has a different *raison d'être*: mass undergraduate and MBA teaching, but as necessary chores in preserving the "publish (for other academics) or perish" academic agenda. Executive development is frequently treated as an extracurricular activity that helps boost faculty income. It is delivered by "senior" faculty who have accumulated enough anecdotes and white hair to perform without state-of-the-art, research-based knowledge.

In addition, the archaic argument of academic freedom, as if business schools needed to be sheltered from certain business realities, is often used to refuse that research activities should be performed in cooperation with a business firm. For example, difficulties often arise with respect to the way a piece of research may be used or disseminated within the corporation.

This setup does not allow the flexibility needed to partner with a business firm to develop the insights needed to deal with its business challenges. It also does not allow bridging the gap between strategic and learning priorities—an activity that is generally performed by business professors as private consultants, or even by consulting firms that then subcontract the "teaching" part of the deal. In any case, it maintains in the business community an image of executive development that would only consist of traditional teaching.

THE OUTMODED TEACHING MODELS

The teaching models used in executive development are extensions of what business schools have always done: undergraduate and MBA teaching. The same teaching approaches are used—silver-bullet sessions on generic subjects—even though executives come with experience and, often, a pressing business issue on their mind. To deal with this impatient audience, good lectureship will prevail, and the structure of "seminars" will be guided by the art of juxtaposing entertaining pieces.

The value added of a business school in offering such executive development activities is limited, compared to what its faculty may offer independently. Indeed this leads to frequent competition between the business school and its faculty, while maintaining in the business community an image of executive development that is more associated with traditional teaching than with learning partnerships. Such requirements as focusing exclusively on strategic priorities, tight integration of the various aspects of the issue addressed, joint inputs from the learning partners—the firm and the business school—will just not be feasible.

THE STRUCTURE OF BUSINESS SCHOOLS

The functional specialization of business schools, often leading to hermetic departmentalization, prevents them from addressing a business issue in its entirety. Experience in working across departments, addressing together a total business issue, is very rare in business schools. No wonder the business community sees the business school as a pool of more or less usable specialists, rather than as a solution deliverer in a strategic challenge.

The mode of operation of business schools also gets in the way. The life of the business school professor is often structured around terms, courses, teaching days, and office hours. In addition to the number of refereed articles published, the output of the academic is measured in number of sessions taught or of hours of teaching. Not only does this structure not encourage teamwork in business schools, it also makes it almost impossible to find the availability needed for a learning partnership—where most of the service is delivered outside of a classroom.

Honestly, under such circumstances, why a business firm might consider a partnership with a business school may only be explained by a fascination with academia.

NEXT STEPS

What should be done? Innovation in executive development clearly calls for a learning partnership between two active constituents: the firm and the business school. The challenge is to create a partnership-based executive development reality.

PROPOSITION ONE

At a minimum, business school should respond with a portfolio of open courses, allowing key members of the firm to learn in a benchmarking context, by comparing themselves with other leading firms and executives. There are several implications of this:

- strong corporate partner input on developing the content of each of the offerings in the portfolio
- allowing only participants who can "give" something to a learning activity; filling up the available classroom capacity to ensure break-even will jeopardize interactive learning from state-of-the-art practices

PROPOSITION TWO

Tailored executive development is a key element of the win–win partnership agenda. This approach allows in-depth, collective work around the formulation and/or implementation of the firm's strategy to take place. Both the firm and the business school progress through such a partnership; it will, indeed, become one of the critical ways for business school faculty members to gain essential insights into the most current business challenges.

One very important implication, however, is that business schools make some very fundamental changes in their modes of operation. The "bottom line" will probably not be perceived as high enough by the typical academic to make this change a smooth one.

PROPOSITION THREE

There must be an underlying network of relationships, primarily between each firm and a business school, but also among the firms, leading to learning networks. These learning networks will support several activities. First, research on selected current strategic issues, to propose reliable generalizations, document effective practices for benchmarking, and anticipate future challenges. Second, tailored executive learning, focused on strategic priorities, through cross-organization teams. Third, a continuous learning process to anticipate future strategic challenges.

In this case, the challenge is a fundamental change in the very nature of business schools. The path to be followed is closer to a consulting firm's way of operating. Business schools, however, could offer a unique one-stop shopping service. Indeed, while consulting firms have also performed high quality research on critical business issues, and while their *raison d'être* is often to help bridge the gap between strategic priorities and specific behaviors, the distinctive competence of business schools should be in engineering executive learning while offering considerable insight into critical business issues—not an insignificant change in the way business schools see their mission. To support this change, the nature of the relationship between the business school professor and the business school will also have to be significantly reviewed: the concepts of partnership and of value creation with a bottom-line impact may have to apply to the business schools themselves.

BIBLIOGRAPHY

Lorange, P. (1996) "Developing Learning Partnerships", *The Learning Organization, International Journal*, **2**(1), Spring, **3**(2), 11–19.

Lorange, P. (1996) "Between Academia and Business: New Challenges for Today's Modern Business Schools", *Management Education and Business Performance*, P. Amdam, (ed.), London: Routledge.

Lorange, P. and Xavier, G. (1994) "National Approaches to Strategic Management— A Resource-Based Perspective", *International Business Review*, Pergamon, **3**(4), 411–423.

The Study of National Strategic Management: A Methodological Discussion

TAÏEB HAFSI, PABLO MARTIN DE HOLAN

For most strategic management scholars, national strategic management is very much like witches: it does not exist, and if it does, no one has ever seen one. Lack of enthusiasm notwithstanding, the increasing globalization of markets has motivated scholars to produce literature dealing with strategy at the national level. Among many others, Quinn (1992) indirectly, and Ohmae (1985) more openly, suggested the importance of being part of the world that counts, the "Triad"; Reich (1989) and Magaziner and Patinkin (1989) show that governments, on behalf of societies, do contribute in achieving prosperity in a "silent war" among firms and nations; Prahalad and Doz (1987) show that a sound multinational strategy is the result of understanding the dynamics of government policy and global competition. In the same vein, Porter (1990) admits that "my theory, and the evidence from our research, does not support the view [that governments are powerless]. Government policy does affect national advantage, both positively and negatively"; finally, Rugman (1990) and Francis (1992) argue with Porter on the mechanics of government influence, but not on its importance.

The influence of government on firm behavior and on firm profitability is ubiquitous in our societies, yet our journals and conferences often disregard the dynamics of government as an important object of study. The reasons are sound: we do not know how to study the behavior of large complex

Strategy, Structure and Style. Edited by H. Thomas, D. O'Neal and M. Ghertman
Copyright © 1997 John Wiley & Sons Ltd.

systems, without a lot of simplification which could defeat the purpose. A country is furthermore a web of intertwined complex systems. Is it possible to study the concatenation of a multitude of factors on a system's behavior?

We "jumped into the dark" a few years ago with an extensive study of 17 country strategies. We started with the assumption that the dynamics of strategy at the national level need not be, in essence, different from strategy for a large complex firm. Then, we proceeded to study countries in the same way scholars have been studying complex firms' behavior for decades: through monographs.

In this chapter, we tackle the methodological issues related to this type of research. In the first section we discuss why it is legitimate to undertake studies of such complex systems as that of a nation. In particular, the conceptual framework that has been used to collect the data is presented. Then, the methodology used in our studies is described. The case of Taiwan (Daleu-Daibé and Hafsi, 1993), is presented as an illustration in section three. Finally, in section four are discussed some of the methodological issues that have been identified. In the conclusion, a few comments and recommendations for research are offered.

THE STUDY OF NATIONAL STRATEGY

Several questions come to mind when one addresses the issue of national strategy. Can one study the behavior of a state and find coherent patterns that would reveal its strategy? Second, is it appropriate to use the state's strategy as a proxy for national strategy? If so, what exactly is to be taken as the state? Third, is it methodologically feasible to study the strategy of the state? If so, what does strategy mean in such a case or, expressed another way, how would the researcher conceptualize the idea of strategy to make it relevant for the study of such a complex organization? Finally, assuming that we are able to come up with a strategy for the state, how useful would that be?

THE STATE'S STRATEGY

The strategy of a nation is an abstract and vague idea. The problem with a nation is that there are too many things happening and too many people involved, many more than anybody can track. The first task then, is to find some coherence in the myriad of actions taking place in a nation. The concept of strategy provides a useful tool.

Strategy has been defined as the pattern of behavior or decisions in an organization that determines objectives, produces policies and plans and defines the activities the organization engages in and its contribution to shareholders (Andrews, 1987). Therefore, strategy is the resulting effect of action, when such effect is not random or chaotic. When looking at past actions of a social actor, strategy can be observed in the patterns of the streams of actions that the actors have taken over time (Mintzberg, 1978; Mintzberg and Waters, 1982).

It is important to be able to simplify and identify among the large number of actors those who are representative of the whole. A useful distinction is presented by Murtha and Lenway (1994), who differentiate between "states" and "governments". States are made up of the various organizations that make "country-specific governance capabilities. . . . together with national factor endowments, influence the international economic strategies that governments can implement". Governments are the "groups of officials" that actuate the state organizations.

When looking for a meaningful and representative body at the national level, three main approaches have been utilized:

1. One that looks only at the top executive levels of government (Neustadt, 1960; May, 1966; Ullman, 1968; Williamson, 1969; Allison, 1971). The focus would then be on the formulation of strategy.
2. Another approach focuses on the government as a unified organization, with an executive group coordinating, integrating the activities of a number of departments or units each involved in conducting business in a different domain (Lindblom, 1955, 1959; Truman, 1951; Neustadt, 1960).
3. Finally, the government has been studied as a set of loosely coupled institutions with limited interactions or coordination among them (Lindblom and Braybrooke, 1963; Wildavsky, 1964; Sayer and Kaufman, 1960; Thompson, 1950; Simon, 1953).

The perspective adopted in this study is managerial; we are therefore interested in how an organization achieves results. What direction, what objectives are developed and how they are developed on the one hand, and to what degree they are realized and how they are realized on the other, are the questions of interest to us. The second option is thus the one that fits best with our purpose. The first option is incomplete and the third option is a negation of the very idea of strategy.

Government* appears to be a complex organization. Standards of desirability are unclear, power is dispersed, and yet it must function as a reasonably unified whole if any result is to be achieved. However, neither state organizations nor governments are omnipotent. They cannot, alone, generate the behavior that they prefer. At best, they can thrust it in the desired

---

* For the sake of simplicity, we shall refer in this article to "government" as being both the groups of officials and the organizations that are under their control.

direction. This is clear in Johnson's (1982) useful taxonomy that distinguishes between "regulatory" and "developmental" states. The former have limited concern or capabilities to formulate economic strategies, and few policy or organizational tools with which to implement them. Developmental states have instruments to pursue "a strategic, or goal-oriented, approach to the economy". Johnson recognizes that most nations display both regulatory and developmental traits, and one has to look at dominant patterns.

As most nations are legally designed, governments have the power to define the rules of the various games occurring on the national territory. This power is significant enough to push every actor to try to influence the decisions of government in its own favor. As is the normal practice in business policy for the study of firms' behavior, looking at what governments do or try to do over time will provide information not only on what that particular body is doing, but also on what the various actors are trying to do. Thus, the behavior of the government over a long period of time is a valid, and probably the best, proxy of a nation's behavior.

A CONCEPT OF STRATEGY IN GOVERNMENT

Even though the idea of strategy is the same for all kinds of organization, simple and complex, there are important differences between the strategy-making process in a simple organization and in a complex system. In essence, strategy starts with the formulation of goals, taking into account the organization's capabilities, and the environmental constraints or opportunities. Then, the implementation is managed through a systematic adjustment of resource, structural and human variables (Christensen, Andrews and Bower, 1978).

Such a view implies that someone takes care of formulation and the others implement. However, it has been shown that as the organization becomes more complex, there is a new and unsuspected specialization of labor among managers (Bower, 1970; Hafsi, 1984). In fact, the study of large complex organizations, both of the private sector (Bower, 1970; Gilmour, 1973; Schwartz, 1973; Hamermesh, 1976) and the public sector (Hafsi, 1981, 1984), shows that the organizations that appear to be performing reasonably well have put in place a system that helps them deal with the cognitive and power limitations that complexity generates for all. Such a system is the result of a vertical specialization among managers whereby:

- Managers in contact with technology and markets are the ones who are generally better able to formulate "product and market" strategies.
- Managers at the higher levels manage the context within which the decisions are made. They provide direction and choose the managers in

charge of strategy and manage their behavior through changes in values, structure and incentives.

● Managers in the middle, who understand better than the top the realities of the lower-level managers, and better than the latter the requirements of the top.

These three layers of management are the system through which decisions are processed so that the organization as a whole keeps humming and moving with a purpose. Strategy, in terms of product/market competitive capacity, is the result of the functioning of such a system, and the strategy-making process is the functioning of the system. The process is actually a process of reconciliation between three sets of logic: the business strategy logic of managers at the bottom, the organizational logic of the top, and the political or interpersonal logic of the middle.

When using such a model, the traditional formulation–implementation distinction is still valid with only one caveat: all three layers of management actually participate in both phases of the process (see TABLE 17.1 for an illustration). The essence of the strategy-making process is the design and the operation of the system so that formulation and implementation are processed in such a way that the general objectives of the organization are met.

The strategy of government is thus the actual design and management of the process of strategy-making. What is important, then, is how to design the system so that the right strategies are chosen, however "right" may be defined.

The study of strategy at the national level should be the study of how the strategy-making system functions. The functioning of the system may be undertaken by looking at how strategies are formulated and how they are implemented. Since both formulation and implementation are influenced by the whole system, their study will reveal how the system works. The overall structure of the system should, however, recognize the vertical specialization of labor among key actors.

TABLE 17.1 The strategy-making process

Level	Formulation	Implementation
Top	Vision, general objectives	Structure, incentives, values, beliefs, resources
Middle	Consensus-building, portfolio analysis, integration	Design (structure, incentives, values) evaluation, sanction, integration, synergy
Lower	Positioning, innovating, adapting	Competitive moves, organization-building, commitment-building

How useful is the study of strategy at the government level? For the moment let us emphasize the importance of revealing the patterns of influence that government has or may have on a nation's competitive advantage. The learning that could come out of the study over a very long period of national behavior may help design better the systems leading to strategic behavior and thus to competitiveness.

METHODOLOGY FOR THE STUDY OF NATIONAL STRATEGY

When studying development, economists are generally interested in the types of strategies that succeed and the factors that appear to be linked to success. They are interested in the content of strategy. Political scientists, for their part, are generally concerned with the strategies that individuals and groups adopt to achieve or consolidate power and political positions.

Both perspectives are an inspiration to a study like ours. Yet, we are specifically interested in what shapes the implementation of a country's strategy. The gist of our conceptual framework comes from the study of complex organizations (Hafsi and Demers, 1989). In that context, the direction that an organization want to take is important; but clearly identifying this direction has become a minor problem in comparison to the tremendous challenges of managing the apparatus needed to move the organization in that direction. In the same vein, managing a country is always a complex undertaking, and the level of complexity increases as the government makes a greater effort to intervene. This effort increases the number of entities to be managed and their interactions, obscuring cause-and-effect relationships.

Knowledge about organizational strategy has been developed primarily through longitudinal, monographic studies on the process by which organizations function. These studies have generally led to case histories. The most famous of these cases are Chandler's (1962). We need to step back in history to appreciate patterns of behavior, finding homogeneous periods within the historical era studied, accumulating a wealth of information on each period, and checking the reliability and validity of the available information (see Mintzberg and Waters, 1982).

The periodization criteria used to study different countries were not necessarily the same for each. What was constant, however, was the exercise of following the systematic and simultaneous variations in a series of major variables, and then to seek patterns in these variations (Mintzberg and Waters, 1982). Changes in economic policy, or in political leadership and direction, were important, essentially to suggest or highlight a breaking point.

Our conceptual framework was used to structure the information collected in a very systematic way (see van de Ven and Poole, 1990). Therefore, it was decided early in the process to structure the information gathered in the same way for all periods and all countries.

Our final decision was to leave analysis to the end of data gathering. In particular, each of the periods was to be described in detail without any analysis, and a monograph covering all the periods for a given country would be written. So far 17 monographs have been written or drafted, covering in excess of 50 periods.

THE TAIWANESE EXAMPLE

Towards 1630, the Manchu dynasty from China recovered Taiwan from the Dutch, and for the following two centuries, Taiwan was Chinese. Since possession of the island was useful for military purposes, the Japanese took it from a vanquished China in 1895. The Japanese colonized it systematically, putting in place a highly sophisticated administration, a good infrastructure and a thriving agriculture. Much later, after the Second World War, the Potsdam declaration (1945) gave Taiwan back to China.

At the time, Chiang Kai-shek, who had replaced the nationalist figurehead Sun Yat-sen, was in trouble in a China which was crumbling under corruption and mismanagement. In 1945, he named the general Chen Yi to administer Taiwan. Chen Yi carried out severe repression and decimated the local elite to suppress opposition. The modern new country of Taiwan emerged when Chiang Kai-shek, kicked out of China, moved to Taiwan with a million refugees.

In 1950, while an attack on Taiwan by communist China appeared imminent, the invasion of South Korea by communist North Korea—heavily supported by China and the USSR—pushed the United States to reinforce its military presence in the region and give Taiwan the support it needed to resist continental troops. The modern economic history of Taiwan was on a roll.

Several strategies, generally explicit, were progressively implemented to ensure the economic development of the new country. These strategies can be grouped into four major periods starting in 1895, 1949, 1960 and 1975:

- We decided to start the study in 1895 with the Japanese colonization. The export traditions, its elites, the balanced interventions of the state, the alliance between the industrial and the political elites and the authoritarian traditions, could not be well understood without reference to the Japanese colonization.
- In 1949 there was the arrival of Chiang-Kai-shek, with a generalized decline of macroeconomic indicators, and the adoption of a new economic policy: protectionism for industrialization.
- The year 1960 is another break in the history of Taiwan. New economic

policy, major monetary reforms, open policy for foreign investment, and dramatic changes in the macroeconomic indicators, all pointing toward the important growth of the economy.

• Finally, 1975 corresponds to the death of Chiang Kai-shek and the beginning of an economic slowdown and a major change of planning policy. The last period was still going on in 1991 at the end of the study.

1. From 1895 to 1949, Japan systematically colonized the island of Taiwan. Besides the usual political and cultural repression, the whole period was devoted to the development of the basic infrastructure, physical, educational, social (health in particular) and administrative.

2. From 1949 to 1960, at the height of the cold war, Taiwan discovered stability. The American support also included assistance for economic development. Under the military umbrella of the USA, the government adopted a strategy of import substitution, with a major restructuring of agriculture and of rural life. The main objective was to use agriculture to create the basic industrial infrastructure.

3. The years 1960–75 were golden ones for Taiwanese economic development. However, many diplomatic setbacks occurred as China replaced Taiwan in the United Nations organization. The strategy was focused on increasing the volume of exports, and opening the country to foreign investment and technology. Socially, the policy of equity begun in the previous period gathered steam and Taiwan became a very equitable society. In terms of leadership, Chiang Ching-Kuo, the President's son and Minister of Defense, emerged as a strong leader, and a possible successor, despite strong competition from Prime Minister Cheng Cheng. The period ended with the death of Chiang Kai-shek.

4. From 1978 to 1990, the authoritarian style of Chiang Kai-shek was slowly replaced by a style more compatible with the aspiration of the Taiwanese to democracy. First, Chiang Ching-Kuo had a more sober demeanor than his father, then his successor Lee Teng-Hui, a Taiwanese of local origin, put the tension and the "war" against China to rest, and allowed much greater political democracy. Economically, the emphasis was more on heavy industry and on technology-based manufacturing.

The strategy-making process was dominated by a number of elements. The values of the dominant coalition were essentially a return to Confucian traditions, after the mistakes of the past in mainland China; integrity, and fight against corruption; economic development as a competitive tool against communist China; modernism based on education and science, search for consensus and legitimacy through effective reform and a management of the economy that emphasizes equity; a privatization program, where the state was to be the instrument of economic development, but the unit of development would be the private sector, essentially small and medium-sized firms; emphasis on exports; priority to human resource development.

The key to implementing these ideas was the planning process. Planning was not, however, bureaucratic or the domination of the top level over productive units. It was simply a mechanism through which the various levels of management, strategic (lower levels), intermediate and institutional (at the top), could interact and define policy or tackle the implementation problems.

The private sector was developed by the state. First, Japanese firms were bought back from their owners and transferred to Taiwanese private entrepreneurs. Similarly, the government did not exclude creating state-owned enterprises (SOEs), but included the need to privatize all those that could be managed by private entrepreneurs. Each SOE status was reviewed at the outset of each plan. Finally, encouragement and support were provided to ensure a smooth and strong development of the private sector, and a fruitful collaboration between both sectors.

Formulation of strategy in Taiwan was considered to be the first step in its implementation. Planning was also the framework through which decisions were debated and consistency maintained among them. This ensured both commitment to the plan and the identification ahead of time of major inconsistencies that could slow down its implementation.

Finally, the other major success was the creation of a public sector entirely devoted to promoting national development and to accepting the prime role of the private sector in the production of wealth. In fact, Taiwan's leadership has not simply imposed a structure on the strategy formulation and implementation processes (see Hafsi, 1994). It has put in place a sort of "meta-strategy" which includes: (1) the expression of grand objectives or vision; (2) the expression of quantitative goals; (3) the development of a structural cadre within which behavior was evaluated and rewarded where appropriate; (4) general rules and procedures to ensure the smooth functioning of the system.

This meta-strategy helped manage the emergence of strategies at the activity (or firm) level. Yet, it had to be kept precise to be helpful; that was a key task among the leading coalition members. The other important task was to keep the coalition united while all this was taking place. Because the Taiwanese leaders have succeeded in keeping the coalition united and the meta-strategy precise enough, they have been successful at generating the product/market strategies that have brought success to Taiwanese businesses in their competition in fast changing global industries.

The Taiwanese may be perceived as an exceptional example. Everything that we expect successful large firms to do, was done by the Taiwanese government. In fact, they are among a large group, of generally Asian countries, South Korea, Malaysia, Singapore, Hong Kong, in particular, that have had great success at this "corporate management" of a country.

In another sense, that is not quite the case. In all the cases studied where strategy-making was conducted without taking into account the complexity of the system with, on the part of government, an emphasis on choosing strategies rather than managing their emergence, success was hard to achieve and, more frequently, hard to maintain. Rules of the game tended to become hazy, generating resistance, infighting and division, even among the ruling coalition, creating political instability and as a consequence little or no growth. So our proposition that strategy-making in situations of complexity has to be different, is confirmed by those cases as well.

DISCUSSION

The research underlying this discussion has generated some important issues. In this chapter, we focus mainly on the methodological issues and on their consequences for research. Since methodological and substantive issues are frequently intertwined it is difficult to separate them neatly; we shall proceed as best we can to highlight the problems of studying such a large and complex organization.

In this discussion we address five questions. First, the characteristics of complexity and their compatibility with the study of strategy at the level of a country. Second, having used the strategy process framework extensively as a research tool, we discuss the problems and limits related to that use. The third issue is related to the problems of quality and amount of data. The fourth issue concerns the appropriateness of the data collected for the study at hand. Finally, the nature and challenges of analysis are taken up.

COMPLEXITY AND NATION

What is the difference between a "simple" organization and a "complex" one? What are the dimensions that foster complexity in organizational life? A leading essay on organization theory (Perrow, 1986) suggests some important pointers: organizations are complex because they have multiple, conflicting goals, because human beings are intrinsically complex and because our ability to understand reality is limited, as well as our knowledge about cause-and-effect relations. All that renders planning and controlling difficult, and as a consequence, unexpected things happen. In addition, organizational complexity is fostered by the norms, values, roles, symbols and cultural dimensions of human actions and the meaning systems created, perpetuated and modified by the organization's members (Daft and Weick, 1984).

Two elements appear central to complexity in organizations: (1) The difficulty to fully understand reality because of cognitive limitations

(Simon, 1957), interpretation (Weick, 1979) or enactment of reality by the individual and the group (Smircich and Stubbart, 1985), and (2) uncertainty about cause–effect relationships, so that the consequences of one's actions are uncertain, and sometimes counterintuitive (Schelling, 1978; Boudon, 1982).

These two elements have remarkable consequences in organizational life: (1) nobody fully understands what is going on in the organization as a whole, and cause–effect relationships may be expressed only in probability terms; (2) wishes or objectives that are appropriate for the whole organization are hard to express; (3) power is dispersed and people at the top have to share it with many others, which reduces their ability to affect the system. These three characteristics constitute our definition of complexity.

How does one manage properly when one does not understand cause-and-effect relations, does not even know how to express goals properly, and has limited power to act? A tentative answer can be found in the general systems theory, which shows why it is acceptable not to worry about every detail of a large complex system's operations, to be able to understand its overall dynamics.

It is the structuration of executive activities with a wide distribution of power that does the trick in large complex organizations. If the system is properly designed, everyone involved would have a stake in its operating well, and would be willing to cooperate to achieve it (Hafsi, 1984, 1985). The framework is not, however, without its problems, to which we now turn.

PROBLEMS RELATED TO THE CONCEPTUAL FRAMEWORK

Our decision to be guided, in the study of national strategies, by an explicit conceptual framework raises many of the important issues that have been highlighted by Popper (1959). It may be argued that the framework is tautological: our data do not prove that strategy-making takes place that way. On the contrary, we are postulating it and gathering data that can only confirm it. Our purpose in this chapter is not to develop a model of the strategy-making process at the national level. Rather, based on existing research, we take this process for granted, and go on to understand the strategy-making behavior of governments.

The problem, however, is that the framework may be misleading, and it may lead the researcher to force the data into a framework that has nothing to do with reality. For example, in countries where the economy is still "simple", one could argue that the framework does not describe the strategy-making process. In fact, in all the countries that have been studied, there always seems to be an early period where the strategy-making process is not the "shared powers" process, which has been proposed, but the traditional top-down process of simpler organizations. In our opinion, this does not really invalidate the framework, even though the importance of interactions among the elite, and the role of intermediate managers, may be exaggerated. The study of leaders, of their characteristics and their powers, generally attracts the researcher's attention soon enough to compensate for the bias.

What is also inaccurate or inadequate with the framework is that it rests on a strong assumption that organizational rationality dominates the actors' behavior. Each of the key actors is assumed to behave so as to further the interest of the organization first and foremost. In some cases, however, individual rationality can and does displace organizational rationality.

Therefore, the framework is not really representative of all situations. It is generally representative, with a better fit in "corporate countries" of East Asia, a regular fit in most, so-called, stable countries, and a poor fit in disorderly, generally developing, countries.

For the purposes of the research, we were aware of the problems that some situations may generate, and have accepted that, in the history of a country, those situations do appear from time to time. Whenever they were diagnosed as potentially disorderly, we have put the emphasis on key individual behavior, while keeping the framework as a guide of potential power positions in the operation of the system.

PROBLEMS RELATED TO THE NATURE AND AMOUNT OF DATA

In studying countries one soon realizes that there are problems with the data available. Two broad categories of data have been found and used: statistical and aggregated data; and essays and analyses, generally partisan with limited expected objectivity.

In terms of quality, most of the statistics and quantitative data on countries pose no major problem. They are compiled by major international institutions, which ensures at the very least their external validity, reliability and consistency. The most significant problem encountered is that of missing data. When the series of figures available are incomplete or more recently compiled, comparison is much more difficult. In some countries, there are important periods for which no quantitative data are available.

The quality of qualitative data and analyses is more questionable since they are more difficult to evaluate. Most documented qualitative analyses are partisan positions or beliefs. Most of the perspectives are acceptable; rarely did we have a convincing reason to eliminate any of them. The question is how to reconcile widely diverging opinions. We have systematically triangulated our sources, and compared the information provided by any one source to other, sometimes contradictory, versions of the events described. This research process is based on the principle that the perspectives of individuals are all valid, but incomplete. Only the researcher, by combining many perspectives, is capable of approaching reality.

A few measures were adopted to make the task manageable and the results more reliable. First, we decided early enough in the process that, whenever possible, each country should be studied by a researcher who had a good understanding of the country's background and current issues. When this was not possible, the researcher was encouraged to spend time to get acquainted with the country.

Second, the researcher was required to concentrate on description. Separating the analysis from description helps reduce the biases coming from the researcher's opinion. Analysis was kept as much as possible out of the first step of the study. The research proceeded systematically through three identifiable steps: (a) acquaintance with the history of the country; (b) development of the periodization. The various periods, once finalized, were presented and discussed within the research team; (c) write-up of each period description, using the structure provided by the conceptual framework. Only one element of analysis was allowed within the framework and that was the assessment of consistency in the formulation process, in the implementation process, and between them.

Third, the whole research was geared to building a data base, so that analysis could be systematically conducted. Each of the descriptions of periods and thus each monograph written up, has the same structure as any other. The data base was constructed with an emphasis on mentioning verifiable facts, and eventually obvious regularities in the data.

Finally, the conceptual framework was also a way out of bias and data glut. Looking through the sources of information, the researchers were looking at documenting the framework. So the latter became a kind of walking stick, a reference against which to decide how to use the data available.

PROBLEMS RELATED TO THE LEVEL OF OBSERVATION

Some of the data available are heavily biased toward explaining the country's fate by describing the behavior of individuals, generally those at the top. The analysis is therefore micro. Some other data are devoted to describing the system, with limited attention to the individuals involved. The analysis provided is therefore macro. The researcher's problem, for any one time period, is to decide which is the more important. In our case, we decided to never leave aside one or the other level of analysis. The framework as designed offers both micro and macro data. But, given the familiarization period, we decided on a case-by-case basis to add more information on one level or the other.

PROBLEMS WHEN ANALYZING THE DATA

This phase is only in its infancy, so here we are only debating the issues as perceived rather than the issues as experienced. There are two major problems in the data analysis; one is related to the purpose of the analysis and the other to the amount of data or information available.

There are two types of analysis. The first looks at the quality of the strategy-making process. This has been integrated into the data collection and monograph write-up, through an analysis of the consistency of and within the process. Consistency within the process looks at the elements of the strategy-making process and evaluates whether they are consistent. The questions are whether those goals or orientation are consistent with the strengths and limits of the country, with the general culture, with the constraints and opportunities offered by the international situation, and with the values and talents of the top leadership. Similarly, consistency among the elements of implementation, structure, rewards, leadership, . . . , is evaluated.

The consistency of the strategy-making process is a measure of the fit among the mechanisms developed to implement strategy and the goals as formulated. This test checks the characteristics of such elements as structure, rewards and punishments, measurements and control, management development and leadership styles, in regard to what is to be achieved.

Consistency is a central idea in strategy, and in our studies was usually associated with good economic performance of the country. A lively debate could be started with the question of causation. Was consistency the cause of good performance or was it the reverse? Unfortunately, no convincing answer can be given here. In any event, consistency is constantly challenged by changing external and internal conditions, especially while breaking new ground, so it is important that fit be not so dominant as to stifle adaptation to changing conditions. Yet, it has to be sufficient to avoid disorienting the organization's key members. That level of consistency or inconsistency is in fact a function of performance. The better performing organizations seem to stand more inconsistency than the others.

The second type of analysis has to do with the search for patterns among the situations described in the various periods of any one country and across countries. The purpose of the study was to discover the relationship between the strategy-making process and the social–economic performance of a country. Therefore the propositions that come to mind are those that relate the nature or characteristics of each of the elements of the strategy-making process to performance. But the most significant analyses are those that reveal the patterns of strategy-making and the relationship of these patterns with socioeconomic performance (Miller and Friesen, 1984).

To conduct the analysis in a more systematic way, we also decided to look at the monographs as a data bank, and design questionnaires to be used as a means of investigating systematically such a bank. This procedure is also intended to further reduce the biases that the monograph writers may introduce in the search for patterns, and increase the credibility of the results.

Finally, the search for patterns requires the use of appropriate clustering techniques. The recent use of neural net programming as a tool of pattern recognition appears to hold out great promise for data that contain a large amount of qualitative assessments.

CONCLUSION

The study of strategy at the national level poses important theoretical and methodological problems. The most important issue is modeling of the state as a complex organization to justify the use of a theoretical framework that has essentially been developed for describing the behavior of large, complex organizations.

Traditional scholars of the fields of political science and public administration may see in the attempt a heresy, a misguided delusion, because the nation or the state is either too complex or radically different to be compared to an organization. Our belief is that many such criticisms are proper and well taken. In particular, we may at times oversimplify the political process or the workings of the multiple bureaucracies of government. We may also assign a high organizational rationality to processes where individual rationality dominates.

Despite these shortcomings, we believe that the proposed conceptual framework is appropriate where overall, rather than specific, behavior is sought. We strongly suggest in this chapter that the behavior of the large complex organizations of the private sector today are dominated by processes that are not dissimilar from those that take place in the large complex organizations of the public sector. In both, the logic of economic, organizational, managerial and political processes is converging, and we hold that what may explain overall behavior in one, explains satisfactorily overall behavior in the other. It is this basic premise that has been at the outset of our research. We take comfort in the fact that the study of a large number of countries over long time periods has provided us with preliminary results that are consistent with the perceptions of the experts.

The more important challenges are elsewhere. They are in our ability to recognize patterns from a very large amount of data on a large number of variables. We do not yet know how to do it convincingly, even though more recent works on neural net programming are very promising. We suggest that the efforts of scholars should focus more on the tools needed to conduct such complex analyses.

REFERENCES

Allison, G.T. (1971) *The Essence of Decision: Explaining the Cuban Missile Crisis.* Boston: Little, Brown and Co.

Andrews, K.R. (1987) *The Concept of Corporate Strategy.* Homewood, Ill.: Irwin.

Bower, J.L. (1970) *Managing the Resource Allocation Process.* Homewood, Ill.: Irwin.

Boudon, R. (1982) *The Unintended Consequences of Social Action.* New York: St Martin's Press (First Edition in French, 1977).

Chandler, A.D. (1962) *Strategy and Structure.* Cambridge, Mass.: MIT Press.

Christensen, C.R., Andrews, K.R., and Bower, J.L. (1978) *Business Policy: Text and Cases,* 7th edn. Homewood, Ill.: Irwin.

Daft, R.L. and Weick, K.E. (1984) "Toward a Model of Organizations as Interpretation Systems", *Academy of Management Review,* 9, 284–295.

Daleu-Diabé, M. and Hafsi, T. (1993) *La stratégie nationale de Taïwan de 1895 à 1990.* Monographies en gestion et économie internationales, Cétai.

Francis, A. (1992) "The Process of National Industrial Regeneration and Competitiveness", *Strategic Management Journal,* 13, 61–78.

Gilmour, S.C. (1973) "The Divestment Decision Process", unpublished doctoral dissertation, Harvard University, Graduate School of Business Administration, Boston, Mass.

Hafsi, Taïeb (1981) "The Strategic Decision-making Process in State-owned Enterprises", unpublished doctoral dissertation, Harvard University, Graduate School of Business Administration, Boston, Mass.

Hafsi, Taïeb (1984) *Entreprise publique et politique industrielle.* Paris: McGraw-Hill.

Hafsi, Taïeb (1985) "Du management au méta-management: les subtilités du concept de stratégie", *Gestion,* February, 1–14.

Hafsi, Taïeb (1994) "Gestion stratégique au niveau national: une étude historique du développement de Taïwan", *Asac Proceedings,* 15(6), 70–79.

Hafsi, T. and Demers, C. (1989) *Le changement radical dans les organisations complexes: le cas d'Hydro-Québec.* Boucherville, Québec: Gaétan Morin.

Hamermesh, R.C. (1976) "The Corporate Response to Divisional Profit Crises", unpublished doctoral dissertation, Harvard University, Graduate School of Business Administration, Boston, Mass.

Johnson, C. (1982) *MITI and the Japanese Miracle: The Growth of Industrial Policy, 1927–1975.* Stanford, CA: Stanford University Press.

Lindblom, C.E. (1955) "Bargaining? The Hidden Hand in Government", RM-1434-RC, Santa Monica, CA: Rand Corporation, 22 February.

Lindblom, C.E. (1959) "The Science of Muddling Through", *Public Administration Review,* 19, Spring.

Lindblom, C.E. and Braybrooke, D. (1963) *A Strategy of Decision.* New York: Free Press.

Magaziner, I.C. and Patinkin, M. *The Silent War: Inside the Global Business Battles Shaping America's Future.* New York: Random House.

May, E.R. (1966) "The World War and American Isolation". Cited by Allison, op.cit.

Miller, D. and Friesen, P.H. (1984) *Organizations: A Quantum View.* Englewood Cliffs, NJ: Prentice-Hall.

Mintzberg, H. (1978) "Patterns in Strategy Formation", *Management Science,* 24(9), 934–948.

Mintzberg, H. and McHugh, A. (1985) "Strategy Formation in an Adhocracy". *Administrative Science Quarterly,* 30, 160–197.

Mintzberg, H. and Waters, J.A. (1982) "Tracking Strategy in an Entrepreneurial Firm", *Academy of Management Journal*, 465–499.

Murtha, T. and Lenway, S. (1994) "Country Capabilities and the Strategic State: How National Political Institutions Affect Multinational Corporations' Strategies", *Strategic Management Journal*, **15**, Summer, 113–129.

Neustadt, R. (1960) *Presidential Power*. New York: Wiley.

Ohmae, K. (1985) *Triad Power: The Coming Shape of Global Competition*. New York: Free Press.

Perrow, C. (1986) *Complex Organizations: A Critical Essay*, 3rd edn. New York: Random House.

Popper, K. (1959) *The Logic of Scientific Discovery*. New York: Basic Books.

Porter, M. (1990) *The Competitive Advantage of Nations*. New York: Free Press.

Prahalad, C.K. and Doz, Y. (1987) *The Multinational Mission: Balancing Local Demands and Global Vision*. New York: Free Press.

Quinn, J.B. (1992) *Intelligent Enterprise: A Knowledge and Service-based Paradigm*. New York: Free Press.

Reich, R. (1989) "As the World Turns", *The New Republic*, 1 May, 23–28.

Rugman, A.M. (ed.) (1990) *Research in Global Strategic Management*, Vol.1. Greenwich, Conn.: JAI Press.

Sayer, W. and Kaufman, H. (1960) *Governing New York City*, New York. Cited in Allison, op. cit.

Schelling, T. (1978) *Micromotives and Macrobehavior*. New York: Norton.

Schwartz, J.J. (1973) "The Decision to Innovate", unpublished doctoral dissertation, Harvard University, Cambridge, Mass.

Simon, H.A. (1953) "Birth of an Organization: The Economic Cooperation Administration", *Public Administration Review*, **13**, 227–236.

Simon, H.A. (1957) *Administrative Behavior*. New York: Macmillan.

Smircich, L. and Stubbart, C. (1985) "Strategic Management in an Enacted World", *Academy of Management Review*, **10**, 724–736.

Thompson, J.D. (1967). *Organizations in Action*, New York: McGraw-Hill.

Truman, D. (1951) *The Governmental Process*, New York. Cited in Allison, op. cit.

Ullman, R.H. (1968) *Anglo-Soviet Relations, 1917–1921*, Vol. 2, Princeton University Press.

Van de Ven, A.H. and Poole, M.S. (1990) "Methods for Studying Innovation Development in the Minnesota Innovation Research Program", *Organization Science*, **1**,(3), 313–335.

Weick, K.E. (1979) *The Social Psychology of Organizing*. Reading, Mass.: Addison-Wesley.

Wildavsky, A. (1964) *The Politics of the Budgetary Process*, Boston. Cited in Allison, op. cit.

Williamson, S.R. (1969) *The Politics of Grand Strategy*. Cambridge, Mass.: Harvard University Press.

18

Uncertainty, Complexity and New Product Performance

RAYMOND-ALAIN THIÉTART, JEAN-MARC XUEREB

The successful design and development of innovation are strategically important to many organizations. Product innovation is a primary means by which these organizations are able to adapt to market shifts, take advantage of new opportunities and technology, respond to competitive changes, or regenerate themselves. A recent survey of over 700 senior managers worldwide found that improving new product development was a predominant managerial priority (Arthur D. Little, 1991). Nevertheless, established firms still experience difficulties in the effective development of new products, and improving product innovation remains a crucial research concern.

Many factors key to successful innovation are well known. The commercial success of a new product has been shown to be dependent upon how well the perceived market opportunity has been identified, analyzed and incorporated into its design (Cooper, 1983; Dougherty, 1990; Lilien and Yoon, 1988; Rothwell, 1977). Commercial performance has also been associated with a strong R&D orientation and the appropriate use of advanced technologies (Cooper, 1984; Kanter, 1988). Cooper (1979) finds that among 18 factors which characterize successful new industrial products, one of the most important is the firm's technological and production proficiency. Studies on competitive strategies have also emphasized the influence of competition on the commercial performance of a new product (Porter, 1980,

1985); for example, Robertson and Gatignon (1986) argue that competitive factors have a vital role in the diffusion of a technological innovation. To date, literature on new product development has emphasized the importance of these individual factors in achieving commercial success. The innovation process has thus been shown to be fraught with three corresponding categories of uncertainty: uncertainty about users' needs, uncertainty about the technology to use, and uncertainty about competitors' moves (see, for example, Souder and Monaert, 1992). What is now crucial for managers is not so much determining whether the firm should pay attention to these issues, but considering how the organization is to be able to deal with the uncertainty and complexity which arises from all three related areas: the customer, technology and competition.

To deal with uncertainty and complexity, firms rely upon their organizational resources (Cooper and Kleinschmidt, 1986; Rubenstein et al., 1976; Souder, 1987; Souder and Monaert, 1992). However, the need for these organizational resources to be appropriately allocated and managed introduces a fourth source of uncertainty and complexity: the organization itself.

Innovations also vary with the degree of product novelty. Products may be more or less different from competitors' products. Although the development of a new product may occasion a clear departure from existing practices, an innovation which is incremental in nature, resulting from minor improvements or simple adjustments to an existing product, may not require any change in the way it is produced, marketed or used (Duschesneau, Cohn and Dutton, 1979; Ettlie, 1983; Munson and Pelz, 1979). Freeman (1974) states that "radicality" is strongly linked to uncertainty. The outcome of a radical product is more uncertain than the outcome of an incremental innovation. Similarly, a product may be more or less complex to develop, depending on whether it is to be targeted at specific customers' needs or aimed at a broader range of users. Therefore, the product itself introduces a fifth source of uncertainty and complexity.

Several authors have suggested that the success of a new product is directly linked to the ability of the organization to reduce the uncertainty and complexity connected with innovation in general (Fidler and Johnson, 1984; Fischer, 1980; Souder and Monaert, 1992; van de Ven, 1986). However, very few empirical studies have investigated how this reduction is to be achieved. Our study is based on the preliminary assumption that organizations develop means to create what we will refer to as "islands of rationality", which serve to circumscribe too complex and uncertain a situation. We have speculated that these means enable managers to act in a "rational" and orderly manner, and consequently improve their effectiveness in managing the innovation project. We will attempt to determine in which ways different approaches to uncertainty and complexity reduction influence the outcome of innovative projects.

CONCEPTUAL BACKGROUND

Managing an innovation project is one of the most unsettling and destabilizing of endeavors. It is a situation in which organizational actors try to find solutions to problems which are loosely defined, and where limits are not drawn. However, project managers continue to make decisions and take actions under these conditions, with consequences which are impossible to accurately predict.

Some companies have solved the paradox of taking action in unpredictable situations by accepting uncertainty as a priori. Wide latitude may be given to organizational actors in which to explore new ground, within a framework of shared values and a common understanding of the ultimate goals of the organization. For example, work by Burgelman (1983) and Bygrave (1989) on entrepreneurship is illustrative of the determination of certain organizations to provide optimum conditions for experimentation with different types of innovations. In giving the organizational actors enough freedom and sufficient resources to explore—without constraint—new areas of growth and new ways of doing things, the organization creates a catalogue of responses ready for different and as yet unknown demands from the competitive environment. This is a catalogue from which elements may be selected, or recognized "serendipitously", as the environment unfolds. Nystrom, Hedberg, and Starbuck (1976) stress the exigency for an organization to develop such a repertory of alternative and novel responses to possible future situations, arguing that, when confronted with a new and therefore uncertain environment, it may be forced to move from its traditional positions. March (1981) and Weick (1977) suggest that activities which are not directly connected with the organization's traditional interests are often an appropriate means of improving its capacity of response to complexity and changing conditions.

However, experimentation, incoherence and diverse activities—especially those which diverge from the organization's usual area of interest—are such sources of instability that the resultant innovations may not necessarily be consistent with the organization's planned objectives. As roots of internal disorder, they may engender major strategic change and reorientation. Some degree of stability and order is also needed to be able to achieve the organization's objectives. If the innovation process was a matter of experimentation and disorder alone it would be a maelstrom of perpetual change and revolution; as Daft and Weick submit, managers would be forced to "wade into the ocean of events that surround the organization and actively try to make sense of them" (1984: 286). According to Daft and Lengel (1984: 192), "in response to the confusion arising from both the environment and internal differences, organizations must create an acceptable level of order and certainty".

Order is also necessary to furnish the facilitating conditions for decision making, and contributes to the closure of too complex a system for a cognitively limited mind. Order helps in "creating" certainty: and with certainty, traditional rational management schemes can be applied to their full extent. In addition, the discomfort which arises when managers are confronted with a problem which they intuitively know impossible to solve or master can be reduced.

This reason, which stresses the apparently nonutilitarian functions of formal approaches, has a psychologically based origin which the cognitive dissonance theory of Festinger (1957) can help to explain. To fight against feelings of powerlessness, that they are in a situation of high complexity and uncertainty which is in total contradiction with their mission and *raison d'être*, managers rely on formal tools to create an illusion: the illusion of managing. As an example, Feldman and March (1981: 177) state that the gathering of information provides "a ritualistic assurance that appropriate attitudes about decision making exist" and that "displaying the symbol reaffirms the importance of (the) social value and signals personal and organizational competence" (p. 182). Managers in this way avoid a reality which seems in complete contradiction to what they are being paid to do. Their purpose in invoking formal management tools is less to improve their performance than to give the illusion and assurance of doing so; it is more the sense of doing and mastering that these tools provide which matters than their practical uses. Managers can thus reduce the dissonance their feelings of powerlessness engender when confronted with a reality which seems too complex and unpredictable to be effectively managed.

If innovation requires some degree of instability and disorder to unfold, innovation project managers need closure of a too complex and uncertain system to be able to understand it. Means to manage innovation and to deal with its surrounding uncertainty and complexity are numerous, and some are more appropriate than others, depending on the degree of uncertainty and complexity faced. We believe that innovation performance depends on the appropriateness of these means. We will now turn to the hypothesized relationships between the level of uncertainty and complexity faced by an organization, and the effectiveness of the means it uses to reduce these, in relation to new product performance.

HYPOTHESES

To close the organization and make it more predictable, managers attempt to control their external environment (Pfeffer and Salancik, 1978) "to translate uncertainty to certainty in order to achieve internal efficiency and stability" (Skivington, 1982, as quoted by Daft and Lengel, 1984: 228). For instance, interlocking directorates and strategic alliances and cooperation with customers and competitors might prevent a situation described by

Astley and Fombrun (1983: p.286) where "organizations act independently in many directions, producing unanticipated and dissonant consequences in the overall environment they share". Spender (1993) also suggests that in a situation of unpredictable external associations, managers can rely on networking and cooperation to develop mutual beneficial relationships. In the same vein, he proposes that in a context characterized by "incompleteness", managers look for more information.

High uncertainty may lead managers to imitate or copy strategies used by others (Milliken, 1987). Managers often assume that their competitors have successfully found the most appropriate response, and tend to emulate their behavior (DiMaggio and Powell, 1983). However, organizations may also actively seek to create uncertainty (Jauch and Kraft, 1986). For example, pharmaceutical firms have been shown to patent their mistakes and failed products to encourage uncertainty about the direction of their product development (*Business Week*, 1984); in order to reduce uncertainty, managers from other firms may be imitating their competitors on the basis of misleading information (Porter, 1980).

Xuereb (1993) suggests that in high-technology sectors, where firms generally lack reliable data about users' needs (Lilien, Brown and Searls, 1990; von Hippel, 1986), managers turn their attention to competitors' projects, through information scanning and networking. To prevent other organizations from developing a competitive advantage, companies tend to include in their own project their competitors' product characteristics. Consequently, in this type of highly uncertain and complex environment, a "virtual market" is created, on the basis of which the new product development takes place; a market defined without any reference to potential users. Conversely, when confronted with more predictable and less complex environments, innovation projects which rely on networking and external information on their competitors should not be adversely affected; in fact a more precise view of what the competition is doing (assuming that market signals are readable) should improve the innovation performance. This leads to our first hypothesis.

HYPOTHESIS 1

Depending on the degree of uncertainty and complexity associated with an innovation project, innovation performance is influenced by information on competitors or by networking with competitors:

(a) negatively when uncertainty and complexity are high;
(b) positively when uncertainty and complexity are low.

The development of a new product in a highly complex and uncertain environment creates the need for more market scanning and networking with users to identify customer needs. In contrast, market scanning and networking are not as effective in simpler and more certain environments, since products are targeted to a more familiar market, and innovation projects do not need to rely on extra information and specific coordinating devices. This leads to the following hypothesis.

HYPOTHESIS 2

Depending on the level of uncertainty and complexity associated with an innovation project, innovation performance is influenced by information on users or by networking with users:

(a) positively when uncertainty and complexity are high;
(b) positively, although to a lesser degree, when uncertainty and complexity are low.

In order to cope with the uncertainty and complexity of their venture, innovation managers also rely on organizational procedures. For instance, Dougherty (1992) shows that each sector of a firm develops a different vision of the prevailing environment, and that the success of an innovation is directly linked to the merging of these different visions. This is especially relevant in a highly complex and uncertain environment, where functions need to be differentiated and specialized, and where organizations tend to rely on group decision making to confront issues related to marketing, R&D, production, finance and engineering. Coordination between functions is also facilitated by intense and frequent face-to-face interactions (Miller, 1987). Project management contributes to a better coordination and monitoring of the diverse tasks the organization has to undertake to develop a new product. As means of coordination, project management is helpful in tackling the cognitive limitations of the organizational actors. But again, in situations where the degrees of uncertainty and complexity are lower, multifunctional team and interfunctional coordination are less essential.

HYPOTHESIS 3

Depending on the level of uncertainty and complexity associated with an innovation project, innovation performance is influenced by the use of project management:

(a) positively when uncertainty and complexity are high;
(b) positively, although to a lesser degree, when uncertainty and complexity are low.

Nelson and Winter (1982) suggest that firms have "routines" for coping with new situations, and that new routines develop slowly and incrementally. Routines allow managers to reduce their perceived uncertainty and complexity, but can hinder adaptation to new environmental demands. A routine readily becomes an end in itself, and an end which needs to be achieved whatever the characteristics of the environmental context. Managers thus frequently find themselves unable to react or adapt to the complexity and uncertainty of their environment. However, in situations which are relatively simple and stable, uncertainty and complexity can be efficiently dealt with using formal rules and procedures (Miller, 1987).

In the same vein, planning is frequently presented as an effective means that firms use to achieve their mission. Sinha (1990) shows that formal planning systems are a useful aid when confronted with decisions perceived as both important and risky. Planning is presented as a means to manage uncertainty. By formalizing the decision-making process, managers sequester zones of certainty and simplicity, within which they can proceed in a rational manner. Furthermore, planning, by providing an information network and encouraging communication (Quinn, 1980), is a means to deal with important decisions; important decisions which are generally characterized by numerous ramifications and complexity. Thanks to the decomposition of a broad mission into elementary tasks, the readability of the organization and its numerous links with its environment are improved. Planning helps in creating enclosures within a system which is too complex to be dealt with in a global manner.

However, the persistent search for order through excessive rationalism can be disruptive; formal approaches, although helpful in closing the organizational system and making it more predictable, increase its resistance to change. According to Quinn (1985: 77): "Managers in big companies often seek orderly advance through early market research studies or Pert planning. Rather than managing the inevitable chaos of innovation productively, these managers soon drive out the very things that lead to innovation in order to prove their announced plans." In his seminal study on the *Apollo 3* mission, Weick (1977) has also demonstrated how the order that formal tools provide can be unsettling. Similarly, Miller and Friesen establish that momentum (the continuity and stability of patterns of change in strategy and structure) derived from past experiences, political coalitions or the existence of formal programs, can be costly when it "protracts an orientation that has proved to be dysfunctional" (1980: 611). In a situation of high uncertainty and complexity, order can sabotage performance.

HYPOTHESIS 4

Depending on the level of uncertainty and complexity associated with an innovation project, innovation performance is influenced by internal routines, rules and procedures:

(a) negatively when uncertainty and complexity are high;
(b) positively when uncertainty and complexity are low.

The fragmentary nature of understanding requires that managers create meaning through organizational culture to create a new focus for their attention (Spender, 1993). As has been said, some firms, in uncertain and complex environments, leave a large latitude for organizational actors to work within a framework of shared values and goals. Burgelman (1983) and Bygrave (1989) show how organizations create the facilitating conditions for innovation through culture specially when the environment is difficult to predict. By giving the organizational actors enough freedom to explore new areas within the limits of shared values, and reinforcing their behavior with the right incentives, the organization finds responses to different and as yet unknown demands from the competitive environment.

HYPOTHESIS 5

Depending on the level of uncertainty and complexity associated with an innovation project, innovation performance is influenced by an innovation organizational culture:

(a) positively when uncertainty and complexity are high;
(b) positively, although to a lesser degree, when uncertainty and complexity are low.

In theory, firm strategy should guide decisions made and actions taken during an innovation project. But new product development may depart from strategic guidelines, to experiment with alternative ideas, new directions and unfamiliar markets (Burgelman, 1983)—all of which arguably keep strategy viable and regenerated (Jelinek and Schoonhoven, 1990). While some authors suggest that innovation should be kept separate from mainstream strategy, Day (1990) argues that such separation might result in *ad hoc* products, as it does not facilitate the development of products which reinforce the strategic focus. Furthermore, strategy is frequently encoded in the organizational structure and decision-making process, and tends to prevail despite external changes (Miller and Friesen, 1984). Such deeply rooted strategic orientations can constrain new product development by systematically forcing new ideas into old pattern (Hall, 1984; Johnson, 1988). When the environment is familiar and reasonably elementary, following a habitual strategic orientation should facilitate management of an innovation project. However, in a highly uncertain and complex situation, following an established strategy might eviscerate such a project.

HYPOTHESIS 6

Depending on the level of uncertainty and complexity associated with an innovation project, innovation performance is influenced by strategy:

(a) negatively when uncertainty and complexity are high;
(b) positively when uncertainty and complexity are low.

METHODOLOGY

SAMPLE

We collected our data through a large-scale mail survey. Some 1800 questionnaires were sent to R&D and marketing executives drawn randomly from a commercially available list of French companies with sales of more than $50 m in nine industrial sectors: durable and nondurable consumer goods, industrial equipment, chemical products, medical and pharmaceutical products, electronic products industrial services, consumer services and computer-based technological products. Of the questionnaires, 193 were not delivered and 213 were returned complete.

For our unit of analysis we asked each firm to select a single past innovation project. The questionnaire was filled out by R&D and marketing executives who have shown in past research to be knowledgeable key informants about the information concerning new product development (Xuereb, 1993). We compiled information on the uncertainty and complexity related to the innovation project, the means that had been used to cope with uncertainty and complexity, and the resultant product "performance". We included data on several other factors which can influence a new product's "performance", to serve as control variables.

In order to verify that the questionnaire was reasonable in length and that the respondents did not have any difficulty with any of the questions, a pretest of the questionnaire was performed on a few R&D and marketing executives. Based on their responses, some questions were reworked and the final questionnaire was sent to the sample. The total of 213 returned questionnaires gives a 13.3% response rate after deducting the questionnaires which did not reach the addressees. This rate is in line with rates reported in similar surveys. An analysis of the characteristics of firms indicates no significant differences between respondents and nonrespondents. Neither was any statistical difference found between early and late responses. Consequently, there is no indication of response bias in our sample (Armstrong and Overton, 1977). Appendix 1 presents the distribution of the observations by classes of industry, and shows the variety of this sample which contributes to the generalizability of our results.

VARIABLES

Multiple-item scales were developed. All items were measured on a six-point Likert-type scale ranging from total disagreement to complete agreement. No objective measurements were sought, and the questions were purposely designed to facilitate subjective (perceptual) responses, primarily because of the difficulty faced by the respondents in retrieving the necessary data, but also because we believe that perception plays an integral role in inducing the organizational actor to select an appropriate means of coping with uncertainty and complexity. Finally, although more objective measures do exist, they are generally only available at the aggregate (firm or industry) level.

On the return of the questionnaires, factorial analysis was performed on each set of items: context, means and performance. We operationalized the variables from the factorial analysis. The first factorial analysis was performed on items measuring complexity and uncertainty. Ten factors, with an eigenvalue greater than one, were retained. They all represented a given dimension of complexity–uncertainty: complexity and uncertainty associated with the organization, with the competition, the technology, the users and the product. The second factorial analysis was done on the items representing the means used to cope with uncertainty and complexity. Eight factors with an eigenvalue greater than one were retained. These factors cover different aspects of what we have referred to as "islands of rationality": organization (routines, rules and procedures, organization values and culture), management (project management), strategy (strategy, partnerships with competitors, and custonmers), cognition (information on the market and competition). A final factorial analysis was run on items of innovation performance, together with items from which our control variables were established. Four factors with an eigenvalue greater than one were retained. These factors cover such variables as: performance; the market-induced transformation following the innovation introduction; the degree of autonomy of the unit in charge of the project; and the relative size of the organization. All the variables were unidimensional, as items load on a single factor. Twenty-two variables were constructed from 80 items and items for each factor were pooled to create the variables used in the research. Appendix 2 gives the constructs of the variables and their associated reliability coefficients.

Dependent Variable

The dependent variable, innovation performance, is based on five items which evaluate:

1. the innovation market growth relative to that of competing products;
2. the innovation return on investment relative to the company's other products;
3. the fulfillment of the innovation project objectives;
4. the commercial success of the innovation;
5. the innovation effect on the overall market share.

Although self-assessment measures of performance are prone to potential bias, they are the most commonly used form of performance assessment in strategy marketing research (Saunders, Brown and Laverick, 1992). In fact, they may be less problematic than more "objective" financial measures which can also be biased because of "the ulterior motives for which they are produced" (Saunders, Brown, and Laverick, 1992: 184). Finally, a number of studies have demonstrated the convergent validity of such scales (Dess and Robinson, 1984; Doyle, Saunders, and Wright, 1989; Venkatraman and Ramanujam, 1986).

Independent Variables

Eight independent variables were used to measure the different means to cope with uncertainty and complexity associated with an innovation project. They were built from item-based additive scales. All items for each variable load on a single factor. These means cover four broad categories. The first category consists of "organizational" means to cope with uncertainty and complexity while managing the innovation project. They are measured by two variables: rules–procedures–plans and culture. The second category consists of "cognitive" means. They are measured by two variables: competitor information and customer information. The third category consists of "strategic" means. They are measured by three variables: strategy, customer network and competitor network. The fourth category consists of "managerial" means. It is measured by one variable: project management.

Control Variables

We isolated three other factors which can influence the innovation "performance" and collected information on these to act as control variables. These three variables are the following: the market-induced transformation following the innovation introduction, size of the organizational unit relative to the competition and the degree of autonomy of the unit in charge of the project.

Contextual Variables

As discussed previously, means used to cope with uncertainty and complexity may vary depending on the degree of uncertainty–complexity associated with the innovation project. Ten variables dealing with different aspects of uncertainty and complexity were used. They were built from item-based additive scales. All items for each variable load on a single factor. These variables are the following: organizational uncertainty, organizational complexity, competition uncertainty, competition complexity, technological uncertainty, technological complexity, customer uncertainty, customer complexity, product uncertainty and product complexity.

SAMPLE CLUSTERING

A stratification of the sample along variables of uncertainty and complexity was performed. The "furthest-neighbour" or "complete linkage" method was adopted for the clustering. Two other methods ("average linkage between groups" and "median clustering") were also used to test the stability of the clustering. Similar results were found.

Although four homogeneous groups (in terms of uncertainty and complexity) were obtained, two were found unsuitable for the study. One did not provide a sufficient sample size. The other could not be easily interpreted. Of the two remaining groups, the first was composed of 77 innovation projects of relatively high uncertainty and complexity. The second group was made of 39 projects of lower uncertainty and complexity. T-tests were performed to identify the characteristics of each group (see TABLE 18.1). A discrimant analysis was performed on these two groups: 98% of innovation projects were correctly classified according to uncertainty and complexity dimensions.

TESTING PROCEDURES

To test the impact on the innovation project performance of the various means used to cope with uncertainty and complexity, we used partial log linear regression models. Partial models were adopted because of the relatively small size of the samples (77 and 39 respectively) and the significant number of independent and control variables (11). Furthermore, as some of

TABLE 18.1   Test of inter-groups means differences

Uncertainty and complexity variables	"High" uncertainty and "high" complexity max: 6 min: 1 $n = 77$ Means	"Low" uncertainty and "low" complexity max: 6 min: 1 $n = 39$ Means	Statistical significance of the means differences * 0.1; ** 0.05; *** 0.025; **** 0.01
Organizational complexity	3.03	2.93	n.s.
Competitive complexity	3.41	3.10	**
Technological complexity	3.87	3.10	**
Market complexity	4.06	2.98	****
Product complexity	5.17	1.93	****
Organizational uncertainty	2.75	2.86	n.s.
Competitive uncertainty	3.21	2.75	***
Technological uncertainty	3.51	3.25	*
Market uncertainty	4.08	2.18	****
Product uncertainty	4.88	3.96	****

n.s. = not significant.

the independent variables were highly correlated (see TABLE 18.2(a) for the group of high uncertainty–complexity and TABLE 18.2(b) for the group of low uncertainty–complexity), a full model estimation would have run into the problem of colinearity. In addition, we were only interested in the statistical significance and the sign of the equation coefficients for both clusters of innovation projects; we did not intend to predict a performance but to test the influence of the different independent variables on the performance of the innovation. Partial equation models were thus adequate for our purposes. Within each cluster—innovation projects characterized by high uncertainty and complexity, and innovation projects characterized by lower uncertainty and complexity—partial equations were estimated. Each partial equation was composed of variables representing the broad categories of means used to cope with uncertainty and complexity: organi-

TABLE 18.2   Correlation matrix between independent variables

(a) High uncertainty–complexity group

	RPP	ICL	ICON	STR	RCO	RCL	IMA	IRA	TAC	AUT
CULT	0.327**	0.2770*	−0.032	0.3106**	0.018	0.4069**	0.3935**	0.2519*	0.3791**	0.0587
RPP	1	0.222	0.5024**	0.376**	0.0846	0.2163	0.3375**	0.2583*	0.4147**	0.0864
ICL		1	0.1149	0.1487	0.0414	0.8249**	0.5505**	0.0923	−0.0148	0.1977
ICON			1	0.1281	0.1567	0.1806	0.1524	0.063	0.0526	−0.1492
STR				1	0.0407	0.1816	0.2921**	0.1434	0.3834**	0.1335
RCO					1	0.1413	0.0497	0.1412	0.0173	0.238*
RCL						1	0.6046**	0.1144	0.021	0.2443*
IMA							1	0.0941	0.0247	0.391**
IRA								1	0.196	0.0803
TAC									1	0.0053

(b) Low uncertainty–complexity group

	RPP	ICL	ICON	STR	RCO	RCL	IMA	IRA	TAC	AUT
CULT	0.7118**	0.5837**	0.3476*	0.572**	−0.3099	0.5893**	0.7065	0.3803*	0.2768*	0.3894*
RPP	1	0.4709**	0.4028*	0.5127**	−0.1861	0.5166**	0.5861**	0.343*	0.3852*	0.177
ICL		1	0.0559	0.4005*	0.0076	0.813*	0.496**	0.2375	0.2043	0.3652*
ICON			1	0.4248**	0.0479	0.2048	0.138	0.2492	0.4694**	0.0984
STR				1	0.0039	0.4056**	0.3933*	0.1496	0.4996**	0.0516
RCO					1	−0.1325	−0.3723*	−0.1817	0.3483*	−0.1807
RCL						1	0.6096**	0.3082	0.26	0.3912*
IMA							1	0.5239**	0.1796	0.4648**
IRA								1	0.2018	0.3983*
TAC									1	0.3616*

* $p < 0.05$, ** $p < 0.01$.

CULT: Innovation "culture"
RPP: Rules, plans, procedures
ICL: Information on users
ICON: Information on competitors

STR: Strategy
RCL: Network with users
RCO: Network with competitors
IMA: Project management

AUT: Organizational unit autonomy
TAC: Relative size
IRA: Innovation-induced market transformation

zational, cognitive, strategic and managerial. Standardized beta-tests were computed to enable intercluster comparisons.

RESULTS

Descriptive statistics are given in TABLE 18.3. From these statistics, a first observation can be made. The different means used to cope with uncertainty and complexity are similar in the two groups of innovation projects. Only two of the variables related to means used—rules and procedures and information on competition—show any statistical difference between the groups. Consequently, it does not seem that managers and organizations adapt their means to the perceived level of uncertainty–complexity (high or low surrounding the innovation projects. From this observation, we can speculate that the choice of means is dependent on other considerations. These may be cognitive, to reduce a dissonance created by the task of managing a project which by nature is uncertain and complex, or psychological, to give the symbols and apply the rites of good management.

TABLE 18.3   Means for "creating" certainty and simplicity: descriptive statistics and means differences

Means used for creating certainty and simplicity: islands of rationality	"High"uncertainty and "high" complexity max: 6 min: 1 $n = 77$ Means and (SD)	"Low" uncertainty and "low" complexity max: 6 min: 1 $n = 39$ Means and (SD)	Statistical significance of the means differences * $p < 0.1$
Innovation culture	4.0133 (1.1055)	3.7853 (1.1933)	n.s.
Rules, plans and procedures	4.0673 (1.2185)	3.6125 (1.3563)	*
Information on users	4.3632 (1.1207)	4.2583 (1.0608)	n.s.
Information on competitors	2.7513 (1.0735)	3.1179 (1.0279)	*
Strategy	4.4071 (1.043)	4.1188 (1.0175)	n.s.
Network with competitors	2.4038 (1.2768)	2.3 (1.28)	n.s.
Network with users	4.2179 (1.1138)	4.0917 (1.1742)	n.s.
Project management	4.5647 (1.142)	4.4075 (1.1536)	n.s.

The hypotheses which we formulated above predicted that some means would prove more effective than others in achieving innovation performance. We measured effectiveness by evaluating the degree of association between the means used to cope with uncertainty–complexity and the performance of the new product. Three sets of partial regressions were run. The results are presented below.

The first set of partial regressions deals with the association between product performance, organizational and managerial means to cope with uncertainty and complexity. TABLE 18.4 gives the six regressions—three per group of homogeneous innovation projects in terms of uncertainty and complexity—run with performance as a dependent variable, and culture, rules, plans and procedures and project management, as independent variables.

Even though rules and procedures are used more intensively when uncertainty and complexity are high (see TABLE 18.3), our results indicate that they are not associated with greater success ($\beta = -0.04$, $p > 0.1$). The sign, which is not statistically significant, is negative.This suggests that strict reliance on rules and procedures might even have detrimental effects on project outcome. However, in the case of less uncertain and complex

TABLE 18.4   Innovation performance as a function of culture, rules and procedures and project management

	High uncertainty and complexity $n = 77$	Low uncertainty and complexity $n = 39$	High uncertainty and complexity $n = 77$	Low uncertainty and complexity $n = 39$	High uncertainty and complexity $n = 77$	Low uncertainty and complexity $n = 39$
	β	β	β	β	β	β
RPP	−0.0491	0.2418*				
CULT			0.2831**	0.2955**		
STR						
RCL						
RCO						
ICON						
ICL						
IMA					0.4008***	0.2524*
AUT	0.1911*	0.2024	0.1737*	0.1217	0.0265	0.1314
TAC	0.0173	−0.1086	−0.1015	−0.066	0.0124	−0.0375
IRA	0.2575**	0.518***	0.2035*	0.5155***	0.2426**	0.5028***
R^2	0.108	0.54***	0.16***	0.55***	0.23***	0.53***

* $p < 0.1$, ** $p < 0.05$, *** $p < 0.01$.
RPP: Rules, plans, procedures   AUT: Organizational unit autonomy
CULT: Innovation "culture"   TAC: Relative size
IMA: Project management   IRA: Innovation-induced market transformation

innovation projects, reliance on rules and procedures seems to have a positive and significant impact on the results ($\beta = 0.24, p < 0.1$).

An innovation "culture" and "values", reinforced by incentives, is shown to lead to successful new product performance. In this we found no significant difference between the two groups ($\beta = 0.28$, $p < 0.05$ in the high uncertainty and high complexity group; $\beta = 0.29$, $p < 0.05$ in the low uncertainty and low complexity group). Using innovation culture to manage new product development seems to be a reliable means for innovation performance whatever the degree of the surrounding uncertainty and complexity.

Furthermore, as we hypothesized, a positive association was found between performance and project management in highly uncertain and complex situations ($\beta = 0.40$, $p < 0.01$). As expected, a weaker, but positive, association was found in the case of lower uncertainty–complexity ($\beta = 0.25$, $p < 0.1$). It is likely that project management enhances the capacity of managers to deal with an uncertain and complex environment through information exchange, dialectical confrontations of opinions and autonomy.

The second set of partial regressions deals with the relationship between innovation performance and the use of cognitive means of product management—information on users and on competitors' projects and strategy—to cope with uncertainty and complexity. TABLE 18.5 gives the results. As predicted, information on competitors is negatively associated with performance when projects are highly uncertain and complex $\beta = -0.19$, $p < 0.1$), and positively with performance in the case of less uncertain and complex projects (but not significant). These results reinforce Xuereb's conjecture (1993) that a "virtual" market is created by firms competing in an uncertain and complex environment, and that new products meet the requirements of an imaginary demand. However, although the association was found to be marginally positive when uncertainty–complexity are low, this was not statistically significant.

Turning to the association between information on users and performance, we observe that in both cases the impact is positive ($\beta = 0.44$, $p < 0.01$ in the high uncertainty and high complexity group; $\beta = 0.23$, $p < 0.1$ in the low uncertainty and low complexity group). The impact of information on users is more pronounced when uncertainty and complexity are high. Innovation projects which are developed with a clear notion of users' needs always have more chance of succeeding. This is even more so when uncertainty and complexity are high.

The third set of partial equations deals with the relationships between performance and the use of strategic means—strategy, networking with users, networking with competitors—to "fight" against perceived uncertainty and complexity (see TABLE 18.6). As was predicted, a positive association is found between strategy and performance in the case of less uncertain and complex environments ($\beta = 0.31$, $p < 0.05$). However, there is no statisti-

TABLE 18.5   Innovation performance as a function of information on users and competitors

	High uncertainty and complexity n = 77	Low uncertainty and complexity n = 39	High uncertainty and complexity n = 77	Low uncertainty and complexity n = 39	High uncertainty and complexity n = 77	Low uncertainty and complexity n = 39
	β	β	β	β	β	β
RPP						
CULT						
STR						
RCL						
RCO						
ICON	−0.2771***	0.0781	−0.1859*	0.0911		
ICL	0.4932**	0.2228*			0.4405***	0.2272*
IMA						
AUT	0.0647	0.158	0.1685	0.2315*	0.1027	0.1482
TAC	0.0384	−0.0872	−0.0034	−0.0977	0.0308	−0.0565
IRA	0.2523**	0.572***	0.2654**	0.5948***	0.231**	0.5825***
R^2	0.36***	0.54***	0.13**	0.50***	0.28***	0.54***

$* p < 0.1, ** p < 0.05, *** p < 0.01.$
ICON: Information on competitors   AUT: Organizational unit autonomy
ICL: Information on users   TAC: Relative size
IRA: Innovation-induced market transformation

cally significant association between the two variables in situations of high uncertainty and complexity ($β = 0.12$, $p > 0.1$)—whereas we had hypothesized that the impact would have been negative. This indicates that in a predictable and simple situation, relying on planned strategies leads to satisfactory results, but it seems that little is to be achieved from this when the innovation environment is too complex and uncertain.

TABLE 18.6 indicates a positive association between the reliance on networks with users and innovation performance when uncertainty and complexity are high ($β = 0.31$, $p < 0.01$). In a situation of low uncertainty and complexity, the association was also positive, but not significant ($β = 0.19$, $p > 0.1$). This again reveals the importance of a close association with users, especially when innovation projects are managed in highly uncertain and complex contexts. Relying on users probably avoids the innovation being developed for nonexistent needs, and consequently enhances its chance of success.

Finally, as was hypothesized, networking with competition has a detrimental effect on performance in environments of high uncertainty and complexity ($β = −0.026$, $p < 0.05$). However, the speculated positive association in the case of lower uncertainty and complexity was not observed

TABLE 18.6 Innovation performance as a function of strategy with users and competitors

	High uncertainty and complexity $n = 77$	Low uncertainty and complexity $n = 39$	High uncertainty and complexity $n = 77$	Low uncertainty and complexity $n = 39$	High uncertainty and complexity $n = 77$	Low uncertainty and complexity $n = 39$	High uncertainty and complexity $n = 77$	Low uncertainty and complexity $n = 39$
	β	β	β	β	β	β	β	β
RPP								
CULT								
STR	0.0341	0.273**	0.1157	0.3094**				
RCL	0.3497***	0.0572			0.3111***	0.194		
RCO	-0.294***	-0.0059					-0.2661**	-0.0696
ICON								
ICL								
IMA								
AUT	0.1515	0.2258	0.1743	0.2607*	0.0994	0.1603	0.2473**	0.207
TAC	0.0028	-0.1908	-0.0421	0.2131	0.0026	-0.0653	0.01	-0.0299
IRA	0.2504**	0.5884***	0.2469**	0.6128***	0.238**	0.5678***	0.2634**	0.5961***
R^2	0.29***	0.57***	0.11*	0.57***	0.21***	0.52***	0.16***	0.50***

* $p < 0.1$, ** $p < 0.05$, *** $p < 0.01$.

STR: Strategy
RCL: Network with users
RCO: Network with competitors

AUT: Organizational unit autonomy
TAC: Relative size
IRA: Innovation-induced market transformation

($\beta = -0.07$, $p > 0.1$). This again reinforces Xuereb's "virtual market" hypothesis, according to which interactions and information exchange between competitors, in highly uncertain and complex environments, lead to innovation projects with little connection to the real market.

CONCLUSION

This study was premised on the assumption that innovation project managers rely on different means to fight against uncertainty and complexity surrounding the innovation project to facilitate their actions when managing innovation. We speculated that these means help to close a system which would otherwise be too complex and uncertain to be managed. They confine the system within an insular field, which we have called an "island of rationality", in which managerial action may be undertaken. We also suggested that these "islands of rationality" enable managers to act with greater effectiveness, and that a variety of means are used to establish them: organizational (rules, procedures, plans, organization culture, values, incentives); cognitive (information on users and competitors); strategic (strategic intent and content, networking and partnerships with competitors and users); and managerial (project management). A twofold approach was adopted. Firstly, we formulated a set of six hypotheses, based on existing literature, on the expected relationships between means for coping with uncertainty and complexity and the innovation performance. These hypotheses were then tested against empirical data collected on 116 innovation projects.

Empirical observations revealed that, as a general rule, there is no statistical difference between the diverse means used for managing highly uncertain and complex innovation projects, and those characterized by lesser uncertainty and complexity. The only remarkable exceptions were the higher reliance on rules and procedures when projects were highly uncertain and complex, and the more intensive use of information on competition when there was less uncertainty and complexity surrounding the innovation project. The implication of the first observation is surprising. Innovation managers, whatever the surrounding uncertainty and complexity, seem to rely on similar means. This suggests that managerial "recipes" are relied upon when managing an innovation project, without necessarily taking into account the context of the particular project. However, as we can see below, a differentiated use of these means makes a difference in terms of innovation performance. We also found a tendency to rely more heavily on rules and procedures in a situation of high uncertainty and complexity, even though such increased reliance does not lead to innovation performance.

We will now turn to the main results of the study. In a situation where surrounding uncertainty and complexity are high, we found that a supportive innovation culture; the reliance on project management; an adequate amount of information on users' needs; and close relationships with prospective users through networks and partnerships are all associated with a successful innovation outcome. These associations were also observed in situations of lower uncertainty and complexity, but to a lesser extent. However, it was only when uncertainty and complexity were less pronounced that reliance on more structured and formalized means such as rules, procedures, plans and strategy was positively associated with performance.

These results highlight the fact that when uncertainty and complexity are pronounced, less formal methods like the development of an innovation culture or project management are more effective in managing new product development than they are under conditions of lower uncertainty and complexity. They also suggest that, although in simpler and more certain situations managers can rely on the more formal means to direct their project, the fact that no association is found between rules and procedures and innovation performance when uncertainty and complexity are higher might reinforce the ritualization hypothesis in the use of organizational means. This is consistent with writings on strategic management which stress that formal tools do not allow managers to react rapidly enough to unplanned events. It is likely that in a highly uncertain and complex situation managers tend to rely on all means at their disposal to reinforce their feelings of certitude and good management, which could explain why rules and procedures are more extensively used in these situations.

The "virtual market" trap hypothesis, in which highly uncertain and complex projects might fall when they rely on information or networks with competitors, is also illustrated by our findings. As, in situations of high uncertainty and complexity, firms have difficulty in deciphering what users' needs are and what the real market is, they tend to rely on competitors' projects to influence their decisions about the direction of their innovation venture. In so doing, they are attempting to prevent competition from developing a hypothesized competitive edge if their project were to fit market requirements. Consequently, firms end up including in their innovation project their competitors' product functionalities—leading to results abstracted from reality. Our findings show that, in this situation, relying on information on competitors and networks is negatively associated with innovation success. Even in simpler and more certain cases, networking and competition information do not seem to have any effect on innovation performance.

We believe we have shown that means to cope with uncertainty and complexity are, to some extent, functional in the management of innovation projects. By creating a greater sense of certainty and simplicity, they probably aid managers to determine meaning and continuity in their day-to-day actions. They may also facilitate communication and coordination between organizational actors by giving them a better understanding of the tasks to be accomplished. However, not all these means are equally effective in leading to innovation performance. More tacit means seem to be better adapted to highly uncertain and complex projects, while more formal means are better fitted to the management of innovation when uncertainty and complexity are less pronounced.

Further research needs to be done, and it is not our belief that our findings are without flaws. The major limit of the present research is that we are using a cross-sectional sample to measure effects that are inherently time sensitive. Technological uncertainty, for example, declines as a technology moves toward maturity (Anderson and Tushman, 1991). In the same vein, a specific means might be efficient at coping with uncertainty and complexity at the beginning of an innovation process and less efficient at the end of the same process. Furthermore, the performance evaluation is assessed by the same respondent who rates the uncertainty and complexity levels as well as the extent to which each means was used during the innovation process. Finally, we are using only perceptual measures. More objective measures exist but they are rarely available for the new product and only at the aggregate (firm or industry) level.

We do feel, however, we have provided some empirical evidence to reinforce certain accepted findings on innovation management; these stress the importance of considering the nature of the innovation context, and also open new doors in our understanding of the means used to cope with uncertainty and complexity while managing innovation.

APPENDIX 1

DISTRIBUTION OF INDUSTRIES REPRESENTED IN SAMPLE

Industries	Percentage of sample
Consumer durable goods	5.7
Consumer nondurable goods	15.1
Consumer services	1.4
Medical and pharmaceutical products	4.2
Industrial equipment	34
Electronic products	4.7
Chemical products	3.8
Computer-based products	11.8
Industrial services	1.9
Miscellaneous	17.4

APPENDIX 2

MEASURES OF MAJOR CONSTRUCTS AND THEIR RELIABILITY

Dependent Variable

Innovation success (or performance). The innovation market growth relative to that of competing products, the innovation return on investment relative to the company's other products, the fulfillment of the innovation project objectives, the commercial success of the innovation, the innovation effect on the overall market share. Reliability coefficient of 0.9043.

Control Variables

Market-induced transformations following the innovation introduction. Modification of competitive rules, modification of the market. Reliability coefficient of 0.8131.

Size of the organizational unit relative to the competition: Relative size, relative market share, relative resources, relative number of employees. Reliability coefficient of 0.9015.

Degree of autonomy of the unit in charge of the project. Overall autonomy, autonomy in strategy formulation, autonomy in resources, autonomy in technological strategy formulation. Reliability coefficient of 0.7965.

Clustering Variables

Organizational uncertainty. Incapacity to develop and implement an agreed-upon strategy, political decision-making process, numerous internal conflicts, no long-term commitment to innovation projects, no long-term resources commitment. Reliability coefficient of 0.8239.

Organizational complexity. Difficulty to know who is doing what in the organization, existence of numerous groups of diverse culture, large number of hierarchical levels, divergence between goals. Reliability coefficient of 0.7647.

Competition uncertainty. Frequent modification of competitor strategies, difficulty to predict competitor actions. Reliability coefficient of 0.6148.

Competition complexity. Very diverse competitor strategies, great competitor diversity, difficulty to understand competitor actions, difficulty to understand competitor strategic moves, variety of competitor strategic advantages. Reliability coefficient of 0.7041.

Technological uncertainty. Duration of technology's life cycle, frequency of technological revolution, frequency of manufacturing processes changes. Reliability coefficient of 0.7184.

Technological complexity. Innovation project complexity, innovation based on very diverse scientific fields, large number of different technologies used in the innovation project, complexity of technologies used in the innovation project. Reliability coefficient of 0.6943.

Customer uncertainty. Difficulty to predict customer needs evolution.

Customer complexity. Difficulty to understand customer needs and expectations, customer heterogeneity, diversity of market segments needs and expectations. Reliability coefficient of 0.7374.

Product uncertainty. Large dissimilarity between the innovation and other competitor products, high final users' perceived difference between the innovation project and other competitor products. Reliability coefficient of 0.6835.

Product complexity. Innovation project based on very diverse customer expectations, diversity of the innovation uses. Reliability coefficient of 0.7258.

Independent Variables

Rules, procedures and plans. Project and product definition, constant project evaluation, existence of standardized rules and procedures to manage innovation process, presence of a carefully planned project management. Reliability coefficient of 0.8301.

Culture. Innovation-based incentives, innovation risk-taking behavior, innovation orientation, innovation organizational culture and values. Reliability coefficient of 0.8916.

Competitor information. Information on competitors' R&D programs, analysis of the competition, simulation of competitors' reaction to the innovation,

innovation project based on competitors' own project, innovation project based on competitors' R&D programs. Relibility coefficient of 0.7816.

Customer information. Innovation project decision based on customers' needs, innovation development based on users' advice and recommendations, innovation development based on working group with users. Reliability coefficient of 0.7119.

Strategy. Innovation based on the firm's competitive advantage, innovation derived from the strategy, innovation based on internal resources, project definition based on the firm's strategy. Reliability coefficient of 0.7168.

Customer network. Partnerships with users to develop new products, participation of users in the definition of new products, information network with users to identify future needs. Reliability coefficient of 0.7788.

Competitor network. Information network with competitors on the industrial sector evolution, partnership with competitors to develop new products. Reliability coefficient of 0.8193.

Project management. Innovation headed by a project manager, multi-disciplinary team, interdepartmental coordination, team autonomy, project management. Reliability coefficient of 0.7889.

REFERENCES

Anderson, P. and Tushman, M.L. (1991) "Managing Trough Cycles of Technological Changes", *Research Technology Management*, 34, 26–31.

Armstrong, S. and Overton, T. (1977) "Estimating Non-response Bias in Mail Survey", *Journal of Marketing Research*, 14(3), 396–402.

Arthur D. Little (1991) *Worldwide Survey of Product Innovation*, Cambridge, Mass.: Arthur D. Little Inc.

Astley, W.G. and Fombrun, C.J. (1983) "Collective Strategy: Social Ecology of Organizational Environments", *Academy of Management Review*, 8(4), 576–587.

Burgelman, R.A. (1983) "Corporate Entrepreneurship and Strategic Management: Insights from a Process Study", *Management Science*, 29(12), 1349–1364.

Business Week (1984) "Business Sharpens Its Spying Techniques", 4 August, 60–62.

Bygrave, W.D. (1989) "The Entrepreneurship Paradigm (II): Chaos and Catastrophes among Quantum Jumps?", *Entrepreneurship: Theory and Practice*, 14(2), 7–30.

Cooper, R. (1979) "Identifying Industrial New Projects Success: Project Newprod", *Industrial Marketing Review*, 8(2), 124–135.

Cooper, R. (1983) "A Process Model for Industrial New Product Development", *IEEE Transactions on Engineering Management*, 30(1), 2–11.

Cooper, R. (1984) "New Product Strategies, What Distinguishes the Top Performers?", *Journal of Product Innovation Management*, **1**(2), 71–95.

Cooper, R. and Kleinschmidt, E. (1986) "An Investigation into the New Products Process: Steps, Deficiencies and Impact", *Journal of Product Innovation Management*, **3**(2), 71–85.

Daft, R.L. and Lengel, R.H. (1984) "Information Richness: A New Approach to Managerial Behavior and Organization Design", in B.M. Staw and L.L. Cummings (eds), *Research in Organizational Behavior*, Vol. 6, Greenwich, Conn.: JAI Press Inc., pp. 191–233.

Daft, R.L. and Weick, K.E. (1984) "Toward a Model of Organizations as Interpretation Systems", *Academy of Management Review*, **9**(2), 284–295.

Day, G. (1990) *Market Driven Strategy*, New York: The Free Press.

Dess, G.S. and Robinson, R.B. (1984) "Measuring Organizational Performance in the Absence of Objective Measures", *Strategic Management Journal*, **11**, 59–78.

DiMaggio, P.J. and Powell, W.W. (1983) "The Iron Cage Revisited: Institutional Isomorphism and Collective Rationality in Organizational Fields", *American Sociological Review*, **48**(1), 147–160.

Dougherty, D. (1990) "Understanding New Markets for New Products", *Strategic Management Journal*, **11**(1), 59–78.

Dougherty, D. (1992) "Interpretative Barriers to Successful Product Innovation in Large Firms", *Organization Science*, **3**(2), 179–202.

Doyle, P., Saunders, J., and Wright, L. (1989) "A Comparative Study of US and Japanese Marketing Strategies in the British Markets", *International Journal of Research in Marketing*, **5**, 265–273.

Duschesneau, T.D., Cohn, S., and Dutton, J. (1979) *A Study of Innovations in Manufacturing: Determination Processes and Methodological Issues*, Vol. 1. Orono: Social Science Research Institute, University of Maine.

Ettlie, J.E. (1983) "Organizational Policy and Innovation among Suppliers in the Food Processing Sector", *Academy of Management Review*, **8**(1), 27–44.

Feldman, M.S. and March, J.G. (1981) "Information in Organizations as Signal and Symbol", *Administrative Science Quarterly*, **26**(1), 171–186.

Festinger, L. (1957) *A Theory of Cognitive Dissonance*, London: Tavistock.

Fidler. L.A. and Johnson, D.J. (1984) "Communication and Innovation Implementation", *Academy of Management Review*, **9**(4), 704–711.

Fischer, W.A. (1980) "Scientific and Technical Information and the Performance of R&D Groups", in D. Dean and J. Goldhar (eds), *TIMS Studies in Management Science*, 15, Amsterdam: North-Holland, pp. 67–89.

Freeman, C. (1974) *The Economics of Industrial Innovation*, London: Penguin Books.

Hall, R. (1984) "The Natural Logic of Management Policy Making", *Management Science*, **30**(8), 905–927.

Jauch, L.R. and Kraft, K.L. (1986) "Strategic Management of Uncertainty", *Academy of Management Review*, **11**(4), 777–790.

Jelinek, M. and Schoonhoven, C. (1990) *The Innovation Marathon: Lessons from High Technology Firms*, Cambridge, Mass.: Basil Blackwell.

Johnson, G. (1988) "Rethinking Incrementalism", *Strategic Management Journal*, **8**(1), 75–91.

Kanter, R.M. (1988) "When a Thousand Flowers Bloom", in B. Staw and L. Cummings (eds), *Research in Organizational Behavior*, Vol. 10. Greenwich, Conn.: JAI Press, pp. 169–211.

Lilien, G., Brown, R., and Searls, K. (1990) "Cut Errors, Improve Estimates to Bridge Biz-to-biz Information Gap", *Marketing News*, **25**(1), 20–22.

Lilien, G. and Yoon, E. (1988) "Determinants of New Industrial Product Performance: a Strategic Re-Examination of Empirical Literature", *IEEE Transactions of Engineering Management*, **36**(1), 3–10.

March, J.G. (1981) "Footnotes to Organizational Change", *Administrative Science Quarterly*, **26**(4), 563–577.

Miller, D. (1987) "The Structural and Environmental Correlates of Business Strategy", *Strategic Management Journal*, **8**(1), 55–76.

Miller, D. and Friesen, P.H. (1980) "Momentum and Revolution in Organizational Adaptation", *Academy of Management Journal*, **23**(4), 591–614.

Miller, D. and Friesen, P. (1984) *Organizations: A Quantum View*, Englewood Cliffs, NJ: Prentice-Hall.

Milliken, F.J. (1987) "Three Types of Perceived Uncertainty about the Environment: State, Effect and Response Uncertainty", *Academy of Management Review*, **12**(1), 133–143.

Munson, F.C. and Pelz, D.C. (1979) "The Innovating Process: A Conceptual Framework", Working Paper, University of Michigan.

Nelson, R. and Winter, S. (1982) *An Evolutionary Theory of Economic Change*, Cambridge: Harvard University Press.

Nystrom, P.C., Hedberg, B., and Starbuck, W.H. (1976) "Interacting Processes as Organizational Designs", in R. Killman, L. Pondy, and D. Slevin (eds), *The Management of Organization Design*, New York: North-Holland, pp. 209–230.

Pfeffer, J. and Salancik, G.R. (1978) *The External Control of Organizations: A Resource Dependence Perspective*, New York: Harper and Row.

Porter, M. (1980) *Competitive Strategy: Techniques for Analysing Industry and Competitors*, New York: The Free Press.

Porter, M. (1985) *Competitive Advantage*, New York: The Free Press.

Quinn, J.B. (1980) "Managing Strategic Change", *Sloan Management Review*, **21**(4), 3–20.

Quinn, J.B. (1985) "Managing Innovation: Controlled Chaos", *Harvard Business Review*, **63**(3), 73–84.

Robertson, T.S. and Gatignon, H. (1986) "Competitive Effects on Technology Diffusion", *Journal of Marketing*, **50**(1), 1–12.

Rothwell, R. (1977) "The Characteristics of Successful Innovators and Technically Progressive Firms", *R & D Management*, **7**(2), 191–206.

Rubenstein, A.H. Chakrabarti, A.K., O'Keefe, R.D., Souder, W.E., and Young, H.C. (1976) "Factors Influencing Innovation Success at the Project Level", *Research Management*, **51**(1), 15–20.

Saunders, J., Brown, M., and Laverick, S. (1992) "Research Notes on the Best British companies: A Peer Evaluation of British leading firms", *British Journal of Management*, **3**, 181–193.

Sinha, D.K. (1990) "The Contribution of Formal Planning to Decisions", *Strategic Management Journal*, **11**(6), 479–492.

Spender, J.-C. (1993) "Some Frontier Activities around Strategy Theorizing", *Journal of Management Studies*, **30**(1), 11–30.

Souder, W.E. (1987) *Managing New Products Innovations*, Lexington: Lexington Books.

Souder, W.E. and Monaert, R.K. (1992) "Integrating Marketing and R&D Project Personnel within Innovation Projects: An Information Uncertainty Model", *Journal of Management Studies*, **29**(4), 485–512.

Van de Ven, A. (1986) "Central Problems in the Management of Innovation", *Management Science*, **32**(5), 590–608.

Venkatraman, N. and Ramanujam, V. (1986) "Measurement of Business Performance in Strategic Research: A Comparison of Approaches", *Academy of Management Review*, **11**, 801–814.

Von Hippel, E. (1986) "Lead User: A Source of Novel Products Concepts", *Management Science*, **32**(7), 791–805.

Weick, K.E. (1977) "Organization Design: Organizations as Self-Designing Systems", *Organizational Dynamics*, **6**(1), 31–46.

Xuereb, J.-M. (1993) "Stratégies d'Innovation dans les Secteurs de Haute-Technologie: Le Piège du Marché Virtuel", *Recherches et Applications en Marketing*, **8**(2), 23–44.

19

Forms of TMT Consensus and Organizational Change: An Integrative Model

BILL WOOLDRIDGE, STEVEN W. FLOYD

INTRODUCTION

Previous research on consensus within the top management team (TMT) has focused on agreement about strategic goals and means. Although contingency theory has made considerable progress explaining the links between consensus and organizational performance, the theory continues to be limited by a relatively narrow "planning" definition of strategy. Assuming a broader framework, our argument is that another form of consensus—TMT agreement on organizational capabilities—may be more important to the coherence among the historical stream of *emergent* decisions made by individual TMT members over time. This form of consensus contributes to the effectiveness of the organization's emergent adaptation process. Consensus on strategic goals and means on the other hand appears to contribute more to the *deliberate* side of the adaptation process. By itself, either form of consensus creates rigidities, and these lead to a deterioration in organizational performance. A performance crisis, in turn, creates the need for radical, frame-breaking change and often threatens the organization's survival. We propose that a dynamic balance between both forms of consensus will lead more consistently to high levels of organization performance.

Strategy, Structure and Style. Edited by H. Thomas, D. O'Neal and M. Ghertman
Copyright © 1997 John Wiley & Sons Ltd.

Research investigating the effects of consensus on organizational performance has, for the most part, focused on the extent to which top managers agree about organizational goals, means, and environmental perceptions (Bourgeois, 1980, 1985; Dess, 1987; Wooldridge and Floyd, 1989). Motivating this research has been the notion that consensus improves performance by promoting unified direction and successful implementation (Dess and Origer, 1987; Hrebiniak and Joyce, 1984; Nielson, 1981; Steiner, 1979).

The logic for this relationship has been built around the organization's need for integration and efficiency. A high level of consensus among a firm's TMT conserves resources, promotes integrative structures, and facilitates smooth implementation (Dess and Origer, 1987). In empirical studies, both positive and negative relationships with performance (Bourgeois, 1985; Dess, 1987; Grinyer and Norburn, 1977–78) have been found, however, and subsequent work has taken a contingency perspective emphasizing the importance of competitive stable context (Dess, 1987; Priem, 1990).

Contingency theory assumes differences among organizations in their need for efficiency and adaptation, depending on the degree of environmental change. The approach in this chapter assumes there is a need for efficiency and adaptation in all organizations and whether strategy focuses on one or the other depends on how the adaptive process unfolds over time (Chakravarthy, 1982; Mintzberg, 1990; Mintzberg and Westley, 1992). Long-term maintenance inevitably requires renewal of the business and the logic by which the organization is managed (Hurst, Rush, and White, 1989), and change of this sort involves emergent, as well as deliberate, decision processes. As usually defined, however, TMT consensus addresses only the *deliberate* side of the process. This ignores the social agreement that influences the decisions made by top managers in the *emergent* adaptation process.

The purpose here is to extend current thinking on TMT consensus by highlighting the connection between consensus and the organization's strategic change process. The following section begins by underscoring the connection between TMT goals and means consensus and deliberate strategy. Since realized strategy includes emergent forces (Mintzberg and Waters, 1985), the chapter develops an additional theoretical connection between consensus on organizational capabilities and the process of emergent adaptation. The balance of the chapter develops links between the strategic process, both forms of consensus, strategic change, and organizational performance. Relationships are summarized in a proposed model and implications for practice and research are identified.

CONSENSUS AND THE STRATEGIC PROCESS

GOALS AND MEANS CONSENSUS

In past research, TMT consensus has focused on product market positions, reflecting short- and long-term profitability goals, and firms' "competitive posture(s) within an industry" (Bourgeois, 1980: 237). Agreement within the TMT has been seen to result from a conscious thought process that provides the coherence needed for implementation efforts. That is, consensus signifies the extent to which top managers have successfully communicated, negotiated, and gained acceptance within their group for an explicit set of goals and strategies. Defined this way, the consensus construct can be seen as a reflection of top management's efforts to pursue deliberate strategy.

A broader definition of strategy considers emergent forces (Mintzberg and Waters, 1985) and recognizes that the TMT's influence extends beyond their explicit group decisions. Strategy making is an interactive learning process (Burgelman, 1983) and includes unscheduled, autonomous behavior by members of the TMT. Our arguments suggest that consensus is important not only because it influences the way TMT members pursue deliberate strategy, but also because it influences how they facilitate and manage emergent strategy. In other words, TMT consensus can be linked to organizational outcomes because it provides coherence among top executives participating in the "real time" strategic management of the organization.

EMERGENT ADAPTATION

How an organization responds to unforeseen opportunities and threats can be characterized as the emergent adaptation process. As a part of this, top managers and others initiate mid-stream adjustments to the deliberate strategy in order to enhance overall strategic effectiveness. These "mid-course corrections" are conceived within the framework of the established strategy and are designed to be consistent with it (Quinn, 1980). Over time, however, their cumulative effect is to change the direction of strategy (Burgelman, 1983; Johnson, 1987).

It is important to distinguish the emergent form of adaptation from more formal, deliberate responses (Ford and Baucus, 1987). Formal change efforts flow from deliberate TMT group decisions that are focused on official goals and means. Emergent adaptation, on the other hand, is triggered by strategic decisions, not considered by the TMT as whole, but taken by individual TMT members. These more incremental decisions and actions sometimes respond to performance downturns (Ford and Baucus, 1987), but also take the form of resource commitments intended to take advantage of unanticipated opportunities (Bower, 1970; Burgelman, 1983).

The importance of emergent adaptation is recognized in the research literature (Chakravarthy, 1982; Mintzberg, 1978; Quinn, 1980), and its relevance to real world organization appears in the use of cross-functional teams, lateral communication, and employee empowerment. These are all attempts to increase organizational capacities for ongoing innovation and flexibility. Indeed, fostering entrepreneurial autonomous initiative has become a primary focus in strategic management (cf. Guth and Ginsberg, 1990; Burgelman, 1983; Hart, 1992; Mintzberg and Waters, 1985).

But, while considerable effort has gone into understanding how innovation, creativity, and entrepreneurial championing are advanced at operating and middle levels, less has been devoted to understanding how top managers choose among the competing initiatives "bubbling up" from below them. Bower (1970) and Burgelman (1983) frame the process as an interaction between middle- and top-level managers where initiatives are proposed, nurtured, or abandoned.

> Top management picks and chooses among these initiatives and thereby legitimizes them. . . . Strategic choice takes place through experimentation and selection (Burgelman and Sayles, 1986: pp. 144–145).

Top management's decision to nurture and select certain potentially adaptive responses over others represents a "putting-up and a shooting-down" process. Proposals are shaped by operating-level and championed by middle-level managers. As someone typically identified with a particular functional background, a top manager's role is one of encouragement and support as well as oversight and control for initiatives that come to his or her attention. Understanding how these judgments are formed to favor some proposals over others is central to a fuller explication of the adaptation process.

CONSENSUS AND EMERGENT ADAPTATION

Agreements tied to specific goals and strategies are likely to be insufficient for guiding the emergent decisions of individual top managers. By definition, emergent initiatives go beyond deliberate strategy and may even be inconsistent with it. What then, is the underlying logic that guides emergent strategy?

Theoretically, the cornerstone of such a logic would seem to emanate from the organizations' strategic capabilities and core competencies (Prahalad and Bettis, 1986). Over time, organizations learn to get good at and take advantage of certain kinds of activities. Strategies lead to the cultivation of specific assets (Dierickx and Cool, 1989), and firms following different strategies acquire different skills. At any given point, therefore, organizations differ in terms of their strategic capabilities and have a finite set of core competencies. These provide competitive advantage and allow firms to take advantage of emerging opportunities (Barney, 1986; Porter, 1991; Prahalad and Hamel, 1990).

For any given organization, certain levels of initiative or proposals for change are likely to enhance capability and improve performance while others "seem a prescription for failure" (Nelson, 1991). Effective emergent adaptation therefore involves a careful balance between changing what the organization does and being realistic about its ability to change. Existing capabilities are not neutral, and management's attachment to existing organizational capacities frequently undermines strategic change. "These deeply embedded knowledge sets may come to represent 'core rigidities' that pose potential problems for all projects, especially those that draw from 'nontraditional capabilities'" (Leonard-Barton, 1992: 118).

Despite the danger of rigidity, emergent adaptation requires a "reasonably coherent and accepted strategy" (Nelson, 1991:69). Otherwise, inconsistent emergent decision-making is likely to produce a reactive strategy (Miles and Snow, 1978) and the worst form of political incrementalism (Johnson, 1987). *In this regard, a collective awareness of core organizational capabilities among the TMT is important because it provides a common framework for the stream of initiatives, proposals, and decisions that make up emergent strategy.* Stated differently, TMT consensus concerning organizational capabilities allows the firm to develop a focused adaptive capacity.

This reasoning suggests a relationship between consensus on organizational capabilities and performance. References to such links can be found in the existing literature. Hamel and Prahalad (1989), for example, assert that Japanese companies have sustained dominant positions by understanding and nurturing their core competencies. Similarly, Wernerfelt (1989) urges managers to develop an understanding of their organization's distinctive resources.

To summarize our discussion so far, FIGURE 19.1 shows that goals and means consensus can be theoretically linked to deliberate strategy and that capabilities consensus can be tied to the organization's emergent strategy. Since "real-world" strategies include a combination of deliberate and emergent elements (Mintzberg and Waters, 1985), however, goals and means consensus and capabilities consensus are unlikely to be independent from one another. The following section then, integrates the two by describing their antecedents, interactions, contingencies, and consequences for organizational performance.

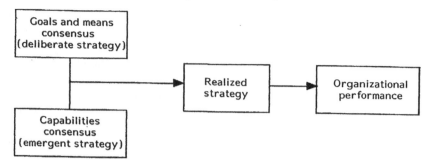

FIGURE 19.1   Forms of TMT consensus and organizational performance

AN INTEGRATIVE MODEL OF TMT CONSENSUS

ANTECEDENTS

Goals and means consensus is generally seen as an outcome of the TMT's decision-making process (Dess and Origer, 1987). While this is probably enhanced when members of the TMT debate and frankly discuss alternative courses of action (Priem, 1990), such agreement may also form as a result of unilateral edicts by the chief executives or a dominant subset of top managers (Brodwin and Bourgeois, 1984). There is room for more research on the events leading to TMT decisions, but what seems clear is that the level of participation in these processes by TMT members varies significantly across top management teams.

In comparison to a finite group process which leads to an agreement on goals and means, the process of achieving an awareness and shared understanding of organizational capabilities among the TMT appears more indeterminate and complex. Knowledge of firm capabilities forms from an awareness of what the firm can actually do, and this requires first-hand experience with middle- and operating-level activities. It is only through observation of success and failure from deploying various resources across different positions that managers come to understand the firm's capabilities. Achieving an awareness of capabilities in one sense therefore depends on the extent of top management's involvement in what is known as the "implementation side" of strategy. Further, this kind of top management involvement is probably self-reinforcing: awareness of capabilities stimulates more involvement in implementation and involvement increases awareness.

Top managers who remain detached from the details of implementation, assuming the role of "strategist" or "planner", are unlikely to gain an in-depth knowledge of how the firm operates and what it can do (Sayles,

1993). Such knowledge develops through immediate involvement in making the strategy work. By managing relationships at the boundaries of key activities, "working leaders" develop an appreciation of the fundamental trade-offs and operational realities (Sayles, 1993). Thus, a necessary, but insufficient, ingredient for TMT capabilities consensus appears to be individual top managers' involvement in implementation activities. All else equal then, we expect the following:

> Proposition 1: *Top management's involvement in implementation is positively associated with their awareness of organizational capabilities.*

As individual TMT members become involved in implementation, each develops a unique understanding of firm capabilities based on their own experiences. TMT capabilities *consensus*, however, requires that these individual interpretations coalesce somehow into a common understanding. This process would seem to turn on the extent to which members of the TMT communicate and share information among themselves about their encounters with capability in the implementation experience. As experiences are compared in formal and informal meetings, individual interpretations are broadened and refined. Over time these conversations result in a common set of assumptions and an accepted set of words to describe firm capabilities. Thus,

> Proposition 2: *There is a positive association between the extent to which members of the TMT share information with each other regarding implementation experiences and the level of TMT consensus on organizational capabilities.*

INTERACTION EFFECTS

The discussion above suggests that information sharing in meetings among members of the TMT is likely to affect capabilities consensus. In deliberate strategy-making contexts where the TMT openly and critically debate strategic alternatives—formally or informally—core capabilities are likely to be explicitly discussed and evaluated. Through this, the learning associated with individual TMT members' experiences is incorporated into discussions of deliberate strategy, and the TMT's collective understanding of capabilities is increased. Indeed, the two forms of consensus are conceptually intertwined, and under the right set of circumstances, it seems reasonable to assume they are associated positively with one other.

In some settings, however, consensus on goals and means may form without a full appreciation of firm capabilities or vice versa. Power differences and pressures for group cohesion (Janis, 1972) sometimes lead to premature closure, and the TMT may exhibit significant consensus on strategic goals and means but lack a common awareness of core capabilities. Alternatively, political and internal forces may preclude agreement on specific goals or means (Lindblom, 1959; Narayanan and Fahey, 1983). Theory predicts that the causes and effects of key capabilities are fundamentally ambiguous, making their comprehension by the TMT difficult or impossible (Reed and DeFillipi, 1990). These ambiguities are likely to impede the TMT's ability to evaluate what the key capabilities are and impede reaching consensus about them. Depending on how TMT members share information, the dynamics of the group's decision-making process and other forces in the organization, then, the two forms of consensus exist to a different degree within a given TMT. In this section we consider how the occurrence of one form of consensus without the other skews the balance between deliberate and emergent strategy and hence, how it can weaken the organization's capacity for strategic change.

When top management's understanding of strategy is driven only by goals and means consensus, there is little basis for coherent emergent strategy. Individual initiatives by members of the TMT may be disconnected and noncumulative, having negative effects on the consistency of realized strategy. Thus, change becomes dependent on the organized, collective efforts of the TMT as a whole. Existing research suggests that formalized rethinking is unlikely to occur until there are major performance downturns (Ford and Baucus, 1987). Until some form of "red flag" appears, therefore, members of the TMT continue to pursue the agreed-upon deliberate course. Opportunities go unrecognized as managers focus on the "benchmarks and milestones" that underlie the established strategy. Thus, when top managers' strategic thinking is guided solely by agreed-to goals and means, the TMT is limited in its capacity to adjust strategy in response to emerging opportunities or minor performance downturns. The capacity for strategic change is likely to be limited to formal, planned reactions.

In contrast, when top management's shared understanding of strategy is limited only to capabilities, the deliberate side of the process appears to suffer. Change may become overly opportunistic, leading to inconsistent decision-making. Lacking common goals and accepted strategies, individual managers have no benchmarks for judging success or failure. This diminishes their collective motivation for planned change. Instead, they are more likely to perceive the need for unplanned, opportunistic change stimulated by problems in subunits and middle managers who champion alternative solutions (Floyd and Wooldridge, 1992). Functional myopia may result from selective perception within the subunits (Dearborn and Simon, 1958), and strategy takes on an increasingly fragmented and emergent character. In sum, the following propositions are suggested:

Propositions 3A–B: *TMT consensus is associated with the organization's change process.*
A: *TMT consensus on goals and means facilitates planned, reactive change.*
B: *TMT consensus on capabilities facilitates emergent, opportunistic change.*

ENVIRONMENTAL CONTINGENCIES

The arguments presented have implications for environmental dynamism as a contingency variable influencing the consensus–performance relationship (Dess and Origer, 1987; Priem, 1990). Theoretically, high levels of TMT consensus on goals and means improves performance in stable environments, while low consensus enhances performance in dynamic contexts (Priem, 1990). This parallels the appropriateness of deliberate strategy in stable contexts. In addition, since more emergent strategy is appropriate as the environment becomes less stable (Mintzberg and Waters, 1985), there is reason to expect a positive association between consensus on capabilities and performance in dynamic contexts. Realized strategies are unlikely to be purely deliberate or purely emergent, however (Mintzberg and Waters, 1985), and most strategy reflects a combination of these. The following sections examine the direct and interaction performance effects of the two forms of consensus in both stable and dynamic environments.

There is strong support for the notion that TMT consensus on goals and means enhances performance in stable environments. (See Priem, 1990 for a complete review and development of this argument). Acknowledging this, the question becomes: What is the role of consensus on capabilities in stable environments? Two opposing arguments appear credible.

First, emergent strategy represents the discretionary responses or autonomous initiatives of organization members (Mintzberg and Waters, 1985), and such behavior typically develops under structures and systems that are not overly constraining. Stable, mature environments, however, are often highly competitive, and looser controls that foster emergent activity inevitably limit management's ability to achieve needed efficiencies. The experimentation that is an inevitable part of the autonomous process, for example, is likely to undermine deliberate strategy formation, dilute resources, and reduce efficiency. Thus, for example, managers may expend resources searching for a product market position or learning how to compete when competitors are already well established (Porter, 1980).

On the other hand, imperfections in the fit between an organization's strategy and its environment appear to be inescapable, and *some* level of emergent strategy is needed even in stable contexts. "Increasing stress . . . [is] . . . the result of a dynamic world, the logical limitations of any given strategy, and changes in human aspirations" (Huff, Huff, and Thomas,

1992: 58). Ideally, emergent adaptation provides incremental adjustments, reduces stress, and maintains strategic fit. When top managers have little common understanding of organizational capabilities, however, emergent responses are unlikely to be coherent. Performance is likely to decline, then, in the face of ineffective responses to the widening gap between the strategy and its context. Thus, emergent processes appear to be incompatible with the need for efficiency and inescapable in the maintenance of fit.

The first argument, that emergent strategy creates inefficiencies and distractions, is based on an assumption that emergent adaptation comes at the expense of deliberate strategy. As more emergent elements become introduced into strategy, intentionality is supplanted, and management loses its sense of purpose. In the second case, however, the notion is that emergent strategy complements or augments deliberate strategy. Rather than displacing it, emergent forces combine with deliberate strategy and maintain the viability of strategic fit.

In short, the effect of emergent processes, and hence the value of capabilities consensus, in stable environments depends on whether emergent strategy and capabilities consensus develop in addition to, or instead of, deliberate strategy and goals and means consensus. When combined with deliberate consensus, consensus on capabilities brings coherence to the adjustments needed even in stable contexts. When it comes at the expense of goals and means consensus, however, emergent strategy and capabilities consensus wastes resources and undermines competitiveness. In the latter case, therefore, we would expect to find a *negative* association between capabilities consensus and performance. Thus,

Propositions 4A–C: *In stable environments,*
(A)   *measures of TMT consensus on goals and means will be positively related to measures of organizational performance.*
(B)   *among organizations with high levels of TMT consensus on goals and means there will be a positive relationship between measures of consensus on capabilities and measures of organizational performance.*
(C)   *among organizations with low levels of TMT consensus on goals and means there will be a negative relationship between measures of consensus on capabilities and measures of organizational performance.*

The existing literature agrees on the desirability of emergent or incremental strategy in dynamic environments (Mintzberg, 1978; Quinn, 1980; Fredrickson and Mitchell, 1984; Fredrickson, 1984; Mintzberg and Waters, 1985). Deliberate or planned strategy is considered untenable in these settings because conditions are continually in flux. Strategy, therefore, unfolds as information becomes available and uncertainty is reduced.

Building on this reasoning, the argument for consensus on organizational capabilities is based on the need for an underlying logic to guide emergent strategy. When ratified by top management, emergent initiatives are likely to change the definition of the strategic context (Burgelman, 1983). While such divergence is inherent to the process, purely random selection is likely to be both inefficient and inconsistent. Without an understanding of organizational capabilities, emergent responses may draw on capabilities that are unavailable to the organization. Another possibility is that proposals drawing on available capabilities are rejected for lack of TMT awareness. Morover, top managers operating with different assumptions about the organization's capabilities may enact multiple, noncoordinated responses that work against each other. In short, without a shared sense of organizational capabilities, an organization's emergent process is likely to be frustrated, and the level of stress associated with a given strategy is likely to increase over time.

The need for emergent strategy in dynamic environments therefore suggests a positive relationship between TMT consensus on capabilities and organizational performance in these settings. Consistent with this assertion and existing contingency theory (Fredrickson and Mitchell, 1984; Hambrick and Mason, 1984), however, Priem (1990) hypothesizes a *negative* relationship between TMT consensus on goals and means and organizational performance in dynamic settings. Again, his reasoning seems to be based on the notion that deliberateness drives out emergent adaptation. As Eisenhardt and Bourgeois (1988) show, however, successful firms are often both deliberately comprehensive and emergently responsive. Consensus on goals and means, when held concurrent with a common understanding of capabilities, may be an effective combination in dynamic environments. In short, the following relationships are proposed.

Propositions 5A–C: *In dynamic environments,*
(A) measures of TMT consensus on organizational capabilities will be positively related to measures of organizational performance.
(B) among organizations with high TMT consensus on organizational capabilities there will be a positive relationship between measures of consensus on goals and means and measures of organizational performance.
(C) among organizations with low TMT consensus on organizational capabilities there will be a negative relationship between measures of consensus on goals and means and measures of organizational performance.

CONSENSUS AND THE CONSEQUENCES FOR ORGANIZATIONAL PERFORMANCE

All organizations face the need for change at some point. In combination, the two forms of consensus improve top management's ability to maintain strategic fit in both stable and dynamic environments. At a fundamental level, therefore, consensus enhances performance because it facilitates effective organizational adaptation.

Even when the environment is relatively stable, developments that weaken strategic fit are inevitable (Huff, Huff, and Thomas, 1992). Without capabilities consensus and effective emergent strategy, the organization becomes dependent on the deliberate, collective, efforts of the TMT as a whole. Formalized rethinking of deliberate strategy by the TMT is unlikely to occur until there are major performance problems (Ford and Baucus, 1987), and this is unlikely to develop as an adjustment in response to routine stresses. Hence, fit and performance deteriorate, and stress continues to build until a critical threshold is reached. This culminates in a felt need for radical change and leads to a frame-breaking strategic reorientation (Gersick, 1991; Miller and Friesen, 1980; Tushman, Newman, and Romanelli, 1986).

When the environment is dynamic, an exclusive focus on organizational capabilities is unlikely to be adequate, and there is a need for goals and means consensus. Technologies and skills driving core competencies unavoidably mature, and experimentation eventually needs to be supplemented by more deliberate, predictable innovation (Nelson, 1991). In addition, since current profitability is often not a priority within emerging contexts, pressures to recoup past strategic investments will increase over time. This is likely to require increased strategic focus and an accompanying set of goals and means in order to leverage the accumulated resource base. Again, therefore, it appears that a critical point may be reached necessitating comprehensive rethinking of strategy.

Thus, either form of consensus, by itself, is likely to lead eventually to a crisis that precipitates frame-breaking change which is highly disruptive and which typically makes things worse before they get better (Gersick, 1991). The presence of both forms of TMT consensus, on the other hand, appears to help avoid, or at least postpone, reaching a crisis of environment–strategy fit. This represents a theoretical ideal that is consistent with Hurst, Rush, and White's (1989) renewing organization and Hamel and Prahalad's (1993) notion of strategy as stretch and leverage. Consensus within the TMT on both deliberate goals and means and organizational capabilities facilitates both planned and opportunistic changes. Thus, capabilities consensus and incremental adjustments reduce the potential that goals and means will become obsolete. Deliberate consensus, on the other hand, focuses capabilities on particular goals and means, thereby increasing the likelihood that resources will be deployed effectively.

In this situation, and perhaps only this situation, should one expect a *consistent* positive association between consensus and performance. Ultimately, revolutionary change may be needed even when both forms of consensus are present, but there is the possibility that some of the negative antecedents and consequences associated with frame-breaking change are avoided. Specifically, since consensus on capabilities facilitates incremental adjustments, revolutionary change may not be precipitated by a long-term performance downturn. Instead, radical change is more likely to occur as a result of new opportunities that take advantage of the firm's core competence. Moreover, openness to emergent opportunities sensitizes the TMT to environmental signals which precede the obsolescence of a particular strategy. Since this encourages deliberate responses before the organization reaches a crisis stage, change is likely to be less disruptive within the organization. Top managers and other key organizational members are not cast as failures to be replaced, and transition plans can be implemented in a more systematic, controlled manner. In short, consensus on goals and means combined with consensus on organizational capabilities is likely to result in a less variable performance pattern, and organizations with TMTs exhibiting this combination of consensus more likely enjoy sustained strategic fit. In short, the following propositions are suggested.

Propositions 6A–B: *Organizations with TMTs exhibiting.*
(A) *one form of consensus but not the other will eventually face a crisis that precipitates radical, frame-breaking, change.*
(B) *high goals and means consensus and high capabilities consensus will experience evolutionary change and consistently high levels of organizational performance.*

FIGURE 19.2 summarizes the relationships proposed in propositions 1 through 6. TMT consensus is shown as a multifaceted construct incorporating understandings associated with both the deliberate and emergent aspects of strategy. Although the two forms of consensus are related, each is associated with a different set of antecedent experiences. Goals and means consensus is seen to flow out of a group decision-making process, whereas capabilities consensus develops from an awareness built from TMT members' implementation experiences. Importantly, the consequences of TMT consensus on organizational performance vary depending on the extent of consensus and whether two forms occur simultaneously. Goals and means consensus facilitates effective deliberate strategy in more stable environments. Capabilities consensus facilitates effective emergent strategy in more dynamic environments. While these contingent relationships are expected to be positive, neither type of consensus alone is expected to improve performance over the long run. By itself each is likely to create circumstances within the TMT which ultimately lead to a deterioration in performance and precipitate the need for frame-breaking change. Thus, the diagram shows a noncontingent relationship between the deliberate and emergent decisions flowing from the combination of the two forms of consensus and organization performance.

370

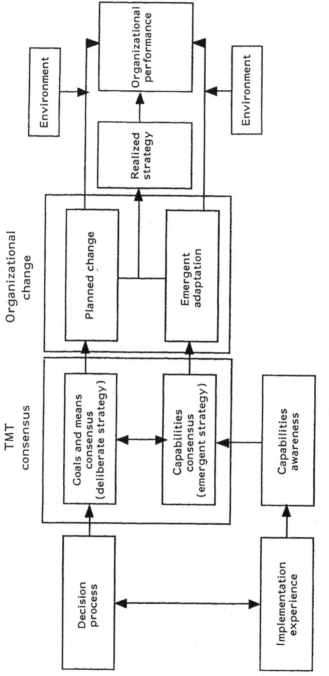

FIGURE 19.2   Antecedents and outcomes of top management consensus on strategy

DISCUSSION AND IMPLICATIONS

REVISING CONTINGENCY THEORY

While recognizing the environment as a moderator of the consensus–performance relationship, the propositions herein suggest primary and secondary roles for the two forms of consensus, depending on the nature of the environment. In stable contexts, consensus on goals and means is of primary importance and is hypothesized to have a positive effect on performance. The effect of consensus on capabilities, on the other hand, is expected to depend on whether it supplants or supports deliberate strategy. In dynamic environments, these relationships are reversed. Capabilities consensus is primary and is expected to positively influence performance. The effect of consensus on goals and means, in turn, becomes contingent on whether it develops instead of or in conjunction with experimentation and learning. Importantly, either form of consensus may be *negatively* related to organization performance when it is observed in isolation and outside its primary context.

By broadening the consensus construct to better reflect both deliberate and emergent aspects of strategy, the present arguments transcend contingency theory. *Regardless of the context*, top management can strike a balance between deliberate and emergent strategy, and the two forms of consensus are both necessary to achieve long-term strategic effectiveness.

IMPLICATIONS FOR RESEARCH

For researchers, the development of measures for capabilities consensus poses an intimidating hurdle. Core capabilities are firm specific (Leonard-Barton, 1992; Teece, Pisano, and Shuen, 1990) and rooted in complex social processes (Barney, 1990). Even insiders may not grasp their significance (Reed and DeFillippi, 1990). Indeed, the tacit character of capability and the experience needed to apprehend it may be one reason to expect low levels of capabilities consensus in many organizational samples. Given the widespread attention in the research literature and business press, however, a growing number of TMTs will likely examine their capabilities as a part of a deliberate strategy-making process. This can be expected to increase the viability of capabilities consensus as a researchable phenomenon.

Still, in order to detect it, researchers will need to begin by identifying core capabilities. This probably means within-industry designs along with a process of preliminary interviews of informed outsiders, such as consultants or investment advisors, as well as the TMT. Using such an approach, recent work (e.g. Aaker, 1989; Hall, 1992; Mehra, 1992) suggests that intangible resources like core capability can be identified and measured successfully.

In addition to research on the consensus–performance relationship, the ideas presented here also suggest the importance of investigating the consensus–change relationship. Past research has measured change on at least four dimensions: business strategy, organizational structure, power distribution, and control systems (Tushman and Romanelli, 1985). Assessment of associations between alternative forms of change and patterns of consensus could greatly enhance the practical utility of consensus-based research. Research of this nature will need to draw on a variety of historical and archival sources (Gersick, 1991) as well as questionnaire data.

In addition, longitudinal case studies may be needed to examine causal directionality. Previous researchers have suggested reverse or simultaneous causality for the performance–consensus relationship (Bourgeois, 1985; Dess, 1987, Priem, 1990). Another concern is that the adaptive process may be deeply embedded in the organization's culture (Johnson, 1987) and world view (Miles and Snow, 1978). Thus, the pattern of change is likely to influence, as well as be influenced by, the level and form of TMT consensus. These causality questions are important to the normative implications and utility of consensus research (Priem, 1990).

The Relevance of TMT Consensus to Management Practice

Several authors (Dess and Origer, 1987; Priem, 1990) have linked interest in TMT research with the success of consensus-based strategy in Japan. Recent economic reversals notwithstanding, the connection appears problematic if the exclusive focus is on top management and consensus on goals and means. Reasoning elsewhere (Wooldridge and Floyd, 1989, 1990) suggests that the involvement and understanding of middle managers and others may be a crucial ingredient of the Japanese model (Nonaka, 1988).

More to the point here, the form of consensus captured in measures of deliberate strategy may not be well tied to the Japanese experience. Where emerging technologies involve continually shifting products and markets (i.e. a highly dynamic environment), a focus on goals and means appears to be secondary. More important concerns may be to gain experience and acquire competencies that position the firm for future competition (Hamel and Prahalad, 1989; Prahalad and Hamel, 1990). Japanese firms invest in technologies and enter partnerships not so much to establish immediate market position, but to learn (Hamel, 1991). Focus within the TMT on organizational capabilities thus contributes to skill-based competition and aggressive pursuit of rapidly changing opportunities (Prahalad and Hamel,

1990) and may more accurately reflect the main concern among top managers pursuing innovation, even in established industries.

Thus, one potentially important normative implication of the ideas advanced here is that top management teams in the USA and elsewhere should begin to incorporate a discussion of core capabilities into their decision-making process (Wernerfelt, 1989). The model in FIGURE 19.2, however, suggests that awareness does not follow from familiar decision-making exercises. Recognition of intangible features of strategy such as capabilities involves an awareness of organizational values and knowledge sets (Leonard-Barton, 1992). Consensus toward capabilities therefore requires the accumulation of shared, real world ("implementation") experiences over time.

CONCLUSIONS

Considerable debate has arisen whether competitive position or core capability is the foundation of business strategy. (See Conner, 1994 or Teece, Pisano, and Shuen, 1990 for a discussion.) Recent writers, however, have begun to synthesize the two schools (e.g. Porter, 1991), and the more complex conceptualization of consensus offered here is partly a response to a more dynamic view of strategy. In addition, relationships between various types of consensus and deliberate and emergent strategy have important implications for models of organizational change. Thus, we would argue that the inconsistencies in previous research may be explained by the need to assess capabilities consensus and that the link between consensus and performance can best be understood in light of the organization's adaptive process.

The central reasoning behind earlier consensus research was that TMT consensus improves organizational performance by promoting integration and efficiency. While consistent with this logic, this chapter points to the role of consensus in the process of organizational adaptation, and in this regard, extends existing theory. We hope the ideas presented here enrich discussion in the area and stimulate additional research.

REFERENCES

Aaker, D.A. (1989) "Managing Assets and Skills: The Key to Sustainable Competitive Advantage", *California Management Review*, Winter, 91–106.
Barney, J.B. (1986) "Strategic Factor Markets: Expectations, Luck and Business Strategy", *Management Science*, **32**, 1231–1241.
Barney, J.B. (1990) "The Debate between Traditional Management Theory and Organizational Economics: Substantive Differences or Intergroup Conflict?" *Academy of Management Review*, **15**, 382–393.

Bourgeois, L.J. (1980) "Performance and Consensus", *Strategic Management Journal*, 1, 227–248.

Bourgeois, L.J. (1985) "Strategic Goals, Perceived Uncertainty, and Economic Performance in Volatile Environments", *Academy of Management Journal*, 28, 548–573.

Bower, J.L. (1970) *Managing the Resource Allocation Process*, Boston, Mass.: Harvard.

Brodwin, D.R. and Bourgeois, L.T. (1984) "Five Steps to Strategic Action", *California Management Review*, 26, 176–190.

Burgelman, R.A. (1983) "A Model of the Interaction of Strategic Behavior, Corporate Context, and the Concept of Strategy", *Academy of Management Review*, 8, 61–70.

Burgelman, R.A. and Sayles, L. (1986) *Inside Corporate Innovation: Strategy, Structure, and Management Skills*, New York: The Free Press.

Chakravarthy, B.S. (1982) "Adaptation: A Promising Metaphor for Strategic Management", *Academy of Management Review*, 7, 35–44.

Conner, K.R. (1994) "The Resource-based Challenge to the Industry–structure Perspective", *Academy of Management Best Papers Proceedings*, 17–21.

Dearborn, D.C. and Simon, H.A. (1958) "Selective Perception: A Note on the Departmental Identifications of Executives", *Sociometry*, 21, 140–144.

Dess, G.G. (1987) "Consensus on Strategy Formulation and Organizational Performance: Competitors in a Fragmented Industry", *Strategic Management Journal*, 8, 259–277.

Dess, G.G. and Origer, N.K. (1987) "Environment, Structure and Consensus in strategy Formulation: A Conceptual Integration", *Academy of Management Review*, 12, 313–330.

Dierickx, I. and Cool, K. (1989) "Asset Stock Accumulation and Sustainability of Competitive Advantage", *Management Science*, 35, 1504–1513.

Eisenhardt, K.M. and Bourgeois, L.J. (1988) "Politics of Strategic Decision Making in High-Velocity Environments: Toward a Midrange Theory", *Academy of Management Journal*, 31, 737–770.

Floyd, S.W. and Wooldridge, B. (1992) "Middle Management Involvement in Strategy and its Association with Strategic Type: A Research Note", *Strategic Management Journal*, 13, 153–167.

Fredrickson, J.W. (1984) "The Comprehensiveness of Strategic Decision Processes: Extension, Observations, Future Directions", *Academy of Management Journal*, 27, 445–466.

Fredrickson, J.W. and Mitchell, T.R. (1984) "Strategic Decision Processes: Comprehensiveness and Performance in an Industry with an Unstable Environment", *Academy of Management Journal*, 27, 399–423.

Ford, J.D. and Baucus, D.A. (1987) "Organizational Adaptation to Performance Downturns: An Interpretation-based Perspective", *Academy of Management Review*, 12, 366–380.

Gersick, Connie J.G. (1991) "Revolutionary Change Theories: A Multilevel Exploration of the Punctuated Equilibrium Paradigm", *Academy of Management Review*, 16, 10–36.

Grinyer, P.H. and Norburn, D. (1977–78) "Planning for Existing Markets: An Empirical Study", *International Studies of Management and Organization*, 7, 99–122.

Guth, W.D. and Ginsberg, A. (eds) (1990) *Special Issue on Corporate Entrepreneurship Strategic Management Journal*, Summer.

Hall, R. (1992) "Strategic Analysis of Intangible Resources", *Strategic Management Journal*, 13, 135–144.

Hambrick, D.C. and Mason, P.A. (1984) "Upper Echelons: The Organization as a Reflection of Its Top Managers", *Academy of Management Review*, 9, 193–206.

Hamel, G. (1991) "Competition for Competence and Inter-partner Learning within International Strategic Alliances", *Strategic Management Journal*, 12, Summer, 83–103.

Hamel, G. and Prahalad, C.K. (1989) "Strategic Intent", *Harvard Business Review*, May, 63–76.

Hamel, G. and Prahalad, C.K. (1993) "Strategy as Stretch and Leverage", *Harvard Business Review*, 71, No. 2, 75–84.

Hart, S. (1992) "An Intgrative Framework for Strategy-Making Processes", *Academy of Management Review*, 17, 327–351.

Hrebiniak, L.G. and Joyce, W.F. (1984) *Implementing Strategy*. New York: Macmillan.

Huff, J.O., Huff, A.S., and Thomas, H. (1992) "Strategic Renewal and the Interaction of Cumulative Stress and Inertia", *Strategic Management Journal*, 13, Summer, 55–75.

Hurst, D.K., Rush, J.C., and White, R.E. (1989) "Top Management Teams and Organizational Renewal", *Strategic Management Journal*, 10, Summer, 87–105.

Janis, I.L. (1972). *Victims of Groupthink*. Boston, MA: Houghton Mifflin.

Johnson, G. (1987) *Strategic Change and the Management Process*, Oxford: Blackwell.

Leonard-Barton, D. (1992) "Core Capabilities and Core Rigidities: A Paradox in Managing New Product Development", *Strategic Management Journal*, 13, Summer, 111–125.

Lindblom, C. (1959) "The Science of Muddling Through", *Public Administration Review*, 19, 79–88.

Mehra, A. (1992) "Strategic Groups, Capabilities, and Performance in the U.S. Banking Industry. A Longitudinal Analysis (1974–1988)", Unpublished doctoral dissertation, University of Massachusetts, September.

Miles, R.E. and Snow, C.C. (1978) *Organizational Strategy, Structure, and Process* New York: McGraw-Hill.

Miller, E. and Friesen, P. (1980) "Momentum and Revolution in Organizational Adaptation", *Academy of Management Journal*, 23, 591–614.

Mintzberg, H. (1978) "Patterns of Strategy Formation", *Management Science*, 24, 934–948.

Mintzberg, H. (1990) "The Design School: Reconsidering the Basic Premises of Strategic Management", *Strategic Management Journal*, 11, 171–195.

Mintzberg, H. and Waters, J. (1985) "Of Strategies, Deliberate and Emergent", *Strategic Management Journal*, 6, 257–272.

Mintzberg, H. and Westley, F. (1992) "Cycles of Organizational Change", *Strategic Management Journal*, 13, Winter, 39–59.

Narayanan, V.K. and Fahey, L. (1982) "The Micro-Politics of Strategy Formulation", *Academy of Management Review*, 7, 25–34.

Nelson, R.R. (1991) "Why Do Firms Differ and How Does It Matter?" *Strategic Management Journal*, 12, 61–74.

Nielson, R.P. (1981) "Toward a Method of Building Consensus during Strategic Planning", *Sloan Management Review*, 22, Summer, 29–40.

Nonaka, I. (1988) "Toward Middle-up-down Management: Accelerating Information Creation", *Sloan Management Review*, Spring, 9–18.

Porter, M.E. (1980) *Competitive Strategy*, New York: The Free Press.

Porter, M.E. (1991) "Toward a Dynamic Theory of Strategy", *Strategic Management Journal*, 12, Winter, 95–117.

Prahalad, C.K. and Bettis, R.A. (1986) "The Dominant Logic: A New Linkage between Diversity and Performance", *Strategic Management Journal*, 7, 485–501.

Prahalad, C.K. and Hamel, G. (1990) "The Core Competence of the Corporation", *Harvard Business Review*, May–June, 79–91.

Priem, R.L. (1990) "Top Management Team Group Factors, Consensus, and Firm Performance", *Strategic Management Journal*, **11**, 469–478.

Quinn, J.B. (1980) *Strategies for Change: Logical Incrementalism*, Homewood, Ill.: Irwin.

Quinn, R.E. and Cameron, K.S. (1988) *Paradox and Transformation*. Cambridge: Ballinger.

Reed, R. and DeFillipi, R.J. (1990) "Causal Ambiguity, Barriers to Imitation and Sustainable Competitive Advantage", *Academy of Management Review*, **15**, 88–102.

Sayles, L. (1993) *The Working Leader*. New York: Free Press.

Steiner, G. (1979) *Strategic Planning*. New York: Free Press.

Teece, D.J., Pisano, G.P., and Shuen, A. (1990) "Firm Capabilities, Resources, and the Concept of Strategy", CCC Working Paper No. 90–8, Center for Research in Management, Berkeley.

Tushman, M., Newman, W.H., and Romanelli, Elaine (1986) "Managing the Unsteady Pace of Organizational Evolution", *California Management Review*, **29**, Fall, 29–44.

Tushman, M. and Romanelli, E. (1985) "Organizational Evolution: A Metamorphosis Model of Convergence and Reorientation", in L.L. Cummings and B.M. Straw (eds), *Research in Organizational Behavior*, Greenwich, Conn.: JAI Press, Vol. 7, pp. 171–222.

Wernerfelt, B. (1989) "From Critical Resources to Corporate Strategy", *Journal of General Management*, **14**, 4–12.

Wooldridge, B. and Floyd, S.W. (1989) "Strategic Process Effects on Consensus", *Strategic Management Journal*, **10**, 295–302.

Wooldridge, B. and Floyd, S.W. (1990) "The Strategy Process, Middle Management Involvement, and Organizational Performance", *Strategic Management Journal*, **11**, 231–241.

Index

Note: Page references in *italics* refer to Figures; those in **bold** refer to Tables

Index compiled by Annette Musker

Printed and bound by CPI Group (UK) Ltd, Croydon, CR0 4YY

23/04/2025

14660956-0002